Sharing Jesus
in the Two Thirds World

*Evangelical Christologies from the contexts
of poverty, powerlessness and religious pluralism.*

The Papers of the First Conference of Evangelical Mission
Theologians from the Two Thirds World

Bangkok, Thailand, March 22-25, 1982

Edited by
Vinay Samuel and Chris Sugden

GRAND RAPIDS, MICHIGAN
WILLIAM B. EERDMANS PUBLISHING COMPANY

First published 1983 by Partnership in Mission-Asia, India

This American edition published 1984 through special arrangement with Partnership in Mission—Asia by Wm. B. Eerdmans Publishing Company, 255 Jefferson S.E., Grand Rapids, Michigan 49503

Library of Congress Cataloging in Publication Data

Conference of Evangelical Mission Theologians from the
  Two Thirds World (1st : 1982 : Bangkok, Thailand)
  Sharing Jesus in the two thirds world.

  1. Jesus Christ—Person and offices—Congresses.
2. Christianity and other religions—Congresses.
3. Christianity—Developing countries—Congresses.
I. Samuel, V. T. (V. Thomas), 1939-   II. Sugden,
Chris. III. Title.
BT202.C664 1982   232'.09172'4   84-4008
ISBN 0-8028-1997-4

Contents

Preface, *David Gitari (Kenya)* vii

Introduction, *Vinay Samuel and Chris Sugden (India)* viii

1. Keynote address
Proclaiming Christ in the Two Thirds World
   Orlando E. Costas (Costa Rica/USA) 1

2. Christology and Mission in the Two Thirds World
   Rene Padilla (Argentina) 12

3. The Liberating Options of Jesus
   Norberto Saracco (Argentina) 33

4. The Image of Jesus in Latin American
Popular Religiosity
   Key Yuasa (Brazil) 42

5. Christology and Pastoral Action in Latin America
   Rolando Gutierrez (Mexico) 59

6. Biblical Christologies in the Context of African
Traditional Religions
   Kwame Bediako (Ghana) 81

7. Dialogue with other Religions—An Evangelical
View
   Vinay Samuel and Chris Sugden (India) 122

8. Christology in an Islamic Context
   Michael Nazir Ali (Pakistan) 141

9. Christology in the Context of the Life and
Religion of the Balinese
   Wayan Mastra (Indonesia) 157

10. Biblical Christianity in the Context of Buddhism
     David Lim (Philippines)   **175**

11. God and Christ in the Context of Buddhism
     Pracha Thaiwatcharamas (Thailand)   **204**

12. Who do you say that I am?—A North American
     Minority Answer to the Christological Question
     George Cummings (USA)   **217**

13. Miracles, Methodology, and Modern Western
     Christology
     Ronald Sider (USA)   **237**

14. Significant Trends in Christology in Western
     Scholarly Debate
     David Cook (Scotland)   **251**

15. Conference Findings
     Towards a Missiological Christology in the
     Two Thirds World   **277**

16. Emerging Issues for the Ongoing Debate
     Vinay Samuel and Chris Sugden (India)   **280**

17. Participants   **282**

18. Christ the Archer—The Cover Painting
     Nyoman Darsane (Bali, Indonesia)   **284**

Preface

During the third week of March 1982, twenty-five theologians from Africa, Asia, and Latin America met in Bangkok to discuss the emerging Christologies in the Two Thirds World. This volume is the result of the deliberations of the conference.

Fourteen papers were read by distinguished evangelical theologians as well as representatives of a generation of emerging young evangelical theologians.

The conference, of which I was privileged to be the chairman, spent much time in discussing each paper in great detail. The conference expressed its findings in a document entitled "Towards a Missiological Christology in the Two Thirds World." We commend this volume and that document to you for study and reference.

This was a historic meeting. It was the first time that theologians of evangelical conviction from the Two Thirds World had met at their own initiative to focus attention on what Jesus from Galilee means in their own contexts and in their attempt to fulfil his mission.

The arrangements for the conference were made possible by Partnership-in-Mission Asia. I would like to thank Vinay Samuel, Chris Sugden, and David Bussau for the part they played in making the arrangements for the conference and also in preparing this volume. I also wish to express my appreciation to Professor Orlando Costas who was the vice-chairman of the consultation. It is my hope that this volume will be a blessing to many.

Embu, Kenya, Easter 1982   DAVID M. GITARI

Introduction

WHY A CONFERENCE?

In the late seventies a group of theologians and missiologists from around the world were preparing for an important consultation. Some months before their meeting, the coordinator received a letter from one of the European delegates suggesting that it would be quite adequate and less expensive for the participants to exchange written papers and conduct the consultation by correspondence. The coordinator replied that the writer would do far more than present a paper at the consultation. He would discover new brothers in Christ.

Sharing Jesus in the Two Thirds World[1] is a book from a conference, the First Conference of Evangelical Mission Theologians from the Two Thirds World, held in Bangkok from March 20–25, 1982. In the keynote address published here, Orlando Costas gives the background to the calling of the conference. But this book seeks to do more than bind together between two covers the papers presented there. For the conference was more than a forum to present papers. It was a creative workshop to facilitate and promote reflection in community. It was a meeting and a fellowship of persons, testing and affirming insights gained from diverse cultural and theological backgrounds to deepen their understanding of Christ.

The product of the conference was thus more than a collection of papers. It was the creation, experience, and development of community. The book tries to capture this dimension by recording the essence and thrust of some of the discussions, which have been edited for conciseness while preserving the speaker's intention. The video and audio cassette tapes of the conference, including a single three-hour video presentation of the highlights (available from PIM Asia, P.O. Box 162, St. Ives, Sydney 2075, Australia) capture this dimension more fully.

Another product of the conference was a sense of unity. The papers and discussions reflect a unity of commitment to Christ and his mission rather than a uniformity of outlook. The concerns of this commitment are outlined in a final chapter which attempts to discern the issues that emerged during the conference.

The purpose of this process was not to produce a catch-all final state-

1. The term refers to the two thirds of the world's population who live in contexts of poverty and powerlessness.

ment which could be cited as Two Thirds World mission theology. The focus was more on the process as time was given for presenters to elaborate their views in discussion, and for the group as a whole to reflect at length on the issues raised. There was no pressure to produce an agreed statement. The final document is only by way of a findings report. It marks the spot on the map where evangelical mission theologians from the Two Thirds World think they are at the moment. It acts as a signpost to direct them in their further action, biblical study, and reflection.

WHY CHRISTOLOGY?

At the heart of Christian mission is our understanding of Jesus Christ, his person and mission. A fundamental unity emerged of commitment to the full and final authority of the Scriptures and to Jesus Christ as Saviour and Lord, both personally and communally. The conference affirmed its commitment to the uniqueness, preexistence, Lordship, resurrection, atoning death, and second coming of Jesus Christ.

Many participants felt unable to give a definitive evangelical Christology in their context at this point in time. To be true to their situations, they felt that so many new areas were only now being opened up which contribute to formulating such Christologies, that they felt able only to set directions and agendas for the process of discerning the meaning of Jesus Christ of the Scriptures in their context. They could only share with us the milestone they had reached.

From North America, black and hispanic Christians stressed that they do not always define who Jesus is in the same terms white evangelicals use. Black American Christians point out that the image of Jesus Christ first presented to their forbears by white slave masters was couched in the dominant structures of society. The black experience forced black Christians to discover for themselves from the Bible a new image of Jesus to replace one which they considered to be inauthentic.

Indonesian Christians pointed out that the Christian message which they received from Europe was already couched in terms of European intellectual and analytical rationalism and expressed in European cultural forms.

African Christians questioned the adequacy of the European and North American missionary understanding of the gospel. They sought new dimensions in understanding the biblical Christ for their people in interaction with the African concepts of ancestor veneration and sacral kingship.

Two distinct images of Christ emerge from the Korean church. One is of a figure of protest against governmental injustice. This leads some Christians to accept imprisonment as an authentic witness to the image of Christ for their society. Other Christians feel that such confrontation with the government only jeopardizes the church's witness to the authentic image of Christ as Saviour of all men.

THE CONTEXT OF THE CONFERENCE

The context in which the conference was held was itself informative and illustrative of our world. While the conference was on, a coup took place in Bangladesh and the travel plans of some members to minister there had to be cancelled. At the same time upheavals in Central America made the return of one participant back to his family very uncertain as borders were closed. Within a month of British and Argentinian theologians dialoguing together, their countries would be at war. One paper writer from Africa was detained during his travel. Since he was unable to produce a vaccination certificate relevant to a transit stop of a few hours, he was held up at a second transit point. He was asked for a small bribe to be allowed to continue his journey. Our contributor refused to pay it, and so was turned back. Another African contributor was refused a visa to leave his country. For these reasons of the setting we live in, the African section of the papers is regrettably reduced in size.

Two contributors brought papers from Europe and North America to affirm that whatever previous imbalances may have existed, we cannot redress them in isolation from one another. Our growth in the body of Christ and as the body of Christ depends on each part continuing to contribute its gift and receive from every other part.

One female participant attended the conference but for varous reasons no paper was presented by a woman. There are many possible arrangements to avoid sexist bias in written language. But such arrangements seem contrived when used in speech. Since these papers were originally presented in speech, we have kept the reference to "men" and "he" where women are clearly included, but hopefully, not suppressed.

We are most grateful to David and Ruth Thorne for their assistance in preparing the manuscript for the press.

Bangalore, Christmas 1982   THE EDITORS

1. KEYNOTE ADDRESS
Proclaiming Christ in the Two Thirds World

ORLANDO E. COSTAS *(Costa Rica, USA)*

Synopsis

We are hard pressed to recognize the face of Jesus Christ as described in the New Testament among the presentations of Christ in the Two Thirds World. Cultural imperialism and the cultural reaction that an oppressive experience provokes have produced distorted reproductions of Christ. A new focus is emerging within the Two Thirds World on the historical Jesus and the active presence of Christ among the struggles of the poor, the powerless, and the oppressed.

This new reflection will be of profound importance for faithful evangelism in the next decade.

THE HISTORICAL CONTEXT OF THE CONFERENCE

In June 1980 the Lausanne Committee for World Evangelization (LCWE) held the Consultation on World Evangelism (COWE) in Thailand in the city of Pattaya.

During the Consultation a group of Africans, Asians, Latin Americans, Antillians, and black North Americans circulated a Statement of Concerns, to which several Western and Eastern Europeans, Australasians, and Anglo-Americans added their contributions. Within a few hours nearly one third of those present had signed the document.

Addressed to the LCWE Executive Committee, the Statement made the following affirmation:

> During the International Congress on World Evangelization (Lausanne 1974) it was affirmed that "Evangelism and socio-political involvement are both part of our Christian duty." The Congress also asserted that "we should share God's concern for justice and reconciliation throughout human society and for the liberation of men from every kind of oppression" (Lausanne Covenant, section 5). . . .
>
> It is a fact, nevertheless, that outside of a few noble and commendable efforts the Lausanne Committee for World Evangelization (LCWE) does not seem to have been seriously concerned with the

1

social, political and economic issues in many parts of the world that are a great stumbling block to the proclamation of the Gospel. This is clearly evident here at Pattaya, Thailand during this Consultation on World Evangelization. We have a working group "Reaching Refugees," but none on those that are largely responsible for the refugee situation around the world: politicians, armed forces, freedom fighters, national oligarchies, and the controllers of international economic power.

Since the world is made up not just of people groups but of institutions and structures, the Lausanne Movement, if it is to make a lasting and profound evangelistic impact in the six continents of the world, must make a special effort to help Christians, local churches, denominations and mission agencies to identify not only people groups, but also the social, economic and political institutions that determine their lives and the structures behind them that hinder evangelism. Indeed to be an effective mobilizing agent for the evangelization of the world, the LCWE (as the visible expression of the Lausanne Movement) will have to give guidelines to Christians in many parts of the world who are wrestling with the problems of racial, tribal and sexual discrimination, political imperialism, economic exploitation, and physical and psychological harassment of totalitarian regimes of whatever ideology and the liberation struggles that are the consequences of such violent aggression.

The Statement urged the LCWE to be given a mandate to continue with its ministry, but suggested that the latter implement four recommendations:

1. That the LCWE reaffirm its commitment to all aspects of the Covenant and in particular provide new leadership to help Evangelicals implement its call to social responsibility as well as evangelism.

2. That the LCWE encourage and promote the formation of study groups at all levels, to deal with social, political and economic issues and provide specific guidance on how Evangelicals can effectively apply the Lausanne Covenant's affirmation of "God's concern for justice and reconciliation throughout human society and liberation of men from every kind of oppression."

3. That, within three years, the LCWE convene a World Congress on Evangelical Social Responsibility and its implications for evangelism.

4. That the LCWE give guidelines on how Evangelicals who support oppression and discrimination (thus hindering evangelism) can be reached by the Gospel and challenged to repent and uphold biblical truth, and how to give encouragement and support to Christians of all races in situations of oppression as they are seeking to be faithful to the Gospel at a great risk.

Though the Executive Committee met with three of the leading sponsors of the Statement, it did not give a formal reply until the entire LCWE met after COWE. The formal response, however, was preceded by the Thailand Statement. In two paragraphs that speak directly to the challenges of faithfulness to the whole of the Lausanne Covenant and not just to parts of it, the Thailand Statement asserts:

> We are also the servants of Jesus Christ who is himself both "the servant" and "the Lord." He calls us, therefore, not only to obey him as Lord in every area of our lives, but also to serve as he served. We confess that we have not sufficiently followed his example of love in identifying with the poor and hungry, the deprived and the oppressed. Yet all God's people "should share his concern for justice and reconciliation throughout human society and for the liberation of men from every kind of oppression" (Lausanne Covenant, section 5).
>
> Although evangelism and social action are not identical, we gladly reaffirm our commitment to both, and we endorse the Lausanne Covenant in its entirety. It remains the basis of our common activity, and nothing it contains is beyond our concern, so long as it clearly related to world evangelization.

The formal response of the LCWE was given in a fourfold motion. The first part simply referred to the fact that the Thailand Statement had already responded to the first recommendation. The other parts of the motion, however, were rather cool and disappointing. The second part of the motion states that:

> The Committee took note of the fact that the Executive Committee last November approved the proposal of LTEG to arrange a small consultation in cooperation with WEFTC on "The Relationship between Evangelism and Social Responsibility" in June 1982, which would be preceded by study groups in different countries and cultures. These study groups will in the Committee's view, fulfil the purpose of their second recommendation. The Committee does not believe that it should convene a World Congress on this topic within three years (the third recommendation).[1]

The third and fourth parts of the motion say that: "The Committee does not consider that it should attempt to give the guidelines requested in their fourth recommendation," and that "The Committee commits to LTEG a further consideration of these matters within the decisions of this minute."

Such a response made some of us wonder how committed indeed was the LCWE to the whole of the Lausanne Covenant. If all that the LCWE would do to implement the Covenant's commitment to social action and evangelism was "to arrange a small consultation . . . on 'The Relation-

---

1. LTEG—Lausanne Theology and Education Group; WEFTC—World Evangelical Fellowship Theological Commission.

ship between Evangelism and Social Responsibility' '' with no more than 40 participants; if the Committee refused, at least, to "attempt to give the guidelines requested in the fourth recommendation"; and if the matter was further referred to a working group which was technically no longer in existence, as the decision was made at Pattaya to formally disband the LTEG, then how seriously were Christians around the world to take the Thailand Statement, which had become the basis for the LCWE's new mandate?

As disappointing and unsatisfactory as some of us found the Lausanne Committee's response, the whole exchange brought to light several important issues.

First, it helped us to see that at the bottom of the evangelistic question there was a Christological problem: what does it mean to proclaim Jesus Christ in a world divided along racial and class differences? How can evangelical Christians expect people of other religious traditions to seriously consider the message of Christ as a personal option when those who are proclaiming that message contradicted it with their lives?

Second, the exchange with the LCWE helped us to see the crucial importance of these questions for evangelical Christians in what will be referred to in the course of this conference as the Two Thirds World, namely, the oppressed people of Africa, Asia, and the Middle East, the Pacific, the Americas, including North, Central, and South America and the Caribbean Islands, Europe, and Australia. We refer here to the oppressed people that live in these various continents. That is what we mean by the Two Thirds World.

Third, the exchange convinced us of the need to reflect on this and similar questions as evangelicals from the Two Thirds World without strings attached, whether organizational, financial, or ideological.

It was out of this threefold conviction that several of us laid the groundwork for a loose Fellowship of Evangelical Mission Theologians from the Two Thirds World, of which this Conference is its firstfruit.

We meet as evangelical Christians seeking to understand what it means to proclaim the name of Christ in a religiously pluralistic world surrounded by situations of poverty, powerlessness, and oppression. We come together not just with a theological but especially with a missiological concern. Our goal is to help the evangelical movement in general and our respective churches in particular to bear a more biblically faithful, spiritually authentic, and socio-culturally relevant witness to Jesus Christ in the Two Thirds World. To reach this goal, we need first to understand the problem of proclaiming Christ in the Two Thirds World.

THE PROBLEM OF PROCLAIMING CHRIST IN THE TWO THIRDS WORLD

Without pretending in any way to be exhaustive, I want to outline briefly several aspects of the Christological problem embedded in the proclamation of the gospel throughout the Two Thirds World.

ORLANDO E. COSTAS

One aspect of the problem is the paradoxical fact that God's incarnate Word has been, by and large, proclaimed in a foreign language(s). By "foreign" I do not mean simply a strange material language. I am not referring therefore to the inability of those who came to our respective countries and communities to communicate the gospel in the local language and idioms. Some mass evangelists and cross-cultural missionaries still depend on local interpreters in their preaching because they never bother to learn the local language. But more than the material ignorance of the vernacular is the fact that the symbolic references which have accompanied the proclamation of the gospel have been foreign to the cultural reality and social experiences of the hearers. Indeed the proclamation of Christ is not a technical linguistic effort, but rather a dynamic communicative event which involves the totality of life. When we look around in the Two Thirds World to see the concrete references that characterize the communication of the gospel, we find in far too many instances church activities which are not congruent with the local situation, liturgies that express the gospel in another culture, an irrelevant architecture, foreign art forms, and music. Is it any wonder that after so many centuries of mission work, no more than 3 percent of people of Asia are followers of Christ; and that both Africa and Latin America have seen the emergence of numerous independent churches and newer religious movements in protest to the foreignness in which the gospel has been proclaimed?

The foreignness of the Word has as a corollary what we might describe as the disfigured face of Jesus. The Jesus proclaimed in far too many situations of the Two Thirds World has been given faces that are not only removed from the cultural, social, racial, economic, and political reality of the people, but also of the very witness of the New Testament Gospels. Indeed Jesus has often appeared in the church's proclamation with every possible face except one that reflects local features.

The disfiguration of Jesus has taken place both at the conceptual and the historically-concrete levels. Thus in South Africa not only has there been a dominant white image in the Christological language of the mainstream church, but also there has been a formal identification of Jesus with the ruling ideology and the elitist power structure. Jesus has become, therefore, a projection of the Afrikaaner, the all-encompassing sovereign Lord who has established a harmonious universe where each part can develop separately.

In the West Indies, Anglophone Africa, and India, several centuries of colonial rule has left a very definite Christological impression in the consciousness of the people of these lands. Along with the British type of architecture and government structures and styles that the British empire left behind, there remained a British-type church, and, therefore, the memory of a British-type Christ.

We can say a similar thing of the disfiguration of Jesus through Anglo-American imperialism and consumerism: an overpowering, pragmatic saviour with a plastic face not only has been impressed on the consciousness of people where the United States has been politically active, but also continues to be reinforced through the consumeristic religiosity that characterizes a good deal of the missionary activities and theology from North America.

For its part, Spain, according to well-known Scottish theologian John Mackay in his famous work *The Other Spanish Christ*,[2] left Latin America the image of a "baby Jesus" and an impotent dying saviour on a crucifix. But then Protestant missionaries proposed a substitution of the image of the Lord of the empty tomb who left behind the cross and his suffering death. Hence "impotency" and "innocence" were substituted in Protestant preaching with the image of "power" and "impassiveness."

In the last decades we have witnessed new disfigurations: the image of the Guevara as a Latin American Christ; in Africa, the image of a freedom fighter; in India that of a Hindu guru or in some places of South East Asia a Christian type of Lord Buddha. Everywhere we go in the Two Thirds World we find distorted reproductions of Jesus Christ. Whether by imposition or reaction, whether as a result of the cultural transplantation that accompanied colonialism or the cultural rebellion that such an oppressive experience provokes, we are hard pressed to recognize the true face of Jesus of Nazareth as described in the New Testament.

How then can we proclaim the Lord Jesus Christ if we have a distorted representation of Jesus of Nazareth?

The Christological problem in the proclamation of the gospel is compounded by the way Christ has been manipulated, being treated as a private possession. Such treatment is often the fruit of an individualistic, pietist religiosity at the service of economic interests from local oligarchical and metropolitan powers. To be sure, lest I be misunderstood, pietism, as an expression of faith, or as an evangelical type of spirituality which stresses personal prayers, Bible reading, and a high personal morality is a positive factor in the proclamation of the gospel. But a spirituality which isolates Christ from reality and interiorizes him in the individual domain of the private self is alienating and deadly for the Christian life and mission. And we cannot deny that in far too many situations of the Two Thirds World this is exactly how Christ has been perceived and proclaimed. It is no surprise to find that such privatization of Christ is characteristic of many expressions of the modern missionary movement and its related churches. Nor is it a coincidence that the financial base of this movement is found by and large in the private enterprise system. Is it not strange that as far back as William Carey and as recent as the LCWE and the WEF the financial backbone of a lot of the churches and missionary societies that *we* represent are to be found among those who

2. John A. Mackay, *The Other Spanish Christ* (London: SCM, 1932; Spanish edition, Mexico: Casa Unida de Publicaciones, 1952).

possessed wealth, knowledge, and power, indeed among those who control?

Are Christological formulations not often subject to forms which are congruent with the theologies and ecclesiastical policies of donor agencies and churches, and the general ideological commitment of their respective countries? This is a very delicate matter not easily admitted by many of us. However, it can be verified by applying sociological tests and analyses to the Christological statements and ecclesial practices of our respective churches and Christian institutions.

The consequence of such privatization, disfiguration, and foreignness has been a distortion of both the theology and practice of evangelization in the Two Thirds World. What kind of evangelism can be carried out with such a distorted Christ? The answer is that it is one that is congruent with its message.

Does not all the emphasis that we witness today on evangelistic strategy and method imply a minimizing of the content of evangelism? And, when the content of an endeavour is distorted, does not endeavour itself end up distorted?

I suggest that as evangelicals we have too easily assumed that the message has been clearly sorted out. The result has been a missiological concentration on strategy and a weakening of its Christological foundation. At Lausanne I talked with a friend from the Third World and asked him why it is that when creativity is handed out, evangelicals never seem to be close by to get their share. He answered me: "If we have the truth why do we need to be creative?" That is part of the problem that we are dealing with. We have assumed too easily that the question of the evangelistic message has been settled. Therefore we have gone on as evangelicals and put a missiological concentration on the "how to" question of strategy and method.

If my suggestion has any validity, then we have reason to be worried not only about evangelism, but about the Christian ethic and the entire life and mission of the church. What kind of church can be built on a faulty Christology? I answer a very weak church. What kind of ethic can come out of a distorted faith? Not a very consistent one—indeed a heretical one.

The problem of Christology in the proclamation of the gospel affects the entire life and mission of the church, the ethical behaviour of Christians in the world, and indeed the totality of our Christian faith.

THE CHRISTOLOGICAL AWAKENING OF THE TWO THIRDS WORLD

Christology in the Two Thirds World is not just an evangelistic problem, however. In fact Christology represents in the Two Thirds World an exciting and dynamic awakening. During the last two decades we witnessed throughout the Two Thirds World the rediscovery of the historical Jesus and the discovery of the Jesus of history. Numerous books and articles continue to appear on the market stressing not only the historical Jesus as a starting point for Christology, but also focussing on the active presence of Jesus in the struggle of the poor, the powerless, and oppressed. Our papers and discussions will contain numerous references to these authors from the Two Thirds World who have concentrated or reflected seriously on the question of Jesus Christ in their contexts. Unlike European theology most of them have stressed the importance of repossessing and recovering the historicity of Jesus of Nazareth as a fundamental starting point for building a Christology from the world of the oppressed.

By the same token, we witness a quest, especially in Asia, for a proper understanding of the cosmic Christ of the Pauline Epistles in the context of other religious traditions of the Two Thirds World. Is there a total discontinuity between the cosmic Christ and the religious traditions as was suggested by some missiologists from the West several decades ago? Or is there a continuity and if so of what kind?

Finally we begin to notice the formulation of Christological categories and themes that are in many ways indigenous to the Two Thirds World and are congruent with the New Testament witness. Among others, two such categories and themes come to mind. One is the concept of Jesus Christ as the man of sorrows, acquainted with grief, as revelation of God's own suffering. This theme was fully developed by the Japanese theologian Kazoh Kitamori, as far back as 1947 in *The Pain of God* (a work which has not been given proper credit in all the discussion on the crucified God in the West in the last several years). The theme is also seen in the work of his fellow countryman, Kosuke Koyama, in his Christological meditation *No Handle on the Cross* (1977).[3] This theme also has a long tradition in Latin America and in the black experience in North America, but it has begun to be worked on in earnest and systematically only in the last ten years in the writings of James Cone, Jon Sobrino, and the Taiwanese theologian Choan-Seng Song.

A second Christological category that has emerged is Jesus Christ as the wounded healer and judge, otherwise identified as "the liberator." This comprehensive category has become the organizing principle for the most well-known theologies of Africa, Latin America, Afro-America, and Asia.

THE CHALLENGE OF CHRISTOLOGY FOR THE EVANGELISTIC AGENDA OF THE CHURCH IN THE TWO THIRDS WORLD

Because the Two Thirds World is not only problematic for the proclamation of Christ but also exciting and fermenting, evangelicals need to put

3. English translation, Kazoh Kitamori, *Theology of the Pain of God* (Atlanta: John Knox Press, 1965); Kosuke Koyama, *No Handle on the Cross* (Maryknoll: Orbis, 1977).

its challenge in the centre of their evangelistic agenda. Faithfulness in evangelism in the next decade will demand of us some deep and profound reflection on Christological themes. For example, the evangelistic church lives by the promise of Christ's continuing presence in history (Mt. 28:19-20). The great commission as given to us in the Gospel of Matthew explicitly underscores the promise of Jesus Christ being present as the church moves through the nations discipling them, baptizing them, and teaching them to observe all that he has commanded us to follow.

The New Testament links this promise of the presence of Christ with the reality of the Spirit. In fact the apostle Paul very bluntly states that the Spirit is the Lord, and where the Lord is there is freedom (2 Cor. 3:17). So the question emerges for our own Christological agendas as evangelicals: where are we to look for the presence of the pneumatic Christ in evangelism in the Two Thirds World?

When John the Baptist asked whether Jesus was the one to come or whether he should be looking for someone else, Jesus answered his disciples with the signs of the messianic age: "Go and tell John what you hear and see: the blind receive their sight and the lame walk, lepers are cleansed and the deaf hear, and the dead are raised up and the poor have good news preached to them. And blessed is he who takes no offence at me" (Mt. 11:4-6). Likewise in answering the question of where is the pneumatic Christ present in evangelism, we will be obliged to point to the signs of the kingdom in our respective ministries. One aspect of Christological reflection in the Two Thirds World will be the task of giving guidelines for the identification of the signs of the Spirit's presence in evangelism.

It is inevitable, furthermore, in speaking of the Christological foundation of evangelism for us to deal with the challenge of incarnating the name of Jesus in concrete historical situations. The incarnation is a fundamental article of Christology and especially of an evangelistic Christology. After all, the pneumatic Christ works in and through the church, which is the body of Christ.

How then does the church incarnate the saving name of Jesus (Acts 4:12) in evangelism? The fact that we cannot talk about incarnation without mentioning the church indicates how closely related is the building of Christ's body to evangelism.

In recent years evangelism has been linked with church growth and in Pattaya it was almost identified with it. We agree that evangelism should lead to and must be verified in terms of church growth. The question, which has not always been answered, is, what kind of church growth are we to talk about and look for? One reason why this question has not been adequately dealt with is because of the weak Christology embedded in a lot of church growth thinking.[4]

4. See further the author's *The Church and its Mission: A Shattering Critique from the Third World* (Wheaton: Tyndale, 1974).

When we start thinking Christologically about evangelism we are forced to think not only about the growth of the church, but especially about the nature of that growth and the ingredients of body-building. Hence comes the question: What does it mean for the church to grow in Christ? If Christology is to serve as a critical principle for church growth thinking and action it will have to develop Christological guidelines also for church growth strategists.

Finally, the proclamation of Christ appears in the New Testament in an eschatological perspective. To proclaim Christ is to announce the dawning of the Kingdom of God. From the gospel narrative we learn that the preaching of Jesus became in fact the proclamation about Jesus: the announcement of the dawning of God's Kingdom became the proclamation of its relevation in Jesus Christ, the Lord and Saviour of the world.

Likewise to proclaim the Kingdom is viewed as the anticipation of the second coming of Christ. This is made clear in the first chapter of Acts. Referring to the coming of the Holy Spirit the disciples ask the question: "Lord, will you at this time restore the Kingdom . . . ? (Acts 1:6). And Jesus told them that it was not their business to go around asking about the times and the seasons, "which the Father has fixed by His own authority." Instead, he commanded them to bear witness to him in Jerusalem, Judea, Samaria, and unto the uttermost parts of the earth (Acts 1:7-8). Then as they gazed at him in his ascension, the angel reminds them that they should not stand there doing nothing, but rather tells them that this same Jesus that had been taken up shall come back (Acts 1:11). Thus they should go out into the uttermost parts of the world and bear witness to his name announcing the dawning of a new age in him. To proclaim that is therefore to anticipate his coming. The question is *"how."* In which ways does the church anticipate the return of Christ through its proclamation?

We evangelicals have traditionally talked a lot about the second coming of Christ in relation to evangelism. But we have rarely worked out the Christological implications of that issue except in very activistic and extra-worldly terms. This remains therefore an important item in the evangelical Christological agenda.

Being a conference of theologians from the world of the poor, the powerless, and the oppressed, we do not pretend to produce in it definitive polished statements. We come by and large from ministries that allow little time for systematic reflection and offer limited research facilities.

We have come, nevertheless, full of courage, hoping to be able to render a service to the church-in-mission in the Two Thirds World.

Our final product is not to be judged by the traditional standards of mainstream western theology, though we recognize that we have learned many good things from it. Indeed not only are we indebted to the West for giving us basic theological tools and concepts, but are also open to learn from its contemporary trends and insights. Hence, we will have in the course of the Conference two papers representing mainstream western perspectives.

Rather, the success of the Conference will be judged in time by whether it helps the church of the oppressed in general and its evangelical variant in particular to proclaim Jesus Christ more faithfully, to communicate his Word more effectively, and to represent him more authentically in the Two Thirds World.

2. Christology and Mission in the Two Thirds World

RENÉ PADILLA *(Argentina)*

Synopsis

The images of Jesus Christ imported from the West into the Two Thirds World are inadequate for the life and mission of the church in situations of poverty and injustice. A search has begun for a Christology which will provide a basis for Christian action in contemporary society.

René Padilla gives a detailed summary and critical evaluation from an evangelical perspective of the contributions to this search by Jon Sobrino's "Christology at the Crossroads," Choan-Seng Song's "Third Eye Theology," and Albert Nolan's "Jesus Before Christianity." Their Christologies stress the historical nature of the Christian life and challenge us to commitment to Jesus Christ for the transformation of the world.

INTRODUCTION

"For some reason it has been possible for Christians, in the name of Christ, to ignore or even contradict fundamental principles and values that were preached and acted upon by Jesus of Nazareth."[1]

"Jesus has been more frequently honoured and worshipped for what he did not mean than for what he did mean. The supreme irony is that some of the things he opposed most strongly in the world of his time were resurrected, preached and spread more widely throughout the world in his name."[2]

The coincidence between these two quotations (the first one coming from Latin America and the second one from Africa) regarding a fundamental problem affecting the church today is quite obvious. It illustrates the growing awareness among Christians in the Two Thirds World of the urgent need to examine the images of Jesus Christ with which traditional Christianity has generally been associated and which have often served as the basis for the Christian mission. At the same time, it shows the importance of a new quest of the historical Jesus for the purpose of letting him speak for himself and, if at all possible, letting him determine the shape of Christian discipleship and mission in the modern world.

1. Jon Sobrino, *Christology at the Crossroads: A Latin American Approach* (Maryknoll: Orbis Books, 1978), p. xv.
2. Albert Nolan, *Jesus Before Christianity* (Maryknoll: Orbis Books, 1976), p. 3.

That has been, in fact, the concern of much of the Christological reflection in the Two Thirds World in the last few years. The images of Jesus Christ imported from the West have on the whole been found wanting—too conditioned by Constantinian Christianity with all its ideological distortions and cultural accretions, and terribly inadequate as a basis for the life and mission of the church in situations of dire poverty and injustice. This has led to the search for a Christology which will have as its focus the historical Jesus and provide a basis for Christian action in contemporary society.

One of the most outstanding contributions to this Christological reconstruction comes from Jon Sobrino, a Jesuit priest, professor of philosophy and theology at Universidad José Simeón Canas of El Salvador: *Christology at the Crossroads.* In the first part of this paper we shall summarize this book; in the second part we shall compare Sobrino's Christology with other treatments of Christology, one Asian and another one African; and in the third part we shall make a critical evaluation of Christology in the Two Thirds World and draw some conclusions from a missiological perspective.

I. "CHRISTOLOGY AT THE CROSSROADS"

In line with the theologies of liberation, Sobrino's Christ emerges out of a commitment to the cause of liberation and aims at making social involvement more critical and creative. The problem for him is not simply to understand reality but to transform it. "The course that Jesus took," says he, "is to be investigated scientifically, not just to aid in the quest for truth but also in the fight for truth that will make people free."[3]

Sobrino takes as his *starting point* the affirmation that Christ is the Jesus of history.[4] According to him, "There can be no Christology of Christ apart from the history of Jesus of Nazareth."[5] For the historical Jesus is the key which provides access to the total Christ. First, because the total Christ, as a limit-reality in this world, can be comprehended only in connection with Jesus' actual course toward fulfilment as the Christ and, second, because Jesus himself demands this, insisting that the fundamental contact with him comes through following his historical life. Furthermore the history of the church shows that faith goes wrong when it concentrates on the risen Christ and forgets the historical Jesus. "If a Christology disregards the historical Jesus," concludes Sobrino, "it turns into an abstract Christology that is historically alienating and open to manipulation."[6]

3. Sobrino, *op. cit.*, p. 35.
4. The "historical Jesus" includes for Sobrino "the person, teaching, attitudes, and deeds of Jesus of Nazareth insofar as they are accessible, in a more or less general way, to historical and exegetical investigation" (*ibid.*, p. 3).
5. *Ibid.*, p. xxii.
6. *Ibid.*, p. 353.

Right from the beginning Sobrino makes it clear that Christology sums up the total meaning of life and history. Consequently, Christology can only be approached on the basis of faith and must take cognizance of each particular historical situation. Sobrino therefore proposes a hermeneutic which does justice both to the concrete Latin American situation and to the history of Jesus as recorded in the Gospels.

Jesus and the Kingdom of God

A Christianity centred around the historical Jesus must follow the events of Jesus' life in chronological order. When that is done, according to Sobrino, it becomes obvious that there were two distinct stages in Jesus' life. The first stage, before the Galilean crisis, was characterized by the proclamation of the Kingdom as an eschatological reality embodied in his work and deeds. The second stage, after the Galilean crisis, was marked by conflict and suffering. Jesus failed with the masses and his life came into jeopardy, with the result that "the Kingdom took on the features of the work attributed to the suffering Servant of Yahweh."[7] All along, however, Jesus did not preach about himself or about God, but rather about the Kingdom of God—he was "In the Service of God's Kingdom."[8]

Consequently, claims Sobrino, the problem of Christ's divinity cannot be broached *directly*, but only in *relational* terms. That is, we must view him as the Son whose relationship to the Father was typified by exclusive confidence in the Father and total obedience to his mission.[9] What Chalcedon affirmed in ontic categories must be reformulated in relational categories. Thus "Jesus *becomes* the Son of God rather than . . . he simply *is* the Son of God,"[10] and in becoming the Son of God he reveals to us the way of the Son, the way to become children of God. "The path of Jesus," says Sobrino, "is the revelation of the Son's path. If it were incapable of incorporating others into it, then Jesus could not be the Son. Hence being the 'first born' is part and parcel of Jesus' divinity. He traverses the way to God and makes it possible for his brothers and sisters to do the same."[11]

Jesus' faith

For Sobrino, the drastic break between the first and the second phase of Jesus' ministry is beyond discussion. It is a break "in the person of Jesus himself," in both his "internal awareness and external activity"[12] and, therefore, "a rupture in his faith."[13] To be sure, after the Galilean

7. *Ibid.*, p. 58.
8. *Ibid.*, pp. 41ff.
9. *Ibid.*, pp. 60ff.
10. *Ibid.*, p. 105.
11. *Ibid.*, p. 107.
12. *Ibid.*, p. 93.
13. *Ibid.*, p. 94.

crisis Jesus continues to have confidence in his Father, but "now that confidence finds nothing in which to root. . . . Letting God remain God now lacks any verification; it is alone in the absence of any verification at all. . . . All that is left is the power of love in suffering."[14] This evaluation of Jesus' faith, claims Sobrino, goes hand in hand with his concrete history. "The faith of Jesus is fashioned through his history."[15]

Each of the two phases of Jesus' ministry, according to Sobrino, results in a different conception of the Christian life. The first phase presumes that God is already known at the start and therefore envisions the Christian life as a journey toward God; the second phase, on the other hand, centres on Jesus himself and sees the Christian life as following him on a journey to a God not yet really known.[16]

Thus understood, Jesus' faith is for Sobrino fundamental to moral theology. Christian ethics, if it is to be *Christian*, is not baptized natural ethics, but ethics that goes back to Jesus. The formal object of moral theology was concretized through the experience of Jesus himself, which was the proclamation of the Kingdom of God and the effort to make it real and present. It follows that the basic question for ethics is, "*What must be done* in order to establish the Kingdom of God in history?"[17] The concern of ethics is therefore "the kind of action that correctly fashions the Kingdom."[18] The concern of moral theology is not what makes a person individually good, but how to make history good, how to fashion the Kingdom of God in history. "The specific question of Christian morality is how individuals become Christians through their efforts to fashion the Kingdom into a reality."[19]

Jesus' death

Sobrino regards Jesus' death as "a central datum of the Christian faith,"[20] insofar as it posits a new revolutionary concept of God. In his view, the models to explain Jesus' crucifixion in positive terms (for instance, as necessary for salvation, according to God's eternal "plan") tend to interiorize salvation. They neglect the question how God can take away an external sin which leads his Son to the cross. Such models are based on two erroneous presuppositions: (1) a conception of God that does not derive from the cross, and (2) a conception of cultic worship as sacrifice that does not derive from Jesus.[21] They are ways to eliminate the scandal of the cross, which consists in the fact that Jesus, being the Son, died in disaster, and that God, being the Father, abandoned him on the cross.[22]

14. *Ibid.*
15. *Ibid.*, p. 100.
16. *Ibid.*, p. 362.
17. *Ibid.*, p. 113.
18. *Ibid.*
19. *Ibid.*, p. 114.
20. *Ibid.*, p. 179.
21. *Ibid.*, p. 191.
22. *Ibid.*, p. 192.

Such an attempt to strip Jesus' death of its scandalous aspect, according to Sobrino, is evident already in the New Testament itself in the fact that the death of Jesus as one abandoned by God is mollified, that the title "Servant of Yahweh" fades from the scene quite early, and that Jesus' death is viewed as reflecting God's design and as having salvific value.[23] "Thus the unfolding logic of the attempted explanation in the New Testament gradually converts the *real-life* scandal of Jesus' cross into nothing more than a *noetic* scandal. Once we correctly interpret the Scriptures, we presumably will not find anything surprising in the cross of Jesus."[24]

According to Sobrino's claim, this tendency to bypass the scandal of the cross, which has its beginning in the New Testament, continues in the history of the church and of theology. The issue at stake here is whether God was revealed only at key points of Jesus' life, that is at his death and resurrection, or all through the history of the Son, "in the process whereby Jesus *becomes the Son* through his concrete history."[25] The choice for Sobrino is clear: Jesus' death was not determined by God's design to arbitrarily use it as a work of redemption; rather, it was the historical consequence of Jesus' life, "the outcome of the basic option for incarnation in a given situation."[26] It was a real-life scandal because Jesus died on the cross abandoned by the Father, condemned for blasphemy and executed as a political rebel. His polemics with the religious authorities of his day centred around his conception of God and his claim that "access to God is to be found in making contact with the very people that the religious mentality of the Jews saw as completely estranged from God: the alien, the heretic, the ritually impure person, the sinner, the disinherited, the poor, the orphan, the widow and the enemy."[27] He wanted to bear witness to God in his concrete situation, and that led him to the cross.

From a theological perspective, however, Jesus' death is meaningful for Sobrino in that it raises new questions about God and the way in which he acts in history. On the one hand, it shows that suffering—political love—rather than power is "a mode of being for God."[28] It therefore sets the Christian faith apart from every other type of religion and brings out the weakness of a theology which, under the influence of Greek thought, does not conceive the possibility of God's suffering; first, because suffering implies change and, second, because suffering is not seen as a source of knowledge of God.

On the other hand, Jesus' death poses the problem of God in terms of *theodicy*, for "Jesus dies in total discontinuity with his life and his

23. *Ibid.*, pp. 184ff.
24. *Ibid.*, p. 188.
25. *Ibid.*, p. 202.
26. *Ibid.*, p. 214.
27. *Ibid.*, p. 207.
28. *Ibid.*, p. 371.

cause.''[29] That raises the question of what justification there is for a God who allows the sinfulness of the world to kill his Son and hence other human beings as well. In Sobrino's words, ''If the Son is innocent and yet is put to death, then who or what exactly is God?''[30] Thus, the theological consideration of Jesus' death forces us to reformulate our very conception of God. Far from being a response, the cross is a new way of questioning, an invitation to adopt a radically new attitude toward God. It shows us that there is no natural access to God, that ''the privileged mediation of God ever continues to be the real cross of the oppressed, not nature or history as a totality.''[31] By being crucified on the cross of Jesus, God takes upon himself all the pain and suffering of history and then reveals himself as the God of love who opens up a hope for the future through the most negative side of history.

What, then, does it mean to be saved by the cross? Sobrino responds that in the cross God has revealed his unconditional love, and that the culmination of that love for us is his work of preparing us to move from passive love to active love, so that we can experience history as salvation. ''We are made children of God by participating in the very process of God. Following Jesus means taking the love that God manifested on the cross and making it *real* in history.''[32] The cross, therefore, invites us to follow with Jesus the road to self-surrender and service through to the end, in the hope of resurrection. To conclude:

> The cross suggests that the reality of God may be viewed as a process that is open to the world. Through the Son, God actively incorporates himself into the historical process; through the Spirit, human beings and history are incorporated into God himself. Thus human life can be described as a participation in God's process.[33]

Jesus' resurrection

Sobrino attempts to understand the resurrection from the perspective of the cross, as the power of God over injustice—the triumph of justice. He observes that the canonical writings do not describe the resurrection itself,[34] but refer rather to the apparitions of the risen Jesus and to the empty tomb. ''The historicity of the 'empty tomb' tradition,'' says Sobrino, however, ''is a moot question.''[35]

In the New Testament, faith in the risen Lord does not depend on the existence or nonexistence of the empty tomb, but on the concrete experience of Jesus' apparitions, about which ''there can be no historical

29. *Ibid.*, p. 218.
30. *Ibid.*, p. 224.
31. *Ibid.*, p. 223.
32. *Ibid.*, p. 227.
33. *Ibid.*, p. 234.
34. *Ibid.*, p. 246
35. *Ibid.*, p. 374.

doubt that the disciples had some sort of privileged experience"[36] leading them to a new faith. In the light of the disciples' new-found faith the alternative posed is: "Either their novel experience can be explained by some natural mechanism or else it was caused by the 'presence of the risen one' that made itself known."[37] The final decision is not a matter of historical science. But historical exegesis can show that the disciples did in fact have faith in Jesus even after the cross had shattered their faith in him: that they tied their faith to the appearance of the risen Jesus, and that the ancient traditions regarding those appearances seem to be authentic, at least insofar as their nucleus is concerned.

What, then, is the meaning of the resurrection? According to Sobrino, the resurrection asserts that God is a deliverative power to be defined in historical terms rather than in terms of abstract characteristics. It asserts that God's action has been a salvific action of pardon and revitalization rather than of retribution, that humanity has been offered a new kind of life based on hope and love, and that Jesus stands in a distinctive relationship to God.[38] It was this conviction regarding Jesus' oneness with God that led Christian reflection to explore the various honorific titles of Jesus ("Prophet," "Servant of Yahweh," "High Priest," "Logos," "Lord," "Son of God," "God") and to develop a theological interpretation of the major events in his life. "The earliest reflection began exploring Jesus' special relationship of oneness with God in terms of the parousia yet to come or Jesus' exaltation in the present. It then went on to consider his oneness with God on the basis of Jesus' earthly life, gradually pushing that oneness further and further back toward the very beginning: transfiguration, baptism, virginal conception, pre-existence with God."[39]

The resurrection posits for Sobrino a hermeneutical problem because it is an eschatological event and, therefore, not immediately comprehensible. If one is to understand it, he says, several presuppositions are necessary: a radical hope in the future, a historical consciousness which sees history as a promise and a mission, and a specific following of Jesus the Messiah.[40] Without these, there will be a one-sided understanding of the resurrection, and the Christ of faith will be separated from the Jesus of Nazareth, as has happened in the past. Once the historical Jesus is forgotten, the Christian existence is turned into "religion," faith is turned into doctrine, the lordship of Christ is used as the basis of Constantinian politics, and Jesus becomes a cultic diety.[41]

All accounts of Jesus' resurrection, says Sobrino, stress mission, and

36. *Ibid.*, p. 375.
37. *Ibid.*, p. 376.
38. *Ibid.*, pp. 376-77.
39. *Ibid.*, p. 378.
40. *Ibid.*, p. 380.
41. *Ibid.*, pp. 381ff.

mission as a proclamation of Jesus, the risen Christ, and as a work of service related to the new creation. To comprehend the resurrection as historical, therefore, is to comprehend it as an event which establishes new history and to participate in the transformation of the world.[42] "We cannot preach the resurrection of Jesus if we do not have the active *intention* to flesh out in reality the hope that finds expression there."[43] This means that the hermeneutics designed to comprehend the resurrection is *political*. In other words, it has to do with a praxis which takes into account the suffering of the cross but also hopes against hope.[44]

Christological dogmas

Classical Christology begins with the incarnation. Sobrino's Christology moves in the opposite direction, from below to above. For him, "Jesus gradually fashioned himself into the Son of God, became the Son of God."[45] He claims that in both types of Christology there is an element of mystery, for "both must include some kind of becoming in order to make explicit the mystery of Christ."[46] But he goes on to affirm that in the classic model, once the Son becomes man, it is difficult to see what is historical in the nature he assumes, while in the model he himself proposes, justice is done to the history of Jesus and the New Testament concept that "he learned obedience" (Heb. 5:8f.). "Both statements are doxological, i.e., the statement that the eternal Son became man, and the statement that Jesus of Nazareth becomes the Son of God. The question is whether the first doxological statement is possible without the second, at least in the light of the New Testament. . . . An authentically orthodox Christology must end up with the ontological affirmation of the Incarnation. Epistemologically, however, it must work in the opposite direction. It must examine the divinization of Jesus."[47]

In conclusion, for Sobrino, Jesus is the way to the Father, not in the sense that he is an epiphanic manifestation of the Father, but *the revelation of the Son*, that is of the correct way to approach and correspond to the Father.[48] The doxological formulation must be verified through the history of Jesus in the Gospels, interpreted in different situations and cultures, and fleshed out in the praxis of Jesus' followers. "The Chalcedonian formula continues to be true insofar as there really continue to be followers of Jesus, people whose concrete discipleship professes Jesus as the Christ."[49]

42. *Ibid.*, p. 254.
43. *Ibid.*, p. 255.
44. *Ibid.*, p. 256.
45. *Ibid.*, p. 338.
46. *Ibid.*
47. *Ibid.*, p. 339.
48. *Ibid.*, p. 340.
49. *Ibid.*, p. 342.

Traditional theology, says Sobrino, begins with the assumption that Jesus knew he was the Son of God, but modern exegesis cast doubts on that approach. The right approach, however, is not to view Jesus' sonship in *absolute* terms, on the basis of what he thought about himself, but in *relational* terms, in the light of his attitude toward the Father and the Kingdom of God. In relation to the Kingdom, he saw himself as playing a decisive role with regard to the "right moment." In relation to the Father, he had an explicit awareness which was expressed in his confident trust in God and obedience to his mission, and he grew in his consciousness through crisis and temptation. As Hebrews 5:8 says, "he learned obedience" and—adds Sobrino—through that learning "he became a human being and God's Son."[50] Here again the concept of two stages in Jesus' ministry plays for Sobrino an important role—the Galilean crisis marked a sharp break in Jesus' consciousness. "After the Galilean crisis Jesus moves toward an unknown future over which he has no control."[51] As a result, he radicalizes and concretizes his relationship to the Father in trust and obedience.

In the light of the foregoing discussion, what is the role of the dogmatic formulation of Christology? Dogmas, says Sobrino, have a positive value. On the one hand, they set limits which are sometimes important and should be respected by all versions of Christianity.[52] On the other hand, they are doxological statements, similar to those of the liturgy, seeking to describe limit-realities. They do not bring out the basic data concerning Jesus which appear in his own history. On the contrary, by centring on the relationship between divinity and humanity in Christ, they prompt us to overlook his unconditional trust in and complete obedience to the Father.[53] The proper logical order of Christology is the chronological order: "We are justified in starting our Christology with the historical Jesus because that is the only way in which our dogmatic formulas can have any real meaningfulness. It is literally impossible to begin with the Council of Chalcedon because the meaningfulness of its statements is made possible only insofar as it takes in the whole process of cognition and praxis that led to Chalcedon."[54]

In the New Testament Jesus' uniqueness and distinctiveness, says Sobrino, are derived from his relationship to the Father, characterized by complete confidence and perfect obedience. That is the historical background behind the doxological affirmation of his divinity in relationship to his Father. To speak of the unity of humanity and divinity in Jesus, therefore, is to speak about something that is verifiable. "We are saying that Jesus is a person who becomes the person he is precisely

50. *Ibid.*, p. 364.
51. *Ibid.*, p. 365.
52. *Ibid.*, p. 333.
53. *Ibid.*, p. 332.
54. *Ibid.*, p. 334.

through his surrender to the One who is the Father."[55] Thus the identification of Jesus with the eternal Son of God is done indirectly, on the
basis of Jesus' historical, tangible, filiation to the Father.[56]

The dogmatic statement is thus maintained, but "instead of beginning with the doxological affirmation of the incarnation of the eternal
Son in Jesus of Nazareth (the theology of *descent*), it ends up with the
doxological statement that this Jesus of Nazareth is the eternal Son."[57]

In the case of the Christological dogmas, they have to do with the
essence of the Christian faith and must be seen as limit-statements
rendered possible by the activity and destiny of the historical Jesus; but
they do not say more (nor say it necessarily better) than can be gleaned
from the life of Jesus as it is presented in the New Testament. On the
other hand, they are based on the Hellenistic outlook. Therefore they
talk about divinity and humanity in abstract terms, assume an *a priori*
knowledge of God and humanity, present an ahistorical interpretation
of Jesus, conceive the divinity of Jesus in ontic rather than relational terms,
and relate Jesus to the eternal logos rather than to the Father. Despite
these conceptual limitations, the Chalcedonian formula does show that
the ultimate meaning of human existence was revealed in Christ. It offers
a model explanation of the person of Christ, and states positively that
Jesus is the eternal Son of God. This last affirmation, however, can only
be understood when it is seen that Jesus' surrender to the Father took
place through Jesus' concrete, historical incarnation in a specific situation, and that it was through that surrender that Jesus became the Son.
Here the author makes the point that if the fact that Jesus is the Son
is taken seriously, the conclusion is that Jesus is not the manifestation
of the Father but rather the revelation of the way one must respond to
God. "In short, the Son reveals the way to the Father, nót the Father
himself."[58]

What, then, are we to make of the notion that the Chalcedonian dogma
has a universal significance? The universality of the formula, says Sobrino,
implies that it must be translated in different local situations. "Without
that process of translation Christ would be universal only for one culture
or one specific situation—a contradiction in terms."[59] Because the dogma
is universal, every human being in every historical situation is offered
the possibility of following the way of Jesus, thus becoming a child of God.

Discipleship or the following of Jesus

As Sobrino sees it, in the first stage of his ministry, Jesus restricted his
summons to discipleship to only a few, whom he called to active service

55. *Ibid.*, p. 336.
56. *Ibid.*, p. 337.
57. *Ibid.*
58. *Ibid.*, pp. 387-88.
59. *Ibid.*, p. 388.

on behalf of the Kingdom. Later on, when he no longer believed that the Kingdom was near, Jesus saw discipleship as following him on his journey to the cross and made his call both basic and universal.[60] Because his view of himself and his mission changed, his concept of discipleship also changed and came to be understood as "following the concrete person in a situation where it is not at all obvious that Jesus himself has very much to do with the coming of the Kingdom as people had envisioned it before."[61]

We gain access to Christ through discipleship and, therefore, through the historical Jesus, since "access to the Christ of faith can only come through access to the historical Jesus."[62] Whenever the historical Jesus is overlooked or forgotten, the Christian faith tends to turn into religion, that is, into "a conception of reality, in which the meaning of the whole is already given at the start because the reality of God is satisfactorily shaped and defined from the very beginning."[63] When the Christian faith takes on a religious structure, it ceases to be Christian.[64] Historically, however, this has been, according to Sobrino, "the most radical temptation facing Christianity."[65] By proclaiming the Kingdom of God, Jesus raises the question of the meaning of history. The definitive answer to this question is given in the resurrection. In order to grasp the resurrection as the answer, however, the following of Jesus in terms of a praxis designed to affect liberation is the essential hermeneutic. "It is only from within such a praxis that human beings can come to comprehend the resurrection as a response to the whole question of history's meaningfulness. Thus *access to the Christ of faith comes through our following of the historical Jesus.*"[66] Since Jesus expected the imminent arrival of the Kingdom, however, Christians must explain the following of Jesus in the context of a history that does not seem to be near its end. So they require religious, social, economic, and political analyses to organize history on its way toward the Kingdom of God. The following of Jesus, therefore, takes account of Jesus' basic attitudes and motives; but it cannot come down to any mere "imitation" of Jesus.[67] Contact with God is made by journeying toward the goal promised in Christ's resurrection in an on-going quest for liberation, trying to fashion his Kingdom.[68]

Discipleship or the following of Jesus is for Sobrino the general paradigm of Christian existence.[69] Such an approach stands in contrast

60. *Ibid.*, p. 116.
61. *Ibid.*, p. 361.
62. *Ibid.*, p. 275.
63. *Ibid.*, p. 275.
64. *Ibid.*, p. 277.
65. *Ibid.*, p. 278.
66. *Ibid.*, p. 305.
67. *Ibid.*, p. 306.
68. *Ibid.*, p. 307.
69. *Ibid.*, p. 389.

with the classical approach to Christian ethics, in which Aristotelian virtues have played a far more important role than discipleship. The outstanding feature of Jesus' lifestyle, according to Sobrino, was his concern to concretize through praxis the meaning of such realities as "God," "hope," and "love." He demanded the same of his disciples—they were to concretize orthodoxy through a praxis which consisted in following in his footsteps and proclaiming the Kingdom. Even after the resurrection, when Jesus himself became an object of orthodoxy along with God and one might have thought that access to Jesus would be possible through the liturgy apart from praxis, the Christian life continued to be the following of the crucified Christ (Paul) or a life of service motivated by love (John).

The supremacy of praxis over orthodoxy is derived from the nature of divine revelation. The object of revelation is not abstract knowledge of God, but a manifestation of God in action; not a message of God's love to be talked about, but a liberating love to be received.[70]

The following of Jesus is thus "the most original and all-embracing reality, far more so than cultic worship and orthodoxy."[71] It can be described as faith, hope, and charity but as faith, hope, and charity which are fleshed out in history in such a way that one is immersed in the historical process even as Jesus was. Christian *faith* is the acceptance of a God who manifested himself in the resurrection but was silent on the cross, and is silent on all the crosses of history. Christian *hope* is a hope that looks forward to the fulfilment of the universe but also takes a stand against injustice and death, hoping against hope. Christian *love* is a love that acts in the midst of alienation and suppression and transforms power into service.

The Christian life is concretized from the standpoint of the cross. It is following Jesus on his journey to the cross, willing to experience God's abandonment on the cross through the experience of injustice in history, and willing to die in self-surrender with hopes of a new heaven and a new earth.[72]

II. CHRISTOLOGICAL MODELS FROM ASIA AND AFRICA

1. "Third-Eye Theology"

In *Third-Eye Theology: Theology in Formation in Asian Settings*, Choan-Seng Song, Associate Director of the Secretariat of the Faith and Order Commission of the World Council of Churches, is concerned with the articulation of an incarnational theology, a theology "open to the mysterious ways of the God who in Christ becomes human flesh in Asia."[73] Although

70. *Ibid.*, p. 391.
71. *Ibid.*
72. *Ibid.*, pp. 393-94.
73. *Third-Eye Theology: Theology in Formation in Asian Settings* (Maryknoll: Orbis Books, 1979), p. 21.

Christology is not the main point on his agenda, the image of Christ which emerges out of the pages of his book is definitely one of an Asian Christ that challenges both the plastic Jesus produced by a civilization where human issues are trivialized[74] and the *logos* projected by a theology which assumes that the reality of God can be grasped by human reason.[75] Convinced that even as Christ had been seen through German eyes, he must also be seen through Asian eyes, Choan-Seng endeavours to do what he calls "Christ-type theology."[76] For the sake of brevity, I will limit myself to mentioning the points of contact between his Christology and that of Jon Sobrino:

     a.   For Choan-Seng Song, as for Sobrino, theology has to be *incarnational*, centred in Jesus Christ and God's salvation in and through him.[77] For that reason, he grounds Christology on Jesus of Nazareth. "The Jesus of history and the Christ of faith," says he, "are essentially one. There is no Christ of faith without the Jesus of history, and the Jesus of history cannot be correctly understood and experienced apart from the risen Christ."[78]

In contrast with Sobrino, however, Choan-Seng does not assume that in order to be historically relevant Christology must be built from below. Theology for him takes as its starting point neither the Jesus of history alone nor the Christ of faith alone but the incarnate Son of God. "We begin with the God-man Jesus Christ on earth."[79]

     b.   For Choan-Seng, as for Sobrino, theology has to be a *theology of the cross*. The new creation comes into being through God's suffering in Jesus Christ. "The suffering God is . . . the redeeming God. Or to put it the other way around, the redeeming God is the suffering God. God commits himself totally to the suffering of this world. This is fundamentally what the incarnation is all about."[80] And again, "Jesus Christ is the God-man in suffering."[81]

What about the concept of the vicarious suffering of Jesus Christ? Choan-Seng accepts that this affirmation, that Christ who is sinless took sin upon himself on our behalf, "has been a central affirmation of the Christian faith,"[82] and that "vicariousness has become essential in the understanding and experience of God's salvation."[83] At the same time,

74. *Ibid.*, pp. 32f.
75. *Ibid.*, pp. 41ff.
76. *Ibid.*, p. 54.
77. *Ibid.*, p. 21.
78. *Ibid.*, p. 188.
79. *Ibid.*, p. 79.
80. *Ibid.*, p. 54.
81. *Ibid.*, p. 101.
82. *Ibid.*, p. 165.
83. *Ibid.*

however, he sees that although Jesus suffered and died *for* the sins of the world, sin and death continue to be part and parcel of life in history. "The vicarious suffering and death of Jesus Christ has not done away with our suffering and death."[84] He then appeals to Jürgen Moltmann's "theology of the crucified God" as offering the important insight that "The God who is crucified on the cross is not so much the God who vicariously suffers and dies *for* the world as the God who suffers and dies *with* the world. . . . The crucified God is the God who identifies all the way with us in our suffering and death. He suffers with us and dies with us."[85] Thus neither in our suffering nor in our death are we alone— "the God of our faith is the God who suffers our suffering and the God who dies our death."[86]

Choan-Seng sees the cross as the basis for hope against hope. By entering into our suffering, God gives us hope. "Jesus Christ is that hope incarnate,"[87] and there is no power in the world greater than the power of this hope rooted in God's suffering love. "Here is precisely," Choan-Seng concludes, "the paradox of the faith: when we embrace the powerlessness, weakness and death of God hanging on the cross in Jesus Christ, we come to embrace his power, strength and life. The mystery of the incarnation is the mystery of this paradox."[88]

c.   For Choan-Seng, as for Sobrino, theology has to be a *political theology*. Because of the resurrection, the powerlessness of God on the cross has become the affirmation of life against death. "The God of the cross is vindicated by the God of resurrection."[89] But the power of the resurrection is none other than the power of the powerless God on the cross. "The cross is the meaning of the resurrection. This is God's politics of resurrection."[90]

It follows that the task of the church is the affirmation of hope and the power of hope in the midst of a hope-denying world. "Evangelization is an act of empowering people with the power to suffer unto hope. . . . The mission of the church must therefore be a mission of promise and a mission of hope."[91] The resurrection is a celebration of life against death, but it is also a call to follow the risen Christ to the cross. "The resurrection faith of a Christian community becomes a historical faith when the cross of the risen Christ becomes its central concern. Apart from this cross, there is no other way for the church or Christian com-

84. *Ibid.*
85. *Ibid.*
86. *Ibid.*, p. 166.
87. *Ibid.*, p. 167.
88. *Ibid.*, p. 168.
89. *Ibid.*, p. 180.
90. *Ibid.*, p. 181.
91. *Ibid.*, p. 172.

munity to become an effective force in the world. The church guided by the cross of the risen Christ is a historical church."[92]

2. "Jesus Before Christianity"

In *Jesus Before Christianity*, Albert Nolan, Provincial Superior of the Dominican Order in Southern Africa, attempts "to take a serious and honest look at a man [Jesus] who lived in first-century Palestine and try to see him through the eyes of his contemporaries."[93] The coincidences between Nolan and Sobrino[94] are striking:

    a. For Nolan, as for Sobrino, the starting point for Christology is *the historical Jesus*. Beginning with his baptism by John the Baptist, therefore, he sketches Jesus' ministry in the face of the impending judgment of Israel announced by his forerunner. He shows that the people to whom Jesus turned his attention were the poor and the oppressed, who were "the overwhelming majority of the population in Palestine—the crowds or multitudes of the gospels."[95] Moved by compassion, Jesus healed the sick and went out of his way to mix socially with the sinners. Furthermore, he proclaimed the good news of the Kingdom of God— "news about a future state of affairs *on earth* when the poor and the oppressed would no longer be miserable"[96]—taught new values, and announced the coming of a new era in which men and women would be totally liberated.[97] His ministry, however, ended up with a trial, sentence, and execution by the Roman procurator Pontius Pilate on a charge of high treason. This well-attested fact shows that the religio-political leaders of Israel did not see him as a religious revivalist who steered clear of politics, but as "a dangerous and subtly subversive revolutionary"[98] who under the cloak of religion was undermining all the values upon which religion, politics, economics, and society were based.

    b. For Nolan, as for Sobrino, *Jesus' death was the historical consequence of his life*. "There is a paradox here, the paradox of compassion. The one thing that Jesus was determined to destroy was suffering: the sufferings of the poor and the oppressed, the sufferings of the sick, the sufferings that would ensue if the catastrophe were to come. But the only way to destroy suffering is to give up all worldly values and suffer the consequences. Only the willingness to suffer can conquer suffering in the world.

---

92. *Ibid.*, p. 193.
93. Nolan, *op. cit.*, p. 1.
94. Both authors published their works in the same year, 1976. (In the case of Sobrino's work, this is the date of the original Spanish edition.)
95. *Op. cit.*, p. 26.
96. *Ibid.*, p. 46.
97. *Ibid.*, pp. 82ff.
98. *Ibid.*, p. 100.

Compassion destroys suffering by suffering *with* and *on behalf of* those who suffer."[99] According to Nolan, the basic fact that Jesus went to death willingly and knowingly is well established by the evidence, but not so the fact that Jesus predicted his resurrection. "Jesus could not have predicted that he would rise before the last day, otherwise all the confusion, doubt and surprise when he did rise would make no sense at all."[100]

Far more important than the question whether or not Jesus predicted his resurrection is whether or not Jesus was in fact raised from the dead. Interestingly enough, Nolan makes the passing remark that some of those who had known Jesus "were convinced that they had seen him alive again after his death" and that "they and the women who discovered the empty tomb said that Jesus had risen from the dead."[101] He asserts: "To believe that Jesus is divine is to choose to make him and what he stands for your God. To deny this is to make someone else your god or God, and to relegate Jesus and what he stands for to second place in your scale of values."[102]

  c.   For Nolan, as for Sobrino, *faith in Jesus Christ is not a question of orthodoxy*. "To acknowledge Jesus as our Lord and Saviour is only meaningful in so far as we try to live as he lived and to order our lives according to his values. We do not need to theorize about Jesus, we need to 're-produce' him in our time and our circumstances."[103] If Jesus' central motivation was compassion and faith, discipleship has to do with a life of trust in God and identification with the needy in the face of evil. "Jesus was immeasurably more human than other men, and that is what we value above all other things when we recognize him as divine, when we acknowledge him as our Lord and our God."[104]

III. CRITICAL EVALUATION

It is quite clear that the image of Christ which emerges out of the writings of Two Thirds World theologians is one that cannot be lightly dismissed in the name of orthodoxy. For the sake of brevity, I will restrict myself to three observations, all of them bearing on the Christian mission:

1. Two Thirds World Christology stresses the humanity of Jesus Christ and challenges us to rediscover the social dimensions of the gospel.

It must be admitted that all too often Jesus Christ has been reduced to intellectual abstractions or encased in ecclesiastical dogmas. Uninformed

 99. *Ibid.,* p. 113.
100. *Ibid.,* p. 116.
101. *Ibid.,* p. 135.
102. *Ibid.,* p. 136.
103. *Ibid.,* p. 139.
104. *Ibid.,* p. 138.

by Jesus of Nazareth, who, when he saw the multitudes, ''had compassion on them, because they were harassed and helpless, like sheep without a shepherd,'' Christology was useless as a basis for meaningful Christian action on behalf of the poor and the oppressed. The rediscovery of the historical Jesus must be welcome as it places service, patterned on him who came not to be served but to serve, at the very centre of mission.

The word of caution needed here is that unless the stress on the humanity of Jesus is balanced out by the recognition of his deity, Christian action is bound to be reduced to mere human effort. It is no mere coincidence that Sobrino should see the Kingdom of God as a utopia to be fashioned by men rather than as a gift to be received in faith.

2. *Two Thirds World Christology stresses the fact that Jesus' death was the historical outcome of his life and challenges us to suffer because of righteousness.*

The word of warning needed here is that unless the death of Christ is also seen as God's gracious provision of an atonement for sin, the basis for forgiveness is removed and sinners are left without the hope of justification.

3. *Two Thirds World Christology stresses the historical nature of the Christian life and challenges us to commitment to Jesus Christ for the transformation of the world.*

The reduction of the gospel to doctrinal formulas goes hand in hand with another misunderstanding of the nature of the Christian life and, therefore, of the Christian mission. All too often the assumption is made that faith means intellectual assent, that the mark of a Christian is inner peace, and that the mission of the church is the salvation of souls. A new emphasis on the practice of truth, and on practice related to God's purpose of renewing his creation, is a necessary corrective.

The word of warning needed here is that salvation is by grace through faith, and that nothing should detract from the generosity of God's mercy and love as the basis of joyful obedience to the Lord Jesus Christ. If it is true that Christianity without the cross is Christianity without Christ, it is also true that Christianity without God's gift of his Spirit to enable us to follow Jesus is not Christianity but a new slavery to the law.

Both the theory and practice of mission to a great extent reflect a specific Christology. The biblical insights of Two Thirds World Christology are a promise of renewal for the Christian mission in today's world.

DISCUSSION WITH RENÉ PADILLA

Q. Is Christology purely the field of writers and theologians? Is the Christology of the Two Thirds World only the Christology of the three writers discussed in the paper? What is the Christology of the thousands of people who are proclaiming Christ every Sunday in the Two Thirds World?

R.P. The question is about the function of theology. My brothers and sisters who are proclaiming Jesus Christ all over the Two Thirds World have an implicit Christology. But often, Christology needs to be corrected in the light of Christological reflections based on the New Testament. Theologians and writers have a critical function in asking "Who is the Jesus being presented to people in the midst of great turmoil as for example in Latin America? Is he a Christ who has to do with their own personal sin and security but nothing whatever to do with injustice, poverty, or oppression?" On the other hand, what do we have to say to people who would make Jesus just another revolutionary, and who say that only the historical mission of Jesus matters?

I am concerned about a proclamation of the gospel which is wholistic, a proclamation that has to do with man's person, with his personal relationship to God and his own personal integration as a human being, with what is going on around in society and with what God wants to do with history. I am concerned with a personal Christianity and a social Christianity. We are not justified in separating the two. Jesus Christ did not and the Bible does not. Our Christianity must be wholistic. One of the functions of theology is to help the whole of the church, especially these many thousands of people who are proclaiming Jesus Christ, to understand better what the wholeness of the gospel is all about.

Q. The basic philosophical presuppositions in both Sobrino and Padilla seem to be fundamentally western. For Padilla's warnings appear to assume that there is a fundamental distance and distinction between the actions of man and of God. The actions of God in practice tend to be miraculous, to be something that man cannot do. The understanding of reality that informs this presupposition is that God's thoughts are not man's thoughts. This presentation supposes a God who is always intervening in history from the outside, and is not related to man. Is this the only possible understanding of reality? Or is there another understanding that helps us see that actually people's actions are God's actions and God's actions are people's actions, yet there is a distinction that not all of the actions of the one are necessarily those of the other?

R.P. The problem lies in dealing with the question in terms of assertions rather than in recognition of who Jesus Christ is. The New Testament never uses the sort of terminology that would give rise to the idea that we are to fashion the Kingdom. It talks about the Kingdom of God being manifested in Jesus' works. There is a close relationship between Jesus Christ and the Kingdom of God. He does not only proclaim the Kingdom. In himself the Kingdom becomes present in history. I agree that God takes up human action to realize his purposes and that we must not state things in such a way as to give the impression that everything God does is miraculously done. We must be careful not to transform Christianity into a new legalism and suggest that somehow through works we fashion the Kingdom. I believe in human action which is a response to something God has done in Jesus Christ and is not simply a way in which we fashion the Kingdom.

Q. Is it true that Sobrino hardly mentions the Holy Spirit, or does he attempt to develop a trinitarian Christology? Does he appear to neglect the Holy Spirit because he speaks of Christ and the Trinity in relational rather than ontological terms?

R.P. I am not quite sure that we should say that the whole problem with Sobrino is that he is trying to get away from ontology and explain the Trinity in relational terms. There is a metaphysics behind any approach to reality.

There are philosophical assumptions whether we want to say this is metaphysics or not. There is a materialistic metaphysic in which everything is reduced to matter and everything can be explained under the basis of history. So we have not got away from metaphysics. A naturalistic metaphysics still remains.

I think we find a relational approach to the Trinity in the New Testament too. I have no problem in trying to elaborate Christology from below as I think this is also found in the New Testament. I am comfortable with everything that is affirmed positively about Jesus Christ becoming the Son of God because the New Testament does say that he learned obedience and that is a perfectly human experience. In the Gospels we find lots of statements that lead us to think that here we have a real man who grows in the understanding of his mission and develops in every possible way. Jesus Christ becomes the Son of God, Jesus Christ is the incarnate Son of God. In traditional theology the whole concept of Jesus Christ who becomes the Son of God is denied or assumed as unimportant.

Q. If we start from below with the historical Jesus, does this necessarily lead us into adoptionism? Why cannot the historical Jesus simply be recognized as divine and human? If Jesus only became the Son of God, how are we to evaluate those passages in Scripture which deal with preexistence? If Jesus only became the Son of God, what precisely is the incarnation? If he only became the Son of God, how is Jesus' divinization different from the divinization of other believers?

Sobrino's adoptionism seems to create a problem in his theology of revelation. He says that the Son is only the way to the Father and does not reveal the Father. How does he interpret John's prologue which speaks of Jesus as the only begotten Son of God?

R.P. Sobrino very boldly says, "Finally we have to conclude that in Jesus we have the revelation of the way to become Sons of God," therefore the revelation is of the Son, not of the Father. Then he says: "This is a shocking statement from the Christian perspective because it reminds us of adoptionism." But I do not think his approach necessarily involves adoptionism.

He says that somehow when the writers of the New Testament tried to understand the significance of Jesus' life theologically, they kept pressing back and enlarging the figure of Jesus Christ. They said that he was not only one who lived an unusual sort of life but that he also had the special experience of the Holy Spirit in which the Spirit descended on him. Then they went back further and said that he was also born miraculously. Then they went back even further and said he was preexistent and then even further back to say he was one with God. Are we talking about the creation of a myth or are we talking about the proclamation of a Jesus who is the Son of God and became the Son of God? The creation of a myth and the proclamation of a preexistent Jesus are not the same thing.

The Christological passages in the New Testament seem to speak of a cosmic preexistent Christ, whose death was not only the historical outcome of his life but also fits into God's eternal purpose and therefore has a significant relationship to the forgiveness of sins. Already in the New Testament there is a basis for a Christology that goes beyond Jesus' historical ministry. Such statements as Jesus' own statement in Mark 10:45 that "The Son of Man came not to be served but to serve and to give his life as a ransom for many" point in the direction of a Christology in which the historical life of Jesus and the transcendant Christ who sacrificed himself have a significant relationship to the forgiveness of sins.

So the ontological Jesus Christ I find in the New Testament certainly cannot be reduced to his history alone. His death and resurrection have to be explained on the basis of revelation if you are to be biblical and therefore I would say Christian.

The difficulty we have in understanding Sobrino is that we live in a world where dogma prevails. We live with no concept of the historical Jesus who identified himself with the poor. That is why it is so shocking to read those who point out that in the New Testament there is a political dimension to Jesus' life and death. This is most relevant to mission today. We like abstract thinking. That is often how the message has been transmitted to us. I wonder whether the development of Marian dogmas in Latin America for instance is related to this problem of abstract thought. Is it because Christological dogmas have meant nothing to people in their historical existence and Jesus Christ is a pale abstract figure, that people have created a Mary who is a mother, who loves them and is close to them?

Q. Choan-Seng Song stresses that Jesus came to identify with our suffering and that God is the suffering God. But where is the deliverance from suffering? Or is suffering itself salvation? What is the hope that we have in suffering? Does he go one step further and ask who are the suffering, why are they suffering, and who caused their suffering? In the Asian situation we have to deal with more than the negative aspect of suffering, otherwise we would indicate that suffering is itself a virtue.

R.P. Choan-Seng Song is the first Asian theologian whom I have read almost in one sitting. You may feel differently because you are in the Asian context but I find him much more orthodox than many other people. On the question of suffering he makes a great effort to rescue the uniqueness of the suffering of Jesus Christ. He makes statements to the effect that Buddha's suffering is not redemption and that there is a unique purpose in Jesus Christ's suffering which is power for redemption. He says that the atonement is a central statement of our faith. I agree with him that it does not explain the suffering which is going on in the world today. We have to discover if there is any light we can get from Jesus Christ's death to understand the suffering of many people today, or our own suffering. We have to ask what is the historical significance of Jesus' suffering in relation to our own suffering.

Q. In Christological thinking should we not take into more serious consideration the basic Christian theocentric outlook from the Old Testament? Our direction must not only be toward incarnation but also toward God. We must not be too influenced by our situation that we forget that in the New Testament the apostles asserted that the same God whom the Jews believed in and were serving, raised Christ.

R.P. Behind the New Testament Christology there is indeed a God who has revealed himself in the history of Israel. But, the starting point in the New Testament is "Who is Jesus Christ? What are we to say about him?" From then on we can say who God is. Otherwise our theology would not be Christian. But, this is a discussion in which it has taken centuries even to clarify the questions.

3. The Liberating Options of Jesus

NORBERTO SARACCO *(Argentina)*

Synopsis

Jesus chose Galilee the land of the dispossessed as the place for his ministry, in preference to Jerusalem the place of power. His message to the scribes and pharisees was mediated through his works in favour of the needy and his identification with their expectations. Jesus' option liberates God and the Gospels from the clutches of an alienating religiosity and from ideologies which maintain dehumanizing relationships. His option is not a struggle for power, but it dynamizes the conscience of the oppressed in a project of liberation, unmasks everything which prevents the full realization of being human, and calls to conversion.

INTRODUCTION

To approach the event of Jesus with the purpose of situating him in his social, economic, and political context may be motivated by multiple interests which extend from the ingenuous biographical purpose to the search for the revolutionary Christ, as well as the intents of psychologizing, historicizing, and scientifizing him. Behind all of this is the old and always new question of who was and who is Jesus. These are questions that we cannot evade if we are serious about our faith, which is no more and no less than a faith in Jesus.

The variety of approaches to the life and work of Jesus are represented in different Christologies. This diversity is even present in the New Testament, especially in the Gospels. This Christological plurality is the reflex of the different "loci," in the light of which the works of Christ are interpreted and conditioned, in good measure, by the historical contradictions.

In our reading of the relation of Jesus to his context, we try to avoid the temptation, always present, of "parallelisms." These lead us to search for situations in the text which compare with ours, with the purpose of establishing an almost magical relationship that does not take seriously the text nor our situation. We prefer to explore, in light of our commitment, the meaning of the liberating options of Jesus. With this we affirm first that Jesus related to his own context through options which were both relevant to the context and in accordance with his redemptive project. The places of ministry, the content of his message, and the addresses are not merely the decorative scene of Jesus' mission, they are his primordial objective. We affirm secondly that these options have "a deposit of meaning" (*reserva de sentido*) which we can and should discover, in the light of our own option and commitment.

THE GALILEAN OPTION

Can anything good come from Nazareth? (Jn. 1:46). With this question, full of doubt and astonishment, Nathanael receives the words of Philip concerning Jesus. Surely, Nathanael's questions transcend the problem of the Nazarene origin of the Messiah. The fact of the matter is that he does not question whether the Messiah could possibly come from Nazareth. Rather he is questioning whether "anything good" can come from that small and unobserved town that is without mention in the Old Testament. The objection is directed to the impossibility of this rural population being able to produce something "good." Undoubtedly, it was not from Nazareth or Galilee that a pious and "real Israelite" (Jn. 1:47) could expect something to which it was worth listening. However, Jesus chose this place as the special and preferential context of his ministry. His Galilean option would have disappointed the expectations of the religious of his era, and also of those interested groups who wanted to have a monopoly on the Messiah. But at the same time, the Galilean option of Jesus has a reservoir of meaning (*reserva de sentido*) and should be viewed from the perspective of the redemptive project.

Because of its mixed population, Galilee, the hometown of Jesus, was despised and even considered pagan by some. The distance that separated Galilee from Judah, and especially from the Jerusalem Temple, had a significant effect on the religious development in the synagogue. During the ministry of Jesus there was in Galilee a group of disinherited people without a country. This was the product of immigration from Judah in search for better living conditions.[1] It is likely, due to the possibilities and opportunities in Galilee, that it became overpopulated. There was an abundance of orphans, widows, poor, and unemployed.

This situation was a contrast to the kind of life the Jews were living in Jerusalem. Things were different there. The mere fact that Jerusalem was the religious centre gave her and her inhabitants a privileged existence. We know that in certain instances the Roman empire reduced their taxes. The rest of the Palestinian population not only bore the major weight of taxation of the empire, but also paid an added tribute to the Temple. The imposed tax was considered an oppression. Because of this benefit to the Jerusalemites there arose a strong Jewish aristocracy, composed principally of the high priests, elders, and scribes. They were zealous in maintaining the status quo as a means of keeping their privileges.

1. Gerd Theissen, *Sociologio del movimiento de Jesus* (Santander: Sal Terrae, 1979), p. 36.

The inhabitants of Jerusalem were also bound in one way or another to the Temple, and likewise to its commercial activity. Among other things, approximately 18,000 individuals were involved in the reconstruction of the Temple which took from 20/19 B.C. till 62/64 A.D. If we add to this the different commercial activities related to religious life we can understand how a town without industry or productive activity lived nevertheless in a state of tranquility and relative economic comfort. This situation caused a convergence of interests between the low and high classes of society. At the same time, it enabled the inhabitants of Jerusalem to assume a conservative stance and attitude.

We can understand the implications of the Galilean option of Jesus in the light of this conflict between Galilee and Jerusalem. His ministry has two important elements: his response to immediate needs (sickness, poverty), and his identification with the expectation of the most needy.

The ministry of Jesus for the most part develops in towns and rural places. The episode of Peter's denial reveals that the majority of the people recognized Jesus' disciples as a Galilean movement (Mk. 14:70). We encounter here a certain similarity between the movement of Jesus and other rival movements, in reference to their ambivalent attitude toward Jerusalem.[2] Although Jerusalem was considered a "holy" city (Mt. 5:36), this holiness was at a loss when confronted with its reality. Essenes, Zealots, and Jesus all distanced themselves from Jerusalem. When Jesus pauses to reflect on the situation of the city, the only thing he does is weep for her (Lk. 13:34).

The confrontation between the expectations represented by Jesus in his Galilean option and the ideologies of the inhabitants of Jerusalem becomes tragically evident in the events that surround the crucifixion. The group which Jesus headed was under suspicion because it originated from Galilee (Mk. 14:67-70). On entering Jerusalem he is hailed by the people who came from the rural areas to participate in the Passover festivities. For this reason the Sanhedrin decides for the moment not to stop Jesus "or the people may riot" (Mk. 14:2). As Theissen asserts, this statement is directed to the rural peasant people who congregated for the feast, because the inhabitants of Jerusalem were always present.[3] In this context they thrust accusations against Jesus that were related to his messianic pretension and to his prophecy of the destruction of the Temple (Mt. 14:58-61).

In this situation, Jesus becomes a threat to the Jewish aristocracy and the people of Jerusalem. Some saw their structure of power in jeopardy. Others were afraid that their source of sustenance would diminish. Because of this, representatives of the Sanhedrin and anonymous elements of the inhabitants of Jeruselem join their voices against Jesus. The critical activity of Jesus in front of the Temple (Mk. 11:15ff.), and his preaching

2. *Ibid.*, p. 49.
3. *Ibid.*, p. 55.

against it constituted a serious threat to the benefits and privileges of the priestly aristocracy. In his Galilean option, Jesus identifies and unmasks the centre of oppression which was hidden behind the religious order, rather than the Roman empire. The common affirmation, that the people who received Jesus triumphantly are the same who one week later crucify him, is incorrect. In reality, they were two groups who represented opposite poles of society.

Neither Jerusalem nor the tomb could detain or enclose Jesus. Before dying, Jesus had promised his disciples a new meeting in Galilee (Mk. 14:28) of which the angel reminds the women at the tomb (Mk. 16:7). Matthew later mentions that, from the mount in Galilee, Jesus commissions his disciples and followers to disciple all the nations (Mt. 28:16-20).

In the Galilean option, Jesus liberates God, the Gospel, and the mission from the clutch of an alienating religiosity. It is in opposition to all ideologies of faith, which tend to sustain and maintain dehumanizing relationships. Mission here has a universal projection in the context of a people who struggle and suffer for their total liberation.

HUMANIZATION AS A PRIORITY

As a point of departure in his solidarity with those who suffer, Jesus designs his ministry with the intention of destroying all that prevents the realization of the total person. His works and words point to a new reestablishment of values imposed or accepted as just or sacred. His provocative attitude makes manifest the alienation of prescriptions and customs whose purpose is self-perpetuation. The sabbath institution allows Jesus the opportunity to execute his pedagogical actions. He moves on the imperceptible line which separates the "sacred" from the "profane" and "obedience" from "sin." The actions of Jesus on the sabbath day put to the test the ladder of values of the pharisees and the guardians of the law. His liberating interpretation concerning the observance of the sabbath is assumed to be an attack on the law (Mt. 12:1-14). The questions of the religious leaders do not side with humanization, but with legalism. Jesus did not rebel against the sabbath but rather against the ideological use of the sabbath, which placed the emphasis on tradition rather than on man. In the name of tradition, doctrine, and sanctity, dehumanizing situations are sustained.

In the same perspective, we need to place or locate the attitude of Jesus toward those who were marginalized by society and the synagogue on account of their condition. Undoubtedly, his option for these is the germ of the gospel, as the good news of liberation.[4] The sick and defeated, the poor and the stranger, the children, the women and sinners lived the

4. J. Saverino Croatto, "La dimencion politica de Cristo Libertador," *Jesus ni Vencido ni Monarca Celestial* (Buenos Aires: Tierra Nueva, 1977), p. 162.

reality of being humans of a second category. The love of Jesus expressed in the healing of the sick (Mt. 12:9-14), his dealing with women (Jn. 4:27), and his identification with the poor and disenfranchised (Mt. 11:28) was a constant cause for scandal. For that reason, he advises the followers of John the Baptist that the blessed ones are those who are not scandalized when the blind see, the lame walk, the lepers are cleansed, the deaf hear, the dead are resurrected, and the poor have the gospel proclaimed to them (Mt. 11:5). We should interpret the signs of the Kingdom not only in reference to what the Kingdom offers as immediate benefit to the needy, but what it contains as a prophetic and provocative confrontation to the religious structure. The gestures of Jesus have the value of returning "the human" back to man, over and above all intent of dehumanization. We can see that the attitude of Jesus to the law and the sabbath, and the way he related and acted with the publicans and sinners, is a "radical option" against those closed circles of the pious, and thus against the representatives of official Judaism.[5]

The relationship of Jesus with the scribes, pharisees, and other factions that participated in power, is not, for the most part, a direct confrontation. On the contrary, it is mediated by his works with the needy. His approach is not a theological-academic discussion about the importance and validity of the sabbath and the law. It is not a conceptualization of poverty behind the backs of the poor and needy. Jesus heals, liberates, and restores. His works are what confront and shake the representatives of the official theology. In other words, the message to the scribes and pharisees is mediated through the works in favour of the needy. Therefore, one as much as the other are the addresses of the liberating love of Jesus.

But the expression of this love assumes different paths. To some it heals. The healing demonstrates to others that the law and the sabbath have meaning if they are directed toward the integral humanization of people (Mt. 2:27). The humanization of some, and the conscientization of others, are two faces of the same redemptive work. All will need to choose or reject it (Lk. 11:14-23).

BLESSED ARE THE UNFORTUNATE

We encounter in the Gospel of Luke three narratives which in context and distinct expectations speak clearly of the options of Jesus in favour of those who suffer need or live under oppression, be this moral, social, or religious. Mary's Magnificat (Lk. 1:46-55), the reading of the prophet Isaiah in the synagogue of Nazareth (Lk. 4:18-19), and the proclamation of the Beatitudes and woes (*oyes*) (Lk. 6:20-26) reveal the character of the redemption brought by Jesus.

The *Magnificat* is a hymn sung to the greatness of God. It exalts the manifestation of his love and power, in favour of the lowly and weak.

5. Gunther Bornkamm, *Jesus de Nazaret* (Salamanca: Sigueme, 1975), p. 44.

At the same time, it relativizes the power of the powerful. The vocabulary employed in this psalm jolts us, due to its clarity and radicalness. It proclaims with catastrophic signs the implications of Christ's actions. For her part, Mary announces and celebrates the inversion of situations. The powerful and arrogant of heart who live in the security of their strength will be dethroned. But the humble ones, accustomed to bending in front of the strong, and those whose rights are trampled on day by day, these shall be exalted (v. 52). All that is part of their dignity will be returned. The hungry and needy will receive abundance, while the rich will be divested of their riches (v. 53).

We need to highlight two elements here. First of all, the liberating action of God is not rooted in hate, but in love. It is not a violation of rights, but justice. Mary is joyful. There is no shadow of resentment (vv. 46f.). The Magnificat does not proclaim that the hour of revenge has come, but rather a time of mercy (vv. 54-56).[6] Secondly the love, justice, and mercy of God are expressed necessarily in conflict. If there is hunger, it is because there are rich people; if there are the fearful, it is because the powerful exist. The only way to satiate the hunger of the hungry and to eliminate the fear of the fearful is to "send the rich empty away" and "dethrone the powerful." According to the manner in which the antagonistic groups live, so the manifestation of salvation is different. Some will be divested while others will be filled with goods. But both are objects of the same love of God. The Magnificat anticipates, in the announcement of the birth, the scandal of the cross.

In *Isaiah's prophecy*, appropriated by Jesus in the synagogue of Nazareth (Lk. 4:18-19), we find the manner in which Jesus interprets the scope of his ministry and mission. His "This day is this Scripture fulfiled before you" (v. 21) expresses his total identification with his reading. The first thing that surprises us is the concrete missionary enunciation. It is a liberating project situated in the context of historical and human needs. We cannot force the text to give another meaning which is not strictly literal about the condition of the poor, sick, and oppressed.[7]

Jesus here connects his mission with immediate problems, but his works transcend the limits of space and time. Before salvation could be universal it needed to pass through the path of the particular. Because Jesus responded in depth to his own concrete situation, his ministry is projected far beyond his own time. His in-depth response not only enables his disciples' response, but the church can have no other mission than that which the head of the church had. The text which recounts his response comes as an "open project" with an invitation to the readers to discover the paths for making this redemptive programme effective.

The *Beatitudes* have a direct relationship with the Magnificat, and with

---

6. Eduardo Hamel, "El Magnificat y la Inversion de las Situaciones," *Selecciones de Teologia* 20 (July–Sept. 1981), 237.

7. Richard Cassidy, *Jesus, Politics and Society* (New York: Orbis, 1978), p. 22.

what Jesus assumed as the objective of his mission in the prophecy of Isaiah. Again an inversion of terms appears. He proclaims, Happy are the poor, hungry, and those that cry and are persecuted (vv. 20-22). But, of course, the happiness does not lie in their present situation, but rather in the fact that they will be liberated from it. The ever-pressing question is, when?

The classical interpretations attempt to translate this "when" way beyond history. Something like, "the present joy is dependent on the fact of a future post-historic reality, when they will no longer cry, or hunger, or be persecuted or poor." Without pretending to negate this reality we consider that to locate the benefits of the Beatitudes only to a life beyond death is to betray the intentions of Jesus.

In the first place, the announcement in the Magnificat and in Jesus' sermon in the synagogue of Nazareth can only be a reality in as long as the Beatitudes are directed to the present. There is no meaning what-soever in saying that the Holy Spirit anointed Jesus (Lk. 4:18) so that the blind could see "in the hereafter."

Secondly, we need to view the Beatitudes as a contrast to the woes. "Blessed are you the poor" (v. 20) is opposed to "woe to you who are satiated" (v. 25). In this perspective both poles of the same reality appear entailed. There is a direct relationship between the rich and the poor; between the persecuted and the persecutor. The Beatitudes and woes bring this situation to light. Because of this, it is honestly impossible to think of a God who takes seriously the sinful situation, and yet transposes its solution to a meta-historical time. It is true that the contradictions will be fully overcome in the eschatological Kingdom. But it is also true that this Kingdom has come near to us in the person of Jesus (Mt. 3:2; 4:1-7).

On the other hand we should beware of falling into the simplistic notion that the Beatitudes presuppose a change in the poles of oppression.[8] This would be to establish a circular relation between poor-rich-poor; or between hungry-satiated-hungry. Such a thought lacks meaning. The event which the Beatitudes point to is the overcoming of causes of poverty, hunger, persecution, and tears. In speaking of causes we implicitly recognize the existence of a causal agent. The rich or poor, the tears or laughter, do not exist per se. There are riches because there are rich peo-ple; persecution, because there are persecutors. The Beatitudes and woes speak to us of the causes, and to them it is directed. Once again, the love of God passes through options which arouse conflict; options which Jesus did not refuse to take and neither should we.

THE COST AND MEANING OF THE OPTIONS OF JESUS

Jesus was not a political leader. He did not organize the people who fol-lowed him with subversive purposes to seize power. He did not rebel

8. J. S. Croatto, *op. cit.*, p. 171.

against the Roman empire, nor did he advocate that others do so. Many of his followers dreamed of such a possibility, but his strategies and objectives did not respond to such expectations. Some of his disciples were to a certain extent disillusioned about this. But Jesus died as a seditious person hung on a cross. The questions that arise are, what did Jesus do to deserve such an end, and what meaning does his life and death have for us?

In the first place, although Jesus did not lead a specifically political movement, nonetheless, his style of life and ministry represented a threat to the established order. Taking his option for humanity as his point of departure he directed his strategies against the dehumanizing elements found in the power structures that had a monopoly on the Temple and the interpretation of the law. For that reason, Jesus is not interested in liberating the Jews from Roman power. That would have provoked fortification of the internal situation of oppression. Since his struggle is not a struggle for power, those who are uncomfortable with his message do not know which excuse to use in order to eliminate him. Without discussing data we are all familiar with, it is sufficient to mention that the confusion and diversity of accusations that surround the trial of Jesus reflect the disorientation of those who wanted to kill him. The only thing they were sure of was the need to eliminate Jesus. The primordial option of Jesus in favour of humanity and not only the Jews cost him his life. At the same time it endows his sacrifice with universal character. The death of Jesus is not enclosed between racial walls. Rather it transcends them all totally.

The options of Jesus constitute a double provocation. On the one hand, they dynamize the conscience of the oppressed, identifying with their expectations. These are found channelled in a project of liberation whose objective is neither vengeance nor power. On the other hand, the options of Jesus have within themselves a prophetical meaning, as long as they unmask all that, in any order, would rise against the full realization of being human.

The options of Jesus are the call to conversion. This is concretized in following him. That is to say, the conflictual dimension of the Kingdom prevents indifference. "He that does not gather, scatters" (Lk. 11:23). Jesus is not identifying with any of the movements of his time, whether they be religious or political, or even the most radical. He is situated in a position that transcends the limits of each one and judges them.

This attitude raises the question of what our responsibility and commitment as Christians have to do with the needs of humankind. A distorted vision of what Jesus accomplished could lead to a spiritualization of the conflicts, or to the search for a neutral position, not contaminated with the processes of history.

Rather, the options of Jesus challenge us to live our faith in such a way that it descends from the subjective plane to historical works. Such an attitude would be marked by the vulnerability and precariousness of our humanity. At the same time, however, it should be a sign of hope and salvation. We should live our faith in such a way that it becomes a sign of contradiction. We make this option, fully conscious that the conflict with the powers of evil places us always in the perspective of the cross. Nevertheless, our faith and hope is in him who arose and waits for us always in Galilee.

4. The Image of Christ in Latin American Indian Popular Religiosity

KEY YUASA *(Brazil)*

Synopsis

An introduction to the Iberian Roman Catholic, African, and Indian components of Latin American civilization and especially popular religiosity which forms the context of Christological reflection.

We will first clarify the concepts implied by the theme: Latin America, Religiosity, Popular, and Indian.

Latin America: Geographically Latin America includes South America, Central America, the Caribbean Islands, and Mexico in the North American continent. Latin stands in contrast to Anglo-Saxon, and means especially the Spanish and Portuguese (Brazil) domains in the Americas, which developed into independent countries. French is also a Latin language and civilization in Haiti, French Guyana, Guadeloupe, Martinique, and French-speaking portions of Canada. Italian migrants, although they did not form an independent country, have come in considerable numbers to the USA, Argentina, and Brazil. Besides these, considerable numbers of Mexicans, Puerto Ricans, and Cubans in varying statuses have been entering the USA and have produced a sizeable Latin American enclave of 23 million Hispanic people inside that Anglo-Saxon country.

HOW LATIN IS LATIN AMERICA?

The expression "Latin America" covers a great variety of cultures, civilizations, languages, and histories. Sometimes the expression is used or heard without taking into account all the various non-Latin realities (languages and civilizations) which coexist in this part of the world. Soon after the discovery, the Spanish and Portuguese started to bring people from Africa in forced migration. This African presence in the Americas (North, South, Central, and Caribbean) was meant to be just a slave labour force. But they soon started to contribute their songs, rhythms, dishes, and languages to the culture and civilization of the Americas. Their contribution was not limited to the labour force and folkways. With time it expanded into all spheres of human activity, where we can see

42

distinguished peoples of African descent active: politicians, novelists, artists, legislators, Christian leaders, sportsmen, and scientists.

In certain cases there has been resurgence of African religions and African divinities. Students of this phenomenon have indicated that in certain instances the organization of sacred space is a sort of reproduction of African geography. Thus people whose language, customs, religion, and dignity had been suppressed sought to relate to the mother country, and thus enhance their self-identity. So we can speak of Afro-America. Nuclei of Afro-American cultures can be seen in Brazil, Peru, Colombia, Venezuela, the Guyanas, and Surinam. They also exist in the USA, in all the Caribbean Islands, in come countries in Central America such as Panama and Nicaragua, and in Honduras, where there was a re-migration from the West Indies. Afro-America is therefore a reality which pervades Latin America and stretches beyond its confines into the Anglo-Saxon world in the Caribbean and in North America.[1]

The original inhabitants of these lands who came to be known as Indians[2] belong to great number of different languages and civilizations. Some groups were just tribes and some were nations. Some were organized in highly sophisticated systems and constituted empires such as the Aztecs in Mexico, the Mayas in Central America, and the Incas in South America. At its height, the Inca Empire extended further than the Roman Empire. But Indians and Indian languages are not simply archaeological remains. They are today a living reality with which our countries have to live. From the matrix of this language and ethos, that which is strange, or violent, or inadequate, or does not give life is constantly checked, ignored, or even rejected.[3]

Guarani is spoken universally in Paraguay. There is even a Guarani Academy of Letters. Quetchua in Bolivia, Ecuador, and Peru, Aymara in the region of Lake Titicaca, Mayan in Central America, and Nauatl in Mexico are languages spoken by millions of people.

Thousands of Indian names for toponymics, fauna, and flora have been

1. Roger Bastide, *Candomblpe da Bahia*.
2. Note the curious meaning that the word "West Indians" came to have. In Portuguese and Spanish the word "Indio" means specifically the American Indians. That which is related to India is "indiano" or hindu. "Indigena" means in Portuguese "that which is related to Indians in the Americas," while in English "indigenous" came to have the meaning of "autocthonous, related to any country."
3. Cultural anthropologists and folklorists have been indicating that the soul of the people is manifested in art forms and popular mythologies. They include messages from the collective subconscious, and reveal all the fears, anxieties, and actual conflicts of a people. Sergio Zapata, Psicoloanalisis del Vals Peruano, writes: "When any element (food, dwelling, myth or a song) shows ability to satisfy the needs of the community, it is kept organically ingrafted to the culture of the group, in a vital way." A. R. Cortazar, *Esquema del Folklore* (Buenos Aires: Columbia, 1959).

included not only within the Spanish and Portuguese spoken in the Americas, but even in English.

Hundreds of languages spoken in our continents have made a rich and varied contribution to the western civilization. This Indo-America is not limited to the geographic space of Latin America but stretches northward through the USA and Canada even to Alaska and Labrador.

In a certain sense the Indo-American universe is both a shrinking and an expanding reality. It is a shrinking reality because the Indians' languages and ways are constantly being westernized.

There are always more children going to schools and less people having only one Indian language as their means of communication. Their customs and religion are changed. There is less space for Indians to be themselves. This includes several aspects: from the crude reality of their land being constantly invaded and taken away to rejection and all kinds of prejudice. A leading newspaper in one of the Latin American cities printed an analysis of the image of the Indian in schoolbooks in that country. The conclusion was that the education about Indians in that country, where hundreds of thousands of Indians live, was immoral and cynical. Indians were clearly rejected as their copartners in living in that country.[4] There was an assumption that a really good Indian is a dead Indian and that Indian civilizations belong to museums.

But Indo-America is also an expanding reality. The voice of the Indian peoples is being heard in ever wider circles. The mass communication systems are carrying more news and defending their cause. There have been more leaders although many leaders are killed. More tools such as grammars, dictionaries, and bilingual schools, regional associations of Indian peoples, and even a World Association of Indian Peoples with connections with the United Nations have been created.[5] According to its president, George Manuel, there are about 350 million Indian (aboriginal) people in the world, in almost all continents, including Europe, Africa, Asia, and Oceania. They would not be part of the Third World. They are the Fourth World.

Latin America has very important Afro-American and Indo-American realities existing within it and interacting in all sorts of combinations. Sometimes the Latin element, sometimes the African, sometimes the Indian element predominates. But somehow, these three basic components are present.

So Latin America has important roots in civilizations that are not Latin. To this complex of the interpenetration of civilizations came further migrants from European countries, Latin or otherwise, from the Middle East, Eastern Europe, the Far East, and from the neighbouring Latin American countries.

4. W. B. de Almeida Mauro, *Educacao imoral and cinical o indio no livro didatico* (Folhetim, *Folha de S. Paulo,* Jan. 20, 1980).

5. Carlos Alberto Luppi, *O Quarto Mundo quer uma tribuna na ONU* (Folhetim, *Folha de S. Paulo,* Jan. 20, 1980).

COMPARISONS BETWEEN LATIN AMERICA, ASIA, AND AFRICA

There are four hundred million Latin Americans, four hundred and seventy-two million Africans, and two billion six hundred million Asians.

Similarities

Let us examine the similarities between them. First, archaeological evidence indicates the antiquity of human presence in Latin America as well as in Asia and Africa. By the time Europeans arrived in the Americas, there were tribes, nations, and empires. By negotiation, treachery, aggression, and war, these lands and peoples were annexed by the European empires. Western countries established colonies in Latin America as well as in Asia and Africa, and European languages became official languages in most of the countries.

These advances were justified on Christian grounds as fostering Christendom. The Iberian conquistadores had political, economic, and religious motivations. Very few people could see injustice in this. Those who saw it and voiced their discontent were considered enemies of the king and of the Christian cause. Since the nineteenth century Latin America has become independent. The independence process is still occurring nowadays in small territories.

Continentally speaking there is an overall growth from mutual isolation toward association and continental solidarity. This can be seen not only on the political level but also in church life.

Latin America has been a missionary field for all kinds of churches and sects and Christian and non-Christian religions. It has been a battleground for opposing ideologies which had their centre of decision making outside the continent. Secularism and consumerism have grown but at the same time there has been a resurgence of non-Christian religions and all kinds of syncretism. Most of Latin America belongs to the so-called Third World.

Dissimilarities

Latin American aboriginal populations have been living in almost total isolation from other continents. Europeans therefore stepped into a practically virgin continent as they arrived in the sixteenth century. They were received as children of the gods. In contrast to Asia and Africa, Latin America has great uniformity in language and religion, at least on the official level. Spanish and Portuguese are closely related and cover almost all of the continent. Roman Catholicism is the religion of the majority of people even when they are participants in other religions.

Latin American Roman Catholicism has differed from European Roman Catholicism in that there is a massive Roman Catholic population and a lack of priests. A century ago one priest might be taking care of up to one hundred thousand people. This was fertile ground for popular religions to develop. Nowadays the world average for Roman Catholics is one priest for 1344 Roman Catholic people. In Europe it is one per 1067, in Latin America it is one per 7000 and in Brazil it is one per 7692. The situation in Latin America is therefore ripe for the development of lay leadership and popular forms of Christian faith.

COMPARISON BETWEEN LATIN AMERICA AND ANGLO-SAXON AMERICA

Let us also make some comparisons between Latin America and Anglo-Saxon America.

Similarities

Latin America and North America were discovered, colonized, and divided into territories belonging to different European powers. Latin America, like North America, has an aboriginal population who were sometimes domesticated, and sometimes converted into slaves. When they resisted, they were suppressed. Latin America, like North America, has a sizeable black population who were bought as slaves.

Dissimilarities

While North America had Anglo-Saxon and Protestant colonization, Latin America had Iberian and Roman Catholic colonization. Somehow the Protestant outlook in sciences, human liberties, and social organization meant that there was a more modernizing attitude compared to Roman Catholic countries. Protestantism represented a rebellion against Papal authority, which used to be absolutist and universal not only in religion and politics but even in the sciences. Although the Council of Trent tried to reform Roman Catholicism, the Roman Catholics were very conservative. For example they tried to revive the Pope's old absolute authority. The discovery of America meant for the Iberian kings and the Pope that their fight in Europe against the Moors was approved by God. They received America as a gift from God, so that their idea of Christendom could be expanded and continued on the other side of the ocean.

One example of the medieval character of Roman Catholicism in the Americas was the presence of the Inquisition, with all its heresy trials, applied not only to the Jews, Protestants, and atheists, but also to the Indians.[6]

6. Here it is not suggested that all Protestant doings were good and all Roman Catholic deeds bad. The testimony of a man like Bartolome de las Casas in Mexico, advocating the rights of the Indians, is unparalleled. He fought a bitter fight with the Spanish conquistadores, the Spanish crown, and the Spanish clergy. He would anathematize all the clergy who forgave the doings of the conquistadores. The following material is something like his spiritual testament. It is a quotation from his official representation to the Council of the Indies in Spain in 1565. It is a resumé of his lifelong battle.

    1. All the wars called "conquista" conquests were highly unjust and tyrannical in character.

One example of the "modernity" of Anglo-Saxon colonization is seen in the land tenure and possession systems. In the North, the colonizers and pioneers marked and took possession of the land according to the measure of their capability to make it produce. Soon land proprietors associated themselves together for mutual defense. In the South, the King of Portugal or Spain gave large expanses of land as a gift to the nobility who would not work and cultivate these lands themselves. This meant land feudalism. The people who worked these lands were quite often serfs, slaves, and others who were not free proprietors. This basic economic and social structure deeply marked the difference between these two societies.

John Mackay in his classic and paradigmatic book *The Other Spanish Christ*[7] was able to see in Latin America a different Christ from the one he was accustomed to seeing. He was able to dig into Spanish history and tradition and discover a real richness of Christian tradition, overcoming the normal biases and prejudices that Anglo-Saxon brothers would have in relation to Latin civilization. He indicated some of the differences he saw in Spanish character: intense individuality, predominance of passion, an abstract sense of justice, and a concrete sense of man and catholicity. His book made many Latin American leaders deepen their roots and their self-identity.

2. All the domains and lordships in the Indies were illegitimately stolen from the Indians.

3. The encomiendas or distribution of lands of Indians therein are extremely evil and "per se" bad and tyrannical and this government is tyrannical.

4. All those who grant them (encomiendas and distribution) are sinning mortally, and if they do not abandon this behaviour, they are damned.

5. The King our Lord (may God prosper him and guard him with all the power he has given him) cannot justify the wars and robberies made against these people, nor the above referred encomiendas and repartimientos, which in reality are worse than the wars and robberies done by the Turks to Christian peoples.

6. All the gold, silver, pearls, and other riches brought to Spain from the Indies, were stolen, and not extracted. Only very little were extracted. And I say extracted because perhaps they refer to gold taken from islands and places which we have first depopulated.

7. If those who have robbed, and stolen do not restitute what they have thus taken illegitimately, and continue to rob and steal through the acceptance of encomiendas and repartimientos, they will not be saved.

8. The natural people at all places we have entered in the Indies have acquired a right to make a very just war against us, and wipe us away from the face of the earth. And this right shall endure until the day of Final Judgement.

From the conclusion to "Representation to the Council of Indies, Memorial al Consejo de Indias" (1565), Fray Bartolome de las Casas. See J. B. Lassegue, "La larga marcha de Las Casas," *Seleccion y Presentacion de Textos* (Lima: CEP, 1974). We have not so far seen any similar indictment from Protestant people.

7. London: SCM, 1932; Spanish edition, *El Otro Cristo Espanol* (Mexico: Casa Unida de Publicaciones, 1952).

RELIGIOSITY

This word is being used very much nowadays in Latin America. It is preferred to the word "religion" when it comes to describing the phenomenon of popular religiosities. A "religion" denotes something identifiable and definable because of a certain degree of coherence, persistence, and systematization. Students of religious phenomena in Latin America are recognizing that people's religions have, besides that part which clearly belongs to one or other identifiable religion, shades, half tones, and mixtures, which though they cannot be catalogued as belonging to the same religion, are important manifestations of what the person is believing or experiencing.

Religiosity includes beliefs, attitudes, the object of cult, and institutional elements. Beliefs refer not only to that which can be articulated as the content of belief, but also realities and experiences in the subjectivity of people, which precede belief. Attitudes include that which can be observed, both of body and mind; facial expressions, voice, words, movements, song, music, dance, processions, stillness, and meditation. The objects of cult include such items as special clothing, beverages, food, water, blood, amulets, crucifixes, altars, images, animals, and divinities. Institutional elements refer to such things as organization of doctrine, sacred space and time, language and grammar of cultic exercises (individual or collective), the division of responsibilities, and specialization of functions.

POPULAR

There is a whole universe of meanings behind the word "popular." It all depends from what perspective the word is viewed. The word "popular" is used in contrast or opposition to a number of realities and notions. "Popular" is that which is not the elite's; that which is not cultured; that which is not patriarchal; that which is not rich and elaborate; that which is not Portuguese or Spanish, but which is more African and Indian; that which is not according to the Roman canon, but which is Latin American; that which is not formal, nominal, or social but is related to authentic life experiences.

The word "popular" will have the meaning that each will give it. If we are working with the people as a partner and companion, this reality will be present when we refer to "popular." If we make the people objects of our studies of our ministry, this reality of reification will also be present. If we are biased against what is the people's or if we move with an ideology of the poor then these realities shall always be present in our talk about "popular."

In Latin America several factors have worked to direct attention to "the people:" the work of sociologists and cultural anthropologists;[8] the work of educators, especially those who, after the orientation of Maria Montessori and Pestalozzi, have worked on the creativity of illiterate people. For example Paulo Freire's method enhances the creativity of people in the educational process: it changes them from receivers of education to active participants in the process. Liturgists are searching for ways to improve people's responses with Latin American music, inspired by the African Missa Lube. Many Latin American churches have been producing masses that include Latin American music. As a result there is much better participation of the people. It even altered Catholic ecclesiology by developing a second focus so that the whole mass did not focus on the clergy alone. (Cf. Missa Criolla, Missa Panamericana, Missa Panamena, Missa Luba.) Since 1930 the Pentecostal movement has become the largest evangelical group. The leaders in many Pentecostal churches have no academic training. Sociologists of religion have noted the resurgence of spiritism, of Macumba and Umbanda. The Liberation theologians, starting in Lima, Peru with Gustavo Gutierrez, have expanded since the sixties. Even if the Roman Catholic hierarchy did not entirely agree with their position, they have taken in much of what was there. In their pastoral orientation all over Latin America they have given preferential priority to the poor people. Further factors are the movement for *Volkskultur* (popular culture and evaluation of popular music, drama, expressions, etc.); the interest of missiologists, studying the religious soil which receives the seed of the gospel and the work of pastoralists developing a "pastoral popular."

INDIAN

A great diversity of situations exist under this category. It is beyond my ability to properly represent their reality, and the meaning of their being our counterparts.[9]

I am poignantly aware that I cannot represent them quantitatively or qualitatively. I do not know even the names of all the tribes living in Brazil. The Institute of Ethnology of the University of Berne, under the

8. In Brazil, Silvio Romero, Nina Rodrigues, Artur Ramos, Euclides da Cunha can be cited as pioneers; then Gilberto Freire, Roger Bastide, Maria Isaura Pereira de Queiroz, a multitude of people in the Roman Catholic Church, and outside also.

9. The Wycliffe Bible Translators have done extensive anthropological and linguistic studies. They have produced dictionaries, grammars, primary readers, and portions of the Bible in many languages. There are many Indian evangelical communities. Close to my home city, Rev. W. Hery is working among Kaingang Indians. There are also descriptions of Indian Christian evangelical communities among the Taba Indians. See also *Church Growth in the High Andes* by Keith Hamilton, and the references in footnote 18.

auspices of the Programme to Combat Racism (WCC), mentions the existence of 205 Indian groups in eleven countries, out of which more than half are in Brazil.[10] But this list does not include Chilean groups, or any of the Central American and Caribbean countries, and nothing is mentioned about Mexico where more than 100 languages are spoken. The list did not include the different Ketchua and Aymara groups in Bolivia, Peru, and Ecuador. The tendency in our countries has been to take the Indian populations as an exotic and marginal reality. Their presence is really massive, and every item must be taken into consideration.

Latin American popular religiosity is therefore the product of the encounter and interaction of Iberian popular Roman Catholicism, Indian religions, and African religions. Each one of these elements has variables. The product of one encounter can cross-fertilize with another. Roger Bastide in his classic study of Afro-Brazilian religions found it necessary to include a chapter on the Pagenlancia and Catimbo, which are a typically Indian heritage. In the region of Maranhao the black people had not only become participants of that form of popular religion without ceasing to be Roman Catholics but also had become leaders of that cult. This exemplifies the meeting and syncretisms which occur. No one cultural universe is closed in itself, but is in living contact with others. In Macumba and Umbanda, African deities are working together and having nice fellowship with the Indian spirits and Roman Catholic saints. Sometimes the syncretism is synchronic in the sense that the people belong to two religions at the same time. They belong to two religions but the two coexist without mixing.

Sometimes the syncretism is diachronic, in the sense of consecutively belonging to different cults, so that a person could have started as a Roman Catholic, become Protestant, and is now following an Afro-Brazilian cult, awaiting the day when he will return to Roman Catholicism.

In the case of Indians, are there common denominators which identify the Indian culture and religions? We do not know the Indian languages and their internal logic and grammar. Though a vast amount of languages are already known, many are still to be discovered or deciphered. But some common experiences in recent centuries since the discovery of America form a possible common ethos.

A common experience to all Indians in all three Americas and the

10. In Venezuela 23 Indian groups were surveyed, in Columbia 63 groups, in Ecuador 10, in Peru 37, in Bolivia 29, Paraguay 17, in Argentina 9, in Brazil 118, Guyana 8, in Surinam 4, in French Guyana 5, totalling 205 groups in these 11 countries. Cf. *La situation del Indigena en America del Sur* (Tierra Nueva, Montevideo, 1972, 514 pp.). In Brazil, the Museum Goeldi in Belém conducts permanent surveys, researches, and expeditions, and publishers in their bulletin a rich collection of factual and interpretative data on Indian tribes and life in general in the Amazon area.

Caribbean was the coming of western people, western Christian missionaries, discoverers, colonizers, and representatives of kings, which suddenly and violently disrupted their life.

This disruption was not just a question of beginning a different way to survive. It was a real destruction of the material aspects of a civilization and also of the core and matrix of that culture. J. C. Mariategui has helped us to understand this in his "Siete Ensayos de Interpretacion de la Realidade Peruana" particularly in the chapters on the Indian, and on the Earth.

> The colonial regime disorganized and destroyed the agrarian economy of the Inca Empire, without replacing it by another one with better productivity. Under the native aristocracy, the Indians were 10,000,000 efficient men, with an organic and productive state. Under a foreign aristocracy, the aboriginal people were reduced to an anarchical and dispersive mass of one million people.[11]

In that context the cult of Pacha Mama (Mother Earth) and of Inty Raimi (the God Sun) had intimate relationship with agriculture so that heliolatry and the cult of the earth were functional, economically speaking. There was a unity in cosmology, cult, agriculture, and state.

The experience of losing the land to which they were attached by the force of animism, and by a form of infantlike attachment to the protection of Mother Earth, left profound and lasting effects which even today can be seen in the form of a deep feeling of being orphaned, alone, and held captive by fate and death.

Mariategui would argue from his sociological and historical point of view, that the problem of the Indian is not a question of race, education, or religion. All stems from the problem of land. They have been dispossessed of their land, and this is the source of all their problems. Some time ago a series of BBC TV programmes in Britain about Canadian and US Indians showed exactly the same problem in the Northern continent.

People have to leave their lands because of political change, discoveries of mineral deposits, or the expansion of farmed lands. An article in the *Folha de S. Paulo,* 10 March 1982, says that the UN High Commissioner for Refugees is denouncing the fact that 12,000 Miskito Indians had fled from Nicaragua to Honduras.

In another South American country, two newspaper clippings dated May 6, 1980 and 16 December 1980 are very illuminating. The first one shows thirty-one Indian chiefs of the Xavantes Nation pressing the government officials in their office about delay in demarcation of their lands. Six months later one of the same chiefs declared that fifteen children of his tribe died in the hospitals from dehydration and pneumonia, and

11. J. C. Mariategui, *Siete Ensayos de Interpretacion de la Realidade Peruana* (Lima: Editorial Amanta, several editions), p. 47.

another six children died from poisoned waters in a stream. The Indian chief accused the authorities of trying to demoralize them.[12]

So when the Pope visited the Amazon area in Brazil in 1980 he made a speech to the Indians recognizing their right to land:

> I trust that the public authorities and the responsible people will take up my will which I express in the name of the Lord, that Indian people have special rights because they have inhabited these lands; having therefore a special right across generations, may you be given the recognition of your rights to live here in peace and serenity, without fear of being expropriated in order to give place to some others, that you may have the security of a vital space, which shall be not only the basis for your survival, but for the preservation of your identity as a people.[13]

The Pope received as an answer a declaration of twenty-six chiefs, produced shortly before in their XIVth Assembly of the Indian Peoples. The document said:

> We have heard that you are going to Manaus and shall listen to Indian songs and dances, but will you not be saddened and even cry, if you know that a people cannot sing and dance while their land is being taken away, their leaders are being killed, and thousands of our companions are working in slave conditions?
>
> You should see the Kaingang people, the Punkarare, the Guajajara, the Tukuna, the Bororo peoples, in order to notice the widows who weep for the violent death of their husbands, see the orphans whose parents were killed by Christians, in the very last three years. . . . It would be good if you could go to the Guapore Valley. . . . The men who studied the situation there, said that the Nambiquara situation and the doings of the government with them, constitute a case of national shame. . . .
>
> . . . If you went there you would certainly say that it is a case for world shame. All the world should be ashamed of what is happening with the Nambiquara Indians, and in higher or lesser degree, with all the Indians, whose lands FUNAI is exploiting. . . . The Kadveu are also living in great misery inside these areas. . . . We ask you to take our message to the world, so that mankind may know that this country is full of injustices, which would be a shame to any country, especially to a country which calls herself Christian. . . . Christ would have hard words to say to the leaders of this nation. And you, the Catholics say that you are a representative of Christ, what do you say? We the Indians who are still alive, and in the name of all those massacred by private and official initiatives, we sign this document.[14]

12. *Folha de S. Paulo,* May 6th and December 16th, 1980.
13. 10 July 1980, Message of Pope John Paul II in Manaus for the Indians.
14. July 4th 1980, *O Estado de S. Paulo.* See also the collection of documents of the National Conference of Bishops on the Indians, *Igreja e Governo* (S. Paulo: Simbolo, 82 pp.).

The following points should be noticed in the dialogue. The Pope included in his speech a recognition of the right of the Indians for their land. He addressed the Indians as loyal members of the Catholic Church. He referred to public authority also as people who should follow his recommendation.

The Indians name some areas where their land is being expropriated at the very moment of the speech. They say that the government authorities are participating in this expropriation. They speak to the Pope not necessarily as his subjects but as the representative of Christ according to the Catholic people. The Indians recognize that the situation is against the teaching of Christ, and ask the Pope to take an attitude. They desperately want the world to know their predicament.

POPULAR RELIGIOSITY ANALYZED

Ribeiro de Oliveira,[15] studying Roman Catholicism in Latin America as lived and practiced by people, characterizes it in an interesting way. He identifies three complexes or focal points in religious exercises which he calls sacramental, devotional, and protectional.

Sacramental experiences are mediated by properly constituted clergy. They refer centrally to the seven sacraments admitted by the Roman Catholic Church. Devotional exercises are those in which the believer enters by himself into contact with a saint or divinity, expecting otherworldly rewards if he keeps himself faithful to the promises he might make. Protectional exercises are similar to the previous ones, but the believer is expecting help for everyday life problems.

Research done by FERES, an International Catholic Social Studies and Sociology of Religion Programme, has disclosed the following results in the area of what kind of religious exercises people are engaging in:

	Sacramental	Devotional	Protectional
Brazil	14.5%	82.5%	75%
Colombia	19%	67%	65%
Venezuela	8.0%	88%	59%

The highest proportion of people engage in the devotional, the second highest in the protectional, and the least percentage engage in the sacramental.

Ribeiro de Oliveira used this chart to arrive at a definition of popular Catholicism. It is that sort of Catholicism in which the devotional and

15. P. A. Ribeiro de Oliveira, "Le Catolicisme popularie en Amerique Latine," *Social Compass* 14/4, *Revue Internationale des Etudes Socio Religieuses* (1972), 567-584. Idem, *Religiosidade Popular na Am Latina Revista Eclesiastica Brasileira* (Petropolis, 32/126, 1972), pp. 354-356, cited by Gunter P. Susse, *Catolicismo Popular no Brazil. Tipoligia e estrategia de uma religiosidade vivida* (S. Paulo: Loyola).

protectional constellations occupy the central position. The sacramental is subordinate and evangelical is insignificant.

G. P. Süsse comments:

> The most important result of this statistical research is the total absence of an evangelical constellation. In the field research only two people read the Bible and this occasionally. No one entered into contact with saints through the Holy Scriptures. The evangelical constellation is the great absentee in the Latin American Catholicism.[16]

If this is true, then there is, as has been the experience of all evangelical groups in Latin America, a vast space, a space providentially prepared where the living Christ as announced in the Scriptures is heartily welcome.

Another constellation of experiences can be called magic. Through magic people search for the solution to their problems, by the mediation of some witch, high priest, sorcerer, or fatherly or motherly figure. This of course would fall a little outside the Roman Catholic domain, but is not alien to masses of Roman Catholic people.

Then there are the widespread spiritists cults. This sort of religiosity interacts very easily with the Afro-American and Amerindian cults, because all three include some sort of spirit possession. This interaction occurs even if the spiritists tend to be prejudiced against more tribal forms of cult including animal sacrifice.

Studies have indicated that people pass from one form to the other along this mediumic continuum (cf. Candido Procopio).[17] One research study in the city of Belém examining hundreds of houses of religious practices showed that in the periphery there were the most tribal forms: trees are adorned, chickens are killed. Then you have a more urbanized form, spiritist, and then in the centre you will have other kinds of sophisticated gnostic religion, like Rosacrucionism or Masonic Temples. The whole thing is amazingly coherent. There is the same religious reality even if you change the garments. The law of Karma of Hinduism is prevalent in all this spiritism. The transmigration of souls is also there. There were no Indian gurus teaching these things but people were following them in the popular religions.

Recent researchers are examining and scrutinizing Pentecostal churches as a form of popular religion.[18] This would add quite a new element to the picture. On the religious soil of the sacramental, devotional, protectional, magic, and spiritist constellations just described, the seed of the gospel is being planted with a certain degree of success.

16. G. P. Süsse, *ibid.*, p. 79.

17. C. P. Fereira, *O Espiritiemo no Estade de S. Paulo*, FERES.

18. K. Yuasa, *Un Movimiento Cristiano entre les Otomies en Mexico* (Cuernavaca, Mexico, mim., 24 pp.). Walter Hollenweger, *Flowers and Songs—a Mexican contribution to doing Theology in Pentecost, Black and White* (Belfast: Christian Journals Ltd., 1974).

So popular religiosity can be said to include at least the following areas: Iberian popular Catholicism which became a member of Spanish and Portuguese Catholicism in the Americas, the Afro-American cults, Amerindian religiosity, spiritism of different levels, syncretistic religions, Pentecostalism, and modernized popular Catholicism represented by base ecclesial communities. All of these are in a process of interaction and change with people moving from one to the other.

POPULAR RELIGIOSITY AND THE OFFICIAL CHURCH

Popular cult places, messianic figures, miraculous apparitions, and pilgrimage locations are all realities of popular religiosity. Generally speaking the phenomenon is mediated by one of the people. Often a poor and illiterate person is the medium by which a cult comes into being. He may be a soldier, captain, businessman, or a clerk, but is always of the laity.

As the cult develops, the official church tries to dismiss or suppress it. Even the army took part in the extinction of some messianic movements.[19] The fact that laypeople develop as leaders in this way indicates a kind of protest against the monopoly of the hierarchy and clergy on religious matters.

If a movement cannot be extinguished, it may be incorporated into the Catholic Church. The sanctuaries of pilgrimage are places where the people give a large amount of money. Quite often a religious order is put in charge of the administration of the place and of the funds. There are also efforts to correct the abuses and move all this popular religiosity slowly inside the Roman Catholic Church.[20]

SOME CHRISTOLOGICAL THEMES ARISING FROM THESE INTRODUCTORY REMARKS

What have you done with your brother?

The encounter with the Indians in the Americas as a theological locus is very important. There are many human situations out of which you can theologize. But meeting with the original inhabitants is a very important task which is not often done. That is the place which we must come to, or go back to, in order to review our western history. Where we read the Bible is a very important theological issue.

Some estimate that of the 200 million people in Latin America, 40 million are Indians. It really depends what you mean by Indians. There

19. The narrative of the events in Canudos, Bahia in 1867–1897 has become one of the Brazilian classics in Euclides da Cunha, *Os Sertoes*.

20. Riolando Azzi, *O Episcopado do Brazil Frente ao Catolicismo Popular* (Vozes: Petropolis, 1977) gives an account of the Brazilian Episcopacy's actions in relation to places of worship, processions, feasts, devotions, sanctuaries, pilgrimages, and religious fraternities (lay).

are people in tribal situations, peasants in rural areas, city dwellers, those who still use Indian garments and still speak Indian languages and those who do not. But in fact all of us from all races are inheritors of the Indian civilization in many ways. We partake in their predicament in some way or other. We cannot confine that predicament to a certain number and say that it is their problem. It is a national problem. Ninety percent of the populations of Peru and Bolivia have Indian ancestry. It is a continental problem. It is vital for Argentina to address this issue otherwise they will continue to be European oriented and not be true South Americans.

As far as I know there is no place in Latin America where you have one ethnic group confined, be it in urban or rural areas. People are always going and coming. In many republics the president is descended from Indians. Sociology in Latin America is not a question of studying assimilation or integration of civilizations. Assimilation and integration may be too ethnocentric categories. We have to do here with a real interpenetration of civilizations, of universes. How does this happen? Someone asked me whether I feel more Japanese or more Brazilian. For me, these two realities do not conflict or exclude each other. I am of Japanese ancestry. I do not deny any of my ancestry, and all that I can learn and speak of Japanese I will. But I am definitely a Brazilian citizen. My identity as a Brazilian must pass through the Indian and African elements, otherwise it is not authentic. It is a truncated Brazilianness. So it is a task as a human being, and as a Christian. To pass through it is to assume what that history means. I must also take what guilt there might be and make it part of my Christian commitment and my Christian expression.

Is it possible to revise the history of western expansion to the Americas and see how the face of the Indian populations reflect how we have been? Has western Christian civilization the courage to see our face reflected in the face of our brethren the aboriginal peoples? The Fourth World confronts not only the Europeans and North Americans. It also confronts the Third World.

There is the theme of the Christo Incognito who comes to encounter us in the person of the suffering Indian (Mt. 25:31-46). This would include a revision of history, as a document like that of Bartolome de las Casas or the encounter of the Pope with the Indians would suggest. Would there be any reparations to be made, and if so how?

The unsaid prayers of Indians and popular religiosity

In theophanies and hagiophanies, the apparition occurs to poor and simple people. For instance our Lady of Guadeloupe appears to an Indian. Christo Morado was a cultic celebration on the outskirts of the city of Lima. Outside the house building, close to a wall, black people used to worship and it has now become a national cult of a black Christ. Our Lady Aparecida in Brazil is a statue discovered by fishermen. Are these not a kind of unsaid prayer that the poor and simple people may receive a revelation from God through poor people; that spiritual good be not something monopolized like everything else, by rich, cultured, elite oriented clergy, with the hierarchy's approval?

Many of these figures are ethnic figures; Guadeloupe is an Indian of Mexico; Christo Morado is the black Christ of black people in Lima; Our Lady Aparecida in Brazil is a dark wooden statue, often represented as a black lady, a negroid lady. Is there not evident here an unsaid prayer that divinities, and those who represent them, may not be just strangers (formally, conceptually, or language wise) but may be really incarnate among the poor? Are the promises of Joel 2:28, 29 and Acts 2 to be taken seriously today, that your children and servants shall receive the Holy Spirit and shall see visions and prophecies?

The theme of woman and family

In all Latin America there is an overpowering woman figure, in the person of Mary, the Mother of God, Queen of Heaven, sometimes even almost as a member of the Trinity. Should we not study Mariology seriously? Quite often we abhor Mariolatry and dismiss Mariology completely. We should study and practice the apostolic recommendation that people who govern their families well should be in charge of the church as pastoral leaders. So since women also govern families, the vocation of women in the church should be on equality with the role of men. The place of pater familias in the family worship in the Jewish tradition should also be considered with a focus on Jesus as a pater familias in, for example, the Passover feast.

The theme of the dispossessed

The experience of the Indians has been one of being dispossessed of their land and their heritage. This suggests important themes for Christological reflection.

The earth is a category which must be worked very seriously. It has basic anthropological, theological, and Christological weight. Since for Indians earth (Pacha Mama) is such an important and vital theme, I would like to indicate some lines for exploration: earth as a constitutive part of man (Admanh—Adam); land and work; cultivating, guarding, and naming (Gen. 1:15) as the sphere of humanity's collaboration with God; earth and land as promised to Abraham; land as belonging to God, and as a gift for his people to become a nation. The extension of the earth as a missiological and eschatological quantity is in focus when Jesus says that when the gospel is to be preached to all the nations, then shall come the end. The earth is, if not an eschatological at least an apocalyptic quantity in the light of the fact that if you blow up the planet, you end the life of humanity on earth. There is a solidarity here between people and the land.

In delineating Christology in relation to God's purpose for the earth, we should also explore the theme of the cosmic Christ in, for example, Colossians 1:15-20, and the theme of the birth pangs of creation in Romans 8, whose fulfilment in freedom is related to the final revelation of God's sons.

There is an ethos of being orphaned, being abandoned, living with solitude, fatalism, and death, among the Indian populations.[21] So we should work on the Fatherhood of God, the Sonship of Christ, the Son of God and Son of Man, joyful sonship, resurrection, and the victorious Christ.

The theme of martyrdom

There is a feeling for martyrdom, and a certian love for the figure of the martyred Christ who reflects the utterly desperate situation in which many Indians find themselves. This would call for a study of the suffering servant (Isa. 53, 49, 41) and the vicarious suffering and servanthood of Jesus (Ps. 22).

Other themes are the theme of those persecuted for the sake of justice, the theme of hunger and thirst for justice, and the theme of those who are treated as foreigners in their own country. There is the theme of the anger of Christ shown in the cleansing of the temple, and the theme of the anger of God against the unjust and those who persecute the weak. There is the theme of liberation (Exodus) and nation building.

The theme of silence

Nowadays we are hearing some voices raised in complaint. But most of the time there has been, and still is, a great and heavy silence. A French historian said:

> The Indians are quiet; they have not yet spoken their word. But how their eyes shine.

Could this silence be a shared silence, like the silence of the Saturday Passover feast, that precedes the morning of resurrection?

21. K. Yuasa, "El Sentimiento de Abandono, Soleada y Muerte, en Algunos Huyanos de la Sierra Peruana"—Estudio de un ethos en la cultura popular peruana de hoy, *INDEF Consultation paper, San Jose, Costa Rica, 1977, and Lima, Peru, 1980* (Escuela Misiologica Latino Americana, 20 mim. pp.).

5. Christology and Pastoral Action in Latin America

ROLANDO GUTIÉRREZ CORTES (*Mexico*)

Synopsis

Beliefs about Christ associated with conquest and colonialism have passed into popular religiosity in Latin America. They undermine the notion of the Christian as a "being-of-the-Kingdom" and weaken the life of the local church as a testimony of faith. They promote the geographical extension of the church and festivals of empty religiosity. Christology in Latin America has thus been used to legitimize conquest, to model the metropolis, and to justify political independence from other countries. Study of the Bible in the power of the Spirit, and Christian obedience in mission-restoring relationships is necessary to recover this life as "being-in-the-Kingdom.

CHRISTOLOGY

We understand Christology to be what is *believed, confessed, taught, lived, said,* and *hoped* about Jesus Christ in the Old and New Testaments, the historical confessions of the church through the centuries, as well as the particular manifestations of this confession in the different cultures and continents.

What the church *believes* of Jesus Christ should be manifested in the intensity of its pastoral action. It is from this belief that the *confession of faith* is given. This constitutes the evangelistic task in which the church fulfils the great commission of announcing the Kingdom of God to the whole world and to every creature; confession that "Jesus Christ is Lord for the glory of God the Father." The *evangelical teaching* undertakes the designs of Deuteronomy to love God above everything and the neighbour as oneself, besides getting involved in "all the things" that Jesus revealed as his Father's will. But to believe in Jesus Christ, to confess faith in him and teach his doctrine, implies to guarantee the mission of *life* which witnesses to this faith through redemptive service. All of this gives sense to the worship and praise offered to the Lordship of the Son until the *coming of the Kingdom* for which the church in hope proclaims Maranatha!

The pastoral action of the church is ruled by the action of the Holy Spirit and the guidance of the Word.

Evangelization is carried out through unity and dispersion. Through unity not for unity's sake, but because Jesus said that we should "be one" so that the world may believe; through dispersion because the disposition to obey in prayer is the Lord's condition for the Holy Spirit to work in his apostles in order to be witnesses in Jerusalem, Judea, Samaria, and to the ends of the earth (cf. Acts 1:8).

Evangelical teaching is constituted by what we call today Christian and theological education. In Christian education we teach people to love God above everything and the neighbour as oneself; and in theological education we teach people to articulate faith at different levels of the family and the local church as well as in a theological institution.

The mission of the church is verified to the world through the faithfulness of her testimony and service, and genuine worship through the exercise of her vocation offered as praise to his glory.

OBJECTIVE OF THE CHRISTOLOGICAL ANALYSIS

We could not make these confessions about Jesus Christ in the Old and New Testaments, as well as in the church through the centuries in our continents, without the Word that communicates the faith that God gives men. For faith comes by hearing the Word of God. Therefore, as Christians we set out from the reality of faith.

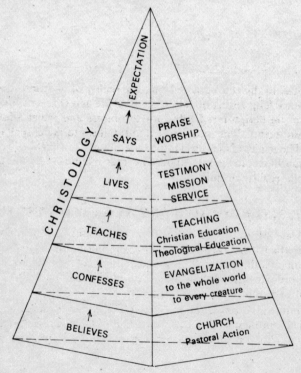

The reality of faith is enriched in each community of believers to the extent that pastoral action is exercised, evangelization carried out, teaching communicated, mission offered, and worship cultivated. The church must be responsible for faithfully fulfilling the Christological task.

We could not deal with the realities of the contemporary world if we could not diagnose the different forms which sin adopts to conceal its destructive task in the life of each person. We must attack every artifice we discover with redemptive attitudes and actions by which we announce the evangelical message. The objective of the Christological task should be to stress how the reality of our faith penetrates the reality of the world.

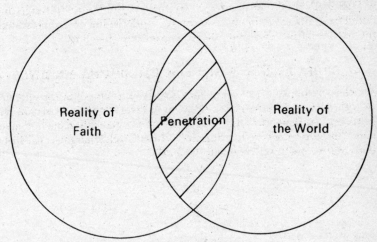

The task of the church is to bring the reality of faith into the reality of the world. This reality of faith is the total life and witness of the church based on the Scriptures. Sadly, our testimony and penetration is not always successful. This is an issue of faithfulness to the gospel and obedience. The reality of the world is the total context in which we live, move, think, and have our being. Sometimes that reality blunts the penetration of the reality of faith.

REALITY OF FAITH AND REALITY OF THE WORLD

When Jesus asked, "Who do men say that I am?", Peter responded, "You are the Christ, the Son of the Living Lord." Jesus identified that confession of faith as something revealed neither by blood nor flesh, but by the Lord who is in heaven. Jesus thus established that faith is not only a gift of God, but has its origin in him.

By contrast the apostle Paul says that faith comes through hearing the word that is pronounced to men on behalf of God. So we find that the nature of faith, in addition to being of divine origin, can be communicated. The writer to the Hebrews declares that faith is essential because without faith it is impossible to please the Lord. Therefore, as a response to Jesus Christ, meditation upon the Bible is an inherent element in the life of the believer. It is necessary to pray in order to meditate on the Word and to assimilate it so that the nature of the reality of faith is understood as divine due to its origin, is such that it must be communicated, and is necessary for every disciple.

Conflict is produced when the reality of faith confronts the reality of the world. For the forces that operate in the world tend to distort the spiritual influence with attitudes such as rancour and ambition that spoil life and its relationships. In the Scriptures this is known as the conflict between the spirit and the flesh, because the carnal conditions in life are so real that the effect of the reality of faith tends to be distorted by this-worldly forces.

What is the condition for overcoming the concerns of the world with the interests of the Spirit? Jesus teaches the urgency of the transformation of the heart because "out of the heart proceed evil thoughts . . ." (Mt. 15:18). To come nearer and nearer each day to the interests of the Kingdom is to achieve the goal that the reality of faith be the victory that defeats the world. It does so through the change of heart that can operate in people through the Holy Spirit and the Word.

LATIN AMERICAN CHRISTOLOGY

The confession of faith that the power that raised the Son from the dead is the power that can transform the life of man, is a reference point for analyzing Latin American Christology.

Its origins are common to the rest of the Christian world. In both the Old and New Testaments the Servant of Jehovah and the Son of Man have been contemplated as an apocalyptic figure for the redemption of this world. The one who in the Old Testament has been identified as the Wisdom that has been with God from eternity is revealed in the New Testament as preexistent by the apostle Peter, as eternal by the apostle John, as a form of God by Paul, as the Son of God by virgin birth in the Gospels of Matthew and Luke, as Lord and God for disciples like Thomas, as Saviour born in Bethlehem for the shepherds of Judea, as the one who will return to the brethren of Thessalonica, and as King of Kings and Lord of Lords in the visions at Patmos. All these enclose the biblical testimony about the Son of God and Son of Man, the promised Messiah, King of the Jews, the Son of David, known as Jesus of Nazareth, the New Man! Having ascended to heaven he will return once more in glory.

Believers from the first through the fifth centuries confessed him as "God of God and Light of Light," "co-substantial with the Father." However, with the discovery of America this theological jargon is

DIAGRAM 3

Reality of faith and reality of the world

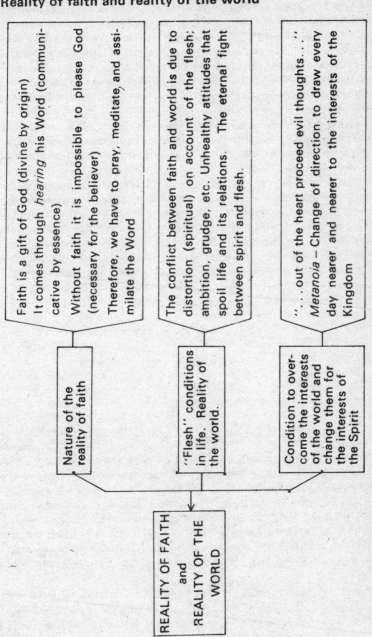

Faith is a gift of God (divine by origin)
It comes through *hearing* his Word (communicative by essence)
Without faith it is impossible to please God (necessary for the believer)
Therefore, we have to pray, meditate, and assimilate the Word

Nature of the reality of faith

The conflict between faith and world is due to distortion (spiritual) on account of the flesh; ambition, grudge, etc. Unhealthy attitudes that spoil life and its relations. The eternal fight between spirit and flesh.

"Flesh" conditions in life. Reality of the world.

"...out of the heart proceed evil thoughts...." *Metanoia* — Change of direction to draw every day nearer and nearer to the interests of the Kingdom

Condition to overcome the interests of the world and change them for the interests of the Spirit

REALITY OF FAITH and REALITY OF THE WORLD

presented to the indigenous population in the form of a cross and sword, baptismal rites, and a liturgy that later takes the form of Roman sacramentalism through which the church will be identified as an institution and not as a confession of faith.

The discovery of America was a milestone in the history of American Christology particularly throughout Latin America. Revolutions such as the industrial one in England and the political one in France and the independence of North America influenced beliefs regarding Christ. These beliefs advanced from notions of conquest and colonialism, to clarifications that later led to popular religiosity.

At that time the purpose of the proclamation of Jesus Christ separated itself from seeking an intimate relationship between the reality of faith and the reality of the world as a confession of faith that nourishes the unity of testimony of each local church. The fundamental bases that make the Christian know himself a being-of-the-Kingdom distinguish the Christian from those who define man solely as a social being or being-in-the-world. Being-of-the-Kingdom includes the element of transcendence and Christian hope. It also includes the knowing of the Kingdom and the language of the Kingdom. These bases ultimately determine the Christological advance. They are undermined by interests inimical to the propagation of the faith. For example, parochialism as a mere geographical extension weakens each local church as a testimony of faith. The only thing that is expressed are the feasts of the underlying Christologies of empty religiosity that become folklore.

It is now urgent for each Latin American context to have perspectives of the Kingdom in which the evangelical calling to repentance invites everyone "to be found faithful" in the day of judgement.

These origins shed light on the Latin American Christological crisis, where proclamation that calls for the confession of faith in Jesus Christ as the only way to salvation is urgent.

POPULAR LATIN AMERICAN CHRISTOLOGY

To set forth popular Latin American Christology, we must first go back to the beginnings of the Christian church. The first Jerusalem community, and every Christian community in the early centuries experienced the activity of the Holy Spirit and persecutions. Christians were both united, and dispersed, and this unity and dispersion had their part to play in the church's task of evangelization.

The dispersion of Christians from the church at Antioch spread Christianity through Asia Minor and Europe. Christianity took on the Greek and Roman cultures as its main point of reference.

Since the arrival of Christopher Columbus in the Americas in 1492, both Roman Catholicism and Protestantism have been part of historical Christianity in our context. The expansion of Romanism from Europe

DIAGRAM 4

Latin American Christology

Latin American Christology

ORIGIN:

—Old and New Testaments

—First to Fifth Centuries

—Discovery of America

—English, French and American revolutions

—Advance: from the conquest to an "*acculturized*" colony, to popular religiosity

OBJECT:

—Relation between the reality of faith and the reality of the world, whose internal bonds nurture the unity of the testimony of the local church

FUNDAMENTAL BASIS OF ITS STUDY:

—Being-of-the-Kingdom: In the last instance it determines the Christological advance

—Local church: A reflection of the underlying Christology

LAWS ON WHICH TO BASE ITS STUDY:

—To be found faithful . . . necessary constant through to the end

* in each context

* in the perspective of the Kingdom

at that time was tremendous, but even then the Roman Catholic Church was experiencing the Protestant Reformation.

Popular Latin American Christology exists among all the different ethnic groups in Latin America and is evident in most of our cities. It is inherited mostly from the popular religiosity that grew up in the process of the cultural adaptation of the Roman Catholic Church. But Protestant and evangelical traditions also had an influence through the foreign and home missions from Europe and North America.

What has been believed, confessed, taught, lived, said, and pointed out about Jesus Christ in our continent, combined with our different traditions and cultures, has affected the fulfilment of the great commission which Christ gave to his church. Therefore, Christology is a critical issue because the image that has been given of Christ has determined the manifestations of faith. Should we regard evangelization as passive or active? Should the proclamation of the Kingdom be active and dynamic?

Today some traditions focus on the images of the Christ Child at Christmas time or on the crucifix at Easter, others on the image of Jesus the healer, and others on Jesus resurrected for our justification. The most recent image of Jesus in some of our Latin American countries is of the "guerillero."

Christology determines pastoral action, ecclesiology, mission, and popular beliefs like syncretism and liberation. For example, the invitation to repentance is a must. Another issue is the proclamation of Jesus Christ as *Lord*, which should be considered seriously because of the semantic problems involved in the use of the term "Lord."

In our Spanish culture, the feudal economic system keeps manifesting itself in our daily behaviour. When a person deserves respect, we call him "Senor Perez" or "Senor Sanchez." The same phenomenon occurs in our politics when we refer to "Senor Presidente" of the republic, whether he is president for a six-year term or a dictator who is a burden to the citizens.

What does the term "Senor" mean in evangelical proclamation? Can we distinguish it from its economic or political usage and give it a theological connotation in referring to Jesus Christ, the Lord of the church, the world, and the cosmos, the eschatological Lord? For we cannot limit this term to an economic or political concept. Neither can we limit it to an ecclesiastical concept and sacrifice its cosmic and eschatological content—that Christ the Lord will deliver the Kingdom to God his Father at the end of time.

To deal with Christology in Latin America is to examine the message that we have regarding Christ. This affects the fulfilment in our continent of the commission to reach out to the whole world and preach the gospel to every creature.

DIAGRAM 5

Popular Latin American Christology

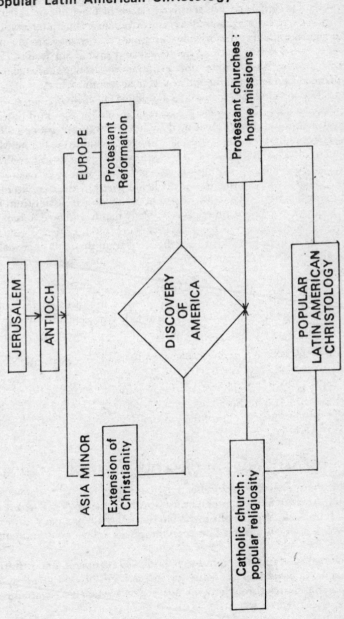

CHRISTOLOGY: ITS PLACE AND FUNCTION IN LATIN AMERICA

There is an urgent need to identify the task of Christology in Latin America so that we may give direction to popular Christologies. The fundamental characteristics of New Testament Christology are given in what is believed, confessed, taught, lived, and said about Jesus Christ in the Scriptures. We must therefore examine what is popularly believed about Christ, in the light of the Bible. We must examine what is popularly confessed in order that we may understand how far the living Son of God who was crucified, dead, buried, and resurrected on the third day for our justification has been substituted by folkloric representations of his birth and crucifixion or by "guerilla" images. We must examine what is popularly taught, lived, and said in confession of faith in Jesus Christ.

The different historical stages in our continent should be examined to distinguish faith in Christ from the belief imposed by the conquistador; to distinguish commitment to Christ that demands self-denial from the cultural adaptation of institutional ecclesiology that has wanted to remove this radical renunciation. Above all, it is evident that criticism silenced by dogmatism in any of its forms is different from the truth that makes free beings and from the liberty of Christ that makes all his disciples participants.

This clarification and differentiation of Latin American Christology will permit us to examine it separately from those Christologies which are used as legitimation of a conquest, as an inherent element of the model of a metropolis or as an image used for independence relative to other countries.

So we occupy ourselves with Christology today, in order that what is *believed, confessed, taught, lived, said, hoped,* and *highlighted* of Christ be thoroughly considered and that our testimony of his life and teachings and our discipleship be both biblical and worthy of our eternal vocation.

This then is the place and function that Christology has at this time in Latin America.

THEOLOGY OF THE CREATION AND OF THE CHURCH

To engage in effective pastoral activity, the church of Christ must examine the reality of the contemporary world. Christology is a necessary part of this task. We find in the Bible that Christ was involved in the very work of creation, and that everything was made "by him and for him."

The reality of the contemporary world is a creation of God distorted by malicious powers. The reality of faith is a gift of God given by his Word to the church through its willing obedience when he reveals himself to her.

DIAGRAM 6

The place and function of Christology in Latin America

CHRISTOLOGY: Its place and function in Latin America

Fundamental characteristics
- What is believed
- What is confessed
- What is taught
- What is lived
- What is said

Stages of the historical development of Christology
1. "Belief" imposed by the conqueror
2. Institutional and ecclesiastic "acculturization"
3. "Criticism" silenced by dogmatism

Cultural development of Christology in Latin America

Christ was:
1. A "legitimation" of the conquest
2. An inherent element to the metropolis model
3. An image used for independence

The Function of Latin American Christology
1. To consider what is believed, confessed, taught, lived, said, hoped and pointed out about Christ
2. To ensure a biblical testimony to his life, work and teaching.
3. To ensure that the testimony of the church be worthy of our eternal vocation

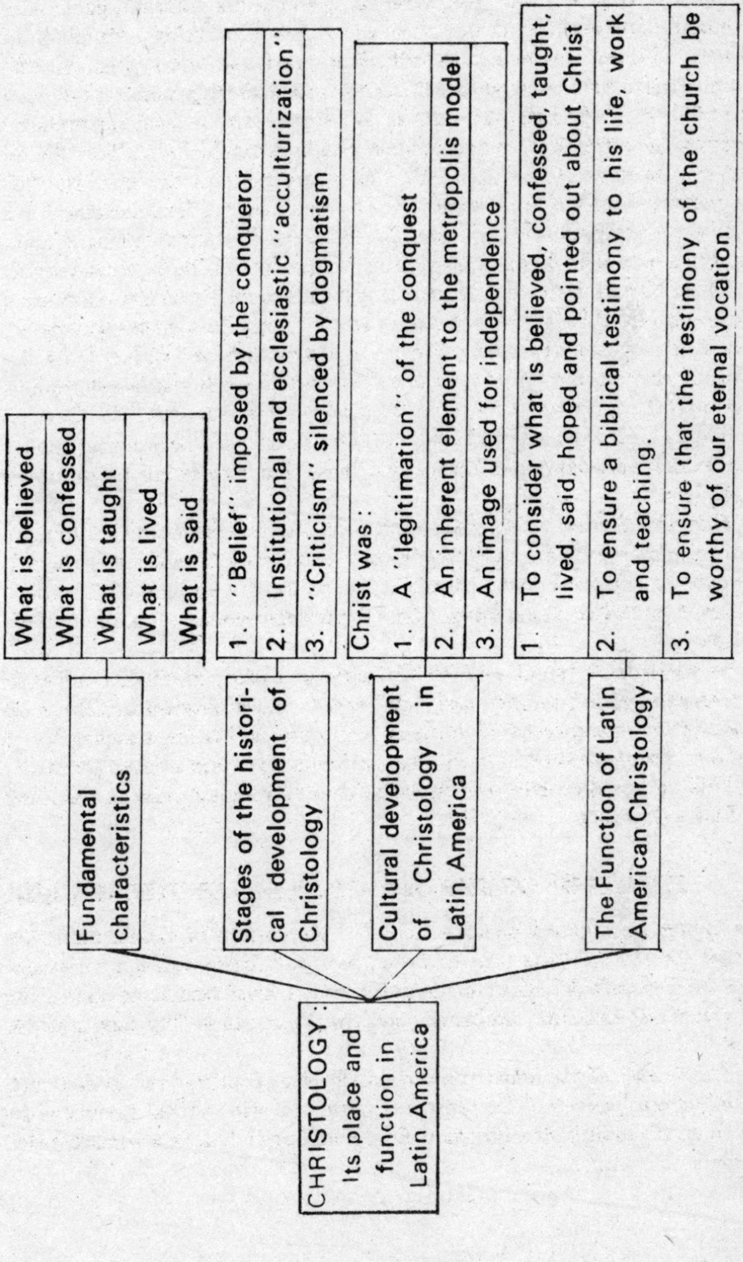

Christology leads us to consider the Scriptures as that which gives testimony to him and permit the articulation of a confession that has constituted us as a church to proclaim him as the Saviour of the world. Being the creator of the world, he is also its Saviour who wants to use his church as an instrument and a witness to be "known and read of all men."

DIAGRAM 7

Theology of the creation and of the church

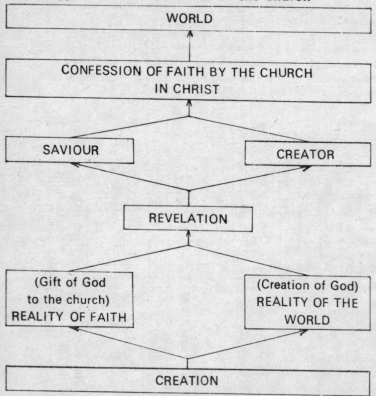

WORLD

CONFESSION OF FAITH BY THE CHURCH IN CHRIST

SAVIOUR — CREATOR

REVELATION

(Gift of God to the church) REALITY OF FAITH — (Creation of God) REALITY OF THE WORLD

CREATION

THE CONFESSION OF FAITH AS THE BASIC ELEMENT IN EVERY ACTION OF THE CHURCH

Each action of the church must contain as a basic element the confession that "Jesus Christ is the Lord for the glory of God the Father." By this belief the church sustains itself as a body. For this reason Paul said that "no one can place another foundation" for her.

We are to obey the mandate that Christ left to his apostles—after he received all power in heaven and earth—telling them "go!" He revealed himself to them as the Lord who gives them that order. That is why in mission he appears as beginning, content, and goal, but only in the

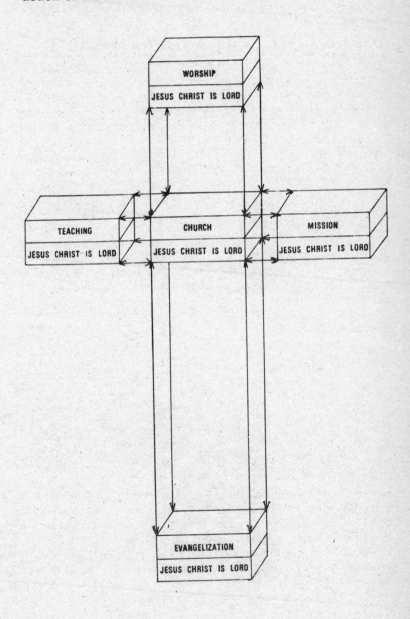

DIAGRAM 8

The confession of faith as the basic element in every action of the church

WORSHIP

JESUS CHRIST IS LORD

TEACHING

JESUS CHRIST IS LORD

CHURCH

JESUS CHRIST IS LORD

MISSION

JESUS CHRIST IS LORD

EVANGELIZATION

JESUS CHRIST IS LORD

DIAGRAM 9

Evangelization through unity and dispersion

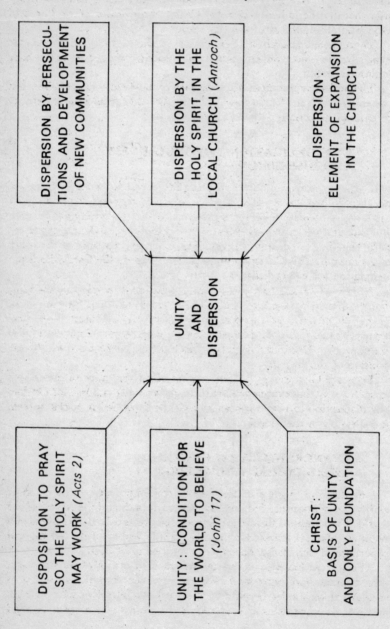

DISPERSION BY PERSECU-
TIONS AND DEVELOPMENT
OF NEW COMMUNITIES

DISPERSION BY THE
HOLY SPIRIT IN THE
LOCAL CHURCH (Antioch)

DISPERSION:
ELEMENT OF EXPANSION
IN THE CHURCH

UNITY
AND
DISPERSION

DISPOSITION TO PRAY
SO THE HOLY SPIRIT
MAY WORK (Acts 2)

UNITY: CONDITION FOR
THE WORLD TO BELIEVE
(John 17)

CHRIST:
BASIS OF UNITY
AND ONLY FOUNDATION

necessary interaction of a church that evangelizes, teaches, and worships. Christ ordered his disciples to go, proclaim that he is the Lord. He sent them to teach, that men should love him as their Lord, and to worship him, because he is believed to be worthy of all praise as the Lamb of God who eliminates sin from the world.

There is no church if there is no mission, no mission without evangelization, no evangelization if there is no teaching, and no teaching without worship.

The necessary interaction among each of these elements requires that the church of Jesus Christ has the confession of faith as a basic element of each of its actions.

EVANGELIZATION THROUGH UNITY AND DISPERSION

The priestly prayer of our Lord Jesus Christ to his Father on behalf of his church, had the objective that we be *one*. In this way, he underlined the unity of all his disciples as a condition that the world might believe. But this unity is expressed in a concrete disposition of the church to remain together in constant prayer. The Holy Spirit works in the unity of the church. This Christian unity finds its base in the Lord who is the foundation for evangelization.

However, we also find in the New Testament dispersion by the Holy Spirit. After the church of Antioch prayed for Paul and Barnabas, the gospel of Jesus Christ was spread throughout Asia Minor. Dispersion was also caused by persecutions that permitted the development of new communities. Unity and dispersion are utilized by the Lord for the expansion of the church.

Does the Christology that we confess affect the unity of the church in such a way that evangelization through her unity is possible? Or does our disposition to pray together so that the Holy Spirit works, foresee a dispersion in each local church?

EVANGELICAL TEACHING AND THEOLOGICAL KNOWLEDGE

To identify the theological task in our contemporary world, we must clarify the relationship between the reality of faith and the reality of the world. Two areas of theological knowledge are involved with these two realities. Natural knowledge opens us to the reality of the world, and supernatural knowledge opens us to the reality of faith.

Theological knowledge can be analyzed in terms of its structure, discernment, and expression. We are involved with the structure of theological knowledge because we must involve ourselves with its *origin* and *goal*. Is *origin* takes us to the Holy Scriptures which we must read

DIAGRAM 10

Evangelical teaching and theological knowledge

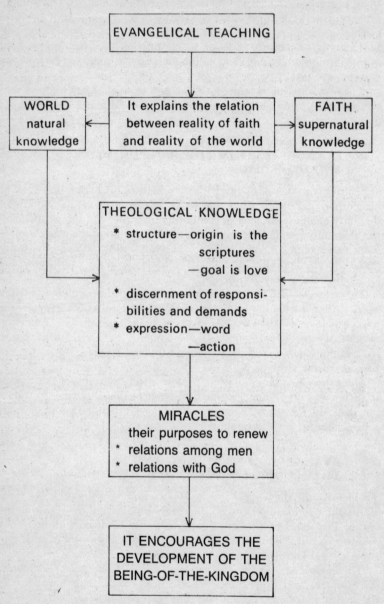

with prayer, meditate on with devotion, and assimilate with fervour as an objective spiritual reality; and as a *goal*, because theological knowledge should be structured so that the ministries of the church grow in love.

We are involved with *discernment*, because we must distinguish the properties and scope of the vocation of God and the responsibility of people in the realm of the reality of faith, as well as the properties and laws of the reality of the world and the demands that God has on their proper functioning. Discernment requires a method of creative work in all the activities that can be stimulated from the reality of faith.

We are involved with its *expression*, because everything we do, be it word or action, should be done for the Lord and not for man. We will express the ideas and images of our conscience in practical and real terms, in oral or written proclamation, or in any other form in which we can intelligibly proclaim the gospel to contemporary man.

We cannot ignore the miracles that the Lord places in his church as unequivocal signs. These give divine meaning to the human significance of the church, and are given for renovation of relationships among men and the relationship with God.

Only with the expression of authentic theological knowledge can we encourage the development of the "being-of-the-Kingdom of God" that he has in each Christian, through the congregation of the redeemed, his church.

CHRISTOLOGY AND MISSION

Each pastoral activity that attempts to fulfil the missionary task found in Matthew 28, requires that the church consider Christ as the centre of its task. It should point out its fundamental belief in him; what it confesses about him as Lord; what it teaches of him as Saviour; how the church lives in him as the Son of God; and what it proclaims and highlights of him as redeemer of the world. This determines the content of its proclamation and the development of its growth through teaching, in which the Holy Spirit and the Word work concretely on the ministries practiced at ecclesiastical and pastoral levels.

Mission renovates the relationships with God and with man. Mission is where the transformation operated by the gospel is overwhelmingly manifested. If the Lord has transformed us, it is in order to transform all natural, technological, and human resources into redemptive resources in this world.

Mission is not an abstraction of religious speculations but restorative action in the world through evangelical transformation. All relationships are affected: those with God in first place and in second place those with other people. Our human relations are affected and in particular our social relationships in the interaction required by our daily work to support our families.

DIAGRAM 11

Christology and mission

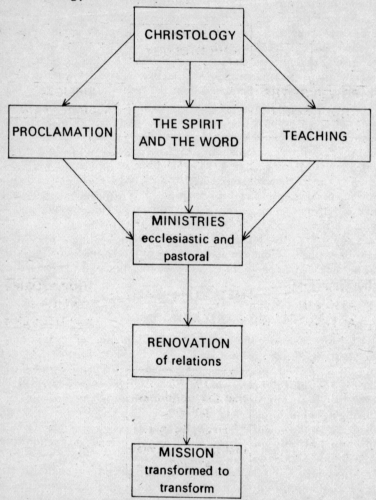

**FROM A POPULAR CHRISTOLOGY TO AN
INTEGRAL TRANSFORMATION**

The syncretism of popular Christology can only be overcome through
the pastoral action of the church where the belief in Christ as Lord is
ruled by the power of the Holy Spirit and the assimilation of the Word.
The power of the Holy Spirit is at work in each cell of the human body
and in each member of the church as an element of the body of Christ.
Biblical assimilation requires meditation on the Word not as a mere

DIAGRAM 12

To the praise of his glory

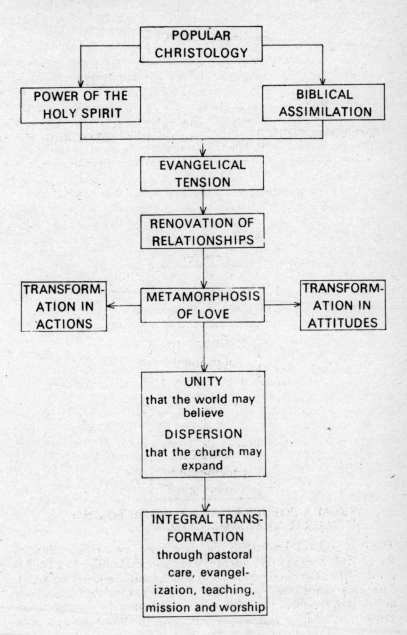

memorization of texts which are usually not digested but as an assimilation of its message that is communicated by word and action in faithful testimony by each local church. The power of the Holy Spirit and biblical assimilation are manifested in an evangelical tension that renews relationships between people.

However, renovation must not be confused with the commonly known term "human relations" which is used in our contemporary world. Renovation is a metamorphosis of love that achieves transformed actions because it has transformed attitudes that lead toward the unity that only in Christ is perfect.

Without this metamorphosis of love that the Holy Spirit pours out in each heart, the unity of which Christ speaks in his priestly prayer as a condition so that the world might believe, cannot be understood. In this unity we can pray, as the church in Antioch did for dispersion through its apostles throughout Asia or Europe, knowing that the church grows through the redemptive message.

It is in this unity and dispersion that the evangelization of the whole world and every creature is explained. They are manifested in a church that believes, in a message that is confessed, in teaching and theological education that is Christian, in mission that is a life of witness and service, in worship that is manifested in vocation and praise, in prayer and in hope, until the coming of the Kingdom. In other words, unity and dispersion are manifested in an integral transformation that goes far beyond souls and men, cultures and generations because it entails pastoral action and teaching, mission and worship, prayer and hope.

THE ROLE OF THE CHURCH AND THE PASTOR IN THE KINGDOM

Therefore, Christology cannot be separated from pastoral action in Latin America. The church was founded by Christ to be his body. He and no one else is its head. For this reason our pulpit proclamation must be characterized by proclaiming him as the only and sufficient Saviour. But we must point out that the church is the recipient of love, gifts, ministries, and talents, so that the pastoral action that is carried out in each local church be performed in the awareness that the role of the church in the Kingdom is to be the receptacle of the Holy Spirit, a community of word and a community of action in the love of Jesus Christ.

The role of the pastor in the Kingdom is to be a permanent stimulus so that fraternal love prevails in everyone; that generous care be cultivated as it was at the beginning of the church when the apostles appointed deacons in Jerusalem.

However, all the members of the church should be dependent on the power of the Holy Spirit in order to act as "beings-of-the-Kingdom" in the world, where their actions must be characterized by creativity and transformation, as faithful witnesses of Jesus Christ.

DIAGRAM 13

The role of the church and of the pastor in the Kingdom

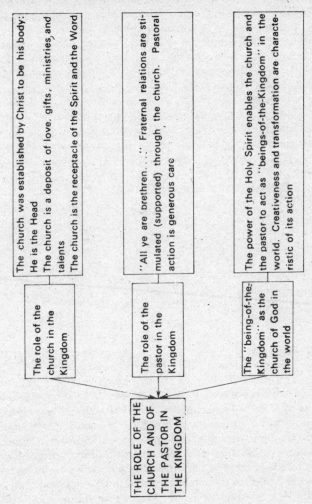

The church was established by Christ to be his body: He is the Head

The church is a deposit of love, gifts, ministries, and talents

The church is the receptacle of the Spirit and the Word

The role of the church in the Kingdom

"All ye are brethren....". Fraternal relations are stimulated (supported) through the church. Pastoral action is generous care

The role of the pastor in the Kingdom

The power of the Holy Spirit enables the church and the pastor to act as "beings-of-the-Kingdom" in the world. Creativeness and transformation are characteristic of its action

The "being-of-the-Kingdom" as the church of God in the world

THE ROLE OF THE CHURCH AND OF THE PASTOR IN THE KINGDOM

Christ does not emerge out of the specific needs of an epoch, but as the gift of God that has been revealed in the Bible. Thus, the church must speak *from* the Bible.

THE ATTITUDE REQUIRED

The discovery of deficiencies as a result of current Christological analysis should not tarnish the relationships within the family of faith.

Many historical, socio-economic, and political reasons tend to divide us. Many mental, personal, and cultural attitudes tend to produce social bitterness. We can even discover political and religious ambitions that harm our fraternal love. In the reality of the world imperialistic practices, economic or ideological, disturb our peace with the intention of diverting our sentiments from Christian love. One can still discover selfish intentions, doctrinal errors, unilateral interpretations, sublimated selfishness, inconsistent discussions, or lack of vision. but the description of a history marked by mistakes does not justify us from ceasing to act on the plane of God's love.

Let us confess the Christ that has been revealed in the Bible. He is the divine and universal guarantee. Our confession of faith in Christ determines our pastoral action. Only Christ transcends all our differences and his immanence must be real among us through the Holy Spirit. May the Holy Spirit guide us and his Word rule our actions.

DISCUSSION WITH ROLANDO GUTIÉRREZ CORTES

Q. Some of us from Africa have benefited a lot from Liberation Theology. This is part of Christology. But I was rather disappointed that, as a pastor who is involved in the situation, you made no mention of this. Those of us from countries which are fed up with a western type of government and are trying to taste other types of governments, socialist or fascist, would benefit a lot from a perspective from your own world in a political kind of conflict. What exactly are the difficulties? Why did you not, as a pastor, tell us whatever you could about this sort of thing?

R.G. My explanation is that first I was offering perspectives on Christology as a pastor. Secondly, in some cases the hierarchy of the church is colluding with oppressive powers and acting against movements for social change. So it is difficult to talk about the involvement of the church in the political scene without being very specific. Sometimes the laypeople in a church congregation may support the oppressive power. And that makes the life of the pastor very difficult.

Thirdly, we must be very clear about what the Word of God is to our own selves and to respect that. We have to be very clear in our obedience to the vocation of God and to respect that vocation. Vocation should be tied up to that single verb in Matthew 28. We must always "make disciples" in mission, in evangelization, in education and in worship. Any church task is a mission task.

Fourthly, I am concerned about the situation of my people and about social injustice. I want to see my own people free. I am doing my theology as an evangelical in the midst of that revolutionary situation. But, I am not just going to say we must go back to the Bible. I realize the hermeneutical problem. The question of hermeneutics is fundamental.

6. Biblical Christologies in the Context of African Traditional Religions

KWAME BEDIAKO (*Ghana*)

Synopsis

A survey of the issues raised for Christian mission and dialogue with African traditional religions, for developing our understanding and presentation of Jesus, expecially examining the understanding of Jesus in relation to the Ancestors and the African concept of Kingship.

The writer appeals for a fresh approach to proclaiming Christ amidst African religions, since previous proclamation suffered from disregard of African religion and an inadequate apprehension of the Good News by the missionaries.

PRELIMINARY OBSERVATIONS: PERSPECTIVE AND APPROACH

Behind the very arresting theme of this conference lies an equally dramatic history, or perhaps histories. To undertake "a consideration of evangelical Christologies arising from the poor, the powerless and the oppressed, and non-Christian religious worldviews" is to presuppose evangelical Christologies arising from the nonpoor, the nonpowerless, and the non-oppressed, and from presumably Christian worldviews. So the theme may have far greater significance in the history of Christian mission than may yet appear. One might even speculate on what it would have meant if the important early Church Council reported in chapter 15 of the Acts of the Apostles had taken place not in Jerusalem, but at Derbe or Lystra, and on the basis of an agenda drawn up by Galatian Christians. After all, it was about them that the Council met.

If we are to have an adequate—holistic—appreciation of the issues relating to the development of our understanding and presentation of Jesus, in our various contexts and in terms of our theme, we cannot avoid trying to understand how the theme has come to impress itself upon us in the first place. Two ways of proceeding were open to me, and I have followed both, though separately, in the two parts of the paper. One approach is to regard the issues raised from Christian mission and dialogue with African traditional religions as relating essentially to questions of contemporary interest and significance. Here mission is taken in a generalized and generic sense, and focusses on the witness in context of our African Christian communities. This approach is required in the second part, where we elaborate and articulate our own understanding and presentation of Jesus in relation to ancestors and the conception of Kingship, although it might be applied to the subject as awhole.

Another crucial approach, particularly in the African context, is to regard mission not so much in its generalized and generic sense, as in its historical dimensions. It is based on the assumption that the emergence in the late twentieth century of evangelical mission theologians from the Two Thirds World, with their own agenda and concerns, cannot be seen in isolation from the massive missionary and evangelistic endeavour of the Christian churches from the "One Third World," in the last two centuries (and more in some places). Our Christian communities and our missiological agenda are connected with that missionary history, even if only as a response to the issues raised as a result of the impact of that history upon our contexts. The realities which confront us in Africa have not been shaped merely by recent forces; they also spring from the quality of the contact which earlier Christian proclamation made with out traditional religious life and spirituality. Our understanding and presentation of Jesus now cannot ignore the understanding and presentation of him in the past. To do otherwise is to deny our history and to fail to learn from the dynamics of the history which has determined the agenda of today. We will begin with this second historical approach in the first part of the paper.

I. WESTERN CHRISTIAN MISSION AMID AFRICAN RELIGION—A FAILURE IN ENCOUNTER?

Our missionary past: presuppositions and implications

The contact which European and North American missionary proclamation in the nineteenth and early twentieth centuries made with the religious lives and spiritualities of African peoples was negative. This fact is sufficiently documented not to require any extensive proof here. A comment by Adrian Hastings about the Roman Catholic side of the missionary story is true of the missionary attitude as a whole, and touches on some significant factors:

> In fact neither in the nineteenth nor in the twentieth centuries did missionaries give much thought in advance to what they would find in Africa. What struck them, undoubtedly, was the darkness of the continent: its lack of religion and sound morals, its ignorance, its general pitiful condition made worse by the barbarity of the slave trade. Evangelization was seen as liberation from a state of absolute awfulness and the picture of unredeemed Africa was often painted in colours as gruesome as possible, the better to encourage missionary zeal at home.[1]

1. Adrian Hastings, *Church and Mission in Modern Africa* (London: Burns and Oates, 1967), p. 60.

Hastings notes further that a natural result of this missionary view of Africa was a tendency "to treat anything pre-Christian in Africa as either harmful or at best valueless, and to consider the African once converted from paganism as a sort of *tabula rasa,* on which a wholly new religious psychology was somehow to be imprinted."[2]

Several reasons can be given to account for this missionary image of Africa. I shall highlight three. First, we must remember the kind of framework in which European-African contact began, as far back as four to five centuries. Philip Curtin has shown in *The Image of Africa*[3] that the foundations for what became eventually the "European Afrikaanschauung" of the nineteenth century were laid in the formative stages of that contact. In the words of a sixteenth century English seafaring adventurer, Sir John Hawkins, he "was among other particulars, assured that Negros (sic) were good merchandise in Hispaniola and that store of Negros might easily be had upon the coast of Guinea." (When Hawkins sailed for the Guinea coast a second time, with the blessing of Queen Elizabeth I, the monarch lent him a Royal Navy vessel called the *Jesus.*)[4] The significant period for shaping those attitudes which would so deeply affect human relations between Africa and Europe was not the later, relatively short phase of imperial rule, but that long prelude to it. This view has been put forward very cogently by Basil Davidson in *Black Mother*, and also by Caribbean political scientist, Walter Rodney, in a book with a rather provocative title, *How Europe Underdeveloped Africa.*[5]

On the specific subject of the European trade in slaves, it is significant that in 1772, the very year in which Chief Justice Mansfield ruled that slavery was illegal in England, the only Anglican clergyman who had at that time served as missionary in West Africa also published a pamphlet justifying the slave trade on grounds of Scripture and Aristotelian ideas.[6] It is understandable therefore that in the early stages of the modern missionary movement, the missionary enterprise itself was frequently considered as atonement for the injuries which, it was felt, the quality of European contact had inflicted upon Africa and her peoples.[7]

2. *Ibid.*

3. Philip Curtin, *The Image of Africa—British Ideas and Action 1780–1850* (Madison: University of Wisconsin Press, 1964).

4. See E. J. Payne & C. R. Beazley, eds., *Voyages of the Elizabethan Seamen—Select Narratives from the "Principal Navigations" of Hakluyt* (Oxford: Clarendon Press, 1907), pp. 6, 9.

5. Basil Davidson, *Black Mother—Africa and the Atlantic Slave Trade* (revised and expanded edition; Harmondsworth: Penguin Books, 1970); Walter Rodney, *How Europe Underdeveloped Africa* (London: Bogle–L'Ouverture, 1972; Dar-es-Salaam: Tanzania Publishing House, 1972).

6. Thomas Thompson, *The African Trade for Negro Slaves shown to be consistent with the principles of humanity and the laws of Revealed Religion* (London, 1772).

7. See Eugene Stock, *The History of the Church Missionary Society—The environment, its men and its work* (Vol. I; London: CMS, 1899), p. 95. Cf. C. J. Phillips, *Protestant America and the Pagan World—The first half century of the American Board of*

In the second place, the development of this rather unhealthy relationship between Africa and Europe did not take place in an intellectual
vacuum, but in the context of some definite intellectual positions and
viewpoints, often put forward as the assured results of science. Within
the terms of reference of the eighteenth-century concept of "the Great
Chain of Being," and eventually of the nineteenth-century evolutionary
scale, African peoples—racially, culturally, and religiously—were the
lowest of the low. This was held to be so, whether imputed to their inherent nature, by the racist scientists, or to their condition alone, as argued
by humanitarians.[8] Missionaries were more influenced by these ideas than
they were aware of. The great radical dissenter, William Carey, did not
believe in the religious superiority of Europeans, or of "those who bear
the Christian name." But he believed Africans to be " . . . as destitute
of civilisation as they are of true religion."[9] The late eighteenth- and early
nineteenth-century editions of the *Encyclopedia Britannica* show that Carey's
view belonged to a general stock of knowledge.

Thirdly, behind these developments lay a whole series of events in
European history which had brought about the virtual identification of
"Christian" with "European." In our missionary story this became the
tie-up of "Christianity" with "civilisation." Max Warren has described
this association of the two realities as "the vestigial remains of Europe's
medieval heritage of ideas, among them the idea of Christendom."[10] As
a result of this kind of outlook,[11] and arising from a combination of all
the factors indicated above, there came to dominate in missionary practice in our context that heavy bias toward European value-setting for
the Christian faith which has become one of the more cumbersome legacies
to our churches.

This brings us to consider what African religions meant to European
missionaries.

THE AFRICAN WORLD IN MISSIONARY THINKING

Rather than attempt to synthesize the mass of information relating to
this very complex subject, I will focus on two international missionary
conferences which took place in the early years of this century, and use

---

Commissioners for Foreign Missions, *1810–1860* (Cambridge: Harvard University
Press, 1969), pp. 206f.

8. Philip Curtin, *op. cit.,* pp. 252-258.

9. William Carey, *An Enquiry into the Obligation of Christians to use means for the
Conversion of the Heathen* (reprinted from the edition of 1792; London: Hodder &
Stoughton, 1891), pp. 63, 65.

10. Max Warren, *The Missionary Movement from Britain in Modern History* (London: SCM Press, 1965), p. 60.

11. See Denys Hay, *Europe—The Emergence of an Idea* (Edinburgh: Edinburgh
University Press, 1957).

evidence from them to indicate some of the trends which have shaped the issues of our context. The two important gatherings are the conferences at Edinburgh (1910) and at Le Zoute, Belgium (1926).

Christian missionaries were, by the very nature of their situation, brought into "religious" contact with African peoples in the nineteenth-century. But, paradoxically, the task of classifying and theorizing on the religion of African societies fell to Europeans who "at the time they wrote, were agnostics or atheists." This critical comment is made by a twentieth-century successor in the same craft, E. E. Evans-Pritchard.[12] He had in mind persons like John Lubbock, E. B. Tylor, J. G. Frazer, who were influential pioneers in the then new sciences of anthropology and comparative religion, both of which finally came into their own on the basis of Darwinian evolutionary assumptions. These historians of the development of culture had minimal contact with African peoples.

For our purposes, E. B. Tylor is the most significant figure. His term "animism" established itself as the standard concept for the religion of all "primitive" peoples. At the Edinburgh Conference, convened "to consider missionary problems in relation to the non-Christian world," Tylor's ideas in his work *Primitive Culture,* supplemented by the researches of Johannes Warneck in Sumatra,[13] provided the intellectual and theoretical framework for the missionary understanding of what W. H. T. Gairdner called, "the religious beliefs of more or less backward and degraded peoples all over the world."[14] This description of what was called "Animistic Religions" took in the whole African field.

From the report of Commission IV—*The Missionary Message in relation to non-Christian religions,* it is evident that "Animism" constituted a religious system like the other categories treated: Chinese religions, religions of Japan, Islam, and Hinduism. However, Animism was probably the most difficult for the missionary to penetrate, since it had neither literature nor scholars to expound its mysteries to the European mind. Therefore, most missionaries were understandably hesitant to suggest that any "preparation for Christianity" existed in this form of religion. Some even concluded that there was "practically no religious content in Animism."[15] Of the fourteen missionary correspondents in Africa who sent in answers to a questionnaire, a dozen were virtually convinced that among the peo-

12. E. E. Evans-Pritchard, *Theories of Primitive Religion* (Oxford: Clarendon Press, 1965), p. 15.

13. Johannes Warneck, *The Living Forces of the Gospel—Experiences of a Missionary in Animistic Heathendom* (trans. from 3rd German edition by Neil Buchanan; Edinburgh/London: Oliphant, Anderson and Ferrier, n.d.).

14. W. H. T. Gairdner, *Edinburgh 1910, An Account and Interpretation of the World Missionary Conference* (London: Oliphant, Anderson and Ferrier, 1910), p. 193.

15. See *World Missionary Conference 1910—Report of Commission IV—The Missionary Message in Relation to non-Christian Religions* (Edinburgh/London: Oliphant, Anderson and Ferrier, 1910), p. 24.

ple to whom they were preaching the gospel, there was "no religion," meaning no "formulated religious observances and doctrines" in evidence. Whatever there was could not be "prized as religious help or consolation."[16] They were all "unhesitatingly" certain that their missionary experience had not "altered in form or substance their impression as to what constitutes the most important vital elements in the Christian faith."[17] When it came to asking what the "Christian Church in civilised lands" (they spoke in those terms then) could learn from their missionary encounter with the rest of the world, it was hard to see how there could be much to learn from what, in the words of W. H. T. Gairdner, was ". . . surely the humblest of all possible teachers . . . and the least sublime of all the five creeds."[18] The European missionary encounter with Africa could not proceed, in missionary thinking, on the basis of a genuine dialogue with African religion and its spiritual quests.

The report of the Le Zoute Conference in 1929[19] shows some interesting shifts in missionary thinking. The conference was convened to discuss specifically African problems. In the meantime, the Great War of 1914–18 had taken place. European attitudes, particularly missionary attitudes, had begun to register a somewhat chastened mood. One of the items listed by Edwin Smith under the heading "favourable factors in the new situation" was "more of respect for the African and his past . . . greater willingness to work *with* rather than *for* the people."[20] Dietrich Westermann produced for the conference a remarkable article on "The Value of the African's Past," which was published in the special Africa number of the *International Review of Missions* for that year. Westermann offered a very sympathetic interpretation of African tradition. He sought to show that it contained "elements of divine education and guidance" toward "a more sublime life," this latter being Christianity. Nevertheless, Westermann's article is equally significant in what he complained about:

> The Africans have been treated by us as having no religion, no language, no tradition, no institutions, no racial character of their own, as empty vessels to be filled with European and American goods.[21]

16. *Answers to Questionnaire for World Missionary Conference. Edinburgh 1910—Commission IV—The Missionary Message in Relation to non-Christian Religions.* Bound volumes of typescripts: vol. I—*Japan, Animistic Peoples, Indochina,* etc. held in Christ's College Library, Aberdeen. I am indebted to Prof. A. F. Walls of the University of Aberdeen for access to this material.

17. *The Christian Message in Relation to non-Christian Religions,* p. 35.

18. W. H. T. Gairdner, *op. cit.,* p. 141.

19. E. W. Smith, *The Christian Mission in Africa* (London/New York: International Missionary Council, 1926). A study based on the work of the International Conference at Le Zoute, Belgium, Sept. 14th-21st, 1926.

20. *Ibid.,* p. 19.

21. Dietrich Westermann, "The Value of the African's Past" in *International Review of Missions* 15 (1926), 426.

Westermann's remarks were not directed solely at missionary attitudes of the past. For, after Edwin Smith has noted that the conference generally took the view that "indiscriminate denunciation of African customs in preaching is merely mischievous—and foolish," he is careful to point out that "not all members of the conference were convinced of this."[22]

Westermann himself does not escape criticism. When he gave the Duff Lectures in 1935 (subsequently published under the title *Africa and Christianity*), he categorically denied African religion any place in what he had spoken of as "divine education and guidance" in African tradition. He urged missionaries to be "ruthless" in uprooting African traditional religions.[23] He has been rightly criticized by Kenneth Cragg: if "giving the new means taking away the old, to what is the new given?"[24] Westermann, in common with others, displays a fundamental misapprehension of the nature of Christian conversion, and therefore of the gospel and Christ. In his case, as in the others', the problem is perhaps not unrelated to missionary ethnocentricism.

I shall not generalize about the missionary attitude to African religion from the evidence provided by these two conferences. But the evidence does indicate the general tendency of missionary thinking about the religion of African peoples. Some missionaries in Africa eventually did become competent students of some important aspects of African religions. In spite of that, it was the generally negative missionary attitude to African religious life which most profoundly influenced African understanding of the Christian faith as presented by missionaries. So far as Africa is concerned, from our present perspective, the Edinburgh Conference belonged to the nineteenth century. Even though Le Zoute showed a more positive missionary attitude to African tradition, European value-setting for the Christian faith was not quite ready to be buried; missionary ethnocentricism was as important as ever.

The kind of outlook we have been describing had one ominous implication—although I doubt whether it was then perceived as such: Africans could only receive and articulate the faith insofar as they kept to the boundaries and models defined by the Christian traditions of Europe. Christ could not inhabit the spiritual universe of the African consciousness except, in essence, as a stranger. It is difficult not to link our missionary connection with the problem of identity which came to weigh so heavily on the Christian conscience of many an African; must we become other than African in order to be truly Christian? The story of many so-called African Independent Churches is often an answer to that kind of question, at least to the extent that these churches take seriously

22. E. W. Smith, *op. cit.*, p. 40.

23. Dietrich Westermann, *Africa and Christianity* (Duff Lectures, 1935; London: Oxford University Press, 1937), pp. 2, 94.

24. Kenneth Cragg, *Christianity in World Perspective* (London: Lutterworth Press, 1968), p. 57.

matters relating to the African religious worldview and the questions it poses.

Yet there is more to this whole problem than missionary lack of understanding or disregard of African tradition. Some have raised the question of missionary misapprehension of the gospel.

THE MISSIONARY LEGACY IN BIBLICAL AND THEOLOGICAL PERSPECTIVE

Why did the kind of genuine encounter and dialogue which one would have expected between the gospel of Christ and African religious life not take place? Instead of producing a real meeting at the specific level of religious apprehension and theology, the missionary enterprise produced what can be called an African Christian identity problem. The most evident indication of this is the theological agenda of African theologians in the last two decades.

When the first African theological scholars, with their own intellectual and Christian convictions, set about interpreting theologically (using admittedly Christian categories) the pre-Christian religious traditions and spiritualities of African peoples, some hinted darkly of "syncretism" and made overt charges of distortion, both of Christian belief and of the "old" religion itself. The dominant drive behind that kind of theological production was admitted to be an effort "to establish the value of African religion and culture before the unjust criticisms made by earlier missionaries."[25] But it was not sufficiently recognized that these African theologians were seeking to come to terms with continuing realities of African life which constituted also their own "ontological" past. Such coming to terms with one's past, and the interpretation, even reinterpretation of it, with the aid of the new understanding and commitment, has outstanding precedent in Christian history. It was crucial for laying the foundations for the vigorous patristic theology of the second and third centuries A.D. in the context of Gentile Christianity. Therefore the well-known "quest for an African theology" by this generation of theologians must be understood as a quest for a framework in which African Christian identity could inhere, in terms meaningful also for the demands of African integrity; for without such integrity African Christian theology would be impossible. If it is correct to link this vital theological quest with Africa's missionary past, it is not surprising that some ask whether the missionary enterprise itself did not proceed on inadequate theological premises.

In the early years of the century, Roland Allen argued convincingly in two major studies, *Missionary Methods: St. Paul's or Ours?* and *Spontaneous*

---

25. Philip Turner, "The Wisdom of the Fathers and the Gospel of Christ: some notes on Christian adaptation in Africa," *Journal of Religion in Africa* 4 (1971).

Expansion of the Church and the Causes which Hinder It,[26] that the outlook
of the western missionary enterprise was hindering the freedom of the
emergent Christian communities of Africa and Asia. The heavy western
bias and cultural assumptions which undergirded much of the missionary
planting of churches, amounted, in New Testament terms, to a "Judaizing" activity, in marked contrast to the outlook and method of St. Paul
in his mission to the Gentiles. At the specific level of theology, missionary
misapprehension of the gospel led to a tendency to preach law in the form
of a westernized gospel as though it were pure gospel, and to a failure
to trust converts sufficiently to the Holy Spirit for the moulding of Christian communities.

In our own time, and with particular reference to Africa, the western
missionary enterprise has been critized in similar terms by a South
African missiologist, G. C. Oosthuizen, in his book *Post-Christianity in
Africa.*[27] Oosthuizen is particularly concerned to explain the phenomenon
of the independent churches, whose leaders he compares with western
missionaries, to the disadvantage of the latter:

> The independent movements accept the fact that they have to do with
> their own world and world-view, and this in contradistinction to many
> missionaries whose motto was, "You must become like us."[28]

Oosthuizen traces the missionary error to "the development of western
Christianity itself," to what he calls "the fallacy that is alive in the concept of western Christian civilisation."[29] His major conclusion is that the
weakness in the western missionary movement in Africa is to be accounted
for by the fact that "Africa had no Paul."[30] According to Oosthuizen,
in the earlier transposition of the gospel from the Jewish cultural milieu
into the Graeco-Roman world, "Paul, well versed in Rabbinic Judaism
and in all aspects of Hellenism, was at the centre of this transposition."[31]
But Oosthuizen ignores the fact that St. Paul's achievement was not obtained without a struggle primarily with positions and attitudes within
the form of Christianity practiced in the cultural milieu of the earliest
mother-church. If Paul's adversaries, the so-called Judaizers, had had
their way, Gentile Christianity and the teaching of the New Testament
itself might have taken a different turn. It is worth pondering what the

26. Roland Allen, *Missionary Methods: St. Paul's or Ours?* (reprinted; Grand
Rapids: Eerdmans, 1979); *The Spontaneous Expansion of the Church and the Causes
which Hinder It* (reprinted; Grand Rapids: Eerdmans, 1978).

27. G. C. Oosthuizen, *Post-Christianity in Africa—A Theological and Anthropological
Study* (London: Hurst and Co., 1968).

28. *Ibid.,* p. 235.

29. *Ibid.,* p. 3.

30. *Ibid.,* p. 235.

31. *Ibid.,* p. 234.

New Testament would read like had its documents been composed from the standpoint of the "Judaizers."

However, Bishop Kenneth Cragg has given us the most searching critique of this "heavy western bias"[32] of the modern expansion of Christianity. In a series of lectures in 1966, subsequently published under the title *Christianity in World Perspective,* he drew attention to the "near monopolisation of Christianity by western possessiveness, . . . the marked dominance of western cultural forms and assumptions in the whole context of Christian thought, worship, custom and practice among the nations of the Gospel's dispersion," concluding that "the geographical universality of the Church, or nearly so, had been achieved only in the context of a deep cultural partiality." Here was a notable point of "contrast between nineteenth century mission in the world, and the apostolic precedents of the first century."[33]

Some have questioned the validity of the comparison of the modern missionary enterprise with the apostolic mission to the Gentiles. Max Warren considered that criticisms of the modern missionary movement in the light of St. Paul's "supposed missionary methods" were irrelevant. However, his criticisms centre on the supposedly different social conditions of the apostolic mission and the modern missionary enterprise.[34] These differences are insignificant,[35] and his objections do not deal with the theological perspectives of the propagators of the faith.

In view of the consequences of the modern missionary enterprise, a theological assessment of it should be in terms of comparison with the best ideals of the faith that it sought to impart, and not on the basis of extraneous factors. Therefore, the apostolic precedent provides the most adequate paradigm for assessing a similar massive transposition of the Christian faith. It is also a scriptural one. Moreover, Bishop Cragg is careful to point out that such critical assessment is made from a twentieth-century perspective, in an era that is postimperial and on the whole postmissionary, and "in the light of subsequent experience and the vantage of time."[36] The present writer enjoys the further advantage of a measure of cultural distance from the western missionaries themselves—an advantage that must surely be worn lightly.

The Edinburgh Conference of 1910 is a witness to the missiological outlook of a major portion of the western missionary enterprise in its heyday. It indicates that missionary thinking about the "non-Christian" world (that is, the nonwestern world) conceived of that world in terms of its religious *systems.* In this respect, the modern missionary enterprise from the West was fundamentally different from the Gentile mission of

32. Kenneth Cragg, *op. cit.,* p. 9.
33. *Ibid.,* p. 9.
34. See Max Warren, *op. cit.,* p. 88.
35. Roland Allen, *Missionary Methods,* pp. 26-37.
36. Kenneth Cragg, *op. cit.,* p. 88.

the early Church as crystallized in the vision and achievement of St. Paul. In a penetrating study of the relationship between the missionary understanding of the first chapter of the Epistle to the Romans and the missionary view of the modern "heathens," Prof. Andrew Walls has shown how during the western encounter with nonwestern, hence "non-Christian" peoples, western categorizations came to overlay the apostolic teaching:

> As systems and ultimately the collective labels for systems which we called the world religions, have slipped into the place of ungodly men in the interpretation of Romans 1, so Christianity, also conceived as a system has sometimes slipped into the place of the righteousness of God. The true system has been opposed to the false system condemned there.[37]

But what the apostle means by the ungodly in Romans 1, are not systems at all, but men:

> It is *men* who hold down the truth in unrighteousness, who do not honour God, who are given to dishonourable passions. It is upon men who commit ungodly and wicked deeds, that the wrath of God is revealed.

Walls further points out:

> It has sometimes, but not always, been realized that "Christianity" is a term formally identical with the other labels; that it certainly covers as wide a range of phenomena as most of them; that if the principalities and powers work within human systems, they can and do work within this one. Man-in-Christianity lies under the wrath of God just as much, and for the same reasons, as Man-in-Hinduism. . . . Man was vile everywhere, not only in Ceylon (sic). The Christian preacher had the same message of *repentance* and faith for the non-Christian world as he had been preaching in the Christian world; for it was not Christianity that saves, but Christ.[38]

In their contact with African peoples, many missionaries were most struck by what appeared to them to be the "sheer paganism" and the "awfulness" of African "heathen superstitions."[39] In the process, mis-

---

37. A. F. Walls, "The first chapter of the epistle to the Romans and the modern missionary movement," in W. Ward Gasque and Ralph P. Martin, eds., *Apostolic History and the Gospel* (Biblical and Historical Essays presented to F. F. Bruce on his 60th birthday; Exeter: Paternoster Press, 1970), p. 356.

38. *Ibid.*

39. Some missionary accounts included descriptions of these as a matter of importance: see, for instance, *A. M. Mackay—Pioneer Missionary of the Church Missionary Society to Uganda,* by his sister (London: Frank Cass, 1970, first published 1890), ch. V, "Heathen Superstitions."

sionaries became considerably less aware of Africans as essentially human, with their utterly *human* fears and joys, hopes and disappointments, and yearnings for salvation. The apostolic contrast has been described by Bishop Cragg, setting forth how profoundly Paul grasped the universal need of all men, Jews no less than Greeks, and on the same terms, for the one and the same universal gospel:

> Through all these runs, as integral to the sense of the universal, the new dimension of the person, the sense of men as men, not of Jews as Jews, or Greeks as Greeks.[40]

The gospel, turning as it does on "grace and personality,"

> . . . has to do with men as men, their sins and their fears, and not with Jews as Jews, òr Greeks as Greeks. Thus its unity majestically transcends the most stubborn divisions of humanity.[41]

By failing to view man-in-African-"heathenism" as *man* in the same terms as man-in-Christianity, they deprived themselves of adequate means for discerning the activity of God in the lives of Africans. They also tended to confuse their particular institutionalized western Christianity with Christ, and to present the former as the giver of salvation. The truth is rather that it is "not Christianity that saves, but Christ."[42]

Paul's encounter with Greeks on Mars Hill in Athens was the symbolical high-point of his ministry.[43] The apostle who grasped perhaps most firmly the significance of Christ for the entire universe (cf. Col. 1:15ff.; Eph. 1:10ff.), and who strenuously preached Jesus to Jews as the fulfilment of the promises of the Old Testament (cf. Acts 13:26ff.), there proclaimed with equal conviction that Jesus was to Gentiles also the fulfiller of their deepest religious and spiritual longings (cf. Acts 17:22ff.; 14:15ff.). From this standpoint, the crucial weakness in the modern missionary enterprise from the West consisted in a failure to appreciate as deeply as Paul did the nature of this fundamental and primary universality of the gospel, of Christ, and hence of his intimate relevance to all our *human* contexts. Therefore none of us can be said, in a strict sense, to be speaking on Christology from a "non-Christian" religious viewpoint, for no one can confess "Jesus is Lord" unless he is guided by the Holy Spirit (1 Cor. 12:3, TEV).

We must further clarify the significance of Paul's achievement in contrast to our own more recent missionary past in view of the contemporary interest in contextualization in the "One Third World" where the view still exists that Christian mission takes place essentially only in the "Two

40. Kenneth Cragg, *op. cit.,* p. 62.
41. *Ibid.,* p. 48.
42. A. F. Walls, *op. cit.,* p. 357.
43. See J. Dupont, *Etudes sur les Actes des Apôtres* (Paris: Les Editions du Cerf, 1967), p. 414.

Thirds World.'' For example, Johannes Verkuyl makes this rather dubious territorial distinction between "evangelism" and "missiology"—in his otherwise very valuable book, *Contemporary Missiology*.[44]

Some imagine that the great achievement of Paul in apostolic times was to have effectually contextualized the gospel *for* the Gentiles, and to have, almost, produced a theology *for* them. Paul surely did have a crucial part in the cultural and intellectual transposition of the gospel from Jewish milieu into the Hellenistic world. But, in a strict sense, the fulness of that transposition could only be the work of Hellenistic Christians themselves. The great significance of Paul in the early mission and for all subsequent cross-cultural Christian mission, lies in his ministry as facilitator and enabler for the Gentiles. Paul ensured that Gentiles would feel at home in the gospel, as Gentiles, on the same terms as Jews like himself—that is, on the basis of faith in Christ Jesus, and not submission to Judaizing demands for circumcision and other ordinances of no import to them. The remarkable achievement of Paul was to work tirelessly to secure the conditions in which Gentile Christian identity could flourish in the subsequent centuries. By his firm grasp of the universality of the gospel of Jesus the Messiah, and by his insistence on the all-embracing inclusiveness of this gospel, he placed at the disposal of Gentile Christians the basic tools for assessing their own cultural heritage, for making their own contribution to Christian life and thought, and also for testing the genuineness and Christian character of that contribution.

Why did this not happen in Africa? The answer to this question has been given with somewhat disturbing acuteness by a Methodist missionary who served in my own country for twenty-six years and died there. In the first in-depth study of the impact of Christian mission upon the life of Akan people of Ghana, considered in the light of the mainline Protestant churches and the Roman Catholic Church, *Akan Religion and the Christian Faith*, S. G. Williamson concluded that "missionary work in general seems to have adopted an attitude at variance with that of the New Testament."[45] In view of the Akan belief in a Supreme Being, as well as in a hierarchy of gods and spirits, Williamson observed:

> It is conceivable that as pure faith, Christianity might have spoken to the Akan in his apprehension of reality. The apostles and missionaries of the New Testament period seem to have approached their listeners on the basis of what they did believe, at least to the extent that they proclaimed Christ as the Saviour of men within a milieu which allowed the existence of "gods many and lords many." The missionary enterprise among the Akan did not take this line, but being

44. Johannes Verkuyl, *Contemporary Missiology—an Introduction* (Grand Rapids: Eerdmans, 1978), p. 9.

45. S. G. Williamson, *Akan Religion and the Christian Faith, A Comparative Study of the Impact of Two Religions* (Accra: Ghana Universities Press, 1965), p. 138.

western in outlook and emphasis, felt bound to deny the Akan worldview, not only on the basis of what was essentially Christian belief,
but on the ground of what was, in effect, a European world-view.[46]

As a consequence of this missionary approach, the implanted Christian
faith "failed to meet the Akan in his personally experienced religious
need."[47] The Akan became a Christian by cleaving to the new order introduced by the missionary, rather than working out his salvation (in
Christ, that is) within the traditional religious milieu. But this latter was
not possible since "the missionary effort was directed toward drawing
the convert away from his traditional life towards what the missionary
considered to be a proper expression, civilised and Christian, of his
faith."[48]

This missionary activity has, therefore, never amounted to a genuine
encounter. The Christian faith as historically implanted by western enterprise has been unable to sympathize with, or relate its message to, the
Akan spiritual outlook. Hence its impact has been blunted.[49] In 1969,
John Mbiti wrote that Williamson's account of the Akan story seemed
to summarize the situation in other African societies.[50]

In the light of the missionary story of Africa, it is not surprising that
when in 1963 John Taylor attempted in *The Primal Vision* to explore how
the Christian presence might be "set more humbly and attentively amid
African religion," he began by posing some of the questions that the
western missionary history had bequeathed to us:

> Christ has been presented as the answer to questions a white man
> would ask, the solution to the needs that western man would feel, the
> Saviour of the world of the European world-view, the object of the
> adoration and prayer of historic Christendom. But if Christ were to
> appear as the answer to the questions that Africans are asking, what
> would he look like? . . . .[51]

II. CHRISTOLOGY FROM AN AFRICAN PERSPECTIVE:
JESUS OF THE AFRICAN WORLD

Some new factors in our present situation

Despite rather negative conclusions from this survey of the western missionary encounter with African religion, the picture must not be over-

46. *Ibid.*, p. 168.
47. *Ibid.*, p. 170.
48. *Ibid.*, p. 171.
49. *Ibid.*, p. 175.
50. John S. Mbiti, *African Religions and Philosophy* (London: Heinemann, 1969),
p. 237.
51. John V. Taylor, *The Primal Vision—Christian Presence amid African Religion*
(London: SCM Press, 1963), p. 16.

drawn, for two reasons. First, the reality of our Christian communities bears evident witness to the communication of the gospel, however inadequate we may now consider that communication to have been. As John Taylor's analysis of the Bugandan Church has shown, there was more to the "hearing" of the Word of God than could be contained in the actual verbalizations of it by the human agents.[52] We must allow the mercy and providence of God to override the inescapably ambivalent character of our human achievements.

Secondly, even if the view is accepted that "Africa had no Paul," in that the missionary enterprise from the West did not produce early facilitators for African theological freedom, African theological thinkers now share in the inheritance of the gospel as Paul proclaimed it. Theological freedom is the freedom of the gospel. Paradoxically, the freedom we now have to theologize in our own terms has also been the result of the efforts of that earlier generation of African theologians who refused to accept the western missionary estimation of the African heritage in religion. Here, I would like to pay tribute to our immediate predecessors in the theological task in modern Africa. It is not necessary to accept without qualification everything that they have said, in order to appreciate the import of their achievement. By affirming consistently the continuity of God from the pre-Christian African part into the Christian present, they have bequeathed to us the assurance that with our Christian conversion, we are not introduced to a new God absolutely unrelated to the traditions of our past.[53] The limitations in our missionary past may now cease to determine the growth of theological awareness and confidence in our churches.

A further dimension in our present situation relates even more closely to the encounter between the Christian faith and African traditional religions. The official account and interpretation of the Edinburgh (1910) Conference described "Animism" as "the religious beliefs of more or less backward and degraded peoples all over the world."[54] Many missionary correspondents felt that Animism was practically devoid of any "preparation for Christianity."[55] At that time, it seemed hardly likely that the scientific and academic study of religion would ever light upon the discovery of a peculiar historical connection between this "form of religion" and Christianity, with probably far-reaching significance for understanding the nature of the Christian faith itself.

52. John V. Taylor, *The Growth of the Church in Buganda—An Attempt at Understanding* (London: SCM Press, 1958).

53. See, among others, E. Bolaji Idowu, *Olodumare—God in Yoruba Belief* (London: Longmans, 1962); J. S. Mbiti, *Concepts of God in Africa* (London: SPCK, 1970); G. M. Setiloane, *The Image of God among the Sotho-Tswana* (Rotterdam: A. A. Balkema, 1976).

54. W. H. T. Gairdner, *op. cit.*, p. 139.

55. *The Missionary Message*, p. 24.

The fact is that the expansion of Christianity has registered its most marked responses in "societies with primal (i.e. animistic) religious systems."[56] These are the Mediterranean world of the early Christian centuries, the ancient peoples of Northern and Western Europe, and the modern "primalists" of black Africa, Asia, Latin America, and Oceania. In an article on the "Primal Religions of the world and their study," published in 1977, H. W. Turner asked whether it was adequate to explain this historical connection as "solely due to their fragility or inadequacies as compared with the great religions? Might there rather not be affinities between the Christian and primal traditions?"[57] Turner points out that the significance of this historical insight is that "the form of religion that might seem farthest removed from the Christian faith has in fact had a closer relationship with it than any other."[58] Andrew Walls, in an article published in *Mission Focus* of November, 1978, argued that inasmuch as primal religions have been "the most fertile soil for the gospel," it is they which "underlie, therefore, the Christian faith of the vast majority of Christians of all ages and all nations."[59] John Mbiti has consistently argued for the view that Africa's "old" religions have been a crucial factor in the rapid spread of Christianity among African peoples.[60]

This argument stands the western missionary view of African religions on its head, and so opens the way for a fresh approach to how we may understand the relation of Jesus as Lord and Saviour to the spiritual realities of our context.

Christology and spirit-power: Jesus and the "spirit fathers" (Nananom Nsamanfo)

Introductory: John Mbiti's contribution

In the late 1960s John Mbiti wrote an article called "Some African Concepts of Christology" which was included in Georg Vicedom's collection of theological contributions from Asia, Africa, and Latin America. Mbiti began by stating: "The title of this paper is misleading because African concepts of Christology do not exist."[61] Yet Mbiti went on to write the article! Drawing on H. W. Turner's study of sermon texts used

---

56. A. F. Walls, "Africa and Christian Identity," in *Mission Focus* 4 (Nov. 1978), 11-13.

57. H. W. Turner, "The Primal Religions of the World and their Study," in Victor C. Hayes, ed., *Australian Essays in World Religions* (Australian Society for the Study of Religions, Bedford Park, South Australia, 1977), p. 37.

58. *Ibid.*

59. A. F. Walls, "Africa and Christian Identity," p. 11.

60. See John S. Mbiti, "The Encounter between Christianity and African Religion," in *Temenos* 12 (1976), 125-135.

61. John S. Mbiti, "Some African Concepts of Christology," in Georg F. Vicedom, ed., *Christ and the Younger Churches* (London: SPCK, 1972), p. 51.

by a West African independent church, the Church of the Lord, Aladura,[62] he gave illuminating insights into Christological points of interest to African Christians, and indicated what the portrait of Jesus in the African conceptualization of the world looked like.

Moreover, Mbiti contributed an article " ὁ σωτὴρ ἡμῶν as an African experience" to a collection of essays in honour of C. F. D. Moule, published in 1973.[63] In that study of how African Christians apprehend salvation, he drew again largely on evidence from "independent" churches. His view was that "it is within these churches that African Christians have more freely externalized their experience of the Christian faith than is otherwise the case in the mission-dominated or historical churches."[64] Though we can now regard the distinctions between "independent" and "historical" (or mainline) churches as less meaningful than they were thought to be,[65] Mbiti's articles did indicate that there was something to write about. In this area, as in much else, he has been a pioneer.

We need not discuss the details of John Mbiti's treatment of the problem here. But I would like to highlight two inferences from those two studies. The first is that Jesus is seen, above all else, as the *Christus Victor*. This arises from Africans' keen awareness of forces and powers at work in the world which threaten the interests of life and harmony. The portrait of Jesus as *Christus Victor* answers to the need for a powerful protector against these forces and powers.[66]

The second inference is that "for African Christians, 'our Saviour' is a term readily interchangeable between God and Jesus, and sometimes the Holy Spirit. In a saving capacity, Jesus mediates and universalises the almightiness of God, . . . so that 'our Saviour' is able to do all things, to save in all situations, to protect against all enemies, and is available whenever those who believe may call upon him."[67] This means that the humanity of Jesus and his atoning work on the cross are considerably less in view, and Jesus is taken to belong essentially to the more powerful realm of divinity, in the realm of Spirit-power. Mbiti criticizes the Christology implied here as "seriously defective"; at the same time he

62. On this church, see H. W. Turner, *An African Independent Church—The Church of the Lord (Aladura)* (Oxford: Clarendon Press, 1967). See also H. W. Turner, *Profile through Preaching* (London, 1965).

63. See B. Lindars and S. Smalley, eds., *Christ and the Spirit in the New Testament* (Essays in honour of C. F. D. Moule; Cambridge University Press, 1973), pp. 397-414.

64. *Ibid.*, p. 400.

65. Cf. A. F. Walls, "The Anabaptists of Africa? The Challenge of the African Independent Churches," in *Occasional Bulletin of Missionary Research* 3 (April 1979), 48-51.

66. John S. Mbiti, "Some African Concepts of Christology," p. 54.

67. John S. Mbiti, " ὁ σωτὴρ ἡμῶν," p. 412.

points out that such a situation requires a reexamination of the methods
and contents of evangelization and also a "deeper appreciation of the
traditional African world, whose grip is so strong that it exercises a powerful influence on the manner of understanding and experiencing the Christian message, however that message may be presented."[68]

These considerations bring us near the heart of the Christological problem as it confronts us now. To make my reflections more concrete, I
propose to relate them as far as possible to the religious belief and
worldview of the Akan people of Ghana. Being an Akan myself, I shall
be dealing with realities with which I can easily sympathize. Further,
theology can be authentic only in context. I shall be setting forth some
of my own wrestlings with regard to my context.

Jesus and the ancestors in Akan worldview

Acceptance of Jesus as "our Saviour" always involves making him at
home in our spiritual universe, and in terms of our religious needs and
longings. So a Christology of spirit-power in the African context is not
necessarily "defective," as against any other perception of Jesus. The
question is whether such a Christological understanding faithfully reflects
biblical revelation and is rooted in authentic Christian experience. Biblical
teaching affirms that Jesus is who he is (i.e., Saviour) because of what
he has done, and can do (i.e., save), and vice versa: Christology cannot
be divorced from Soteriology (cf. Col. 2:15ff.). Since "salvation" in the
traditional African world involves a certain perception of the realm of
spirit-power and its effects upon the physical and spiritual dimensions
of human existence, Christology must address itself to the questions posed
by such a worldview. The needs of the African world require a Christology
that meets those needs. Accordingly, who Jesus is in the African spiritual
universe must not be separated from what he does and can do in that
world. The way in which Jesus relates to the perceived importance and
function of the "spirit fathers" or ancestors is crucial for such Christology.

The Akan spirit-world on which human existence is believed to depend
consists primarily of God, the Supreme Spirit Being (Onyame), Creator
and Sustainer of the universe. Subordinate to God, with delegated authority from God, are the "gods" (abosom), sometimes referred to as children
of God (Nyame mba) and the ancestors or "spirit fathers" (Nsamanfo).
The relative positions of the gods and the ancestors is summed up by
Dr. Peter Sarpong, the Catholic Bishop of Kumasi and an authority on
Akan culture:

> While God's power surpasses all others, the ancestors would appear
> to tilt the scale in their favour if their power could be weighed against
> that of the lesser gods. After all are the deities not often referred to

68. *Ibid.*, p. 413.

as ''the innumerable gods of our ancestors,'' the spokesmen of the human spirits?[69]

John Pobee of the University of Ghana has underlined the importance of the ancestors in the religious worldview of the Akan. He has devoted a whole book to developing some aspects of an Akan Christian theology. He concludes that ''whereas the gods may be treated with contempt if they fail to deliver the goods expected of them, the ancestors, like the Supreme Being, are always held in reverence or even worship.''[70]

We shall not discuss here whether ancestors are ''worshipped'' or simply ''venerated.''[71] We only need to recognize that the ancestors form the most prominent element in the Akan religious outlook, and provide the essential focus of piety. Pobee's comment on the ancestors is therefore well founded:

> Perhaps the most potent aspect of Akan religion is the cult of the ancestors. They, like the Supreme Being, are always held in deep reverence or even worshipped. The ancestors are that part of the clan who have completed their course here on earth and are gone ahead to the other world to be elder brothers of the living at the house of God. Not all the dead are ancestors. To qualify to be an ancestor one must have lived to a ripe old age and in an exemplary manner and done much to enhance the standing and prestige of the family, clan or tribe. By virtue of being the part of the clan gone ahead to the house of God, they are believed to be powerful in the sense that they maintain the course of life here and now and influence it for good or ill. They give children to the living; they give good harvest, they provide the sanctions for the moral life of the nation and accordingly punish, exonerate or reward the living as the case may be.[72]

Ancestors are essentially clan or lineage ancestors. So they have to do with the community or society in which their progeny relate to one another, and not with a system of religion as such, which might be categorized as ''the Akan religion.''[73] Thus, the ''religious'' functions and duties which relate to ancestors become binding on all members of the particular group who share common ancestors. Insofar as Akan religion has to do with the ancestors and their significance for individual and corporate well-being or otherwise, the crucial Christological question is, as John Pobee rightly puts it: ''Why should an Akan relate to

69. Peter Sarpong, *Ghana in Retrospect—Some aspects of Ghanaian culture* (Accra-Tema: Ghana Publishing Corporation, 1974), p. 43.

70. John S. Pobee, *Toward an African Theology* (Nashville: Abingdon, 1979), p. 48.

71. Peter Sarpong, *op. cit.*, rejects ''worship'' as applicable to ancestors.

72. John S. Pobee, *op. cit.*, p. 46.

73. Peter Sarpong, *op. cit.*, pp. 34, 36.

Jesus of Nazareth who does not belong to his clan, family, tribe and tradition?''[74]

Hitherto, our churches, following the pattern of earlier missionary attitudes, have tended to avoid the question, and have presented the gospel as though it was concerned with an entirely different compartment of life, unrelated to traditional religious piety. As a result, many of our people are uncertain about how the Jesus of the church's proclamation saves them from the terrors and fears which they experience in their traditional worldview. This shows how important it is to relate Christology—the essential focus of Christian understanding and experience—to the realm of the ancestors. If this is not done, many of our fellow African Christians will continue to be men and women "living at two levels"—half African and half European—but never belonging properly to either. We need to apprehend God in the Lord Jesus Christ speaking immediately to us in our particular circumstances, in a way that assures our people that we can be authentic Africans and true Christians.[75]

John Pobee suggests that we "look on Jesus as the Great and Greatest Ancestor," since, "in Akan society the Supreme Being and the ancestors provide the sanctions for the good life, and the ancestors hold that authority as ministers of the Supreme Being."[76] He is well aware of the problems involved, but by approaching the problem largely through Akan wisdom sayings and proverbs, he does not seem to engage sufficiently with the "religious" nature of the question. Moreover, in his attempt to fit the traditional, dogmatic formulations of Christology to Akan categories of thought, he does not let the biblical revelation speak sufficiently in its own terms into the Akan situation. He too easily assumes similarities between the Akan and biblical (for him "Jewish") worldview, and so underestimates the potential for real conflict, and does not achieve genuine encounter. For if the full prerogatives of the Greatest Ancestor are claimed for one who, at the superficial level, "does not belong to his clan, family, tribe and nation," the Akan non-Christian might well feel that the very grounds of his identity and personality are taken away from him. It is with such fears and dangers, including the misconceptions which may underline them, as well as the meanings and intentions behind the old allegiances, that Christology has to deal.

The Universality of Jesus Christ and our adoptive past

My own approach is to read the Scriptures with Akan traditional piety well in view. In this way, we can arrive at a Christology that deals with the perceived reality of the ancestors. I also make the biblical assump-

74. John S. Pobee, *op. cit.,* p. 81.

75. Joshua Kudadjie, "Theological training for our time and for our society" (unpublished address delivered at the 2nd Graduation Ceremony of the Christian Service College, Kumasi, Ghana, 2 July 1977), p. 4.

76. John S. Pobee, *op. cit.,* p. 94.

tion that Jesus Christ is not a stranger to our heritage. My fundamental premise is the primacy of the universality of Jesus Christ, as against his particularity as a Jew. This premise does not disregard the incarnation; rather, it affirms that the incarnation was the incarnation of the Saviour of all men, of all nations, and of all times. Furthermore, by insisting on the primacy of Jesus' universality, we do not seek to reduce his incarnation and its particularity to a mere historical accident. We hold on to his incarnation as a Jew because by faith in him, we also share in the divine promises given to the patriarchs, and through the history of ancient Israel,(cf. Eph. 2:11-12). So those promises belong to us also, precisely because of Jesus. Salvation, though "from the Jews" (Jn. 4:22), is not thereby Jewish. It is a distortion to stress the cultural particularity of our Lord's incarnation to the point of making him little more than a "typical" Jew; there is clearly more to him than Jewishness. Through our faith in him, we show that we are also children of Abraham, who was the spiritual father of all who put their faith in God (Rom. 4:11). Consequently, we have not merely our "natural" past; we have also an "adoptive" past, the past of God, reaching into the biblical history itself. This also—aptly described as the Abrahamic link[77]—is our past.

John 8:43-44 shows that a Jew could have for father, not Abraham at all, but the devil! It all turns on how we respond to Jesus Christ. Here we find one of the clearest statements in Scripture that our true human identity, as men and women made in the image of God, is not in a strict sense to be understood in terms of racial, cultural, national, or for that matter lineage, categories, but in Jesus Christ. Himself the image of the Father, by becoming one like us, he has become also a partaker of our *human* heritage. It is within that *human* heritage in which he finds us, and speaks to us in terms of its questions and puzzles. He challenges us to turn to him and participate in the new humanity for which he has come, died, been raised, and glorified.

The Good News as our story

Once this basic, universal relevance of Jesus Christ is granted, it is no longer a question of trying to relate, or accommodate, or even contextualize, the gospel; we learn to read and assimilate the Good News as *our* story. Our Lord has been, from the beginning, the Word of God for us as for all men everywhere. He has been the source of our life, and illuminator of our path in life, though, like all men everywhere, we also failed to apprehend him aright. But now he has manifested himself, becoming one of us, one like us. By acknowledging him for who he is, and by giving him our allegiance, we become what we are truly intended to be, by his gift, the children of God. For he himself is the Son of God, originating from the divine realm. If we refuse him that allegiance, we

---

77. A. F. Walls, "Africa and Christian Identity," p. 13.

forfeit that right of becoming children of God. Our response to him is crucial, because becoming children of God does not stem from, nor is it limited by, the accidents of birth, race, culture, lineage, or even "religious" tradition. It is realized through "the common energies of grace, and the common denominator of faith."[78]

This way of reading the early verses of John's Gospel, from the standpoint of faith in Jesus Christ as *our* story, is valid and necessary. The beginning of the Gospel echoes the early verses of Genesis 1. We are meant to appreciate the close association of our creation and our redemption, both effected in and through Jesus Christ (Col. 1:15ff.). We are to understand our creation as the original revelation of God to us, not as it is often taken, in the rather weak and abstract sense of the realm of "nature." Rather, it was in the creation of the universe and especially of man, that God first revealed his Kingship to our ancestors, and called them and us freely to obey him. Working from the perception of our creation as the original revelation to, and covenant with, us, we, from African primal tradition, are given a biblical basis for theologizing within the framework of the high doctrine of God as Creator and Sustainer, which is deeply rooted in our heritage. More significantly, we are enabled to discover ourselves in Adam (cf. Acts 17:26) and come out of the isolation which the closed system of clan, lineage, and family imposes, to recover universal horizons.

However, "as in Adam all die, so in Christ shall all be made alive" (1 Cor. 15:22). Adam sinned and lost his place in the garden. What the biblical account depicts under the symbol of the expulsion of man (Gen. 3), African myths of origins represent under the symbol of the withdrawal of God, so that he is continually in people's thoughts, yet is absent from daily living in any practical sense. The ambiguity which attaches to the mediation of lesser deities and ancestral spirits, whose power is at once beneficent and malevolent,[79] presents a dilemma whose solution is only in a genuine incarnation of the saviour from the realm beyond. But trinitarian doctrine is preserved. For the God who has become so deeply and actively involved in our condition, is the Son (Jn. 1:18), whom to see is to "see" the Father (cf. Jn. 14:15ff.; Acts 2:38f.).

Jesus as "Ancestor" and sole Mediator

Thus the existential gulf between the intense awareness of the existence of God and also, paradoxically, of his "remoteness," is bridged in Christ alone because "there has been a death which sets people free from the wrongs they did while the first covenant was in force" (Heb. 9:15). How does this death relate to our story and particularly to our natural "spirit fathers"? Some suggest that ours is a "shame-culture" and not a "guilt-culture," on the grounds that public acceptance is what determines

78. Kenneth Cragg, *op. cit.*, p. 48.
79. Peter Sarpong, *op. cit.*, p. 41; also John S. Pobee, *op. cit.*, p. 47.

morality, and consequently a "sense of sin" is said to be absent.[80] This view is oversimplified, and is challenged by African theologians and sociologists.[81] However, in our tradition, the essence of sin is in its being an antisocial act.[82] This makes sin basically injury to the interests of another person, and damage to the collective life of the group. Busia's comment on the Ashanti (also Akan) is significant:

> The Ashanti conception of a good society is one in which harmony is achieved among the living, and between the living and the gods and the ancestors. . . . [83]

Such a conception of morality leaves unresolved the real problem of the assurance of moral transformation, which the human conscience needs. For the real problem of our sinfulness is the soiled conscience, and against this, purificatory rites and sacrificial offerings to achieve social harmony are ineffectual. And yet the view of sin as antisocial seems to be also biblically valid: sin is indeed sin against man and the community's interest. But man himself is the creation of God, created in God's image, so social sin is also sin against God. The blood of Abel cried to God against Cain (Gen. 4). The Good News introduces the valid insight about the social nature of sin and brings the need for expiation into a wider context. Sin is more than the antisocial act; the sinner sins ultimately against a personal God who has a will and purpose in human history.

Seen from this angle, our needs in our tradition make the Christological insights of the Epistle to the Hebrews perhaps the most crucial of all. Our Saviour has not just become one like us; he has died for us. It is a death which has eternal sacrificial significance for us. It deals with our moral failures and the infringements of our social relationships. It heals our wounded and soiled consciences, and overcomes once and for all, and at their roots, all that in our heritage and our somewhat melancholy history brings us grief, guilt, shame, and bitterness. Thus, our Saviour is our Elder Brother who has participated with us in our African experience in every respect, except in our sin and alienation from God; an alienation with which our myths of origins make us only too familiar. Being our true Elder Brother now in the presence of God, his Father and our Father, he displaces the mediatorial function of our natural "spirit fathers." For these latter themselves need saving, since they originated from among us. It is known from African missionary history that

---

80. See F. B. Welbourn, "Some Problems of African Christianity: Guilt and Shame," in C. G. Baeta, ed., *Christianity in Tropical Africa* (London: Oxford University Press), pp. 182-199. Cf. John V. Taylor, *the Primal Vision,* pp. 166-169.

81. John S. Pobee, *op. cit.,* pp. 102ff. Cf. K. A. Busia, "The Ashanti," in Daryll Forde, ed., *African Worlds—Studies in the Cosmological Ideas and Social Values of African Peoples* (London: Oxford University Press, 1954), p. 207.

82. Cf. John S. Pobee, *op. cit.,* p. 118.

83. K. A. Busia, *op. cit.,* p. 207.

sometimes one of the first actions of new converts was to pray for their ancestors, who had passed on before the gospel was proclaimed. The Christological point is that their action is an important testimony to the depth of their perception of Jesus as sole Lord and Saviour. Jesus Christ, "the Second Adam" . . . from heaven (1 Cor. 15:47), becomes for us then the only mediator between God and ourselves (cf. 1 Tim. 2:5). He is the "mediator of a better covenant" (Heb. 8:6), relating our human destiny directly to God. He is truly our high priest who meets our needs to the full.

From the kind of understanding held about the spirit-world, the resurrection and ascension of our Lord assume singular importance. He has now returned to the realm of spirit, and therefore of power. From the standpoint of Akan traditional theology and cosmology, Jesus has gone to the realm of the ancestor spirits, and the gods. We already know that power and the resources for living are believed to come from there but the terrors and misfortunes which could threaten and destroy life come from there also. But if Jesus has gone to the realm of "spirits and the gods," so to speak, he has gone there as Lord over them in much the same way that he is Lord over us. He is therefore Lord over the living and the dead, and over the "living-dead," as the ancestors are also described. He is supreme over all "gods" and authorities in the realm of the spirits. So he sums up in himself all their powers and annuls any terrorizing influence they might be assumed to have upon us.

The guarantee that our Lord is Lord also in the realm of the spirits is that he has sent us his own Spirit, the Holy Spirit, to dwell with us and be our protector, as much as to be Revealer of Truth and our Sanctifier. In John 16:7ff., our Lord's insistence on going away to the Father includes this idea of Christ's Lordship in the realm of spirits, as he himself enters the region of spirit, and also the idea of the protection and guidance which the coming Holy Spirit will provide for his followers in the world. The Holy Spirit is of course sent to convict the world of its sin in rejecting Jesus, and to manifest, to the shame of unbelievers, the true righteousness which is in Jesus and available only in him. But he is also sent to reveal the spiritual significance of God's judgement, not this time upon the world, but upon the devil, who deceives the world about its sin, and blinds men to the perfect righteousness in Christ. Our Lord, now entering the region of spirit, sends the Holy Spirit to his followers to give them understanding of the realities of the realm of spirits. The close association of the defeat and overthrow of the devil ("ruler of this world") with the death, resurrection, and exaltation of Jesus (cf. Jn. 12:31), may be significant here. Furthermore, the thought of the "keeping" and the protection of his followers from "the evil one" forms an important part of Jesus' aptly described "high priestly" prayer (cf. Jn. 17:9ff.).

These are some of the areas for us to investigate when we begin to reflect on the Good News from the standpoint of the worldview of our heritage. Some quite important insights are in store for us, not from isolated passages of Scripture, but from entire and very significant bodies of teaching.

The Lordship of Christ amid sacralized power

The position of the Chief: the problem of ambiguity

The Lordship of Christ in relation to the natural "spirit-fathers" or ancestors finds its concrete focus in the way in which Christ's Lordship may be related to the significance of Kingship in the society. This close connection between the place and function of the ancestors and the meaning of Kingship, on the one hand, and Christology, on the other, is due to the fact that the reigning Chief (or King) occupies the stool (or throne) of the ancestors, particularly his royal ancestors. There is more to the Chief's position than simply succession to the office of his deceased predecessors. In the Akan worldview these do not die but simply go "elsewhere," i.e., into the realm of the "spirit-fathers," from where they continue to show interest and to intervene in the affairs of the state. The installation of the Chief renders his very person sacred. This is done by bringing him into a peculiarly close contact with the ancestors. The esoteric ceremony at which this is effected is known to be quite simple.[84] Upon the ritually preserved stool of his most renowned ancestor, the Chief is briefly lowered and raised three times. Once thus installed (enstooled), the Chief, as Dr. Sarpong explains, is "now more than just a head of state. He is, in a sense, an ancestor himself. From that moment everybody must call him Nana (grandfather)."[85] The Akan royal title, Nana, is itself an ancestral title. The ancestors are Nananom Nsamanfo, i.e., ancestor spirits or "spirit-fathers."

Since the cult of the ancestors is the most potent aspect of religious life in traditional Akan society, the Chief's sacred office becomes heavily invested with religious significance. Because the belief is that "the well-being of the society depends upon the maintenance of good relations with the ancestors on whom the living depend for help and protection," the Chief acquires a crucial role as the intermediary between the state and the ancestors. He is the central figure at the organized religious ceremonies which ensure the maintenance of the desired harmony between the living and the spirit-fathers.[86] So integral is the religious aspect of Akan kingship that in his authoritative study of Ashanti kingship, Dr. Busia concludes:

84. Eva L. R. Meyerowitz, *The Sacred State of the Akan* (London: Faber and Faber, 1951), p. 66. See also K. A. Busia, *The Position of the Chief in the Modern Political System of Ashanti:* A Study of the Influence of Contemporary Social Changes on Ashanti Political Insititutions (London: Frank Cass, 1968, first published 1951), pp. 12-13. Cf. Peter Sarpong, *The Sacred Stools of the Akan* (Accra-Tema: Ghana Publishing Corporation, 1971), p. 537.

85. Peter Sarpong, *The Sacred Stools of the Akan,* p. 54; cf. p. 26.

86. K. A. Busia, *The Position of the Chief* . . . , pp. 26f.

No one could be an adequate chief who did not perform the ritual functions of his office. There have recently been elected as chiefs in different parts of Ashanti men who are both literate and Christian. But they have all felt an obligation to perform the ritual acts of their office. They were enstooled in the stoolhouse, where they poured libations to the ancestors whom they had succeeded. . . . It is as successors of the ancestors that they are venerated and their authority respected, and they could not keep the office without maintaining contact with the ancestors through the traditional rituals.[87]

While Busia rightly insists that "the chief's position is bound up with strong religious sentiments,"[88] his conclusions also indicate that a measure of ambiguity attaches to the position of the Chief in terms of the Christian faith. Busia himself points to the enstoolment of men "who are Christian," in order to emphasize the significance of his central thesis that the institution of Chiefship or Kingship is fundamentally of a sacral nature. Furthermore, Dr. Busia was well known for his view that our churches must come to terms with the Akan understanding of the universe and the nature of society, particularly in its religious dimensions.[89]

Since Busia wrote in the 1950s, the ambiguity that characterizes the relation of the Chief to the Christian community in our society has continued. It has remained as a crucial area of confrontation between the Christian faith as generally understood in our context, and the religious traditions of Akan culture. When the Moderator of the Presbyterian Church of Ghana inaugurated, in March 1981, a committee charged with the specific responsibility of studying the relation of the church to traditional culture, he drew attention to the persisting ambiguity that attaches to the Chief. According to the report, many Chiefs have been baptized and confirmed, but their positions debar them from becoming full members of the church. The question which he posed was: "What can bring these Chiefs and the Church together?"[90]

The problem of the Chief's authority

The Moderator is not the first to ask that question. Behind the decision to set up this committee lay the desire of some Chiefs, with their traditional Councils, to understand more fully the relation of the Christian faith which they now cannot ignore, to the cultural tradition in which they themselves stand. And this is not the first instance of such an initiative by our Chiefs. In 1941, the Chief and Elders of the Akan state of Akim-Abuakwa sent a memorandum to the synod of the Presbyterian Church

87. *Ibid.*, p. 38.
88. *Ibid.*, p. 39.
89. He made an important contribution to the Conference of the Christian Council of Ghana (then Gold Coast), in 1955, on the subject *Christianity and African Culture*. See S. G. Williamson, *op. cit.*, pp. 157ff.
90. *Christian Messenger* 4 (April 1981), 3.

which was meeting in the Chief's capital, Kibi. The memorandum criticized the church on several counts, and particularly complained about
what the state authorities saw as the disruptive effect of segregating Christian converts into a separate community in each of the towns in order
to guard against what were considered to be "pagan" influences. This
undermined the unified authority of the Chief over his natural subjects.[91]

Another state response to the Christian presence occurred in the same
year, 1941, from Ashanti. The Ashanti Confederacy Council decreed that
farming on Thursday, the natal day of the earth deity, Asaase Yaa, was
to be regarded as an offence. Since the Christian community had, in the
meantime, become quite a significant factor in the state, it is understandable that the traditional authorities were disturbed by evidence of increasing violation of this law, mainly on the part of Christians.

The Christian churches concerned responded to the state authorities
on each of these instances of state criticism. In the earlier case, the church
pointed to the social and educational benefits of its work, and asserted
Christian loyalty to the state. In the second case, the Christian churches
in Ashanti presented a memorandum to the King of Ashanti (Asantehene)
on the relations between Christians and the state.[92] The memorandum
asserted the rights of Christian belief, and while protesting the loyalty
of Christians to the state, attempted to secure a dispensation from the
law for Christians. The crux of the churches' argument, for our purposes,
seems to have been formulated by paragraph 6:

> On the part of the chiefs we would ask that they accept as a fact the
> existence of Christians as members of their state and lay down ways
> by which they can show their allegiance to their chiefs without at the
> same time offending their Christian conscience.

I shall not discuss in detail the issues raised in these two instances of conflict between Akan traditional authorities and the Christian churches
within their jurisdiction. But while the Christian faith was obviously assail-
ing the institutions of sacral kingship as well as the position of the Chief
in some of its most vital aspects, i.e., its specifically religious dimensions,
none of the Christian responses seem to have addressed themselves to
these issues. The memorandum to the Asantehene attempted to apply
western ideas on church and state to a cosmic sacred order which made
no sharp distinctions between religious and political institutions. Busia's
comment on this controversy provides a useful insight into the deeper
issues at stake:

> In a society in which political and religious office are combined, the
> chiefs regard the request for the recognition of the existence of the

91. See S. G. Williamson, *op. cit.,* pp. 152-153.
92. See K. A. Busia, *The Position of the Chief* . . . , pp. 220-222; cf. pp.
133-138.

Christians and for the adaptation of native law as a request for the surrender of authority. As they see it, the Christian Church requests that they should not have power to legislate on certain things for certain members of the community, because the Church desires the right to legislate on these for those of the chief's subjects who have embraced the Christian Faith. Christianity challenges the traditional position of the chief as the religious as well as the political head of his tribe.[93]

The Christological dimension and the desacralization of political power

Behind this conflict between two authorities—the Christian church and the traditional state, *imperium in imperio*—lies two conceptions of power, and differing views as to the source of power. In the religious cosmology which undergirded Akan social organization, the power of the reigning Chief as the channel through which cosmic forces operated for the well-being of the society, was based on his position as one "who sits on the stool (throne) of the ancestors." The power of the Chief among the living, sacral power, is therefore the power of the ancestors, just as his title (Nana) is also theirs. Consequently, a Christology which fundamentally undermines and removes the power of the ancestors over the living, by the same token, desacralizes the power of the reigning Chief or King. We may wonder how many of our Chiefs who desire closer links with Christian churches are aware of how far their power as well as their own persons would need to be desacralized. Perhaps some of our natural rulers may rather be men among men. A Christology which alters so radically the nature and source of power carries, inevitably, immense implications for politics in our societies.

Here, I mean politics in a wider sense than the political organization of our sacred states. Historically, biblical faith has been a desacralizing force in the world,[94] and the story of Christianity in Africa has also demonstrated this quality in the Christian faith.[95] Much of the prestige which attached to Kingship in the past has been lost in the process of social change. New forms of political administration have been forged with the emergence of the new nation-states and their elected presidents. The natural ruler who sits on the stool of the ancestors is compelled now to seek ways of coming to terms with the new realities.

However, sacralization of political power is not the prerogative of the "old" ontocratic order. Sacralized power can find its way into the new ideology of states, as a secular parody of the old, genuinely religious social organism. Some modern African republics need to be understood from

93. *Ibid.*, p. 137.

94. Arend van Leeuwen, *Christianity in World History: the Meeting of the Faiths of East and West* (London, 1964).

95. Cf. H. W. Turner, "The Place of Independent Religious Movements in the Modernization of Africa," in *Journal of Religion in Africa* 2 (1969), 43-63, esp. pp. 49ff.

this angle. In so many of our modern nation-states, the leaders who achieved political independence often insisted on wielding power even when they became unpopular. This may well reflect the role of the royal ancestor who never ceases to rule from the realm of spirit power! Certainly the praise-names and titles of some African presidents would seem to bear ancestral overtones. When Dr. Kwame Nkrumah accepted the title of "Osagyefo," he must have known what he was doing. Nkrumah was not concerned to promote the interests of the "old" sacral rulers, and he was not from a royal house himself. But the designation "Osagyefo" portrayed him as the "Saviour" from British colonial rule. Under his presidency, Ghana's coins bore his image and the inscription: Civitatis Ghaniensis Conditor. Nkrumah was, for all practical purposes, an ancestor in the old sacral sense. It is not surprising that the Young Pioneers recited: Nkrumah never dies!

I have not drawn attention to the modern secular politics of African societies, to detract from the significance of the old order. On the contrary, if we are to know how to deal theologically with the problems of contemporary politics in our societies, we may need to find ways of coming to grips with the forces at work in the old order which have not yet been adequately encountered with the gospel. To do this through a genuine encounter with the realities behind the traditional institutions, and at the level at which our people experience them, it is important that the gospel of Jesus Christ be seen also as *our* story. If it is true that "the sovereignty of the world has passed to our Lord and his Christ, and he shall reign for ever and ever" (Rev. 11:15, NEB), this must find its meaning also in our context. In terms of the old sacred cosmic order, it is understandable that one King of Ashanti should say:

I am the centre of this world around which everything revolves.

And one of his subjects is reported to have said of him:

Everything comes out of him, he is holding the source of power, force and generation.[96]

However, what happens when the spirit-fathers who ensure such power to the reigning King become subservient to Christ the Lord? What happens to the position of the Chief who "sits on the stool of the ancestors," when it becomes evident that Christ himself is the Great Ancestor of *all* mankind, the mediator of *all* divine blessing, the judge of *all* mankind, and that access to him is not dependent on inherent right through royal lineage, but through "the common energies of grace and faith," and repentance from the heart? Will the Chief be a man among men, honoured but not venerated or worshipped?

96. See Eva L. R. Meyerowitz, *op. cit.,* p. 57, note 1.

The relevance of Christian history

These questions are not peculiar to our context, and certainly are not new in Christian history. The most instructive period of the Christian story for our purposes is the very early centuries of the Christian era. Those early Christians were convinced that in the Good News about Jesus Christ, and through Jesus Christ, they found access to the God beyond the gods, and that Jesus Christ met their spiritual needs and inspired higher hopes.

For this reason they were able to make the definite break with the cult of the emperor. Many earnest men and women though perhaps disapproving of much in the popular and state cults, did not make that break; they were not apprehended by the gospel. For such, the gospel was alien, if not distasteful. But not so the Christians; the gospel assured them that the sovereignty of the world had indeed passed to their Lord, and so they were able to relativize all other claims to sovereignty. And they won, as the visionary was shown:

> . . . by the blood of the Lamb and by the truth which they proclaimed; and they were willing to give up their lives and die (Rev. 12:11, TEV).

The message is quite clear: the heart of the encounter of the Good News with our context is Christology; the significance of our faith in Jesus Christ, crucified and risen, for our existence and destiny in the world. Such faith implies a firm conviction that in and through Christ, we are apprehended by ultimate truth, utterly dependable, and coherent with experience. We also are bound to discover that we are involved in a struggle to the death. It is not with flesh and blood, but with more subtle powers and intelligences who would hinder men and women from perceiving the nearness of Christ as one who has opened for us a new way, a living way, into the presence of God, through his own body, and as one of us! (cf. Heb. 10:20).

Christology . . . as power encounter

Christology, then, at the heart of our missiological struggle, has to do with encounter, "pulling down strongholds," "destroying false arguments," levelling "every proud obstacle," taking every thought captive and making it obey Christ (cf. 1 Cor. 10:4-5). But this kind of encounter does not wait for the "specialists" and "experts"; it takes place in the normal worshipping, witnessing life of the congregation, as the following incident shows:

Drumbeat in Church

A sharp conflict recently erupted between the Christian churches and the traditional authorities in the Ghanaian town of Akim Tafo over violation by the churches of a ban on drumming during a traditional religious festival.

During the two weeks preceding the "Ohum" religious festival, drumming, clapping of hands, wailing, firing of musketry, and any other noises likely to disturb the gods is not permitted.

But Christian churches in the town ignored the ban and continued to allow drumming during their worship services, arguing that drumming was an essential part of the Ghanaian form of worship.[97]

Obviously, it is the fact of drumming in church, which, in view of our missionary past, the reporter found most striking. I am more interested in the fact that the controversy took place in the context of worship. We have, therefore, an encounter of experiences, and of apprehensions of reality. We have a power encounter. It is equally interesting that the Christians claim their drumming in church to be "an essential part of the Ghanaian form of worship." They do not say *Christian* form of worship. However, since they are Christians, we have to assume that their worship has to do with Jesus Christ and not with the gods of the "traditional religious festival." So, we may ask, who are maintaining the authentic *Ghanaian* form of worship?

Our Christian brethren here have grasped the insight of the early Christians, that the issue at stake is not the confrontation of two "religions" or religious systems. The gospel turns, as Bishop Cragg has pointed out, "upon grace and personality," and has to do with God manifesting his love for us in and through Christ, touching our hearts and opening our eyes through his Spirit, so that we can respond to his love where he finds us in our heritage of culture and religious tradition. Could it be that in their own way the Akans of Akim Tafo have understood that Christian identity (for salvation has to do also with identity—God calls us by name), has to do with the discovery of personality in Christ, personality which is validated at both individual and social levels of our existence, and that this discovery, which is a gift of Christ, itself becomes the basis of confidence?

I doubt whether I have claimed too much for the theological awareness of the Christians of Akim Tafo. Their attitude seems to have something of the understanding that I have described. This enabled them to confront the traditional authorities on the common ground of a belief in the value of worship and to challenge the devotees of the "old" gods (and ancestors) to recognize that their own Christian worship with the aid of drums, even though it might be in violation of a religious ban, is in its own right authentic Ghanaian worship.

Such incidents and actions give me hope. They show me that my approach to Christology coheres with the Christian experience of those who share in the cultural heritage which my reflections presuppose.

Some concluding observations

Objections might well be raised against some of the solutions suggested in the second part of this paper. Does the primacy of the universality

97. *Voice Weekly,* Sept. 3-9, 1980, p. 6.

of Christ allow sufficiently for the uniqueness of the incarnation? Is not the attempt to begin with the basic relevance of Jesus to our tradition in some sense a reduction of his Jewish historicity? Might there not even be a danger of "docetism" in this approach to Christology?

I do not intend to answer these objections as I have stated them. I think the approach can be validated on biblical grounds. I will only make a few brief comments about the significance of the Epistle to the Hebrews in our context and for our methodology.

The problem of theology in New Testament times has often been assumed to be related to the church's encounter with Gentile cultures and traditions. The meaning of Christ for Jewish religious tradition was thought to be relatively simple. The Epistle to the Hebrews, however, corrects that misapprehension. The writer appears aware that some Hebrews might be tempted to turn from the proclamation of the great salvation. His frequent warnings about apostasy may sometimes sound hypothetical. He balances them with assurances that his readers would not fall away from their Christian discipleship. Yet he was also conscious that he was seeking to impart "solid food" and that some of the readers might not be used to such heavy diet.

The clue to the whole lies, I think, in his Christology. Hebrews is the one book in the New Testament in which Jesus Christ is understood and presented as High Priest. His priestly mediatorial role is fully probed and we are given one of the highest and most developed Christologies in the entire New Testament.

One of the most significant statements in the Epistle must be chapter 8:4: "If he were on earth, he would not be a priest at all. . . ." It may seem obvious that our Saviour does and did fulfil a High Priestly function in the redemptive work for us.

The problem arises when one has to validate that insight on the basis of Old Testament prophecies and anticipations. The fact is, "he was born a member of the tribe of Judah; and Moses did not mention this tribe when he spoke of priests" (Heb. 7:14). Thus the Christology of Hebrews involves making room in the tradition of priestly mediation for one who, at the purely human level, was an outsider to it. How were Hebrews to take this demonstration? "Why should an Akim relate to Jesus of Nazareth who does not belong to his clan, family, tribe and nation?" My suggestion is that a similar question must have occurred to some Hebrews in time past and the Epistle to the Hebrews was written to answer that question.

The Epistle takes us to the sublime heights of Christology. This is done by working *from* the achievement of Jesus *into* the biblical tradition. In this process, the *universality* of the Lord from heaven forms the basis for his *particularity* as the Messiah of the Jews. His High Priesthood is not after the order of Aaron, but of the enigmatic non-Hebrew, Melchizedek. I have tried to do something similar.

If this understanding of Hebrews is correct, then this Epistle not only gives us a remarkable instance of the kind of problem which our Christology must deal with, but also provides a biblical paradigm on how we may proceed.

SELECT BIBLIOGRAPHY

Kenneth Cragg. *Christianity in World Perspective.* London: Lutterworth Press, 1968.

Afua Kuma. *Jesus of the Deep Forest-Prayers and Praises of Afua Kuma.* Accra: Asempa Publishers, 1980.

John S. Mbiti. "Some African Concepts of Christology" in Georg F. Vicedom, ed., *Christ and the Younger Churches.* London: SPCK, 1972, pp. 51-62.

John S. Mbiti. " ὁ σωτὴρ ἡμῶν   as an African Experience," in B. Lindars and S. Smalley, *Christ and the Spirit in the New Testament.* Cambridge: C.U.P., 1973, pp. 397-414.

John S. Pobee. *Toward an African Theology.* Nashville: Abingdon, 1979, esp. Ch. V.

John V. Taylor. *The Primal Vision—Christian Presence amid African Religion.* London: SCM, 1963.

S. G. Williamson, *Akan Religion and the Christian Faith, A Comparative Study of the Impact of Two Religions.* Accra: Ghana Universities Press, 1965.

DISCUSSION WITH KWAME BEDIAKO

A missiological issue

K.B. I am concerned with ancestor worship as an instance of wrestling with a problem in context. The paper is limited to my own specific culture and to my own situation in the Presbyterian Church of Ghana. The issue is a theological and missiological one, not just an evangelistic question. It is the issue of affirming the Lordship of Christ which I accept and by which I live in context. The context is the awareness of the importance of ancestors in the Christian organization of the people. The question is: How does Christ who is God according to Christian confession, not simply remain something abstract but become an existential experience and reality of the church? How does that relate to their perception of the role of ancestors in the communal life of the people and in their individual perception of themselves?

I do not have the full-blown answer. I am wrestling with the problem of how does this Jesus Christ, whom some would say is essentially a Jew and therefore has nothing to do with my national heritage, relate to me, who believes in him as my Saviour? What categories do I have to articulate that faith to myself and to my environment so my people can also recognize themselves in Christ in whom we have become children of the Father? I must find some theological and biblical framework, in which I am at home in Christ, where I can begin to exist and answer these questions.

Personal testimony

On the back of my hand I have the marks of protection on me. My father loves me, I am his eldest son, he is Kwame and I am Kwame so we are also brothers, i.e., soul brothers, for Kwame is a name for a male child born on a Saturday. He is concerned that his son should not be lost because he has got some enemies in his family. So he has to do something for me to protect me from evil spirits and his enemies. I go to school, away from home, to new territory. In his trip to Mesopotamia, Jacob went beyond his home territory. He asks God at Bethel: "Will you go with me? If you will go with me and protect me then I will come here and worship you" (Gen. 28:18-22). But what about my father who does not understand that Christ is Lord? He knows the ancestors are here. But I am going abroad and the ancestors are not there. They are buried here. So he wonders how will I be safe there? Christology comes in here. Christ is available everywhere. So my father says, "We will just do this thing again. We have done it so many years back." But in the meantime, I become evangelical and become ordained into the church. When my father comes and says, "Kwame, we must do this thing again, we must renew the protection," I begin to expound my Christology to him.

My father replies, "If Christ protects you that is all I am interested in. Let us not go on with this any more." I explain, "He protects you too, father. He is the wall around us. Do you understand that?" He says, "Yes." That is the end of the argument. Now he could have turned the other way. But he understood and he turned this way. Christology liberates us from fears; fears which are not irrational, but are real fears of demonic oppression. Only Christ can liberate in this way.

Are ancestors good or evil spirits?

The Holy Spirit helps us to discern spirits and protects us. For while ancestors are not demons, demons can masquerade as ancestors. Demons can take on identities. Human ignorance and sinfulness can open us to demonic manipulation. Ancestors themselves need to be saved, so how can they have control over us? Once we reach this understanding, demons can take over. For the demons understand that we have now understood, and so we become targets. That is why the Holy Spirit comes to be a protector.

In discussing the question whether Jesus can be Lord of these spirits, we must probe first into the intention of all forms of worship. We must not assume that the respect for the elder, ancestor, or father is necessarily evil.

We must probe into the meaning and intention behind this respect and concern for ancestors. We must probe into the intention of the belief in some societies that the child in the womb is the reincarnation of an earlier ancestor.

We have known the ancestors. They have lived among us. Because they know us and are our fathers, they care for us. It is simply an extension of the filial relationship in life.

Behind this may lie social organization, the solidarity of the family, the concept that the family continues through death. The dead are alive. Because they know us they are the best guarantee of our security.

To what do we attribute the notion of filial piety? Does not Christian tradition and the Scripture affirm it? So we may discover in the practice something of God's revelation which belongs to Christ. The heart of that revelation is, of course, Christ and his Kingdom. The question then really is, what happens when Christ comes? When we see Christ as the real Lord in the realm of the ancestors and power encounter takes place, I claim that not everything in the tradition will be seen not to have belonged to him. Something of him has been there all along; but it is only discovered with Christian confession, not before. We cannot theorize from the outside at this point. We must probe behind the meaning and intention of the concern for the ancestors and not assume that because it does not have to do with the Christian tradition historically defined, that it has nothing to do with Christ.

What then happens when Christ comes? The nature and destiny of man is affected here. The ancestors were mere men. They did not come from above. Jesus said, ''I am from above, you are from below.'' So Christology from above is valid. But what kind of Christology deals with fears of what the ancestor might do and also with the belief that he is a source of blessing? In terms of Christology the ancestor ultimately cannot be a source of blessing. Because Jesus has come, history is significant and important. The revelation of God in Christ creates a new history. We are brought into a new history. Salvation history becomes our history, because of faith in Christ.

So once Christ has come the ancestors are cut off as the means of blessing for we lay our power lines differently. Blessing comes from Christ. Our concern with ancestors and their concern with us has to do with social organization. We can now alter our relationship with them. They simply become members of the community. We may even include them in our intercessions.

Suppose my father who has gone ahead is in the hands of God. I can rejoice and every now and then I can address him through Christ. Not that I will hear something back. But if God so desires and chooses he may give me a message from my father because he knows what my father means to me. If Jesus knows that the only way he will speak to me or get through to me is through my father, he will give me a word from my father. I am willing to let him do that and open myself to that; but on the understanding that I am now in Christ and I do not depend upon my father for power any more apart from complete dependence on Christ as a source of power and blessing. Once you open yourself to that you are in the realm of the occult.

The realm of occult power and the manipulation of evil by the learning of witchcraft is different from the realm of veneration of ancestors. Witchcraft is the effect of ill-will in the community. Imagine what would happen here if we begin to lose our love for one another and begin to hate. Jesus said you kill through hatred. Do you think that says anything about witchcraft? If we begin to lose love, things will happen in our midst which will simply be witchcraft operating. By his training the medium can see into the realm of spirit power and can tell you who has done what. He may also be a "quack," as there are fakes. That is another matter altogether. But it is power that we are talking about here and once Christ comes, the power is conducted.

Christ and the ancestors

I approach this by sketching a framework in which I can live, do my hermeneutics, and face the kind of questions that will meet me on my pilgrimage. I have the framework that Christ is universal, as I think the Bible really presents him. The uniqueness of Christ consists in this universality. Christ is the only saviour who is available to all people on the same terms everywhere and for all times. His uniqueness is not a narrow and exclusive uniqueness. In his inclusiveness he is universal and unique.

How does Christ change the context? First of all, who is this Christ who I say is in the heritage? He is the Christ of the Scriptures, who is the Son of God; the Christ from heaven who became incarnate in his specific historic incarnation but who died and rose again and is now in the realm of spirit. Therefore he is available everywhere to everyone. He was all the time available but now is available more clearly because of the Holy Spirit. Now we can have an experience of Christ which is authenticated by the Scriptures where Spirit and Word agree. We can know Christ now in a way which in our pre-Christian existence we could not articulate in the same way.

We have got the Scriptures, the incarnation which has taken place, and our own experience of the reality of Christ. This is not just an abstraction. God himself vouches in our hearts and in our minds that what we are saying is true. We know it from the Scripture and from our experience of the Holy Spirit who is the Spirit of Christ. Jesus says, "If somebody loves me he will be loved of my Father and we will come to him and dwell with him." How does that happen but in the coming of the Holy Spirit? So then we find ourselves in an area where Christ is close to us in faith. We have him, he has us. How does he change us? He comes in as Lord and Saviour. But in our own tradition before he comes, we have a concept of salvation, we have ideas of expiation, mediation, placating our ancestors. We have an idea that if we harm them, they do something to us.

My view is that Christ comes in and assumes all those roles. I think

Paul is saying that in Colossians. Christ assumes the roles of all these points of our piety which we addressed in our understanding to various sources of power; it could be God, it could be deities, it could be ancestors. So he changes us in terms of our worldview. He changes us from within. It is no more a matter of what elements of the culture must go and what elements must stay. That was the superficial missionary approach which has left us with the problems which we have. Paul did not proceed like that. In the New Testament (in Acts 14), we never find Paul arguing about a false religion against the true religious system. When we find him in Lystra and Derbe healing the paralyzed man, the priests of Zeus come and want to offer him presents because they believe that only God could do this and therefore these men who have done it must be gods. Paul and the people of Lystra agree on the basic point that there is such a thing as divine intervention in the lives of humans. They agree that only God can do this. They, after all, have their own god of healing. The question is, how does God work? What does Paul say? "Turn away from these idle things and worship the Living God who himself has given witness of himself to you, by giving you food and rain and happiness in your heart." In the past, the people prayed to Zeus, Hermes, and Neptune and received answers to their prayers. Paul is saying— "you pray to Zeus but also to the God I am preaching." He is not saying your religion is false and this is the true religion. Paul is saying—"you prayed to Zeus for these things, but who gave the answer? It is the God I am proclaiming to you."

In my society, people go to put a little bit of food before the ancestor's spirit and pray for the things that concern people in my society, such as for a child. If a woman is barren and has no child the society looks on her askance. She goes to pray at the tomb. Then nine months later she has a child. Now in our church what is happening to people who come from this background? When they have a baby because they have prayed for one they come to church and say, "Thank you, Jesus for giving me a baby." What has happened? The power conduit has simply been relaid differently. This is what we are wrestling with. I am claiming that Jesus is involved here. He has saved us, he finds us and changes us into his image so that he creates new problems for us to solve. He creates new allegiances in the people of God. We have to relate to somebody outside our lineage. Ancestors are clan ancestors. They do not belong to everybody. They belong to families and lineages. The people of God relate to someone, that is Christ, who is not within their immediate family. They find a new family. These are the areas of change.

It is a dynamic process. It is not a matter of what elements go before we start. It is a dynamic process of discovery, discipleship, of reading the Scriptures and believing all the time that Jesus is with us, not to leave us where we were but to take us on. That gives us hope and confidence.

*Participants' comments on ancestor veneration in Asia
and other parts of Africa*

Bali

The Holy Spirit is the creative power of God active in the creation, the birth of Jesus, the initiation and baptism of Jesus, and at Pentecost. In Bali the spirit of ancestors is real. When people get sick, they still consult the spirits of the ancestors through a medium. It is difficult not to believe when they speak through a medium because everything becomes real. So cannot you harmonize these two? When the ten commandments mention honour your father and mother, it means your ancestors also: give them a role also in your life.

The Balinese like to harmonize things. In the world you have a right hand and a left hand. Each one plays a role. In Bali, if we give something to people we use the right hand. With the left hand we pick up dirty things. When we eat we are not afraid if we do not wash, because we always take clean things with the right hand, so it is always clean. But the left one is dirty. It is not proper to give something with the left hand. In the world also there is man and woman. Both play a specific role. Can you not give a role in your Christology to this spirit of ancestors? The Jewish people also respect the God of the fathers, the God of Abraham, Isaac, and Jacob. They always like to relate themselves to their ancestors so that they play a role in their life.

Korea and Taiwan

In Asia now we are constantly battling with this concept of ancestor spirits. Let me explain what the Chinese and Koreans believe about the spirits.

When a lady conceives there is a spirit the Chinese call "poor." At the time of birth the "poor" joins with a spirit known as "shine," the "hun."* The "hun" will remain in the body until the person dies. It is extremely important in the minds of the Koreans and the Chinese to treat these spirits, the "hun," well because they will receive either benefits or harm out of the "hun" depending on the way in which the people treat their ancestors. If a father dies, his spirit, his "hun," will either become an evil spirit or a good spirit.

Therefore the sons and daughters treat this deceased father well by performing a funeral service. They burn paper money and decorate the paper house in which the deceased father is going to live. The children do their best to treat this deceased father's spirit well in order that this father's spirit would come to bless the family. If the children do not give the proper treatment, then the spirit becomes evil. These are the spirits which we confront today in the Far East.

The Protestant churches in Taiwan and Korea have condemned ancestor worship because it deals with the spirits worshipped in the

---

* These transliterations are only approximate.

Buddhist and Taoist temples. Buddhist homes have their ancestral shrines and the daily activity starts with the burning of incense in the morning. The Protestant church has taught that this is contradictory to scriptural teaching. On the other hand the Roman Catholic Church takes a different position, and in Taiwan allows ancestor worship. That goes with the Roman Catholic tradition and their teachings of praying to the dead. Their Bibles have extra-canonical books and their praying to the dead comes from Second Maccabees. That fits into the Chinese mentality of having this ancestral worship in the family.

Africa

I will offer some further clarification from the African point of view, on the whole question of ancestor worship and its relationship to Christian faith. My own experience is among the Bantu people. In Africa, there are many ethnic groups. African religions cannot be homogeneous. There are many primitive religions in Africa. Among the Bantu people, we do not worship the ancestors, we venerate the ancestors. We give them respect. There is a strong feeling that when a person has died, he is still one of us. In the English language as soon as a person dies we start talking of him as "he was." In the part of Africa from where I come, you do not speak of a person who has just died, as if he was. You still say "he is," "he is a good man," or "these are his children," not "these were his children." There is a strong feeling that a person who has died is still one of us. The living and the dead have a kind of a connection.

When the Bantu people go to the grave for whatever they might do there they are worshipping, because they know one supreme god whom they worship. But they can placate the spirits of the dead if they feel they have annoyed them and that they have therefore been covered with misfortune. They will try to placate them so that they do not find this misfortune. I also find the idea of veneration among Christians in the West. At graves people are very busy, planting flowers and weeding the graves. In the newspapers notices say "so and so still we love you so much." I do not know whether they expect the dead man to read the newspaper or not. A sense of veneration is still there. And in certain sections of the African community, there is what we call the communion of saints. We have communion with those believers who have died and would like to remember them in our prayer.

The high Anglican Church which takes strongly the whole question of the communion of the saints is probably closer to the African culture than the low Anglican Church which does not want to think about the people who have just died. But there is a strong feeling among the African people that the living and the dead form one big family. The extended family is not just extended among the living but among the dead. You cannot be a person without relating to the whole group of people, including the living and the dead. I think Professor John Mbiti says that as long as a person is still being remembered by those who are living he is the living dead. Though he is dead he is still living. On the question of what is man, he says, "I am because we are. We are, therefore I am."

Understood from the African point of view, I am very prepared to think that it is possible for us to look at the whole question of ancestors and our contact with them. I do not fear that anything will come from them because the Lord Jesus Christ has now become their Lord and we are one with them. As a Christian, I am not going to worship them. If they are saints, then it is the communion of the saints and it becomes part of Christian worship.

Missionaries' encounter with nonwestern forms of Christianity in Africa

K.B. By the nineteenth century, it was generally believed that the best form of Christianity was Protestantism. This was the age of Protestant missions. Catholics and papists were vile and immoral. They did not know the gospel. The Greek churches and the Eastern Orthodox tradition were allies but needed the gospel and the Bible.

The way in which the Ethiopian church was seen is very interesting because the Portuguese Catholics in the earlier sixteenth century had missionary work in East Africa and had some contacts with the Ethiopian church. The legend of Prester John who was supposed to be a Christian monarch excited much interest. As part of the explorations initiated by Henry the Navigator, Vasco da Gama made an attempt to discover this Christian prince. The idea was that if they could make an alliance with Prester John, they could conquer the Muslims and Arabs in the North. Ideological baggage was worked into what was ostensibly missionary outreach. But it did not yield much fruit because the whole Catholic Portuguese enterprise in Africa was vitiated by the slave trade. It never got down to real, genuine, lasting encounter. The work never really took root. In Ethiopia they found the church to be on the whole moribund according to their view of what a Christian church ought to be like. Their traditions seem to have overlaid the Christian tradition as they understood it and when the Portuguese empire collapsed, the mission collapsed.

The African Independent Church is another form of nonwestern Christianity. Very early on, Africans were making their own response to the gospel without the agency of the West. In fact, the moments of breakthrough in the stories of many western missions came through an African evangelist or an African preacher. But that is not recorded in many of the basic histories. In my own church in the south of the country, a breakthrough was made in the region of Accra by a converted traditional healer when the missionaries stalled.

The same is true of the opening up of Ashanti to the Methodist mission. Before 1941, the church was a minimal factor in Ashanti.

It did not pose a threat. An illiterate Ashanti man, a jailbird in prison on the Ivory Coast, met a certain Moses who spoke to him about the gospel, became a Christian in prison, and got a dream from Jesus that he would be released and be a preacher. He knew not a word of English. All he had was an oval stone from which he read off Scripture texts and preached. He became the spearhead opening up the entire region of the Ashanti to the missions.

William Wade Harris in West Africa blazed from Liberia right across to Western Ghana. At the same time in the first two decades of this century Simon Kimbangu's story was being lived out in Zaire and Isaiah Shembe's in South Africa. In 1915, a prophet called Gary Braide, a Nigerian, was called into renewal and preached. The missionaries called him a trouble-maker because he would not take orders from missionaries. Through his preaching there were mass movements into the church. I have read a report of a missionary writing to Britain in that year to ask for more missionaries. It did not mention the one man through whom God was doing this new work. The missionaries were completely unaware that there could be other "Christianities" than the form that they knew. This problem persists right up to our day.

7. Dialogue with other Religions— an Evangelical View

VINAY SAMUEL and CHRIS SUGDEN *(India)*

Synopsis

The paper examines the emergence of evangelical social involvement in response to the needs of the context in Latin America and calls for a similar response to the context of religious pluralism by evangelical involvement in dialogue. The paper evaluates evangelical hesitancy to be involved in dialogue, and examines the evangelical understanding of mission from Tamburam to Lausanne. The paper suggests an agenda of Christological issues for dialogue with other religions.

INTRODUCTION

A vital context for considering Christology among the poor, the powerless, and the oppressed is the context of religious pluralism. This requires engaging in dialogue with religions in our context. By dialogue we mean being open to other religions, to recognize God's activity in them, and to see how they are related to God's unique revelation in Christ. We do not mean a process which carries the assumption that all religions are the same, nor that they carry within them an essence from which we can create one universal religion to which Christianity would be a mere contributor. The goal of dialogue is to affirm the Lordship of Christ over all life in such a way that people within their own context may recognize the relevance of that Lordship to them and discover it for themselves.

As evangelicals have not yet entered into the process of dialogue, we do not feel that it would be true to the situation to describe an already formed Christology in the context of religious pluralism. We suggest only an agenda for such a Christology. Therefore a prior task must be to outline an adequate methodology for evangelical theology in addressing world religions. Since we write from an Indian context, we will use Hinduism as the particular religion in focus. It appears that the kairos has come to engage in such a task.

HISTORICAL PERSPECTIVE

The focus of the international missionary conferences at Edinburgh in 1910 and in Jerusalem in 1927 was, according to Archbishop Simon Lourduswamy, how to communicate the Gospel to men of other religions. The initial attitude was one of confidence: only Christianity could survive the shock produced by the scientific and technological changes which broke down religious customs and traditions on which religions like Hinduism were supposed to be based. The principal questions proposed for study were: What are the sources from which men whose minds have been moulded by other faiths than Christianity draw strength and comfort? In what ways does Christian revelation deepen, enrich and supplement the insights given by other faiths?[1]

The Tamburam Conference of 1938 moved the debate on. The uniqueness and incomparability of Christian revelation (as distinct from Christianity) was the main point of emphasis. In his preparatory volume for the conference *The Christian Message in a Non-Christian World,* Hendrik Kraemer insisted on the strict discontinuity between non-Christian religions and Christian revelation: non-Christian religions had to die and be replaced by Christian revelation. But this Christian revelation to be grown in non-Christian cultures was decisively not the same as western Christianity.

Kraemer outlined four clear guidelines for this process of developing Christian revelation in non-Christian cultures.[2] His first principle was the principle of "Evangelistic Adaptation." Christian truth must be "expressed against the background of, and in conflict with, the moral and religious context of the non-Christian religions" (p. 308). Paul and John are our models for such adaptation: they "expressed and formulated the essential meaning and content of the revelation in Christ against the background of and in conflict with the moralistic and legalistic conception of religion in Judaism, and with the naturalistic and gnostic mysticism of the paganism of that time" (p. 308).

The second principle was the legitimacy of different incarnations of Christianity. "Europeans can proffer no reasonable objection to adaptations in the sense of various characteristically Asiatic or African expressions, because their own national and regional Christianities, which they often cherish highly, are all adaptations" (p. 313). To posit one or more of the historical forms of Christianity as its finality would be "one of the most subtle forms of idolatry."[3]

1. Simon Lourduswamy, "Meeting of Religions I Indian Orientations," in *Meeting of Religions,* ed. Thomas A. Aykara (Bangalore: Dharmaram Publications, 1978), p. 8.
2. This summary is from M. M. Thomas in "Christ Centred Syncretism," in *Varieties of Witness,* ed. T. K. Thomas and Preman Niles (Christian Conference of Asia, n.d.). The page references to Kraemer are from *The Christian Message in a Non-Christian World* (International Missionary Council, 1947).
3. In "A New Theology from Latin America," *The Churchman* 88:2 (April-June 1974), p. 114, Andrew Kirk makes just this point about the incarnation of the gospel in the social milieu of Latin America: that the authority of the Scriptures must not be identified or linked with one particular set of dogmatic formu-

Thirdly, Kraemer defines syncretism as an amalgamation of religious elements without reference to the criterion of revelation. Kraemer identified such syncretism in the following approaches: "To assimilate the cardinal facts of the revelation in Christ as much as possible to fundamental religious ideas and tastes of the pre-Christian past" (p. 308) is syncretistic. The attempt to substitute Scriptures of other religions in place of the Old Testament is also syncretistic.

Fourthly, Kraemer "points out that the history of the 'adaptation' of Christianity afer the New Testament period is generally mixed with a good deal of syncretism. . . . 'The whole history of Christian dogma, is so to speak, the story of the perennial tension and war between the mysterious wisdom of God in the acts of Revelation and the various foreign tongues' (p. 327). Syncretism universally remains a constant danger to Christian authenticity."[4]

The younger churches in the former "mission fields" were encouraged and released by Tamburam and by Kraemer's advocacy of evangelistic adaptation to take their contexts seriously in framing their mission. Their contexts were the end of the colonial era, the political independence of their nations, and their own independence from the sending churches. The younger churches in the Two Thirds World found themselves as independent entities in newly emergent nations. Due to their origin in western missions and links with the colonial rulers, they had to demonstrate their loyalty to the new nation and commitment to the process of nation-building. They took this to mean that the church had to be deeply involved in the quest for social justice. The churches interpreted the new-found national independence to include true self-sufficiency in all spheres of life. This task required common action by followers of all religions. For the churches such common action involved a dialogue with other (often majority) religions as part of the process of building a Christianity which would be at home in the new context.

Thus the church's understanding of mission, shaped by the challenge of the context of nation-building and of religious plurality, extended beyond verbal proclamation to involvement for social change in the context. The denominational missionary societies in the West which maintained links with the young churches followed the lead they gave, and allowed them to define what Christian mission was in their contexts. Thus it is no wonder that leaders from the first independent nation, India, Paul Devanandan and M. M. Thomas, made an important contribution on the world scene in this area. At the same time, parallel concern for the context in the West was giving birth to movements such as the Civil Rights movement which had a strong basis in the churches.

---

lations of the gospel. Evangelicals have heard Kraemer in the social milieu; we need to hear him in the religious milieu.

4. M. M. Thomas, *Varieties of Witness, op. cit.*, pp. 11-12.

MISSION THINKING IN THE W.C.C. AFTER 1948

Between 1948 and 1961 the development of mission thinking in the W.C.C. on dialogue with other religions was, according to Archbishop Lourduswamy, as follows:

> The focus of the problem was shifted to the anthropological context, the one common humanity, and the solidarity of all men. The central problem was the basic values of modern man as well as the interaction of changing social ideals as reflected in World Religions in their relation with the Word of God, the Biblical understanding of man and society, and the once for allness of the redemptive act in Jesus Christ. . . . The basic outlook is stated thus: "The Gospel is addressed to men and not to religions. Hence the question is not between Christianity and other religions nor between the Gospel and the religions, but the relationship of the Gospel to man, whatever be his religion."[5]
>   Since 1961 the focus . . . shifted from anthropology to salvation history. . . . In the face of secularism and humanism religions seek to provide a firm spiritual basis, and in this Christianity has to enter into a dialogue at the deepest level with other living religions on the nature and destiny of man and on the nature of ultimate truth. Here the task is not to oppose one religion to another but to acknowledge the unique contribution of each religion in the total plan of salvation by a sort of critical solidarity with men of all faiths. . . . We cannot detach man from his beliefs . . . we encounter man, individuals and groups adhering to certain religions, holding particular beliefs.[6]

To the emphasis on nation-building was added the concern to take the religions of the context seriously and work with them in the process of social change, or at least to tap their spiritual resources in the process of social change. Dialogue essentially was not to attack or undermine other religions but to understand and develop a common base with them in the common task of nation-building. So, the concern to convert people from other religions became secondary at best and often did not come into the picture at all, lest it undermine the fragile commonality that was being discovered after decades of distance.

MISSION THINKING AMONG NONCONCILIAR EVANGELICALS AFTER 1948

A different perspective on world mission took increasing organizational form after 1948. This movement was ideologically and organizationally structured to continue the crusade of the Great Century of the expan-

5. Lourduswamy, *op. cit.*, pp. 9-10.
6. *Ibid.*, p. 10.

sion of the Christian faith. Its focus was on new mission fields, new converts, and greater numbers. It reacted to the postcolonial period rather
than adapted to it. The movement looked for new unevangelized fields
in which to carry on doing the things that it had always done.

This movement was confined largely to the western missionary enterprise and within that to the missionary societies from the United States
of America. We suggest a number of reasons for the growth and increased
visibility of this movement.[7]

First the transition to the postcolonial era did not affect relations
between the North American missionary societies and their churches in
the newly independent nations. Secondly, the enormous growth in wealth,
resources, and confidence of the North American churches promoted a
rapid expansion of these missionary societies. Thirdly, the private enterprise view of western mercantile capitalism shaped this expansion. The
effects of these three factors on missionary expansion paralleled the activity
of free enterprise business. Once one market closes down, the natural
way forward for any enterprising businessman with a product to sell is
to seek new markets. So with the emergence of independent national
churches, who would now be responsible for mission in their own context, these mission societies went into areas where the church was not
planted, among for example primitive tribes. In the fifties and sixties,
the evangelism of the Auca Indians was projected as what world mission
was all about. The evangelism of the Auca Indians was a brave and
courageous undertaking. Our point is that the fact that it became a legend
and an inspiration for tens of thousands of western Christians and dis-
placed all the struggles of national Christians to witness to their faith in
newly independent nations in the minds of the western evangelical
churches, is indicative of the prevailing understanding of mission.

The Berlin Congress on Evangelism in 1966 gave visible expression
to this movement. The agenda of the congress appeared to promote views
which would justify a "free market" understanding of mission(s). The
voice of the younger churches engaged in mission in the unevangelized
fields of their own context was not heard. The spotlight fell instead on
the Auca Indians.

This "free market" understanding of mission attempts to validate itself
in two ways. First it faults the national church for not doing the task of
evangelism, for diluting the mission of the church with concern for social
issues, and for undermining the gospel with syncretism and universalism.
This charge was made at the Berlin Congress of Evangelism in 1966.

7. With the increasing confidence of independent nations and the increasing
affluence of some of them, for example, Korea, Taiwan, Indonesia, Nigeria,
Brazil, and India, indigenous missionary movements are emerging from these
nations which now number 15 percent of all Protestant missionaries. But in terms
of their ideology they are only a younger church version of the same western missionary enterprise.

The new churches had changed both the message and the methods of missions:

> The use of the term "mission" in the new sense represents an attempt to depart from the narrow verbal proclamation with evangelism considered to be ineffectual, or ineffectual without the wider area of service. The use of the word "mission" represents a symbolic departure from the heaven and hell concepts of historical missions. It represents not only a change of *method* but also of the *message* of missions.
>
> The use of mission as the "mission of the church" has been used to describe the penetration of the values of Christianity into other cultures and religions and has, consequently, precluded the need of first winning individuals to Christ.
>
> The "church mission" communicates the sense of the brotherhood of man under the fatherhood of God whereby service becomes an act of reconciliation by the "church in mission." Sin is not individual but corporate deeds, alienating man from God and rending or tearing the human fabric of peace.
>
> God, according to D. T. Niles, has performed reconciling acts in all religions, to which men have responded in faith without accepting the Christian's God in Christ.
>
> The consequences of this form of universalism lead to a syncretism of all religions and faith—a new universalism.[8]

Secondly, it claims that the Bible and mission tradition affirm that verbal proclamation of the gospel to individuals is the sum total of mission. Arthur Johnston writes:

> Edinburgh 1910 saw evangelism in terms of the individual and missions; Jerusalem 1928 established a partnership between missions and the younger churches. Madras focused upon the Church universal, as the divine answer to the needs of men. . . . The entire Church should participate in evangelism. . . . This means of evangelism— the Church—was no longer a "soul-winning" Church that supposedly concerned itself with the inward part of man, to the exclusion of his physical needs. It was the Church, rather than the individual as a disciple of Jesus Christ, which brought others to the life of the Christian community. "Personal evangelism" by the Church replaced "soul-winning" by the individual believer.[9]

According to Johnston, the authentic gospel is committed to individuals over against the church, to win souls over against personal evangelism, directed toward the inward part of man to the exclusion of his physical needs. Johnston uses the above formulation of the gospel to support his

8. Arthur M. Climenhaga, quoted in Arthur Johnston, *The Battle for World Evangelism* (Wheaton: Tyndale House, 1978), p. 195.

9. Johnston, *op. cit.*, pp. 71-72.

claim that the tradition of mission is on the side of verbal proclamation. Not unnaturally he sees the Lausanne Covenant and John Stott's book *Christian Mission in the Modern World*[10] as declensions from the biblical mission of the church.

This "free market" analysis of evangelical missions is not a new one. As early as 1900 an editorial in an Indian magazine noted:

> We admire the power of these missionary gentlemen to organize and institute foreign missions as easily as their secular brethren promote joint stock companies and banks.[11]

DEVELOPING A FOCUS ON THE CONTEXT

We stand in the tradition represented by the Berlin Congress. Since Berlin, increasing numbers of evangelicals committed to the Scriptures, the Lordship of Christ, and evangelism have begun to take their contexts seriously. At the follow-up to Berlin, the Lausanne Congress of 1974, the presentations made by evangelicals working among students in Latin America stimulated the drafting of a statement on Radical Discipleship which went further than the Lausanne Covenant in linking evangelism and social concern in the mission of the church. These Latin American evangelicals put this question firmly on the evangelical agenda. At COWE in Thailand in 1980, a concerted effort was made to put the clock back to Berlin. But at least one third of the participants, and even more according to the highest authority, resisted this attempt and said so in both a Statement of Concerns and the texts of some of the booklets emerging from the Consultation. The subject remains on the evangelical agenda and will be debated at the Consultation on the Relationship between Evangelism and Social Responsibility (CRESR) in June 1982, eight years after Lausanne.

For the same reasons as our Latin colleagues put social action on the evangelical agenda, it is time for us to put dialogue with other religions on the agenda also. Evangelicals are still at the same place as mission thinking was fifty years ago. For example, in 1978, Ernest Oliver, a past chairman of the Missions Commission of the World Evangelical Fellowship called on "faith missions" to get better acquainted with the psychological and religious sources of non-Christian religions. He spoke positively of the "strength and comfort" other faiths provide for their adherents.[12] This is the same position as was taken at the Edinburgh conference in 1910.

10. Falcon, 1975.

11. Vedanta Brahmavadin, July 1900, p. 607, quoted by Graham Houghton, *The Development of the Protestant Missionary Church in Madras 1870–1920*, Ph.D. Thesis presented to the University of California Los Angeles 1980, p. 198 (Madras: Christian Literature Society, forthcoming 1983).

12. Quoted by Waldron Scott, "No other Name—an Evangelical Conviction," in *Christ's Lordship and Religious Pluralism*, ed. Gerald Anderson and Thomas Stransky (Maryknoll: Orbis, 1981), p. 68.

However, in order that the gospel might become relevant to a context, it must take the total reality of the context seriously. The context in which millions of the "unreached" live is dominated not only by poverty but also by living religions from which is derived the entire value system of the worldview on the basis of which people live, act, and move. In addressing social change, mission strategists have been discovering a new method of praxiology and contextualization which has tremendous potential to enable us also to approach the religious context. We need to examine that methodology carefully.

A NEW METHODOLOGY

The praxiological approach is to go into a context with deep convictions shaped by the gospel. The goal is not to apply ready-made formulations of the gospel, but to understand the focus, emphasis, and the very meaning of the biblical gospel in that context.

The approach is increasingly being accepted by evangelical mission theologians, especially from the Two Thirds World. We are discovering that this process affirms the gospel and does not distort or undermine it. It brings new insights and makes the gospel excitingly relevant. It liberates rather than enslaves both the Scriptures and our own persons. The process has begun to give birth to more wholistic expressions of the gospel and wholistic strategies for evangelism. Thus evangelicals have been able increasingly to affirm social change as part of the mission of the church.

Just as evangelicals working in Latin America have brought the issue of social change to the fore, evangelicals from Asia in the context of the plurality of religions need to bring this issue of interreligious dialogue to the fore. For in countries where the plurality of religions is the dominant reality, social change on its own is an inadequate way of applying the gospel. The plurality of religions must also be addressed.

In the context of religious pluralism, no social change can take place without a religious reality that promotes this change. Where religion is part of the whole worldview of a people, any Christian claim to bring the truth about life must be related to their worldview if it is to have any meaning and stimulate any change.

The experience of the Indian church is that lasting social change cannot be achieved unless a religious dimension promotes this change. A clear example of this is the Rural Health Project at Jamkhed run by the Doctors Arole. An evangelical leader visited them recently and noted four ways in which the villagers had become de facto Christians; that is they are not yet baptized or part of any existing church structure.

First, fear has been eliminated from the villages. Villagers used to be afraid to have surgical operations on certain days because the day was inauspicious. The Aroles taught them that God is in control of every minute of every day, so every day is auspicious to have an operation.

This fear of forces which meant they could not control their own lives has gone. The villagers believe that in Christ God has come to the village to control every aspect of their life. There is no need to fear because God is present.

Secondly, there is a sense of social justice. Slowly the bitterness that arises from the experience of inequality emerges and is articulated by the villagers. Through stories of the way Jesus dealt with people and inter-acted with the authorities they accept that in the Kingdom of God all people are equal, and that the Brahmin is not really a better person than they.

A third area is a corollary of the growth of the awareness of social justice. Women have been raised to a point of equality. They no longer live in abject fear of their husbands. Women play dignified roles in the villages. Some are mayors of their village. The premise of this is Jesus' relationship to women. The Aroles "walk" people through the gospels and show how Jesus related to women. The villagers are happy to accept Jesus' authority as God incarnate. And on his authority, women have a new dignity and freedom.

Fourthly, each village has an awareness of the supreme God. A deity represents that in each village. This usually turns out to be some person in the village who lived four to five generations ago. That person, in essence regarded as a saint, becomes the villagers' deity. Confronted with the Jesus of the gospels, the village deity is no longer attractive. After they have gone through various phases, they have come to accept Jesus as their deity. In time, they accept the whole gamut of Christian theology of Jesus, the Son of God who came, lived, worked, died, and rose again.[13]

Further, other religious systems are now providing their own challenges. Kraemer maintained that the Christian faith had never been a closed system. It had constantly interacted and changed with its con-text. But he insisted that other religions were closed monistic naturalistic systems with only one focus. This is not so. M. M. Thomas has shown that these religions have interacted with the march of westernization and Christianity across the world, and in interaction with them have developed a second focus as a counterpoint to their central monistic focus. They have become elliptical systems growing in tension rather than monistic systems growing round one central core. Thomas identified this process in his *Man and the Universe of Faiths*.[14] The historical horizontal (man to man) and prophetic challenge of western Christianity has met a response within the vertical, naturalistic religions of the world. They have developed their own prophetic movements and their own concern for justice and society.

13. For a description of the Arole's work at Jamkhed see *Health by the People*, ed. Kenneth Newell (Geneva: World Health Organization, 1975).

14. M. M. Thomas, *Man and the Universe of Faiths* (Madras: Christian Literature Society, 1975).

These religions are undergoing a form of renewal and resurgence and are developing a new confidence. They are now being imported into the very homelands of western Christianity. They are scoring significant successes. They are addressing the issues of materialism in the West, which Christianity seems to have both produced and yet apparently failed to adequately answer. Their evangelistic strategy is based on the assumption that western Christianity has failed to give a wholistic answer to all man's needs. Thus a new attempt at religious dialogue may be a real contribution to our brothers and sisters in the western church. For as we enter it in the context of Asia, we may well come out of it with directions and suggestions that will help the western church with its real quest.

Evangelicals are therefore beginning to see the fundamental necessity of grappling with the reality of other religions, from the basis of evangelical presuppositions, for the sake of the total impact of the gospel.

Why have evangelicals not been involved in dialogue?

Why have evangelicals been hesitant to enter this field? The current attitude among western evangelicals is dramatically illustrated by an incident recounted by Waldron Scott:

> At a recent consultation on theology and mission, David Hesselgrave . . . called on evangelicals to review their attitude of disinterest and non-participation in dialogue. . . . Hesselgrave had several types of dialogue in mind. These included dialogue on the nature of dialogue, interreligious dialogue to promote freedom of worship and witness, dialogue concerned with meeting human need, dialogue designed to break down barriers of distrust within the religious world, and dialogue that has as its objective mutual comprehension of conflicting truth claims.
>
> . . . the response that participants in the consultation—all evangelicals—made to Hesselgrave's call . . . was virtually nil. Consequently Hesselgrave concluded that "for whatever reasons, evangelicals are not really ready for any of the five types of interreligious dialogue proposed in my paper." . . . "Certainly until such a time as the position of evangelicals is clearly understood by both non-evangelical participants and a wider evangelical constituency, the cause of biblical Christianity, at least, is better off without their participation."[15]

This incident clearly illustrates the apparent crisis of identity that evangelicals experience when the subject of interreligious dialogue is raised. Hesselgrave does not give any reasons for their diffidence. We venture to suggest the following.

15. Waldron Scott in *Christ's Lordship and Religious Pluralism, op. cit.,* pp. 66-67.

The fear of syncretism

The main reason why evangelicals have not gone into the field of religious dialogue is that evangelicals have heard Kraemer's warnings about evangelistic adaptation, but not his challenges. They have made his warnings central and the substance of his argument peripheral. They are afraid that any dialogue would lead to syncretism.

This fear is not substantiated by those who take part in dialogue. Albert Nambiaparambil writes:

Actually experience does not give any room for this doubt. Though involved in different kinds of dialogues, I have had no occasion to feel there was any such risk resulting from religious dialogues; the opposite was often heard mentioned, that so and so returned home confirmed in his or her faith-commitment.[16]

Dr. Lynn A. de Silva, Director of the Study Centre in Sri Lanka, said, at the Nairobi session of the W.C.C.:

Dialogue, far from being a temptation to syncretism, is a safeguard against it, because in dialogue we get to know one another's faith in depth. One's own faith is tested and refined and sharpened thereby. The real test of faith is faiths-in-relation.[17]

We suggest that a number of questionable assumptions about the nature of the Christian faith and other religions lie beneath this fear.

The first assumption is that both Christianity and paganism are closed systems which are both already clearly defined. The evangelical approach to other religions has been to view them as systems which are pagan, heathen, and closed to the activity of God in history. They are anti-Christian systems which have no signs of redemption in them. Only the people in them are redeemable. The system itself is not redeemable. Therefore the approach is to confront the systems by hurling gospel grenades over the boundary walls in a process designed to raze the religious system to the ground. While this siege is in progress, the at-tacking forces rescue what inmates they can, clean them up, baptize them, and then use them as front line troops in the siege operations.

An alternative approach has been to look for God-prepared "landing strips" within the system which can be used in the service of evangelism. These are cultural analogies of redemption, such as Don Richardson's example of the Peace-Child among the Sawi.[18] The system is still irredeemable, but from these landing strips which God has himself prepared, people can be taken out of the system.

The second assumption is the stress on the uniqueness of God in Christ

16. Albert Nambiaparambil, "Religions in Dialogue: Indian Experience Today," in *Meeting of Religions, op. cit.,* pp. 81-82.

17. Quoted by Nambiaparambil, *op. cit.,* p. 82.

18. Don Richardson, *Peace Child* (California: G. L. Publications, 1974).

at the expense of the universality of God at work throughout all history. This stress can be seen in the Lausanne Covenant paragraph 3 on the Uniqueness and Universality of Christ:

> We affirm that there is only one Saviour and only one Gospel, although there is a wide diversity of evangelistic approaches. We recognise that all men have some knowledge of God through his general revelation in nature. But we deny that this can save, for men suppress the truth by their unrighteousness. We also reject as derogatory to Christ and the gospel every kind of syncretism and dialogue which implies that Christ speaks equally through all religions and ideologies. Jesus Christ, being himself the only Godman, who gave himself as the only ransom for sinners, is the only mediator between God and man. There is no other name by which we must be saved. All men are perishing because of sin, but God loves all men, not wishing that any should perish but that all should repent. Yet those who reject Christ repudiate the joy of salvation and condemn themselves to eternal separation from God. To proclaim Jesus as ''the Saviour of the world'' is not to affirm that all men are either automatically or ultimately saved, still less to affirm that all religions offer salvation in Christ. Rather it is to proclaim God's love for a world of sinners and to invite all men to respond to him as Saviour and Lord in the wholehearted personal commitment of repentance and faith. Jesus Christ has been exalted above every other name; we long for the day when every knee shall bow to him and every tongue shall confess him Lord.[19]

There is no grappling in this section with the issue of whether God is at work in other religions.

The third assumption is about the nature of religious phenomena. Evangelical religion is very reformed and cerebral. It focusses on faith and belief. It assumes that the same is true of other religions. So, it abstracts belief systems from religious practices and worldviews, and confronts them with its own belief system. Since evangelicals are already convinced that their belief system is totally right, any other set of beliefs which are not the same must automatically be wrong.

This assumption is based on a number of false premises. First, it neglects any critical basis for the analysis of religious truth. The centre of gravity of western evangelicalism as far as it impinges on missions is the United States of America. North American Christianity has in general not gone through the fires of the Enlightenment and rationalist tradition of Europe. In North America the Christian religion is usually regarded as good per se until it is proved fraudulent. There is no tradition of self-critical analysis of religions. The two alternatives for the encounter with

19. The following references are cited at the end of the paragraph: Gal. 1:6-9; Rom. 1:18-32; 1 Tim. 2:5-6; Acts 4:12; Jn. 3:16-19; 2 Pet. 3:9; 2 Thess. 1:7-9; Jn. 4:42; Mt. 11:28; Eph. 1:20, 21; Phil. 2:9-11.

other religions are therefore perceived to be only total rejection of them or syncretism with them.

A second false premise is a failure to take account of the functions which religions and belief systems have in a society. A religion is an integral part of a worldview. A worldview is not just a matter of beliefs. It forms each society's basic model of reality from which the conceptual and behavioural forms (linguistic, social, religious, and technical structures) find their unified meaning. Such a worldview explains how and why things exist, continue, or change, evaluates which forms are proper or improper, systematizes and orders the varied perceptions of reality in that society into an overall integrated perspective.[20] Thus a worldview is not just a matter of beliefs. It is the whole model of reality which is held and practiced by a society. If we merely try to discredit certain beliefs, we neither understand them nor the role they play in society.

The fear of being misunderstood

A second reason why evangelicals have not gone into this field of religious dialogue is, we suggest, possibly the fear of being misunderstood. Some evangelicals have welcomed and others have at least tolerated the new interaction between evangelicals and their social contexts. Those of us involved in this interaction may be accused of getting the priorities wrong in the mission of the church. But our central identity and Christian affirmation has not been called into question. There was no question of dialogue with the fundamentals of the faith.

Because evangelicals have not worked out the uniqueness of Christianity vis-à-vis other religions, the fear is that the admission of truth in other religions raises questions about the nature of this uniqueness.

Fruitfulness in other fields

A third reason why evangelicals have not been involved in religious dialogue is that over the last thirty or forty years they have experienced great fruitfulness in missions among so-called primitive cultures. Two hundred years of witness to Hinduism and Islam has borne little fruit. So there has been a move away from them to more fruitful labour among primitive tribal peoples, and among those practicing magically oriented popular religion within Hinduism and Islam.

Studies in anthropology, sociology, and linguistics have been adequate for the success of mission in these areas. This success, however, does not imply that there was never any need for dialogue with these religions. These religions are very coherent logical systems with worldviews. But the mentality of mission has been to conquer these religions, and a limited range of studies has been adequate for this conquest.

But dialogue must take place with animism and magically oriented

20. For this understanding of worldview see Charles Kraft, *Christianity in Culture* (Maryknoll: Orbis, 1978), pp. 53ff.

popular religion. The people who follow tribal religions and magical popular religion are non-high caste, lower economic classes, whose lives are ruled by fears of beings and spirits who control their day to day destiny. Their worldview is as complex as any other, but because of the presentation of Christ as the conqueror of all fears, they respond more quickly. This does not rule out dialogue with their worldview because, as recent research has shown, converts retain a magical orientation and practices even for generations.[21] A Christian veneer has been papered over a continuing worldview which is animistic and dialogue has never taken place with their religious worldview. Dialogue is thus not just an intellectual exercise in discussing conflicting views on the origin, purpose, and destiny of the cosmos. It is a vital necessity for adequate Christian pastoral care.

Fear of decline in evangelism

A fourth fear is that dialogue will lead to being lukewarm about evangelism. Evangelicals can mistake fanaticism for firmness of conviction. If we are firmly convinced about Christ we will want to see Christ apprehend others and be apprehended by them. Christology will be at the centre of our focus. The centrality of Christ would seem to be the biblical motivation for evangelism. ''God has exalted him therefore. . . . '' By contrast some motivations for evangelism seem to owe more to the sociological factor to reinforce and expand one's own in-group over against other groups. This may lie behind the desire to act as those who would prevent people falling over a big cliff into a ravine. To do this more effectively they would tend to emphasize the depth, darkness, and danger of the chasm. So there would be the temptation to emphasize the darkness and demonic nature of all other religions and ideologies. People with this perspective would tend to view those who did not have such a sect mentality and who did not paint such a black picture as therefore being lukewarm about the desire to win others.

But this fear is unfounded. Albert Nambiaparambil writes:

> Conversions do occur as the result of dialogue; often this is in the form of liberation from ignorance and prejudices about others. Some return home more confirmed in his own religious tenets, but less fanatical.[22]

AGENDA FOR DIALOGUE

We suggest the following possible items for an agenda for dialogue.

21. For example, research carried out in Madras in 1982 by graduate students in a programme of the Association for Evangelical Theological Education in India showed that, for problems of sickness and decisions, many Christians revert to astrologers, magicians, and local deities.

22. Nambiaparambil, *op. cit.,* p. 82.

The doctrine of man

What are the assumptions about the nature of man upon which the very possibility of dialogue is based? Dialogue assumes a degree of self-transcendance of one's own religion. What concept of man is adequate to understand that a man can transcend his own religious convictions, commitments, language, and praxis to dialogue with another religion? On what doctrine of man can we posit such a degree of self-transcendance?

Those who assert the individuality of each religious context maintain that we comprehend what we comprehend only in terms of concepts and categories given in our context. There is no conceptual experience apart from the immediately given linguistic structure that shapes our ordinary human experience. So it is with our perception of religious realities. Therefore whatever it is that is given as the gospel, is given to us in, through, and never apart from the linguistic and conceptual structures of our context.

Is such a view compatible with a Christian doctrine of man, and even with the practice of dialogue? Or at the end of the day is it solipsistic?

What is the nature of the common ground between religions?

Both dialogue and proclamation-evangelism presume some common ground. These committed to dialogue tend to assume that there is a common human experience of which all religions are expressions. The philosophical tradition identifies this common experience as the universal categorical moral imperative. Bimal Motilal, the Spalding Professor of Eastern Religions and Ethics at Oxford, writes:

> If we can locate an autonomous moral system which is commonly shared by the dominant religions of India, then we can explain different religious systems as only different combinations of this moral system with different worldviews.[23]

Many from a Two Thirds World context identify the common experience as social relationships. Satish Gyan writes:

> Positively religion acts as a cementing and integrating force, preserves and sustains social relationships, and negatively it has been applied for subjugation, manipulation and domination.[24]

Nineteenth-century western Christianity of the tradition emanating from Schleiermacher, and Indian Christianity of the Bhakti tradition of personal devotion, identify the commonality of religion as man's religious feelings of dependence on a higher power.

Evangelicals have by and large vigorously criticized attempts at

23. Bimal K. Motilal, "Towards Defining Religion in the Indian Context," in *Meeting of Religions, op. cit.*, pp. 40-41.

24. Satish Gyan, in *Religion and Society* (Christian Institute for the Study of Religion and Society 27 [June 1980]), p. 2.

dialogue which seek for common ground between religions because they hold that it will dilute what they perceive is the uniqueness of historic Christianity. They define Christianity by the way in which it differs from everything else.

But evangelicals themselves also appeal to common ground. Their presentation of the gospel assumes that a presentation addressed to man's reason and to his felt needs will meet with a response. They assume a common rational faculty in all men and common needs. Often they base this on an understanding of man as made in the image of God.

The whole issue of the nature and definition of the common ground needs to be addressed. Evangelicals appear to make a philosophical mistake when they define the uniqueness of Christianity by stressing its differences from other religions. This is like defining a bicycle by its differences from all other wheeled vehicles and ending up with the definition that a bicycle is a wheeled vehicle which will fall over if left free-standing. This is not a very satisfactory definition, nor one likely to attract customers.

Others who enter dialogue in order to seek a common ground and who seek to define the essence of all religions as morality, justice, or feelings of dependence also make a philosophical mistake in seeking a definition of religion by excluding all differences between religions. This is like defining games by excluding all the differences between games and ending up with a definition that a game is anything governed by rules.

Wittgenstein suggested that definitions should be treated as a matter of seeking family resemblances rather than defining by the differences or commonalities in various groups. Thus both those who have evaded and those who have overstressed the uniqueness of Christianity in dialogue with other religions may have both been in error. We need to look again at the whole issue of what constitutes commonality in man's experience of religions and the part that it should play in interreligious dialogue.

The watershed of karma

The Asian context is a context of a vast number of people formed by the Indian religious worldview of Hinduism and Buddhism. In this context, A. G. Hogg has shown in his scholarly studies that the watershed between Christianity and the Hindu-Buddhist worldview is the concept of karma, and its corollary of the transmigration of souls and doctrine of rebirth.[25] The concept of karma is the concept of the just requittal of wrong, of automatic cause and effect justice. This is the issue of theodicy.

Many scholars claim that Hinduism contains all the religious concepts of Christianity except its concept of theodicy. Hinduism speaks of the knowledge that we gain of our true identity, which parallels the Christian claim that the Spirit witnesses with our spirit that we are children

25. See, for example, A. G. Hogg, *Karma and Redemption* (Madras: Christian Literature Society, 1923).

of God. It speaks of a personal God who gives salvation through grace. The watershed is the area of determinism and responsibility. Karma is a watershed because it seems to answer the problem of suffering phenomenologically, but not metaphysically or morally.

Karma, it must be noted, is not necessarily a watershed between Indian Christians and Hindus, because many Indian Christians would hold a de facto Hindu worldview on this point. They have baptized karma into the Christian understanding of providence. If a person suffers it must be because he has sinned. This can also dry up the wellspring of Christian compassion. Often a deep seated sense of guilt and reproach attends those who suffer. Thus dialogue on this issue is most important for the pastoral growth of Christians as well.

The Christian tradition has wrestled long with this problem. It is the central problem of the book of Job. Would the book of Job be a valuable resource for the religious dialogue with karma in Hinduism? Another area for study would be the question of the link between karma and Indian pessimism. Is karma a fruit or root of the pessimism which so deeply pervades Indian society?

Where is God at work?

Is the Kingdom of God at work in any sense in other religions? We have noted that there are many prophetic elements in other religious traditions where movements have arisen to struggle for equality, justice, the fulfilment of people, and devotion to God in contrast to materialism.

Can we say not just that God has left himself a witness in these religions, but is actually at work in them? In the same way that God is at work in non-Christian movements for justice, can the prophetic movements in other religions be seen as the work of God? For example Gandhi's movement developed as a prophetic movement in dialogue with his experienc of western education and western Christianity. Western Christianity has also learned from him in its quest to seek an alternative to both passive nonresistance to evil and the increasing military aggression which the just war theory seems powerless to restrain. Was Gandhi's movement a movement of God or of the devil?

This question should be one of the main items on the agenda. The central issue of dialogue is to discover where the Lord of history can be seen at work, which instrument he is using and what truths he is pointing to. Authentic dialogue on this topic will take place between those committed to change society in the direction of justice. If Christian participants speak from the reality of servanthood in the context, they will be sharing a Christian faith which has taken genuine shape in the total religious, personal, socio-economic, and political context. They will be communicating to a fundamentally religious people who in common with many others are seeking, we believe, for a divinity active in the struggles of history.

CHRISTOLOGY

Many of these questions find their focus in our understanding of the uniqueness and universality of Christ. There are three important areas of Christology which must be on our agenda.

The decisiveness of the Christ-event and its meaning for the world of religions

Christians claim that God has acted decisively for the redemption of the creation in Christ. All of creation must relate to him. Evangelicals have been coming to accept that the Christ-event is affecting the area of ethics throughout the world, for example through the liberation of women and the process of social change. But the area of religious belief is just as much a part of history as the areas of ethics, law, and order. The religions of the world arose out of certain historical contexts. The renaissance of these religions has been due to their interaction with the historical processes of colonial and missionary history. These religions are part of man's history now. They are not beliefs unrelated to history.

Evangelicals have tended to be a-historical, because they think in terms of belief systems. They have not really taken the historicity of Christian revelation seriously. So when they think of other religions they also tend not to take their historicity seriously. But if the event of Christ was decisive for all history, then the world of religions as part of history is affected by it. Our agenda is to discern how.

What is meant by the universality of Christ?

Dialogue may lead to an increased understanding of the universality of Christ by understanding his activity in other religions. Does the universality of Christ necessarily entail universalism in soteriology or not?

The place of Christ at the crossroads between East and West

Jesus Christ lived in the Middle East, and the faith which he founded has profoundly shaped and been shaped by the West. We are considering the task of communicating the faith in the religiously pluralistic contexts of the East.

We must first recognize that there is an important difference in the thinking of East and West. Eastern religion tends to be unitive and experiential. It is utilitarian in its outlook and is primarily concerned to win liberation (salvation). Systems of belief and conceptualization of truth are secondary.

Western thought forms are more analytical. They stress truth often in contrast to experience. We well remember the discipleship adage ''don't trust your feelings, look at the facts.''

What Christological understanding enables us to be truly biblical to bridge this gap, to communicate both to the unitive experiential East and the analytical West? John records Jesus as the way, the truth, and the life. What understanding of "truth-experience" would enable us to develop a Christology for dialogue?

Conclusion

The agenda for this dialogue and its results are very important, for they will vitally affect our strategy for evangelizing the millions who as communities live with these worldviews.

SELECT BIBLIOGRAPHY

Gerald Anderson and Thomas Stransky, eds. *Christ's Lordship and Religious Pluralism.* Maryknoll: Orbis, 1981.

Thomas A. Aykara, ed. *Meeting of Religions.* Bangalore: Dharmaram Publications, 1978.

David Hesselgrave. *Communicating Christ Cross-Culturally.* Grand Rapids: Zondervan, 1978.

C. D. Jathanna, ed. *Dialogue in community: Essays in Honour of S. J. Samartha.* Mangalore: Karnataka Theological Research Institute, 1982.

John R. W. Stott. *Christian Mission in the Modern World.* London: Falcon, 1975, Chap. 3, "Dialogue."

8. Christology in an Islāmic Context

MICHAEL NAZIR ALI *(Pakistan)*

Synopsis

The paper concentrates on the Christology of Christians living in Islāmic contexts but does not neglect Muslim views of Jesus Christ.

The fundamental issue between Islām and Christianity is that God has become flesh and dwelt among us men. Much of the task of Christology in an Islāmic context is to show the Muslim that the incarnation is not a contradiction. Terms which describe Jesus as the Word of God, the Truth, and the Spirit proceeding from the Father make a useful point of departure for talking about the person of Christ. The Muslim would be less offended by the language of procession than he is by the language of generation which is alien to his whole tradition. Christ's obedience is the most effective way to begin talking to the Muslim about the atonement, and his ethical teachings are a most important alternative to the Islāmic system.

INTRODUCTION

Christology in an Islamic context is not the same as an Islāmic Christology. The latter would be a specifically Muslim view of Christ,[1] whereas the former is a Christian Christology developed within a Muslim socio-cultural situation and addressed to it.

RADICAL AND ORTHODOX APPROACHES

The person of our Lord has been of late the subject of much controversy between professional theologians in the West. The more "radical" have so overstressed his humanity that they have either neglected or, in some cases, denied his divinity and, as a necessary consequence, any notion of his incarnation. Their views are little different from the orthodox Muslim view of the person of Jesus Christ. Muslims rightly claim affinity between their own view and that of these "radical" theologians.

The "orthodox" reply to these theologians has been of a high order but has often been couched in the traditional language of Christian theology and is, therefore, opaque to the Muslim. Also, the reply often

---

1. For an example see Mahmoud N. Ayous, "Towards an Islāmic Christology: An image of Jesus in early Shi-c-i Muslim Literature," *Muslim World* (July 1976).

141

takes the form of an exploration into the terms used in the New Testament. Although this is a valid procedure within the confines of the Christian church, it can only be used with great reserve with the Muslim as he is not convinced of the authenticity of the New Testament. The ancient Christian Churches of the Islamic East have generally confined themselves to reaffirming traditional Christological doctrine whether in its Chalcedonian or non-Chalcedonian form.

Is a more dynamic approach possible?

THE PERSON OF CHRIST

The whole question of the person of Christ is intimately linked to the doctrine of the Trinity: if Christ is God and the Holy Spirit is also God, why are there not three gods but only one God? The traditional answer that there are three persons who all share the one substance of the Godhead is not easily understood by the Muslim. For him God's individuality is absolutely unique and brooks no plurality, certainly no plurality of persons.[2] The ordinary word for person in Arabic and some other Islamic languages is Shakhs, which carries with it connotations of psychological autonomy. This makes it difficult to speak of three persons and one God at the same time. Augustine himself used the word person in this context with great reserve and only because he considered it better than keeping silent on the issue. The Latin "persona" was a translation of the Greek προσωπον which means face or aspect and even as little as an actor's mask. The exact Arabic equivalent is Shakl which means a form, aspect, figure, or mode. The traditional Eastern Christian word for a person of the blessed Trinity is Agnūm (pl. Aqānīm). This is the exact equivalent of hypostasis and can, in other contexts, mean "constitutive element." When Muslim commentators like Al-Tabari discuss the Christian doctrine of the Trinity they often use this last term.[3]

Modalism

Those who have attempted to articulate a more or less conservative Christology within an Islamic context have often tried to do so in two major ways.

One group begins with a consideration of the Trinity. After rightly rejecting the error that the persons of the Trinity are in some way persons in the modern psychological sense, they conclude that the only alternative is some kind of modalism. The temptation to come to this conclusion is strong as the Qurān itself speaks of God manifesting himself in different ways, e.g., in the burning bush to Moses (20:10f.). Sūfī tradition

2. M. Iqbal, *The Reconstruction of Religious Thought in Islam* (Oxford, 1934; Lahore, 1971), pp. 62f.

3. A. Rudvin, *The Gospel and Islam: What sort of dialogue is possible?* (Rawalpindi: Al-Musheer, 1979), p. 101.

also talks of God's many modes (Gūna) of revelation.[4] The temptation is to translate προσωπον by Shakl and to speak of God as manifesting himself in different modes or Ashkāl. Jesus Christ then becomes the particular manifestion (Tajallī) of God at that particular time. This is the doctrine of τροπος αποκαλυψεως or of the Trinity of manifestation and is most associated with the name of Sabellius (3rd century A.D.). The different modes of the Trinity are regarded as successive and the problem arises as to which, if any, of the modes reflects the nature of God as he is in himself? If the "hidden" God has manifested himself in these ways, none of which necessarily reveal his essential self, what advantage has the Christian doctrine of God over the Islāmic doctrine? For that also teaches that God manifests and reveals his will but remains hidden in himself. Furthermore, why should there be only these manifestations of God? Is he not free to manifest himself, as the Ṣūfīs claim, in a hundred thousand different ways? If any kind of modalism is permissible, it must regard the different "modes" of the Trinity as modes of being, as being "aspects" perhaps but not successive manifestations. The aspects must be seen as "constitutive elements" of the being of God, as permanent rather than passing, as revealing God as he is in himself. If the word Ashkāl is to be used of such modes it must be clearly understood that these Ashkāl of God are coexistent aspects or faces of God and are not successive. It may be, however, that in the economy of salvation they are successively *revealed*.

Nestorianism

The second group begins with the person of Christ. After rightly claiming that one must have both Christ's humanity and his divinity in mind, it often arrives at a radically Nestorian solution to the problem of how to explain Christ to the Muslim. Some come to this conclusion as a result of a Qurānic exegesis which insists upon solving the problem of Christology in the Qurān by claiming that wherever the divinity of Christ is denied, only the human Jesus is meant, whereas wherever it is affirmed the indwelling λογος is meant.[5] This makes for a Nestorian Christology with the two natures of Christ rigidly separated. It substitutes for the doctrine of the incarnation a doctrine of Hulūl or indwelling. The consequence is that God's "distance" from the world is maintained and his impassibility is preserved. This has some interesting results.

For example, much preaching on the passion of our Lord in Pakistan claims that only the human Jesus suffered on the cross and that the divinity abandoned him in order to preserve its impassibility. This is the commonest exegisis, in certain circles, of the cry of dereliction. Christians thus tend to lose sight of the important truth that God has, in Christ, suffered for us, that he has given up his transcendence and omnipotence

4. Rūmī, *Fīhi mā Fīhi* (Teheran, 1959), pp. 148f.
5. R. C. Zaehner, *At Sundry Times* (London: Faber and Faber, 1958).

in order that he might identify himself with us in our weakness, poverty, and death. Certainly, Christ has two natures but they are such a close union that they may also be spoken of as one. The humanity has been taken up into his divinity. Whatever happens to the human nature also affects the divine logos. This is why Ignatius, for example, can speak of the "passion of our God."[6]

Much recent theology rightly takes God's involvement with man, as supremely manifested in the incarnation, as a point of departure for making a case for Christian involvement with the poor, the deprived, the sick, and the oppressed.[7] Such an argument is impossible on the Nestorian view of the nature of Christ since here God's presence is half-hearted at best and does not in any way involve a kenosis.

To put forward a Nestorian view in an Islāmic context may buy us cheap approval for a while. But it does not come to grips with the fundamental issue between Islām and Christianity that God has become flesh and dwelt amongst us. Strictly speaking, the Islāmic God can be merciful but he cannot be compassionate. He cannot share our suffering because he has never been incarnate. Iqbāl tries to articulate the dilemma of the sensitive Muslim in this regard:

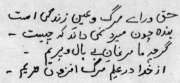

God is beyond death and is the essence of life,
God does not know what the death of man is,
Though we be as naked birds,
In the knowledge of death we are better than God![8]

This is the logical result of believing in an utterly transcendent and impassible God. It would not apply to the Christian idea of God who tastes suffering and death in the person of Jesus Christ, where the humanity of Jesus Christ is so closely united to his divinity that what happens to the one can be said to happen to the other.

Dāūd Pahbar, in a letter to his friends explaining why he has become a Christian, argues that the Qurānic doctrine of God's justice demands that such a God be himself involved in suffering and be seen as involved in suffering. Only then can he be a just judge of suffering humanity. A God that is preserved from suffering will be an arbitrary and capricious judge. Dāūd believes that God's suffering is focussed supremely in the birth, life, and death of Jesus of Nazareth. It is here that God's involve-

---

6. Eph. 1:1; 18:2; Smyrn. 6:1; cf. Acts 20:28.
7. E.g., J. Moltmann, *The Crucified God* (London: SCM, 1974).
8. *Jāvid-Nāma* (Lahore, 1974), p. 38.

ment with humanity reaches a climax and that God's justice is seen as love. God's presence in the innocent suffering of Jesus "for righteousness' sake" justifies and redeems humanity.

GENERATION OR PROCESSION?

One of the doctrines regarding the person of Christ which Muslims find most offensive is that he is the only-begotten Son of God. Sūrah 112 of the Qurān makes it clear that God neither begets nor is begotten. It has been suggested that this Sūrah was originally directed against the pagan Arab belief in the daughters of Allāh as intercessors with Allāh. It has also been suggested that this Sūrah is directed primarily against the teaching of St. Cyril of Jerusalem which was widely known among the Christians of Arabia.[9]

Whatever the original intention of this Sūrah, it inculcated a prejudice in the Muslim mind regarding language which associates generation with God. In the Muslim mind the generation of the Son often means his birth of the Virgin Mary. Christians often encouraged this error themselves. For example, when Muḥammed denied the Sonship of Christ in the presence of the Christians of Najrān, they are reputed to have asked him who Jesus' Father was—clearly referring to his earthly birth. Some Christian literature published in the Middle East claims that Jesus is Son of God, because he had no human father. And yet whenever the early Fathers refer to the generation of the Son they mean his "eternal birth." They nearly always referred to the earthly birth as the incarnation. It is a moot point whether the ecumenical councils and the Fathers were mistaken in using the expression, "the eternal birth." Could, for example, the fact that "time" was often seen as coming into being with creation have led to the view that the Son was born "eternally:" he was created before our "time" but one could, nevertheless, picture the Father at first without the Son and then picture the Son coming into being. It is clear that this view was taken in some circles. Nevertheless when most of the early writers spoke of the Son's "eternal birth" they meant that the Father was the source of being and that the Son proceeded from the Father. The Father, then, was the *ratio essendi* of the Son. The doctrine of the eternal generation was concerned to show that the relation between the Father and the Son was analogous to the logical relation between ground and consequent.

We may agree that the Fathers and the councils were using and, to some extent, were bound by the very inadequate categories of Hellenistic metaphysics. For example, many of the Fathers tried to "save" the Hellenistic doctrine of the impassibility of God despite the early conviction that God had been involved in human suffering in the incarnation. Again, the generation of the Son was sometimes interpreted in neo-

9. Rudvin, *op. cit.*, p. 98.

Platonic emanationist terms which tended to hold that the generation of
the λογος preserved the essential isolation of the One. We must, however,
view the dilemma of the early church in sympathetic terms. The Fathers
were grappling with realities which challenged all the old presuppositions
and at the same time demanded a response. Quite often the response
was in the form of paradox.

For example, Ignatius (d. 108 A.D.), in a famous passage in the Epistle
to the Ephesians, tries to articulate certain aspects of the paradox in this
way:

> There is one Physician, of flesh and of spirit, originate and unoriginate
> God in man, true life in death, Son of Mary and Son of God, first
> passible and then impassible, Jesus Christ our Lord.[10]

Ignatius refers to Christ as both αγεννητος and as γεννητος , i.e., as
both ungenerate and as generate. He recognizes that to speak of the generation of the Son is only a metaphorical way of referring to the Father
as the Ground of Being of the Son. The Son could equally be called
ungenerate as he has no beginning in time. In this connection Ignatius
speaks of the Son "proceeding"προελθοντα from the Father. Later on
he refers to Christ as, "His Word, coming forth from silence. . . . "[11]
Tradition has always considered Ignatius to have been a disciple of St.
John. It is therefore interesting to see that John also speaks of Christ as
proceeding ἐξηλθον from God (Jn. 8:42).

In our Islāmic context it may be worth stressing this aspect of "procession" (which could be translated by Ṣadara in the way the procession
of the Spirit is) over and against the language of generation. Qurānic
Christology, such as it is, lends itself much more to "processional" than
to generational language. We must use the Qurānic titles of Jesus with
great reserve as Muslims invariably ascribe similar, if not higher, titles
to Muḥammed. When however, we declare Jesus to be the Word of God
or the Truth or his Spirit, we are using terms which a Muslim cannot
deny though he may qualify them. Such terms, therefore, often make
a useful point of departure for talking to the Muslim about the person
of Christ.[12]

Most of the titles used of Jesus in the Qurān are susceptible of a processional interpretation.

The sent one

He is referred to as "rasūl" (4:171) or "the sent one." This is paralleled
in the very passage in John where Jesus refers to himself as proceeding
from the Father (Jn. 8:16, 29).

10. 7:2.
11. Magn. 7:2; 8:2.
12. For a Christian interpretation of Qurānic Christology see G. Bassetti-Sani's
highly controversial book, *The Koran in the Light of Christ* (Chicago: Franciscan
Herald, 1977).

For the Muslim, a rasūl is a special kind of prophet to whom a book has been vouchsafed. There are, generally speaking, only four rasul recognized by Islam: Moses, David, Jesus, and Muḥammed. Bishop Cragg in a very original but neglected article[13] has tried to show that the Muslim idea of rasūliyyah or "sentness" can be developed in such a way as to narrow the gap between Muslim and Christian ideas of revelation. Both Muslims and Christians believe that God has sent prophets. The one who sends is somehow "associated" with those whom he sends. The one who is sent is somehow full of the one who sends. The Qurān repeatedly speaks of the prophets and other believers, as aided by the Holy Spirit (ruḥal-Quds. Q. 2:87, 253, where the reference is to Jesus, 58:22). For Cragg, the belief in the sending of the prophets and in the aid of the Holy Spirit means that the Muslim acknowledges God's special "presence" in the revelation through his prophets and apostles and in the community of believers which this revelation brings into existence.

Revelations with a strong ethical imperative, as Cragg believes Islām to possess, argue necessarily for divine involvement in the human. Two questions, however, remain. First, to what extent is God's presence, for the Muslim, presence *with* and not presence *in*? Orthodox Islām always maintains the human-divine divide quite strictly. It is only in Ṣūfi mystical speculation that this divide sometimes appears to have been overcome. Even here the identification of the divine with the human is often more apparent than real. Secondly, to what extent is the Christian distinction between revelation *through* the prophets and revelation *in* the Son, one of kind and not simply of degree (cf. Heb. ch. 1)? Although the Christian may accept "God's presence *with*" as a model of revelation through the prophets when he speaks of the incarnation, a totally different kind of model is needed. The revelation through the prophets is fragmentary precisely because divine distance is maintained. In the incarnation it is definitive precisely because this distance has been overcome. The divine is not only present *with* but present *in*. Divine involvement is complete. The paradox at the heart of the gospel is that the sender is also the one who is sent. It is this paradox which the Muslim rejects as an antinomy. Much of the task of Christology in an Islāmic context lies in showing the Muslim that the incarnation is not a contradiction in terms.

Spirit of God

He is explicitly referred to as a Spirit proceeding from God (Ruḥ[un]Min[hu]) in Q. 4:171. A common Muslim title for Jesus is Rūḥ Allāh or Spirit of God. Whatever Christian apologists may say, the Muslim does not intend this title to ascribe divinity to Jesus. Jesus *is* a spirit from God but he is a created spirit. The Qurān refers to Jesus as a spirit proceeding from God. In sharp contrast, the New Testament refers to the Holy Spirit as the Spirit of Christ (Rom. 8:9; Acts 16:7). Whether

---

13. K. Cragg, "Islām and Incarnation," in *Truth and Dialogue*, ed. J. Hick (London: Sheldon Press, 1974), pp. 126ff.

or not this argues for a double-procession of the Spirit, as the western church would have it, it is at least certain that the Spirit is *given to the church* by Christ.

The Word of God

He is called the Word of God (4:1710) and (possibly) the Word of Truth (19:34), i.e., the Word which proceeds from God. It is around this phrase that controversy is centered. In 4:171 Jesus is called the Kalima of God. The ancient Christian apologists like John of Damascus (7th—8th c) and Timothy of Baghdad (8th—9th c) understood this to mean that Jesus was being identified with the eternal Word of God in the Qurān. They used this as an argument to show the divinity of Jesus Christ as follows. Muslims believe that God has no partners or equals. Nothing can, therefore, be eternal but God alone. But Muslims also believe the Word of God to be eternal. Therefore, the Word of God must be God. Jesus is called the Word of God in the Qurān, therefore Jesus must be God.

John of Damascus says, for example, that if Christians are accused by the Muslims of Shirk (of ascribing partners with God) the Muslims may rightly, if the Quran be true, be accused of mutilating (qatˡ) God by separating from him his Word and Spirit.[14]

Also, in Arabic usage the phrase Kalimatullāh is used of the Scriptures which the Muslims believe to be the eternal speech of God.[15]

In recent years, however, modern scholars of Islām and of Arabic have claimed that Kalima means the ordinary, created words (such as commands) of God and may not be confused with the eternal Word of God, for which they would use the word Kalām. They would equate Kalima with ρημα which they would take to mean the individual, contingent words of God. They would equate Kalām with λογος which they would take to mean the eternal Word of God. Whether there is an exact equivalent to logos in Arabic is uncertain. But when Greek philosophy began to influence Muslim thought, λογος was usually translated Kalām. It remains open, to my mind, whether this was not an arbitrary choice and whether Kalima might equally well have been chosen.

God's creative command "Be" is his Amar, often called Kalima. This creative command is associated in the Qurān both with the birth of Jesus and with the creation of Adam.[16] Both were de novo events brought about by God's creative Kalima. The significant difference for the Christian apologist is that Adam is never identified with this creative Kalima of God, whereas Jesus is.

14. *Disputation against the Saracens* (Migne's ed.); cf. Patriarch Timothy's dialogue with the Caliph Mahdi in W. C. Young, *Patriarch, Shah and Caliph* (Rawalpindi: Christian Study Centre, 126 B, Murree Road, 1974), Appendix D, pp. 198ff.

15. H. Wehr, *A Dictionary of Modern Written Arabic* (London: Allen and Unwin, 1971), p. 838.

16. Q. 3:57.

It would seem then that the Muslim would be less offended by the language of procession than by the language of generation which is completely alien to his whole tradition.

THE WORK OF CHRIST

As far as the work of Christ is concerned, the Qurān rejects the whole idea of vicarious atonement (6:164). The Muslim translator and commentator of the Qurān, Yusuf 'Ali, says inter alia about 6:164:

> We are fully responsible for our acts ourselves: we cannot transfer the consequences to someone else. Nor can anyone vicariously atone for our sins.[17]

But the situtation is not so unambiguous. Fuad Accad points out one place in the Qurān where the idea of a ransom sacrifice is clearly mentioned. The passage is Q. 37:107 and the context is Abraham's preparedness to sacrifice his own son (who is not named in the Qurānic text). The narrative in the Qurān follows the biblical account and ends with God ransoming the boy with a "tremendous victim." Here, the idea of one life being substituted for another is clearly present. Abraham's preparedness to sacrifice his son is still commemorated by Muslims at the ʿĪd-ul-Aḍhā when a thanksgiving sacrifice is offered. The treatment in the Qurān of the death of Christ is ambiguous too. Some passages clearly speak of his death (1:33). Others go so far as to suggest that Jesus died according to "the definite plan and foreknowledge of God" (Q. 3:55). The passage that has dominated Muslim thinking about the death of Christ is 4:157;

> that they (i.e., the Jews) said in boast: "We killed Christ Jesus the Son of Mary, the apostle of God." But they killed him not, nor crucified him, but so it was made to appear to them and those who differ therein are full of doubts, with no knowledge, but only conjecture to follow, for of a surety they killed him not.

Muslims traditionally believe this verse to mean that Jesus was not crucified but that either Judas or Simon of Cyrene was substituted in his place while he was taken up alive to heaven. In order to reconcile this view with other passages in the Qurān which speak of Jesus' death, Muslim commentators often adopt the view that although Jesus *was* taken up alive, his death will occur at his second coming (a belief in Jesus' second coming is quite common among Muslims). Some ancient Muslim commentators on the Qurān accept that Jesus died on the cross but that his body was then assumed into heaven. Certain modern sects like the Aḥmadiyya believe that although Jesus was crucified, he did not die on the cross but was taken down in a coma. He subsequently revived and

17. A. Yusuf ʿAlī, *Text, translation and commentary on the Holy Qurān* (Leicester: Husami Book Depot, 1975).

travelled to Kashmir where he finally died a natural death. There is even a tomb in Kashmir alleged to be that of Jesus.

Both Prof. R. C. Zaehner and Prof. Geoffrey Parrinder in their exegesis of Q. 4:157 refer to the view that the verse is not denying that Jesus was crucified but does deny that it was the Jews who crucified him. In other words, it was God himself who was ultimately responsible. This view accords well with both the Qurān (Q. 3:55) and with the New Testament (Jn. 19:11; Acts 2:23).[18] In this connection, Parrinder remarks, "there is no futurity in the grammar of the Qurān to suggest a post-millenial death. The plain meaning seems to be his physical death at the end of his present human life on earth."[19]

For the Christian apologist, the fact that most Muslims are reluctant to admit that Jesus died is in itself remarkable. The Qurān repeatedly accuses the Jews of killing the prophets of old (2:61, 71). It even discusses the possibility of Muhammed's own death (3:144). Why then was it so impossible for Jesus (a prophet, from the Muslim point of view) to have been crucified? Is there an implied docetic Christology here? Whatever the Qurān may say about the death of Jesus, it is clear that this death (if it is acknowledged at all) is not in any way understood as an *atoning* death, at least as far as the Qurān is concerned.

In the Şūfī or mystical tradition in Islam, Jesus is often the pattern for self-denial and sacrifice. His death is often seen as the culmination of a life of self-sacrifice. Some modern Muslims too are beginning to see the redemptive value of Jesus' suffering. Their emphasis is generally upon his willingness to suffer for righteousness' sake rather than upon the actual crucifixion itself. They see in this willingness a complete surrender to God's will and lay stress upon the constructive aspect of suffering when it is it endured for God's sake.

Christ's obedience is surely the most effective way to begin talking to the Muslim about the atonement. The Muslim often understands concepts of solidarity very quickly. It may be possible to explain to him that just as we, who are Adam's progeny, share in the sinfulness which he brought into the world, so also Christ as representative man, as the second Adam, returns us to the obedience for which we were created. He came to do what we, of our own nature, cannot do and are not inclined to do. God accepts this offering of free obedience as *Man's* return to God's obedience and, therefore, to his favour. (This, I suppose, is more or less a reworking of the old doctrine of Acceptilation.) Cardinal John Henry Newman summed all this up beautifully in his hymn "Praise to the Holiest in the height":

> O loving wisdom of our God!
> When all was sin and shame,

18. R. C. Zaehner, *At Sundry Times* (London: Faber and Faber, 1958), and G. Parrinder, *Jesus in the Qurān* (London: Faber and Faber, 1965).
19. Parrinder, *op. cit.,* p. 105.

A second Adam to the fight
And to the rescue came.

O wisest love! that flesh and blood,
Which did in Adam fail,
Should strive afresh against the foe
Should strive and should prevail.

God invites men to offer themselves to him in union with Christ. It is only through and in this representative sacrifice that any offering is accepted and any reconciliation effected. It remains true that the giver of this invitation also *enables* us to accept this invitation and that this "enabling" is, potentially at least, for everyone.

The resurrection

One cannot talk about the atoning death of Christ, without discussing God's seal of acceptance upon this supreme act of obedience, the resurrection. One expression that the Qurān uses for the raising of Jesus has to do with the root verb rafᶜa and is rightly translated as Assumption or Ascension into heaven.[20] However, another word is used for the raising of Jesus from the dead and this is baᶜathᵃ (19:33). This word is used of others in terms of a physical resurrection from the dead at the last day (e.g., of John the Baptist in 19:15).

The Qurān, however, does not leave Jesus dead (assuming that it does speak of his death) but speaks of his glorification immediately after his death. Most Muslims believe that Jesus was taken up body, soul, and spirit into heaven. This argues for a resurrection from the dead. So far as the Ahmadiyya are concerned, they do not give sufficient weight to aspects of their own Islāmic tradition, to the testimony of contemporary secular historians, and to the unanimous witness of Christians down the ages regarding Christ's death on the cross. Nor do they take seriously enough the Qurānic testimony to the glorification and bodily assumption of Jesus into heaven.[21]

The ethical teaching of Christ

Christ's teaching as recorded in the Gospels is very important in the task of developing a Christian theology in the Muslim world. A theologian working in a Muslim context will, it is to be hoped, like any other theologian, take full account of textual criticism and the results obtained by it in determining the original texts. He will also be aware that it was the needs of the early church which gave rise to our New Testament documents and that they are, to some extent, shaped by these needs. He will, however, also be aware that the early church was not cavalier in adapting Christ's teaching to its own needs but was extremely conscien-

20. Q. 3:55; 4:158.
21. For a summing up, see my *Islām—A Christian Perspective* (Exeter: Paternoster Press, forthcoming).

tious and conservative in recording the *ipsissima vox Jesu* even where it
did not fully understand it. An example might be the Son of Man sayings which are faithfully recorded in the Gospels but not much used in
other early Christian writing, canonical or otherwise. In other words,
his attitude must not be reductionist. At the same time he should not
eschew his critical faculties. Muslims often look upon the teaching of
Christ as a radical alternative to the Islāmic system. (Whether they accept or reject such an alternative is quite another matter.) Of particular
importance are Christ's teachings on revenge, adultery, divorce, prayer,
and fasting, and on the relationship between "exterior" and "interior"
religion. In these areas the contrast between the Islāmic system and the
gospel is most clearly seen. The Christian emphasis on "change of heart,"
whether understood individually or socially, as opposed to a mere
manipulation of structures provides a credible alternative to the enforce-
ment of Sharīʿah.

No mere metaphysical subtleties are going to win the Muslim to Christ.
Until he is confronted by the person of Christ as found in the Gospels
and in the life of the church, he will not find it possible to acknowledge
Christ as Lord. The character of Christ, as Andrae points out, is
immeasurably superior to any other human character[22] and the excellence
of his teaching, the power of his miracles, the commitment of his obedience
unto death, and his glorious resurrection all conspire together to convict
men and women as to who he really is.

DISCUSSION WITH MICHAEL NAZIR ALI

Q. If we suggest that God breaks his law of transcendence and non-
involvement and does intervene in the creation in the case of this one
man, Jesus, does that give us a positive lead for encounter with
Muslims?

M.N.A. The Islāmic view of God's transcendence is not the same as
the deistic view. God's distance is maintained from the world, but he
is closely involved through the sending of the prophets. If there is any
breaking of this law it is in the passage in the Qurān where God is
spoken of as saying to Jesus: "Jesus, I will first cause you to die and
then I will take you up to myself." It sounds very scriptural. Just before
that it says that the Jews were conspiring together to kill Jesus. So
the Jews conspired and God conspired. It says in the Qurān that God
is the best conspirator. So somehow he got the better of the Jews by
what he did. How he got the better of them is the question which needs
to be clarified.

There is only really one passage in the Qurān where docetism is
implied, and that is influenced by some docetic sect. It seems odd that

22. T. Andrae, *Mohammed: The Man and his Faith* (London: Allen and Unwin,
1936), p. 191.

the Qurān could speak so easily of all the other prophets, of the fact that the Jews caused their deaths and of Muḥammed's own death and yet it cannot speak of Christ dying. Why not?

Q. I am getting a confusing image of Islām. On the one hand we hear that Islām is the religion of Allāh and therefore the fundamental problem in Islām is the question of God, and on the other, contemporary Muslim apologists are insisting that the fundamental problem of Islām is man in terms of the laws and the living of the good life.

M.N.A. Certainly, there is the revealed aspect that Muslims are concerned about as far as the person of Jesus is concerned. But in the Ṣūfī mystical tradition, which is the Islām of the majority of Muslims, Jesus is looked upon as an exemplar. He is looked upon as the ideal guide, Murshid, the ideal peer, as one would say in the Persian. Orthodox, fundamentalist Muslims are aware of this tradition of devotion to Jesus in mystical Islām and they are trying to counter it by saying "Why is Jesus such a perfect exemplar? He did not marry, he did not wage war, he did not have any wealth. How can you get guidance for your life from Jesus? You should look to Muḥammed. He married, he waged wars, he had wealth, he experienced poverty." They are now saying he was a more rounded personality than Jesus.

As far as the God-man question in Islām is concerned the fundamentalists are saying (they are the loudest but not the only voices in Islām) that in the end all that matters to Islām is God. They have written a new song about Pakistan which starts, "The meaning of Pakistan is Lā-illa, the meaning of Pakistan is there is no god but God."

But, the problem for Islām is that as soon as you say "God is all that matters," you suddenly come across the other aspect, that God has given a Sharīʿah. God has given his law and the application of that law in its entirety to the world is a must, however barbaric it may sound and however difficult it may be to apply in contemporary situations. It is part of God being God. This takes all sorts of forms. I was reading an ordinance recently published in Pakistan which provides for adulterers to be stoned. It sets out how a person is to be stoned in very modern legal phraseology borrowed from the British system. But they are both different aspects of the same thing.

Q. Can you comment on the centrality of Sharīʿah, the social structure with the tendency to almost integrate that into the whole religious worldview of Islām? Somehow the Christological confession does have an intimacy with the community that emerges from that confession, the new ecclesia. What implications and possibilities are there for missiology and for theologizing in Islāmic contexts for the Christian community, the community of those who have come into this faith in Jesus? Does it have any Christological value in confession? It seems

the most visible dimension of the gospel would be that there are people who live differently, who act differently, and who have a different
social relationship?

M.N.A. Firstly, Muslims do not believe that Jesus founded a community. In Islāmic tradition, even among the Ṣūfīs Jesus is looked
upon as a loner, the man who went it alone, the hermit par excellence.
Then he is contrasted with Muḥammed. The prophet is reputed to
have said that their is no monasticism in Islām. The congregation is
a mercy. But, our witness as Christians is that Jesus did inaugurate
a community, the church. It is a matter for debate among Christians
about how the church is to witness to this. Some take the Kingdom
of heaven as a kind of umbrella term, and try to set up a revival kind
of Sharīʿah based on the Sermon on the Mount. There has been a
serious attempt to do this. The temptation is very great. If Muslims
are organized by their strict laws why should we not be equally
organized by our laws? The Government will write to the bishop asking what is your law about such and such if the case comes to the court,
and you have to reply in those terms.

The temptation has to be resisted. We have to reaffirm that the
community founded by Jesus is a community of free individuals drawn
together by grace, continuing their life in grace, received in the
preaching of the word and the sacraments; that it is this freedom and
God's grace which enables us to live as a community; that we do not
have a kind of constitution or Sharīʿah which we rigidly follow.

Q. You appear to be saying that the issues of the person and work
of Christ are not really central in evangelism among Muslims. The
excellence of his ethical teaching is the most attractive thing that can
be presented. So Christ must be made real through his teaching, the
power of his miracles, and the commitment of his obedience. That
focusses on the person and teaching of Christ rather than the person
and work of Christ. Is that strategy being suggested in evangelism
among Muslims based on a particular understanding of theology in
the context of Islām?

M.N.A. The person and work of Christ is very important in dialogue
with Muslims. But the point of entry often is the teaching of Jesus.
In my experience there are two kinds of Muslims who are open to
the gospel. One is the strongly ethically motivated Muslim seeking
for justice. He is usually attracted to the gospel message by the teaching
of Jesus in the Sermon on the Mount.

The other is the person who has had an overwhelming religious
experience of some kind. He has seen Jesus in a vision or something
like that. There are many Muslim converts (Christians who were

Muslims) today who are of this kind. Bilquist Sheik who wrote *I dared to call him Father* is of that kind. For them the person and the work, of course, count very much.

Q. As I study the Chinese religions, Confucianism, Taoism, and Buddhism, I see that they are man-centered religions, based on man's own religious experience. Islām has a Judaeo-Christian background and is more a revelatory religion. This means that God has intervened in human history in the Old Testament through Israel, in the New Testament through Christ and the New Testament church. Then of course the Muslims claim that there was a further revelation of God in Islām.

The Eastern religions and the Chinese religions are basically syncretistic. They are willing to include any other religions and beliefs into their systems. Islām is different. Muslims are very emphatic that Islām is the true religion and that they have the final authority. This is why we do not see as much religious dialogue between Christianity and Islam as between Christianity and Buddhism and Christianity and Hinduism. So what are the effective ways of dialoguing as Christians with the Muslims in your country?

M.N.A. One part of your question is about syncretism, the other is about dialogue. They are both related.

In a sense, at its formative stage, Islām was syncretistic. You have referred to the Judaeo-Christian influence. There was also and still is a great deal of pre-Islāmic pagan Arab influence and this is vital to understanding Islām. Early Islām absorbed a great deal from Greek thought mediated to them through the Eastern Christians which is why the Eastern Christians are so important to us. Islām then became fairly static.

Coming to the second point about dialogue, I do not agree that there is no dialogue with Islām. There has always been dialogue with Islām of one kind or another. I have referred to John of Damascus and to Timothy of Baghdad. J. W. Sweetman in his book *Islām and Christian Theology* * lists eight Christian apologists between the seventh and tenth centuries whose works have survived.

Two kinds of dialogue have been conducted by Christians and Muslims throughout the centuries. One is called discursive dialogue. It is a discussion of doctrine: who Jesus is and so on. The other kind of dialogue is mystical, and is called interior dialogue. The Muslim mystical tradition acknowledges the influence in its formation of the Christian monks of the Eastern Christians of Egyptian and Syrian monasticism of the desert.

* J. W. Sweetman, *Islām and Christian Theology,* Vol. 1, *Origins* (London: Lutterworth Press, 1945).

Comment

In Indonesia I find it very difficult to preach the gospel to the Muslims. Not only is Indonesia the only Muslim country in which the Christian church grows fairly fast but the Muslims in Java are not real Muslims. They are only Muslim on the surface, but inside they are Hindus and practice ancestor worship. In other areas such as West Sumatra the Muslims are very fanatical and it is very difficult for the church to grow in those areas.

I find that the best way to preach the gospel to the Muslims is not in dialogue, trying to confront them with the divinity of Christ but just to let the love of Christ show. In a Muslim country, love is not very clear because I find that the king and ruling clans are usually descendants of Muḥammed or are a special group of people. Only the ruling class are rich. In Indonesia, for example, in the old days people were ruled by the chief of the clan. When the Hindus came, the chief became Raja and when the Muslims came, the chief became Sultan and now after independence they become General. But they used the people. They never tried to show concern for the people but were only concerned to get benefit out of the people for themselves. That is why in our preaching to the Muslim we just stress the love of Christ. This is the love that they are missing, because they are usually oppressed by their ruling party.

Q. Islām is one of the three visible religions in my country and I find when we go on house to house visitation for evangelism that the Muslim families are the most hospitable and receptive. They will open the door, invite us to sit down and we can have a very good discussion on Christianity and Islām. The Chinese Buddhist families will not even open the door. They just say they are not interested. But we have found the resurrection a big stumbling block when we talked with Muslims about the death of Christ. Can Islām not face the death of Christ because of the Christian teaching concerning the resurrection?

M.N.A. I do not see why the resurrection should be a problem for Muslims because the Qurān speaks of the resurrection at the last day. One of the fundamental doctrines in Islām is to believe in the resurrection in the last day. There is not the kind of conceptual difficulty that a Buddhist or Hindu might have about the resurrection. Also there is a very strong Muslim tradition that when the prophet died they did not bury him immediately. They waited for three days to see whether he would rise again in the way that Jesus is supposed to have done. When after three days the body began to smell, Abu Baka, the first caleb, got up and said, "Glory be to Allāh, he who believes in Muḥammed, Muḥammed is dead, but he who believes in Allāh, Allāh is alive." So I do not see why there should be a problem.

9. Christology in the Context of the Life and Religion of the Balinese

WAYAN MASTRA *(Indonesia)*

Synopsis

The paper gives an overview of the history, customs, and religious beliefs of the Balinese. Their religious beliefs are centred on the immortality of the soul as expressed in ancestor worship. In this context the spirit of the resurrected Christ available to direct encounter and experience, is most meaningful. Eighty percent of the people are poor tenant farmers, oppressed and exploited by the ruling class. In this context Christ is the redeemer who loves them and liberates them from poverty, oppression, ignorance, and harsh spirits.

INTRODUCTION

The New Testament testifies that there is a bewildering number of ways of looking at and understanding Christ. Christ is described in the understanding of Matthew, Luke, John, Peter, James, and Paul. In history there is Christ in the versions of Justin Martyr, Irenaeus, Origen, Augustine, Anselm, Thomas Aquinas, Luther, Calvin, Schleiermacher, Barth, Bultmann, Bonhoeffer, and many others. As a corollary to the different understandings of Christ there come different churches, such as Roman, Orthodox, Lutheran, Calvinist, Baptist, Free Church, and Sectarian Churches.

The contemporary world is divided into four categories. So there will be the possibility of four different ways of understanding Christ. The First World consists of people who live in the western block in mostly capitalist and affluent societies. They may have one version of Christ. The Second World consists of people in the eastern block or socialist countries in relatively affluent societies. They may have another version of Christ. The Third and Fourth Worlds consist of people who live in developing and underdeveloped countries as poor people who live from day to day. They may look at Christ differently from those who live in prosperous and affluent societies. In the First and Second World people may look at Christ chiefly as liberator from this materialistic world and their own self-centred tendencies. In the Third and Fourth World people may look at Christ mainly as deliverer from poverty and ignorance.

Because there are many religions such as Hinduism, Buddhism, Islam, Judaism, and Animistic religion one cannot avoid looking at and understanding Christ in different perspectives based on people's religious background.

In this paper I will try to express my understanding of Christ, and examine the issues of Christology raised from Christian mission and dialogue with Balinese traditional religion and from the Third World perspective. It will be biblical in nature.

THE BIBLICAL MATERIAL

Christ becomes the revelation of God himself by becoming flesh and real man in order to show his genuine concern for man and the world. The famous passage of John 3:16 records, "For God so loved the world that he gave his only Son, that whoever believes in him should not perish but have eternal life." In this incarnation God who is Spirit has become flesh in the person of Jesus Christ of Nazareth in order to have contact with people and to meet people in their deepest need. Moreover in this incarnation God has revealed and emptied himself by leaving the glory of heaven, becoming man to be one of us. He humbles himself by taking the form of a servant and even gives himself to die on the cross for the salvation of humankind (Phil. 2:5-8). So Christ is God himself who manifests himself as man. He can do so, because he is spirit who can manifest himself in many ways: Creator, Redeemer, and Counsellor. But he is basically the same. He is the Spirit of God who was active in the creation story (Gen. 1:1). He is the same Spirit of God who is active in the birth narrative (Mt. 1:28), in the initiation or baptism of Jesus (Mt. 3:16), in the temptation of Jesus (Mt. 4:1), and who in the Pentecost event restored the courage of the dispirited disciples after the crucifixion (Acts 2:1-47). He is also the same Spirit who brought the dried bones of Israel to be alive again (Ezek. 37), and who brought Joel to prophesy (Joel 2:29-31).

We can describe him in many ways: Father, Son, Holy Spirit, Shepherd, Mother, Brother, or Sister, because he is the one who cares for our salvation. It is because he is Spirit that we can name him in many ways. His name depends upon his manifestation, or how we would like to look at him or picture him, while he cares for us, whether as Father, Son, Holy Spirit, Shepherd, Mother, Brother or Sister, and even man and woman. In a world which is dominated by men, he will be called a man. In a patriarchal society he will be looked upon as Father or Son. In a matriarchal society he will be looked upon as Mother or Sister. Among the shepherd groups naturally he will be looked upon as the Good Shepherd. In Bali people do not have sheep. But they do keep ducks, so God will be looked upon as the Good Duckman.

He is the same yesterday, today, and forever (Heb. 13:8). He is the same Spirit of God who cares for and loves his creation. He does not love only Christians; he loves the world. He is like the sun that sends its rays to the flowers as well as to the dung. In the biblical words: "The Father in heaven, he makes his sun rise on the evil and on the good, and sends rain on the just and on the unjust" (Mt. 5:45). In the story of the Prodigal Son, the father does not love only the son who lives with him, but also the son who runs away. It is difficult for the older son to understand his father's love, when he sees his father express his love and concern to the lost son. He is the Spirit of God who wants Christians to stay with him, to work with him, to be salt, leaven, and light of the world in order to show his genuine concern and compassion especially to those who are in trouble and in need, as he calls: "Come to me, all who labour and are heavy laden, and I will give you rest" (Mt. 11:28).

He is the Christ who teaches his disciples to follow his example by crucifying their own will and the desire of their own flesh. He said: "If any man would come after me, let him deny himself and take up his cross and follow me" (Mt. 8:34). He gives us an example in the temptation story, in which he rejects the temptation of the devil. So he is quite different from Adam. Adam is the man who likes to follow his own will or the desire of his flesh, by following the temptation of the devil in order to know good and bad. But Christ rejects the temptation of the devil by crucifying his own will to know the good and the bad. In this way Adam follows his own will, while Christ crucified his own will. He wants his disciples to follow his example. He even gives himself to be crucified on the cross in his obedience to his Father, who sent him to the world.

In this incarnation God was made flesh in the person of Jesus Christ so that God's initiative in restoring the relation between God and the fallen man, which was broken because man followed his own will, becomes a historical event in the historical person of Jesus Christ. In Christ the communication of divine grace really takes place in history, so that in him all things are reconciled to God. Christ has overcome the broken relationship between God and man, by reopening the way of communication. In that way the salvation of man is not only an idea, it is also a historical fact. John expressed what happens in Jesus Christ in terms of the incarnation very clearly in his own words: "The true light that enlightens every man was coming into the world. He was in the world, and the world was made through him, yet the world knew him not" (Jn. 1:9-10). In Jesus Christ the mystery of God is revealed, the image of God in which man was created becomes gloriously visible and tangible. It makes Christianity the best possible religion, because of its peculiar and unique relation with God. It has experienced the way in which God has communicated himself to man, so that in no other religion does God reveal himself so clearly and directly.

Jesus said: "I am the way, and the truth, and the life, no one comes to the Father, but by me" (Jn. 12:6). The church can join the early Christians to claim: "And there is salvation in no one else, for there is no other name under heaven given among men by which we must be saved" (Acts 4:12).

As a corollary of this belief the church must go out into the world to represent Christ, that people may encounter him, and surrender themselves to him, who is the Truth, and the Christ, the Son of the living God, as Peter confessed in front of him (Mt. 16:16).

BALI, ITS LIFE AND RELIGION

Bali, an island of 5,623 square kilometres east of Java, is one of thirteen thousand islands in the archipelago of Indonesia. It is very small compared with many other islands, but is perhaps the most famous and unique of all, with epithets such as the "last paradise," "morning of the world," and "island of many temples."

The mountains that run across Bali from its western to its eastern tip divide Bali into two parts, South and North Bali, and play a very important role in the life and religion of the Balinese. They are the source of three essential elements for human life: fire, water, and air.

The mountains are volcanic. As there are two active volcanoes, the mountains are considered the source of fire. The mountains are also the source of water. The heavy forests on their slopes cause a lot of rain and the water is gathered in the craters of the dead volcanoes. These act as our reservoirs. The rivers flow south and north from the mountains.

Water plays a very important role in the life of Bali. As the rivers flow to the ocean south and north, they give life to the rice in the *sawah* (wet rice paddies) as well as to the people who live on the plains and low lands. The rivers then continue their journey to the sea, taking all the dirt and filth with them.

Because the mountains are high above the sea level, the weather there is very refreshing. So the mountains are the source of fresh air. So the three elements, fire, water, and fresh air, which are essential for human life, are found in the mountains. In the human body there are also the three elements, fire, water, and fresh air. If one of the elements is missing from the human body, then the human body will die. The source of these three essential elements for human life is in the mountains.

The soul of a man can be compared with fire, water, and fresh air. The source of the soul is the celestial mountains. That is why according to the Balinese, when a person dies the spirit will go to the mountain, especially to Mount Agung, the tallest mountain in Bali. The Balinese build their temples and monasteries on the slopes of the mountains. And on the slope of Mount Agung they built "Pura Besakih" the mother temple of Bali. The people believe the soul of the dead person will go to "Pura Besakih" after having the proper ceremonies. All the clans in Bali have shrines in the mother temple in connection with ancestor worship. On a special day when there is some trouble in the family, quite often the family accompanied by relatives and a medium will go to the mother temple in order to consult the spirit of the ancestors.

Animist beliefs

The native beliefs in Bali are basically animist in nature. The Balinese believe that every thing and every creature has a soul. Souls are the natural forces that give life and movement to all things. The Balinese worship such natural forces as the wind, the sea, volcanoes, springs of water, valleys, jungles, rivers, and big trees, which they consider to be spirits. They bring offerings for these spirits, in order to prevent them from becoming angry at the people. When someone is hurt in an accident or killed, the Balinese believe that the spirit of the thing that caused the accident is angry. In such a case, the injured person needs someone who knows how to deal with the angry spirit. Usually they would go to a *balian* or *pemangku* or priest-magician or medium, whom they believe to have extrasensory perception and to be able to make an advantageous exchange with the spirit for the recovery of good health. The priest-magician or medium would tell the family what to do in order to charm the angry spirit.

The belief that everything has a soul entails that a man also has a soul. This belief leads the people into ancestor worship. The people consider that the souls of their ancestors are still alive after the death of their bodies and dwell at the temple of the dead. The spirit is called *pirata* (a wandering soul). After they have performed a cremation ceremony the *pirata* will be changed to be *pitara* (a settled soul). Then they will perform another ceremony which they call "mukur or Maligia," that will lead the *pitara* to be *betara* or deified soul. This soul will stay in the temple and be worshipped by his descendants in the family temple or the mother temple at Besakih on the slope of Mount Agung (literally "big mount"). Hence in Bali there are still many people who claim to be mediums and clairvoyants or priest-magicians capable of talking with the souls of the dead.

The coming of Hinduism

When the Buddhists and the Hindus came to Bali around A.D. 700 (according to the monument which is found at Blanjongan, Sanur, Bali), they did not change the beliefs of the people, but merely gave new names to the spirits or divine beings in which the people already believed. Since animism, pantheism, and polytheism basically believe in the presence of the soul and spirit in every thing or creature, there was an easy transition from animism to Buddhism and Hinduism.

For example, when the Hindus came to Bali, they gave the name *Brahma* to the spirit of fire, *Vishnu* to the spirit of water, and *Siva* to the spirit of air or ether. These three main spirits manifest themselves in the sea, in volcanoes, and in the jungle, and receive a special name in each manifestation. The present generation of Balinese Hindu priests and leaders have formed a doctrine of the Trinity out of these three main spirits or deities. When the spirit manifests himself as creator, he is Brahman, as maintainer, he is Vishnu, and as destroyer, he is Siva. They claim, however, that this trinity is monotheistic, because the Brahma, Vishnu, and Siva are the manifestations of the one true God, i.e., the *Sang Hyang Widhi Wasa* in Balinese.

The Hindus also introduced the caste system to the indigenous Balinese. Fortunately it was not as bad as in India where it brought untouchability and segregation even in the matter of interdining and other common aspects of daily association. Perhaps this was due to the innate strong sense of self-worth of the freedom-loving indigenous Balinese.

The caste system was introduced by a Sivaist Hindu priest, Dang Hyang Nirarta, an expert in Hinduism and Sanskrit, who came to Bali about A.D. 1355. He dilgently went from one village to another teaching Hinduism. His sons were honoured as members of the highest caste, the *Brahmana*. The families of the king who ruled Bali at that time were called *Ksatria*; their helpers were called *Vaisya*. These three honoured groups, the *Trivangsa*, all came from Java as conquerors after A.D. 1353, when Gajah Mada of the Kingdom of Majapahit in East Java conquered Bali. He managed to unite under his rule Malaya and all the islands that presently belong to Indonesia. This was the last and greatest of the Hindu kingdoms in Indonesia.

The Javanese hold over Bali was tightened after the fall of Majapahit to Islam in A.D. 1478. At that time the entire court of Majapahit, with priests, artists, and intellectuals fled to Bali. They were the most "civilized" in the whole region, the cream of Javanese people. They transplanted their art, religion, and philosophy to Bali which have flourished ever since. They also became the ruling class of Bali. The native Balinese were pushed aside. They were called *Wong Jaba* meaning "people who live outside," because the Javanese Trivangsa, the Brahmana, Ksatria, and Vaisya, built walls around their houses since they feared an uprising of the native Balinese. Later on foreigners who knew the caste system in India came to Bali and called these native Balinese the *Sudra*. Among the Balinese those who rejected Javanese Hindu influence went to the jungle or remote areas and built their villages and called themselves the *Bali Aga* or native Balinese. And those who accepted the Javanese Hindu influence were called *Wong Majapahit* or the people of Majapahit. They later on considered themselves higher in position than the Bali Aga. In this way Hinduism penetrated Balinese life.

Although the process of Hinduization went on for many centuries, the original character of the Balinese remained. This may be seen in the way people dealt with the dead, or in the way they built their temples. They introduced new deities, but ancestor worship remains intact. The shrine for the spirit of the ancestors and the new deities of Brahma,

Vishnu, and Siva were erected side by side. The Hindu priests descended from Empu Dang Hyang Nirarta, the first Hindu priest who spread Javanese Hinduism to Bali, worked in coexistence with the native priest, the *pemangku*, who functioned like the shaman or priest-magician among the people of central Asia and Polynesia. The Hindu priests are from the Brahmana caste, and are the scholars of sacred vedas and mantras who can be compared with theologians. They work side by side with the pemangku or priest-magician who comes from the native Balinese. They are chosen through a trance from within the clan.

The Bali-Hindu religion

The Hindu religion, ancestor worship, and animism of Bali have moulded Balinese life and religion. That is why originally the religion of Bali was called the Bali-Hindu religion. It was exclusively related to the Balinese people. Now they call themselves Hindu-Dharma, in order to give room for non-Balinese to join. But in fact no non-Balinese can join, because the main sanctuary or temple or shrine in Bali is related to the ancestral spirits. Each Balinese family is related to its forefathers in a mystical union between the living and the spirits of the dead. The Balinese are very proud of their ancestry. They are eager to trace their family tree, because a family tree can give them a feeling of dignity and identity as well as pride. Only non-Balinese women can join and become Balinese by marrying a Balinese, because the woman does not bring her family gods or ancestral spirits to the home of her husband. Her husband's gods or ancestral spirits become hers.

From the term "Bali-Hindu" it is obvious that this religion is a mixture of Hinduism and the native Bali religion. So Hinduism in Bali is quite different from Hinduism in India. The temples in Bali do not have statues of the three main deities. The people believe the deities are spirits who live in heaven, and come down to the temple occasionally, whenever they have a festival in the temples.

When the people get sick or want something they do not pray to Brahma or Vishnu or Siva or the Sang Hyang Widhi Wasa. They pray to the spirits of their ancestors. They believe that the spirits of their ancestors are the helpers, maintainers, and sustainers of their lives. So the main belief in the deities is basically the belief in spirit, the real mover of every thing and every creature. The spirit does not have any form, so no one can imagine its form. But it is present everywhere at any time.

The basic principles of the Balinese Hindu belief are expressed in Pancha Shradha or Five Creeds, which are:

1. Belief in Brahman, the life principle pervading all and everything.
2. Belief in Atman, which is the name of this life principle as it resides in man.
3. Belief in the law of Karma, the eternal law of cause and effect.

4. Belief in Punarbhava, the reincarnation or rebirth.

5. Belief in Moksha, the freedom from samsara (the cycle of rebirth) and the attainment of eternal happiness.

But one who has observed the life and religion of Bali can say that most Balinese remained ignorant of true Hinduism. They were not interested in the philosophical and doctrinal part of their religion. There was really very little in common between Hinduism and Balinese Hindu religion except in the similarity of the names of the deities and the existence of the caste system. The Bali-Hindu religion is Hinduism of a particular brand. Their main concern is in the immortality of the soul as expressed in the ancestor worship. This immortality of the soul has been affirmed by the belief in Punarbhava, the reincarnation or rebirth of the spirit of the ancestors. Thus ancestor worship is the main concern of the people. They are very eager to display their concern for the spirits of the ancestors in their lavish ceremonies and complex ritual, for example in the cremation of their dead ancestors.

Bali is predominantly Hindu-Balinese in religion, and out of 2.5 million people in Bali 98 percent are Hindus. About 0.5 percent are Christian and 1.5 percent are Muslims and other groups. As opposed to this the religious situation for the whole of Indonesia is 87 percent Muslims and 8 percent Christians with the remaining 5 percent Hindus, Buddhists, and Animists. That is why culturally Bali is quite different from the other islands.

The social situation

The majority of the people in Bali (about 80 percent according to recent statistics) are tenant farmers. They work on rice paddies owned by the ruling class of Bali. They do not own land, because most of the land is owned by the small elite of the ruling class. There is not much land, and no other industry except tourism.

So it is very difficult for most people to find a job and quite easy for the ruling class to exploit the masses of people who desperately need jobs. In many cases in rural areas crops of rice paddies are divided into five parts. Four parts of the crops belongs to the owner of the rice paddy fields. Only one fifth of the crops goes to the tenant farmer. It is very difficult for the average person to move away from the land. There would be very little opportunity for him in any other area of work if he were to do so.

The government of Indonesia is now trying to move the people from the densely populated islands of Java and Bali to sparsely populated islands such as Sumatra, Borneo, Celebes, Moluccas, and Irian Jaya. The Christians have responded quite well to this offer. That is why the Christian Protestant Church of Bali has more members in Sulawesi (Celebes) than in Bali. The church has a transmigration programme through which it is trying hard to share to the burden of the Balinese.

STUMBLING BLOCKS TO BALINESE
ACCEPTING CHRIST

Ancestor worship

The main concern of the Balinese is the belief in the spirit of the ancestors. When a person dies, his spirit will sleep for three days and on the third day will rise again and depart from the dead body. The relative will come to the cemetery to bring an offering for the risen spirit. (That is why it is not difficult for a Balinese to believe in the event of Easter when Christ rose from the dead. Of course in the Easter story the dead body rose, but in Balinese belief only the spirit or the soul of the dead rises.) After the proper ceremony has been performed the spirit will go to the celestial mountains and remain there until it comes down to the family temple whenever there is a religious festival in the temple, or to reincarnate again in its descendant.

The Balinese will bring offerings regularly to the spirit so that the spirit will protect them in their daily life. They pray to the spirit whenever they are in trouble or need. They will go to a medium to consult the spirit whenever there is trouble or difficulties in the family's life. Quite often the medium speaks very clearly about the spirit whom they consult, so that it is difficult for them not to believe in the reality of the spirit. That is why most Balinese are very strong believers in the presence of the spirit.

There are many trance dances in which people can invite all kind of spirits to come and enter the people who dance the trance dance. These are the fire dance, the horse dance, and the angelic dance. They believe that if the spirit of the fire enters a person in the dance, then he will be able to be on friendly terms with fire, and the fire will do no harm to him. So when a person in trance walks on the fire he will not be burnt. When the spirit of a horse enters a person then the person will act like a horse. When the spirit of a *bidadari* or angel enters a person, she will act very graciously like an angel.

Because people still practice the trance dance and consult the spirit of the dead through a medium, they have no problem in believing in the existence of spirits. They also can very easily believe in the Spirit of the resurrected Christ, whom he sends during Pentecost.

All Balinese have a clan temple in which one clan worships the spirits of their ancestors. They come once a year to the clan temple to have a big celebration. The clan temples give them a sense of belonging and identity as well as pride in their roots and ancestries. So it is quite easy for a Balinese to understand the story of Mary and Joseph who went to Bethlehem because they were descendants of David. In Bali all the male descendants of the clan must be registered in the clan temple. That is why Balinese Hinduism is exclusively for a Balinese, because every temple is stricly related to the spirit of the ancestors. No non-Balinese can join their religion.

For this same reason it is difficult for a Balinese to be a Christian. When a Balinese becomes a Christian, he is considered to be a betrayer of the spirit of the ancestors. In worshipping Jesus, who does not belong to their clan, he is considered to be worshipping the spirit of another clan. So the Hindu Balinese consider Christians to be people who leave their own ancestors and worship the spirit of another ancestor.

In a situation like Bali where the people very strongly believe and worship the spirit of the ancestors, it is not at all easy for them to accept the claim of Christ that he only is the way, the truth, and the life, and no one will come to God except through him (Jn. 14:6). They believe quite easily in the Spirit of Christ, but it is difficult for them to accept his exclusive claim. Moreover he is not the spirit of their ancestors. They do not have any problem in coming to a Christian faith healer in cases of sickness in order to be healed as long as they do not have to leave the spirit of their ancestors. This is one of the big stumbling blocks in mission to the Balinese.

Syncretism

Another stumbling block is the syncretistic nature of the Balinese belief. It is not difficult at all for the Animists to convert to polytheistic and pantheistic Hinduism. Animism, polytheism, and pantheism are very close to nature which is governed by the spirits. They are the very spirits of the world, the mover as well as the life of the world as it is found in every man.

The Balinese perceive man as the microcosm and the world as the macrocosm. Man has a soul that is *atman* or *jivatman* and the world has a soul that is *Brahman*. When a man dies, the jivatman will go to Brahman, in *moksha* (deliverance). The process can be compared with water which eventually will go to the ocean, and then evaporate through heat to become rain, at which point it will water the land and go to the ocean again. Thus the cycle of reincarnation follows the law of *Karma*.

That is why there was an easy transition from Balinese Animism or ancestor worship to polytheistic and pantheistic Hinduism. Hinduism did not try to demolish the people's belief but rather tried to enrich it by mingling Hinduism with Animism, which was indigenous, and so produced a new syncretistic religion which was also indigenous and different from the Hinduism in India. This process was the result of the syncretistic character of Hinduism. The Hindu believes that all religions are the same, all are seeking an experience with God, just like all rivers, although taking different routes, flow eventually into the sea. The difference between religions lies in their stages of development whereby one religion may be higher or lower than another. This syncretic attitude toward other religions produces a religious tolerance which in turn leads to syncretism. So the spirit of Animism and ancestor worship remains, but the name is changed according to the new religion.

The religious history and development of Bali illumines the process by which the people became very syncretistic. When one presents Christ to the Balinese and expresses the claim of Christ as the only way, truth, and life, one should not be surprised when the people say "All religions are the same. Let every one embrace his own religion. All religions have the same *telos*. All religions are like rivers that flow to the sea. It may be that one religion becomes plainer than the other. It may be that one religion is symbolized as a car, another as an airplane, and another as a carriage, but all are vehicles, no matter which one is plainer than the other. The most important factor in religion is its *telos*, and the *telos* of every religion is the same."

Most Balinese from the peasant to the intellectual consider all religions to be the same. They speak of religions as rivers, vehicles, or clothes so that they do not feel the necessity to change from one religion to another. They like to believe in all religions or at least to possess a small part of every religion in a syncretistic fashion. In their temples there are shrines for the ancestors side by side with the Hindu trinity of Brahma, Siva, and Vishnu. They are very eager to add another shrine for Christ. Thus syncretism literally enthralls Bali. It has become a stumbling block for Christianity that preaches the claim of Christ as the way, the truth, and the life and that no one can come to God except through him (Jn. 14:6).

A RELEVANT MESSAGE FOR THE BALINESE

Religious experience

In approaching non-Christians in our missionary endeavour we must not approach them with a judgement, but must come in a positive manner to share the joy which we find in our encounter with the resurrected Christ with those who have not yet experienced this joy. Paul in his personal encounter with Christ felt that necessity had been laid upon him to preach the gospel to other people. Parallels to this feeling of the weight of necessity can be found in Jesus' parable of the shepherd who wanted to share his joy with his friends because he had found his lost sheep, or of the woman who recovered her lost coin and went to her friend saying: "Rejoice with me, for I have found the coin" (Lk. 15:4-10).

Religious experience is a very important factor in witnessing Christ to other people just as it was in Paul's personal encounter with Christ. Paul later tried to witness to Christ as he had known him through his religious experience. Paul's experience of encounter with Christ is neither nearer to nor further from us, because he also encountered Christ who had been crucified, buried, resurrected from the dead, and exalted to heaven to reign with God. If one believes in the resurrected Christ, there is no reason to doubt that one can have a direct personal encounter with Christ, just as Paul did, because Christ is the same yesterday, today, and forever (Heb. 13:8).

Without this religious experience our faith becomes merely a theoretical conviction. Genuine religious experience enables a person to witness to Christ with authority. This is what the psalmist meant when he said: "O taste and see that the Lord is good" (Ps. 34:8). Without some kind of religious experience one cannot invite people to come and taste the goodness of the Lord.

Religious experience also enabled Andrew to say to his brother Simon: "We have found the Messiah" (which means Christ). "Come and see" (Jn. 1:39, 41-42). That is why the most important thing in approaching the Hindu Balinese is to present Christ as available to direct encounter and experience. And we hope and pray that Christ will meet them and open their eyes.

By accepting that religious experience plays a role in mission, we allow for the Holy Spirit who was sent by Christ to reveal himself. He is the Spirit of God, the creative power in the world. The Holy Spirit is the real power and energy behind the creation story. It was by the Holy Spirit that Christ was incarnate, and by the Holy Spirit the world is convinced of its sin, and of God's righteousness and judgement (Jn. 16:8). Moreover it is by the compulsion of the Holy Spirit that the disciples preached the gospel and witnessed to Christ (Acts 2). Thus the mission of the church is none other than the mission of God's chosen people who have been saved by Christ through the Holy Spirit. God is Spirit. In that way he operates only in Spirit and through Spirit. God sent the Spirit of his Son into the believer's heart, so that he can call him: "Abba! Father" and he will be no longer a slave but a son as well as an heir (Gal. 4:5-7; Rom. 8:15, 16).

The whole person

Another important aspect in mission is the role of the body. In the Bible the body is important, because it is the shrine of the Holy Spirit (1 Cor. 6:19), and as its dwelling place (Eph. 3:17). Moreover God created the body before he put breath in it. The incarnation of God in the person of Jesus Christ of Nazareth means that God uses a body of a person for his incarnation. Jesus cured the sick and healed the rotten body of a leper. He fed the hungry and freed the body that was possessed by evil spirits. Lastly he raised the body of Lazarus who was dead.

Christ's saving activity as redeemer is related to the body. His saving activity can be compared with the jubilee year in which people are freed and redeemed from their debt. In a slave culture someone pays the price of the slave in order to free or to redeem him from slavery and make him a free man. It is related with a physical thing, the body, which means transforming the physical thing into a new being. Whoever is in Christ is a new creation, his body, mind, and spirit have been transformed into a new being.

As Saviour, Christ is related with souls—to free the soul from the bondage of sin to enter into eternal life. But this is not separate from his concern for the body. Quite often Christian preachers say that they are looking for lost souls. What are they going to do with the bodies if they get the souls? The Bible testifies: "For God so loved the world that he gave his only Son, that whoever believes in him should not perish but have eternal life" (Jn. 3:16). God has shown his genuine concern for the world by becoming flesh in order to meet man's deepest need. It is the need of the whole person.

One cannot approach a person fragmentarily. The Balinese consider themselves to have three basic needs. We have to meet the three needs of the people: the need of the head, for intellectual or mind development; the need of the heart, for spiritual satisfaction, and the need of the stomach, for the body or physical growth. Hence the saving act of Christ must be preached in terms of meeting these three basic needs. That is why a good pastor in Bali is a person who knows three things. He must be a guru or a good religious teacher, an exorcist, and an economist, so that he can meet the three needs.

When Christ sends a man to a given place, he must first of all look at the need of the people. In one area the need of the stomach may be greater, in another the heart and in another the head. He deals with different people in different ways.

In Indonesia and in Bali in particular most people live in poverty. They are exploited and oppressed by the ruling class. The spirits who live around them are very harsh, so people are very afraid of them. That is why they bring many offerings for the spirits so that they do not disturb them in their daily lives. Ethically the people live good lives. They believe very strongly in the law of karma and reincarnation. These lead them into a life of purity, of non–bad-doing. In this way the Christ that the people are looking for is the Christ who can liberate them from poverty, oppression, and the harshness of the spirits who live around them. Naturally Christ calls them: "Come to me, all who labour and are heavy laden, and I will give you rest" (Mt. 11:28).

They are not interested in Christ being preached as a person who will convince them concerning their sin as well as the righteousness and the judgement of God (Jn. 16:8). In the First and Second Worlds, where the people mostly live in prosperity and tend to follow the desire of their flesh, Christ reminds them about crucifying the desire of their flesh.

The Christ whom we preach must meet the need of the people as well as be relevant to their situation and condition. We do not change Christ, but we stress the one that is needed most by the people. It is similar to when we make clothes. In Europe we need thick clothes, but in Bali we need thin clothes. In Europe church leaders replace baptism by immersion with sprinkling because no one will be eager to be baptized in the wintertime by immersion. It is very interesting to note that the Baptist Churches are very strong in the southern part of the U.S.A., while in

Australia the Baptist Churches are much stronger in the northern part of Australia where the weather is warmer. So the doctrines and ritual of the churches as well as the Christology however lofty and noble in principle, eventually, I believe, cannot escape a certain conditioning due to the situation and condition of the people as well as the nature and climate of a given area.

Love in times of crisis

In Bali where people are surrounded by oppressors in the form of the ruling class, the caste system, and the harsh spirits, the people most need love. We have to stress the Christ who loves them most as Redeemer.

That is why we come to the people with a message about Christ who is full of love and compassion. He is the same yesterday and forever. He is the Spirit who is much mightier than all other spirits. He is a liberator from oppression, poverty, ignorance, and harsh spirits. He is real and true as Paul has experienced him. He approaches the people in their situation and condition.

Christianity can be called a religion of crisis. Most people who encounter Christ in Bali are those who are in a crisis because of sickness, poverty, anxiety, calamity, oppression, or ignorance. In many ways Jesus Christ's words about the rich young ruler are quite true: "Truly I say to you, it will be hard for a rich man to enter the kingdom of heaven. . . . It is easier for a camel to go through the eye of a needle than for a rich man to enter the kingdom of God" (Mt. 19:23-24). In the experience of the Bali church most people who are converted to Christianity belong to people who are *"kelepekan,"* which means they are in a state of crisis stricken by sickness, poverty, oppression, or nervous breakdown. Then they encounter Christ either through prayer or through some help of Christians.

Balinese who transmigrate to other islands convert to Christianity more easily. Firstly in the new land they are away from the oppressors, so they are not afraid to become Christians. In my opinion people who transmigrate to other islands can be compared with plants which are taken by force from the ground and then are replanted in another place. They are taken away from most of their roots. So they are in a state of crisis. They need help and compassion. Most people who are converted to Christianity are those who get help or compassion from some Christian friends in that first six months. After the first six months, usually they remain in the old religion, because they have passed the crisis and they begin to be settled in the new environment.

Many people are attracted by Christianity because it is a religion of love. The basic character of Christianity is love. God is love, and he has shown his love in Christ to us (Rom. 5:8). Those who have experienced his love will be able to express his love in their life, because people who do not experience love will not be able to express his love.

Whoever is in Christ, is a new creation (2 Cor. 5:17). He will walk in Christ and in love. In Paul's words to walk *in Christ* is similar to walk *in love*. The words "Christ" and "love" are interchangeable in many sentences written by Paul. In Colossians 2:6 he writes "live in him" and in Ephesians 5:2 he says "walk in love." Furthermore in Colossians 2:7 Paul says "rooted and built up in him (Christ)," then in Ephesians 3:17 he writes "rooted and grounded in love." Moreover it is no longer he who lives but Christ who lives in him (Gal. 2:20). He will be motivated by love.

He will walk with an offer of living water. He will walk with a sharing of joy in accepting Jesus Christ as his Saviour and Lord. Let the people who are in a state of crisis, thirsty and hungry, encounter Christ who has a sincere interest, a genuine concern and a deep compassion for those in need and trouble.

CHRISTOLOGY AND MISSION

In his *humanity* Jesus will be looked upon as an example of obedience to God. He is a man who is willing to sacrifice himself by leaving the glory of heaven and even to die on the cross for the sake of the welfare and salvation of humankind. He is a man who can give an example of how to crucify and reject the desire of the flesh which is strongly influenced by the desire of the five senses. He is a contrast to the first Adam, the natural man, who liked to follow the desire of his flesh, or five senses.

Moreover, Jesus is not afraid of bringing some changes or reformation to society. His teaching does not merely preserve the mores of society. In the parable of the seed that grows, the growing seed is not static. It does not remain forever. It is very dynamic. It will grow by changing form from time to time. From a mere seed comes the root, the leaves, the branches, the flowers and the fruits. Churches are often very static in the name of preserving their heritage. They lose their dynamic. They are not in line with Jesus' teaching.

In his *divinity* Jesus will be looked on as the Spirit of God who is ever present like the wind that gives fresh air as well as brings destruction. He is also like the fire that gives warmth and comfort as well as spreads destruction. And he is also like water that gives satisfaction to the hungry and thirsty soul. But water also can be very destructive. The Spirit of God works in both ways. He is like a sword with two blades. He can express love and concern, and can be very angry and destructive in his judgement. He is much more powerful than any spirit in the world, because he is the creative power of God in dealing with the world.

The mission of Christ is the work of the whole body of Christ, that is, the church which has been redeemed and saved by Christ. Mission is just like the ocean. Even though all the waters and rivers are flowing to the sea, the ocean will never overflow. Moreover all the churches in the world have become a minority in their own environment either among secular people in the First or Second Worlds, or among non-Christian people in the Third and Fourth Worlds. So churches, no matter where they are, have become a minority group who live among a largely nonbelieving people. They need missionary activities. Mission itself is the sign of its own life. If there is no water which is flowing from the land to the sea, it means there is a drought. If there is no mission activity that comes out of the church or a Christian, it means that the church or the Christian is dead spiritually. Mission is the work of all churches and all Christians in the world no matter where they live. It is just like the water itself. All waters are flowing to the sea or ocean. But they evaporate again and eventually they will become rain or snow that falls to the land. In that way there will be a circulation or recycling of water that gives life to the vegetation and all creatures on land and in the sea.

SELECT BIBLIOGRAPHY

Wayan Mastra. "Contextualization of the Church in Bali—a Case Study from Indonesia," in *Down to Earth: Studies in Christianity and Culture.* John Stott and Robert Coote, eds. London: Hodder and Stoughton, 1981.
——————————. *Gospel in Context.* April 1978, p. 4

DISCUSSION WITH WAYAN MASTRA

Q. You suggest that the most important thing is to present Christ to the Balinese so that they can have a direct encounter experience with the resurrected Christ. But do the Balinese themselves also have their own religious experience in their encounter with the spirits of the ancestors?

W.M. I stress religious experience because people in Bali have many religious experiences. In fact I became a Christian at the age of twenty-one because I had a religious experience.

One day I got into difficulties. I was away from Bali at school in Java. The ruling class did not like me to go to school at that time because as a native Balinese, I do not belong to the ruling class. In fact nobody used to go to college from East Bali where I come from. I was the first. The village chief asked my parents to tell me to quit college because it was against the religious law.

You should know that when people meet in Bali the first question they ask is "Where is your place on the stairs?" If you belong on the bottom stair, you have to stay there to preserve harmony. Harmony is when people stay on their stair. You must not change the situation. Since I did not belong to the ruling class I had to stay on the bottom. I did not like this.

The post office was in the chief's house and he kept all my letters to my father. So my father did not get any of my letters. He did not know my address and could not send me any money. So I was thrown out of my lodgings because I could not pay the lodging expenses. The school was a Christian school and I remembered that we learned about the Lord's prayer and how Jesus encouraged the disciples to pray: "Seek and you will find, ask and it shall be given." So naturally I went to church to express my needs to God. The next morning I met a Christian friend in school who was my classmate. He said "I saw you in church yesterday. I thought you were a Hindu. What brought you to go to church?"

I told him my problem and he said "I live in a dormitory in which the principal is a Christian. So I will ask him whether you can move to that place because of your difficulty." After school was over, he talked to the principal and I was allowed to move to his dormitory. Then about a week afterwards, I received a letter from my father who wrote that he had gone to the chief's house and found all my letters and my address. I worked out that he had done this exactly while I was in the church. So I believed that God was alive. I decided to become a Christian and joined the catechism class. After one year I was baptized and confirmed.

This is one religious experience. I believe strongly that Christ is the same yesterday, today, and forever. If Paul can encounter him, why can we not encounter him? Why can we not present him as a person who can be encountered by people? In Bali, Hindus lead good ethical lives. They are fairly honest people. When we come to a Hindu who believes strongly in spirits, if we speak about sin, he cannot understand. So we do not preach about sin first. But when they are in the church, then we begin to preach about sin. Let me illustrate. People drive on the left hand side of the road in Bali. We do not talk about driving on the right side of the road, we just leave them to drive on the left. But when they move to other countries where driving is on the right side, then we start teaching them to drive on the right. It is the same with teaching the people about sin. If they do not understand, we wait until they come to the church.

Q. Are you not defining ethics and morality too narrowly? Is not the oppression caused by the caste system to do with morality? It was recognized as a deeply moral question by many Hindu reformers like Raja Ram Mohan Roy.

W.M. If we look at the caste system and oppression from outside, it is a form of oppression. But the Balinese feel that this is natural. Let me illustrate. If the United States embraced Hinduism and I was born in one of the ghettoes in the United States, people would believe that this would be a punishment for my former life. I would have to follow the religious requirements and, if I do, when I reincarnate in the next life, I will have a better life at a higher level of human existence. This happens because the soul of man is like water. You can put water anywhere and the shape it will take will depend on the container you put it in. If you put it in a glass it will take the form of a glass, if you put it in a cup it will take the form of a cup. A soul can enter a black man, a woman, a white man, a yellow man depending on their former acts. If I kill another man, when I reincarnate, that man will take my soul and I will take his body. That will be my punishment. So, that is why the Balinese do not feel that the caste system is a form of oppression. It is merely the result of their deeds in their former life.

10. Biblical Christianity in the Context of Buddhism

DAVID LIM *(Philippines)*

Synopsis

This paper explores the various philosophical issues raised from the Christian dialogue-in-mission in Buddhist cultures. The critical categories include the question of epistemology, the essence of reality, the problem of liberation or salvation, and the problem of contextualization. The paper suggests that the approach of some Christians who adopt Christian symbols and fill them with Buddhistic meaning is a nonhistorical and nondoctrinal secularistic model incompatible with the biblical worldview.

INTRODUCTION

This paper surveys the issues raised from the Christian mission and dialogue in Buddhist cultures,[1] with special attention to the trend among

---

1. This paper recognizes four important qualifications for this academic study.

First, we (and even those within a religious tradition) cannot apprehend *fully* what a religious tradition means to those within. Why? Because religious symbols represent the infinity, that which is greater than the symbols and traditions themselves and the human mind. What we can do is try to understand what the majority of its adherents generally understand.

Second, symbols can mean different things at different levels to different adherents. People belonging to the same religion may interpret their faith differently, as a Buddhist philosophical scholar would somewhat differ from a Buddhist folk religionist, etc. As W. C. Smith notices:

"There is more behind our own tradition, and behind other people's than any one man can grasp. Meaning is in part for each participant by his particular experience, and by his capacity, sensitivity, imagination, intensity and whimsy. We can generalize, but we should remember that is what we are doing. . . . All interpretations, then, must be suggestive rather than conclusive." Wilfred Cantwell Smith, *The Faith of Other Men* (New York: Harper and Row, 1963), p. 43.

Third, we cannot assume uniform structure and categories for both religions under study (as positivists once attempted). Tai Dong Han criticizes Paul Tillich for setting up four criteria of comparison between Christianity and Buddhism by using Christian terms and concepts (e.g., heaven, hell, person, and transformation) which are not equally essential to Buddhism. Such discussion becomes a sort of Christian monologue while forcing Buddhism to stay under the Chris-

some Christians to adopt Christian symbols and fill them with Buddhist content.[2] The paper will examine the basics of the Buddhist worldview, the issues for dialogue with Buddhists, and the trend to "Buddhistise" Christian forms.

BASICS OF A BUDDHIST WORLDVIEW

It is necessary to understand the intricacies of the total worldview of the Buddhists to give us an overall view of what we face. The following are the typical and significant elements in Buddhist philosophy which shall form the basic background knowledge for intelligent interaction.

The heart of Buddhist faith is the Four Noble Truths which Buddha preached following his enlightenment. They are: life is suffering; suffering has a cause; there is release from suffering; and the way of release.

The First Noble Truth does not mean merely that life in this world involves suffering; it means that the very nature of existence is such that to live is to suffer. While we live, we suffer. Our existence is marked by three things: impermanence (anicca), nonsubstance (anatta), and suffering (dukkha).

Second, the basic cause of suffering is desire for life. Behind such craving is ignorance (avidia) of the true nature of our existence.

The Buddhist "good news" is the Third Noble Truth: those who really

---

tian shadow. See Tai Dong Han, "Mediation Process in Cultural Interaction: A Search for Dialogue between Christianity and Buddhism," in *The Northeast Asia Journal of Theology* 2 (Oct. 1969), 88-105.

Lastly, the issue actually lies in basic philosophical worldviews. Thus to find apparent morphological similarities between both religions is quite superficial. Dr. Han also cites a case of the shallow study of some Christian scholars in using apparent similarities of Buddhist Trinity—Buddha as substance, spirit, and redemptive power—and Christian Triune God. Such correspondence is just mere coincidence, for Buddhists also believe in bi-nity (two in one), quadrinity (four in one) and deca-nity (ten in one). The only proper method of comparative study is on the overall structural level, so that the set of terms together in their appropriate configuration is the focus of evaluation (*ibid.*, pp. 88-89). Takizawa also believes that it is more legitimate to compare both religious systems on an ontological basis in regard to the fundamental structure of their respective religious outlooks than to compare them in individual phenomenological points and detailed dogmatic conceptions. The latter are "expressions of ontological and existential facts realized in each religion and often form a closed world of ideology which is not important as such" (see Katzume Takizawa, *Buddhism and Christianity* [Tokyo: Hozokan, 1964]).

2. The study will focus on the book *Taking Leave of God* (New York: Crossroad, 1981), written recently by Don Cupitt. This approach bypasses the laudable attempt of some Christians, like Aloysius Pieris and Lynn De Silva of Sri Lanka, to express their Christian faith in terms of the Buddhist model of reality and symbols.

believe the first two truths can be released from suffering. But it is very difficult to accept this Truth because of man's blindness and craving to enjoy life (whereby many are bound more and more to live and suffer). Rare and blessed are those who can escape the wheel of rebirth (samsara), the operation of the law of Kamma (Pali form of Sanskrit Karma, the principle of universal causality, that each act brings on its own inevitable return).

The way of escape is called the Eightfold Path (often called the middle way): right understanding, right mindedness, right speech, right actions, right livelihood, right efforts, right mindfulness, and right concentration. The first two require the peculiar perspective of anicca, anatta, and dukkha, the Four Noble Truths, the law of Kamma, and the law of Dependent Origination (paticcasamupada, which lists twelve phenomena lined together to explain the origin of life and suffering).[3] The next three are Buddhist ethical disciplines involving day-to-day relationships with their fellowman—avoidance of harming others and oneself.[4] The last three are "mental disciplines" which provide peace of mind and mental clarity which are not in themselves the final key to escape.[5] They make it possible for one to "realize" (going beyond intellectual understanding and coming to an intuitive grasp of) the Truth and set one free in Nirvana, a transcendent state free from craving with its attendant sorrow and suffering.

Buddhist concern focusses on pain and suffering. Knowledge or wisdom is supremely important. Misery comes from ignorance. Thus the Eightfold Path starts with right understanding and right mindedness and ends with three "mental disciplines."

From here on, Buddhist thought can be divided into two main branches: Theravada and Mahayana. The first emphasizes austerity and more literal interpretation of the Buddha's teachings, the second espouses a more expansive and liberal interpretation.[6]

3. The vulnerable links of the chain are *ignorance* and *desire*, which provide the points at which the Buddhist hopes to break the chain and thus to end sufferings. H. G. Grether, "The Cross and the Bodhi Tree," *Theology Today* 16 (Jan. 1960), 449.

4. This is done through refraining from taking life, from taking property without the owner's consent, from indulging in sexual license, evil speech, and use of narcotics and intoxicants. Also, one must not engage in a means of livelihood which dispenses wrong-doing to others. However, these cannot result in ultimate release from suffering but they help to improve one's situation and are necessary for pursuit of the next three.

5. For a fuller treatment of the Middle Way, see Kenneth W. Morgan, ed., *The Path of the Buddha* (New York: Ronald Press Co., 1956), pp. 28-32.

6. These are the two *general classes,* since Buddhism has a great variety due to its flexibility and adaptability, especially in the Mahayana branch. There have been tendencies toward monism, dualism, atheism, and theism, enlightenment by faith and/or by works, salvation to a blissful heaven or to a blissful nothingness.

Theravada (also called Hinayana, "lesser vehicle") Buddhism, the more primitive of these branches, has different expressions in Southern Asia (Sri Lanka, India, Burma, Thailand, Laos, Kampuchea, and Vietnam). But they all view Truth as far beyond the common life of man with its relationships, so that the ethical distinctions of man's life are lost. To know and discern good and evil (and one cannot be known without the other) is to suffer. Higher wisdom or "enlightenment" (bodhi) is attained as the ultimate in the highest degree of concentrated reflection.

One is responsible to walk the path to ultimate enlightenment as Buddha's own individual search ended with the discovery of freedom from the chain of rebirths. When one is released, he is absorbed into Nirvana (the ultimate "nothingness" or "emptiness"). Actually, there is no self to be denied or known for the nature of all existence is nothingness. One must come to "realize" the impermanence and nonexistence of all things. The ideal is that one becomes the Arahant (perfected one) who is a solitary, self-contained, and self-dependent figure.

On the other hand, Mahayana ("greater vehicle") Buddhism developed in Northern Asia (Bhutan, China, Japan, Korea) into a more theistic kind where numerous buddhas and bodhisattvas ("beings of enlightenment") and Gautama Buddha himself have been deified. The Buddha is considered the greatest of the series of eternal Buddhas who had appeared on earth to spread the dhamma (way of truth) to suffering humanity. Bodhisattvas (especially the Japanese and Chinese Amitabha or Amida-Buddha) bestow merits on those who trust them because these mythical heroes who attained perfect knowledge (like Buddha) refrained from entering Nirvana, and helped preach the dhamma of the middle way.

To Mahayanas, Nirvana is a place of restful happiness where enlightened beings will have their continued existence. What is extinguished is not life itself but the craving and vain attachments which have to be destroyed if one is to reach Nirvana. The idea is to become a bodhisattva, as one who has attained release from sufferings but chooses to remain with fellow beings to help them until all creatures are set free, and ultimately become Buddhas.

ISSUES FOR DIALOGUE WITH BUDDHISTS[7]

Although this section cannot claim to give an exhaustive survey of the

---

At the same time much Buddhist conceptualization has been mixed with folk-religiosity based on local spiritistic and animistic beliefs which include gods, demons, rituals, spells, incantations, and prayer formulas; an elaborate example is Lamaism which developed out of the context of Tibetan Bon beliefs. Conservative and liberal sects and parties came from reform movements within Buddhism and have developed their own doctrines and practices. Thus this great variety cautions against any simplistic approach to Buddhists, for much depends on which Buddhist individual or group one is addressing.

7. Notice the more frequent use of "Buddhist" instead of "Buddhism" in this paper. The author agrees with Kosuka Koyama's claim that "*ism* and *ist*

issues raised in Christian dialogue and mission[8] to the Buddhists, it aims
to describe the critical categories which Christians have used for presenting the Christian faith in the light of Buddhist philosophical thoughts and
worldview.

Epistemology

Christians generally believe that the supernatural may be known and
believed because of divine revelation, human reason, and/or intuitive feelings. Buddhists differ in their theory of knowledge and knowledge
acquisition when one is "enlightened." Theravada Buddhists seem to
be agnostic about metaphysical questions. Buddhist scholars Suzuki and
Matsuzi see that we are to move toward a "thought-sphere which centers
in the tremendous mystery of nature. All is secret since all such
metaphysical questions lead to an ultimate mystery and are impossible
to answer";[9] there can be no conclusive evidence or reason to believe
or disbelieve. These Buddhists do not say we do not know whether the
supernatural exists, but they say *we know* that the question whether or
not the supernatural exists is unintelligible and nonconclusive.

But Drummond finds in Mahayana Buddhism some idea of revelatory
knowledge. Though no certainty is included, it is compensated for "by
the achievement of 'insight' through the practice of meditation in the
context of 'faith' and strenuous intellectual and moral discipline."[10]
Japanese Roman Catholic Kadowaki also finds the Buddhist San Gaku's
threefold learning (trisikas) compatible with the Thomist connatural
knowledge. The trisikas include both intellectual and moral aspects in
order to gain satori (Nirvana).[11] And connatural knowledge is gained

---

are related," but we should use "a crucified mind" to communicate the Christian faith and relate to others as "living persons in the concrete historical and
existential situation" rather than to think of the "idea of Buddhism" or "logy"
about them; in short, the difference between "library Buddhism" and "street
Buddhists." See Kosuke Koyama, *Waterbuffalo Theology* (Maryknoll: Orbis, 1974),
pp. 130-32, 209-11.

8. In this paper, "dialogue" means the mutual attempt of two or more persons of different faiths to understand with respect each other's beliefs; for the
evangelical Christian, this is *dialogue-in-mission*, for he hopes that the discussion
would lead his partner or respondent to the saving or liberating faith in Jesus
Christ.

9. Nobuhiko Matsugi, "A Contemporary Buddhist's Evaluation of Scientific
Culture," *The Japan Christian Quarterly* 46:2 (Spring 1980), 83-85. See also on
Madhayanika agnosticism Hseuh-Li Cheng, "Nagarjuna's Approach to the Prob-
lem of the Existence of God," *Religious Studies* 12:2 (June 1976), 207-16.

10. Richard Henry Drummond, *Gautama Buddha* (Grand Rapids: Eerdmans,
1974), p. 193.

11. Kakichi Kadowaki, "Ways of Knowing: A Buddhist-Thomist Dialogue,"
The Northeast Asia Journal of Theology 20 (March 1978), 53-73. *Trisikas* include *adhisila
(kai)* as virtuous conduct, *adhicitta (Jo)* as concentrative absorption, and *adhiprajna
(e)* as learning of wisdom.

through intuition and experience when one practices the moral virtues of charity and chastity; one then rises to the higher plane of speculative thinking, not by scientific inquiry through reason, but through intuitive experience. Also Japanese New Testament scholar Yagi finds the "discriminating intellect" (funbetsu) comparable to intuitive awareness in some Christian views.[12]

However, Smart finds that both the Theravada and Mahayana Buddhist nonpropositional way of cognition (as in many modern Christian theologians) differs from the general Christian view of direct divine communication in history. Though admittedly words are indirect expressions which point beyond themselves, Christian knowing is based on the divine historical acts (especially in the Jesus-event) while Buddhists seek mystical union with the Ultimate Reality through contemplation. For Buddhists, the fleshly manifestations of the Absolute remain at the lower empirical level and one has to see beyond the fleshly manifestation to the Absolute.

Thus the issue is: Can man acquire metaphysical knowledge and sure understanding? If yes, what is the proper way? If not, is all knowledge illusory? And what is the point of seeking enlightenment? The focus for further discussion seems to be the study of mystical experience in Buddhism and in Christianity.

Essence of reality (ontology and teleology)

Traditionally, Buddhists are known to believe in the illusory nature of all reality, while Christians claim the essential beingness or the reality of the cosmos. Thus, different related issues about ultimate reality, historical existence, and the human situation are raised.

Basic structure of reality: monism or dualism?   Christians have often presupposed the dualistic subject-object structure of consciousness and existence. Consciousness presupposes a subject who makes it possible and it intends an object about which it is aware of; and existence presupposes a subject which lives or becomes and it relates to an object for or by which it exists.

To most, if not all, Buddhists, reality is tathata, meaning wholeness, perfection in one, that all things without exception are one.[13] Any plurality (including duality) belongs to the illusory distinction of imperfect knowledge and existence. Even in Mahayana Buddhism, heaven (and God who dwells in it) is still imperfect because it coexists with hell.[14] It is not absolutely perfect until all is comprehended in one single reality.

---

12. Seiichi Yagi, "Buddhism and Christianity," *The Northeast Asia Journal of Theology* 20 (March 1978), 1-18.

13. J. Y. Fenton, "Buddhist Meditation and Christian Practice," *Anglican Theological Review* 53 (Oct. 1971), 247.

14. See Kuo Huo-Lieh, "Buddhism in Taiwan Today: Attitudes Towards Changing Society," *Southeast Asia Journal of Theology* 3 (Oct. 1961), 51-52.

All distinctions—emptiness and fulness,[15] good and evil, particular and universal, subject and object—are transcended and exist as complete unity, as Nirvana.

Thus all things in this world (man, animals, plants, dust, etc.) and Nirvana exist in complete equality and union. All things (not just man) are becoming buddhas, for the "Buddha spirit" in everything moves each "to realize the buddha nature" in self-transcendence.[16] This seems to be in contrast with the Christian sense of pluralistic (not uniform) value for various beings (man, animals, plants, minerals) according to their respective "natures."

This problem goes back to the presuppositions of both faiths regarding the basic structure of reality: Is nonsubjective or nonobjective thinking and existence possible? How is right thinking and meaningful existence possible? Can a gesture or sound mean anything significant without playing the role of a subject to an object for both its originator and its perceiver? Can there be meaningful consciousness and existence without the subject-object structure?[17] Dialogue on this level seems to be in favour of the dualistic view since any statement made to say anything meaningful during the dialogue already presupposes a subject (who states it) and an object (which is referred to); otherwise, what is the point of doing dialogue? Nonobjective communication appears as empty and meaningless talk or even self-deception.

Essence of existence: real or unreal?   Does an ultimate reality or ground of being really exist? Will human and other individualities remain eternally? Christians answer "yes" to both and may qualify the second one by adding that "they will exist as long as the ultimate causes or allows them to exist."

Though Buddhists (especially Theravadins) also seek the ultimate goal beyond the impermanent and changing realm of our senses, they deny its actual existence and define reality as "nothing." Nirvana is sunnata, meaning emptiness or "pure nothing." Thus, self (atta) is impermanent because it does not exist; it is a bundle of physical and mental actions and their results which occur very rapidly so as to create the illusion of a "doer" who really does not exist.[18]

15. See Lynn De Silva, "The problem of the self in Buddhism and Christianity," in Douglas J. Elwood, ed., *What Asian Christians are Thinking* (Quezon City: New Day Publishers, 1976), pp. 116-18.

16. Nohuhiko Matsugi, *op. cit.*, pp. 83-85, and also described in Kuo Huo-Lieh, *op. cit.*, p. 52.

17. Fritz Buri, "The Fate of the Concept of God in the Philosophy and Religion of Keiji Nishitani," *The Northeast Asia Journal of Theology* 8 (March 1972), 54, raised this as a key issue for dialogue.

18. See U Kyaw Than, "Man in Buddhism and Christianity," *Southeast Asia Journal of Theology* 3:1 (July 1961), 20-22 for a better description. C. G. Williams

The Buddhist ideal is detachment, becoming an arahant who has no concept of self and who escapes from all forms of existence.[19] He goes out from the illusion of personal significance into nonentity, out from an identifiable particular into indistinguishable totality as the general goal of Buddhist purpose,[20] creating the paradox of a self which is the locus of a will of such unwilling.

Some Christians have found that some Buddhists believe in the reality of the Absolute and other beings. Korean theologian Lee Jung Young thinks that the double negation (neither this nor that) and the state of extinction as "incomprehensible, indescribable, inconceivable, unutterable" are Buddhist expressions of the nonsymbolic nature of Nirvana, that man cannot adequately describe the Supreme reality which transcends the differentiation of existence and essence, subject and object.[21] Suzuki defines God as "a zero full of infinite possibilities . . . a void of inexhaustible contents."[22] Reality exists but man cannot superimpose ideas upon it.

U Hla Bu mentions the reinterpretation of some Burmese Buddhist scholars who stress the positive aspect of Nirvana as a blessed state or a goal of perfection (not as a state of absolute extinction). He quotes

---

quotes E. Conze, *Thirty Years of Buddhist Studies* (1968), pp. 2ff.: "There has been a persistent tendency to attribute to primitive Buddhism the Upanishads' teaching of the self or *atman*. Little can be adduced from the existing Scriptures in support of this thesis, but it has been the curse of Buddhist studies that people will persist in believing that the Buddhists have radically misunderstood the Buddha, and so they hanker . . . after a soul-affirming primitive Buddhism followed by a soul-denying scholastic Buddhism," C. G. Williams, "Selflessness in the Pattern of Salvation," *Religious Studues* 7 (July 1971), 160-61. Williams concludes that the Buddhist concern for developing a virtuous self is only a preliminary discipline to an utter uprooting of the very notion of "self," by negation of selfhood, not by the Hindu absorption of the many into the One Over-Self (p. 163).

19. Koyama, *op. cit.*, pp. 137-43, and Lily Quintos, *The Moral System of Buddhism according to the Milainda Panha with a Christian Theological Reflection* (Quezon City: Ateneo de Manila Press, 1977), pp. 186-88. Fritz Buri, *op. cit.*, p. 54 also finds Buddhist Nishitani's "great death" quite problematic: who really doubts and dies? Doubt, dying, and being enlightened can be meaningful only if there is a self which consciously doubts and indeed dies.

20. Kenneth Cragg, "Buddhism and Baptism," *Theology* 82:688 (July 1979), 260.

21. Jung Young Lee, "Can God be Change Itself?" in Douglas J. Elwood, *op. cit.*, pp. 177-78, believes *Nirvana* can be translated "pure consciousness and eternal subject." To clarify he mentions three examples: 1) Huston Smith's "After we eliminate every aspect of the only consciousness we know, how can we speak of what is left?"; 2) Smith's analogy of the suprasonic which is empty of sounds our ears can detect; 3) Nagasenas' analogy of the wind which exists but cannot be shown by colour or configuration.

22. In Douglas J. Elwood, *op. cit.*, p. 189.

U Thittila's definition of the ultimate as "a lasting state of happiness and peace to be reached here on earth by extinguishing fires of passion," as neo-Buddhists also say "here in our flesh."[23] Thus anatta is not the denial of an individual existence but the denial of individualistic egoism or futile self-love.[24]

Drummond finds this interpretation in the proto-Sankhya teaching of the eternality of separate selves; meditations are expected to move beyond the empirical self not to be extinguished, but to participate in deeper levels of reality. To attain Nirvana is to find "life" at the level of a higher self; to deny self is "to change life-orientation from the selfish, separate self and its roots in attachment to phenomenal existence to the 'other,' which is 'lovely.' "[25] All changing phenomena (the physical cosmos and human beings) are not illusion, but not truly real for only the Absolute is ultimately real and changeless and permanent.

Yagi finds in pratityasanutpada (causality, dependent origination, conditioned genesis) the Japanese Buddhist affirmation of the existence of "beings" through overcoming of the "discriminating intellect" (funbetsu). The reality man believes he knows well is not reality as it is, but as conceived by his funbetsu which is conditioned socially and historically; this objectifying of reality as beings and regarding their self-identical contents as their essence and expressing it by distinct words should therefore be transcended. "Beings" are to be considered not as entities but as "poles." All distinctions are in mutual dependence, mutual implication, and mutual reflection in the whole (not nothingness) of polar relations.[26] The difference between the Christian and Buddhist views is thus just a matter of emphasis: the former on faith in a transcendent subject and the latter on the immediacy of union with the Real Absolute.

Also De Silva from Sri Lanka finds in Theravada Buddhist anatta and Nirvana, the affirmation of self without amounting to "eternalism" (sassatavada) and the negation of self without amounting to "nihilism" (uccedavadaditthi). Transcendence over one's self and beyond oneself is losing oneself in communion with Reality; and this perfect communion implies a differentiation of individual centres of participation and relationship. The underlying principle is that union exists by negating exclusive individuality and perfecting personality. "Perfect communion implies the 'extinction' of the self, i.e., the dying out of separate individuality, by one fully participating in the other."[27] The self is con-

23. U Hla Bu, "The Nature of the Resurgence of Buddhisms in Burma," *Southeast Asia Journal of Theology* 3:1 (July 1961), 20, similar to the Christian idea of "eternal life."

24. *Ibid.*, p. 29.

25. Richard Drummond, *op. cit.*, pp. 194-95; cf. pp. 185-88.

26. Seiichi Yagi, *op. cit.*, footnote 12, pp. 1-13.

27. Lynn De Silva in Douglas J. Elwood, *op. cit.*, p. 116 in the context of pp. 114-18.

tinued in Nirvana as individuality-negating but personality-fulfilling existence. In the experience of individual negation, one discovers the being-transcending reality of both emptiness and fulness, both in one.[28]

Matsugi, quite consistent with his Buddhist assumptions, disregards the question of essence, and focusses on existence: the origin of all existing things is relationship. We as subjects and air as object are not to be recognized as singularities; for "I" alone or "air" in-and-of-itself does not exist in actuality; these entities exist only in mutual relationship.[29] The question remains: Are there entities in-and-of-themselves which relate as subject or object to one another?

Which is the Buddhist view? Is there an "I" which is the locus of personal being and becoming, and responsible for authentic consciousness and existence? Does Buddhist "emptiness" means "nothingness" of being or the "all-embracing self-consciousness"[30] of being? Does the fact of historical transcience necessarily require us to adjudge "nonexistence" and thus "pointlessness" to reality?[31] Should the following two paragraphs be regarded as true or false?

Christianity demands the suppression of selfishness; Buddhism demands the suppression of self, with the one object of extinguishing all consciousness of self. In the one, the true self is elevated and intensified. In the other, the true self is annihilation of the Ego, the utter extinction of the illusion of personal individuality.[32]

The fact that the Buddha expressed the goal for man in "emptiness" while Christianity uses the opposite term "fulness" indicates a real difference between the two religions. Even if many of the Buddhist images could be used to give expression to the Christian ideal, the reverse does not seem to be true. A Buddhist would not use the parables of the Gospel to indicate the meaning of Nibbana as they point too strongly at a positive reality: the union of man with his God, the fulfilment of human desire. . . . The Christian ideal is one of union, of divinization, where the self is important. The Buddhist ideal on the other hand denies the idea of self completely because it is precisely this which causes dukkha and samsaric existence.[33]

28. In De Silva's words: "The realization that one is *anatta* leads to the experience of emptiness and fullness *(sunnatta-punnata, natthi-atthi)* all in one." Douglas J. Elwood, *op. cit.,* pp. 117ff.

29. Matsugi, *op. cit.*, p. 83, which is compatible with Yoshinobu Kumazawa's view of *creative relations,* "God's Being is Being in Relation," God is neither absolute nor relative, but always God becoming relative, which traditionally expressed is "God is love." Yoshinobu Kumazawa, "The Absolute and the Relative in the Problem of God," *The Northeast Asia Journal of Theology* 20 (March 1978), 80-93.

30. Used by Fritz Buri in "My Encounter with Buddhist Thought in Contemporary Japan," *The Northeast Asia Journal of Theology* 3 (Oct. 1969), 50.

31. Implied in Kenneth Cragg, *op. cit.*, p. 261.

32. C. G. Williams, *op. cit.*, pp. 153-54 quotes Monier Williams, *Buddhism* (1890), p. 558.

33. Lily Quintos, *op. cit.*, pp. 195-96.

The issue for dialogue boils down to: Is Buddhism an "as if" philosophy[34] or not? Does the basic transitoriness of existential reality *become* a "not yet" of reality in the positive, concrete sense? When Buddha calls the Absolute as "unborn, unbecome, unmade, unconditioned," does he refer to an actual existence of transcendent Being? Though the self changes, is there a self to know and to direct the change?[35] Does anything including Nirvana exist? And perhaps more basic what does "existence" really mean?

Nature of existence: personal or what? Christianity has traditionally insisted on the existence of God as a personal Being or Creator and the existence of spiritual personalities, both human and angelic. Should Christians insist on such understanding?

Some modern Christian theologians have challenged the traditional language of attributing personhood to God (and have also called into question the concept of "Being" and the preference to speak of God as "Process" or "Becoming").

Khin Maung Din suggests that Buddhist "God" be understood not as impersonal "that," but as a combination of both "thou" and "that." He asks, "Is it not closer to the truth to say that God is a Person as well as not-a-Person; that God is a Being as well as a Becoming; that God exists and also does not exist?"[36] The oriental mind (Buddhist, Taoist, Hindu, or Confucian) understands the *both-and* predication of reality, rather than the *either-or* of classical theology.[37] The alternative is to broaden our concept of God to include nonpersonal and nonexistential categories of God's transcendence, and to understand self (ego, spirit, Hegel's geist, Jasper's "all comprehensive" Umgreifenden, etc.) functionally and not ontologically or metaphysically. The Absolute should and can not be described by relative human terms because this will distort and relativize its true nature. Williams suggests the term "supra-personal" to describe Nirvana.[38]

Drummond suggests a different term, "quasi-personal" Nirvana. Buddha taught and practiced concern and responsible interpersonal relationships among men, thus dhamma (the way, truth) includes intimate friendship with the "lovely" as an integral and necessary part of the life of "dharmamen."[39] People are invited to "come and see." Thus personhood is affirmed in the Buddhist worldview.

Others see the impersonal nature of Nirvana and beings. They hold that in Buddhism the natural law of Karma (cause and effect) takes the

34. Used by Kenneth Cragg, *op. cit.*, p. 260.
35. Question borrowed from Lily Quintos, *op. cit.*, pp. 182-84 and 195-96.
36. Khin Maung Din in Douglas J. Elwood, *op. cit.*, p. 91.
37. *Ibid.*, pp. 90-94, refers to Lee Jung Young's "The Yin-Yang Way of Thinking," also in Douglas J. Elwood, *op. cit.*, pp. 59-67.
38. C. G. Williams, *op. cit.*, p. 160.
39. Richard Drummond, *op. cit.*, p. 193.

place of the personal God as the final cause and exclusive principle of the universe, beyond which no divine personality exists.[40] The ultimate cause of dukkha (suffering) is the impersonal law instead of the broken personal relationship between God and man; thus Buddhism tends to engender fatalism, indifference, and hopelessness.

The key issue then is: Do personality and personal relationships exist in reality? Is there the I-Thou personalistic otherness of beings who can know and relate truly?

Nature of existence: moral or what? Christians have traditionally maintained the moral quality of distinguishing between good and evil, right and wrong. What do the Buddhists believe?

Some Christians see the Buddhists aiming at freedom from a moral samsaric (cycle of rebirth) process in a suffering world, and not from a morally evil condition of existence. Instead of trying to attain goodness or heaven and avoid evil or punishment, Buddhists try to gain Nirvana which is beyond good and evil, liberation from all finite conditioned existence where there is no more becoming or suffering (not sinning!).[41] Quintos and Park see the Buddhist view of dukkha (suffering) as nonmoral and mystical, with no sense of sin or guilt,[42] in contrast to the Christian ethical worldview.

Others find that Buddhists have some sense of goodness or rightness. Gosling finds in Buddhadasa's (Putate in Thai) reinterpretation of rebirth in Thailand that "each person is born at every moment in his life. The individual who thinks evil is born at that moment as an evil being, whereas someone who thinks compassionately is reborn to be increasingly kind and good."[43] Some believe that it is bad or sinful to remain attached to things or to oneself, and Buddha taught the monks that this consciousness of personal responsibility is the good efficacious means of conquering sin.[44]

Besides, Cobb suggests that the Buddhist concept of sunnata (emptiness) focusses on the one cosmic Buddha who is its supreme, eternal

40. Sundar Singh, *The Search After Reality* (Madras: Christian Literature Society, 1968), pp. 26-27, and Alex G. Smith, *The Gospel Facing Hindu Cultures* (Taichung: Asian Theological Association, n.d.), pp. 4-6. Also Paul A. Eakin, *Buddhism and the Christian Approach to Buddhists in Thailand* (Bangkok: R. Hongladaromp Printer and Publisher, 1956), pp. 56-63 notices that *Karma* encourages the self-preoccupation of Buddhists due to the lack of a sense of relationships, man to man, and man to God..

41. Lily Quintos, *op. cit.*, pp. 10-12, 171.

42. *Ibid.*, pp. 184-85 and Park Pong Bae, "Christianity in the Land of Shamanism, Buddhism and Confucianism," *Southeast Asia Journal of Theology* 14:1 (Jan. 1972), 33-34.

43. David Gosling, "Honest to Buddha," *Frontier* 18 (Winter 1975), 222.

44. Taymans d' Eypernon, *Les Paradoxes du Buddhisme* (Brussels and Paris, 1947), pp. 137-38, quoted in Lily Quintos, *op. cit.*, pp. 172f.

realization, the principle of rightness beyond the distinction of good and evil; this is related to one's realization of oneself as an instance of dependent coorigination of all things[45]—and this transcendence of the duality is good in-and-of-itself.

> Although there is much talk of transcending the duality of good and evil, and although cheap imitations of Buddhism sometimes lead to amorality or immorality, authentic Buddhism does not have this character. The result of transcending the duality of good and evil is a pure and spontaneous good.[46]

To be "completely empty" is to be completely open, "to be spontaneously formed by the rightness of that moment. Thus to be truly open is to be spontaneously good. By being wholly indifferent to right and wrong, the Buddhist achieves a perfect conformation to the immanent principle of rightness."[47]

The issue thus is: Do Buddhists believe in transcendent goodness which finalizes all human action and confers upon it a moral weight linked intrinsically to this final goal?[48]

The problem of liberation (Soteriology, Buddhology, and Christology)

Existential questions raise more profitable points for dialogue. Buddhists and Christians find an unquestioned contact point in the search for liberation or salvation. Both presuppose that each person is unconditionally responsible for his behaviour, and that this is enacted in existential conditions of being (or becoming) a person. Both believe that faith or enlightenment is needed to break the false conception that ignorance or sin is impossible to overcome. However, a closer comparison of both faiths seems to produce some differences. These may be discussed as three main issues: the nature, the means, and the agent of liberation.

Nature of liberation: intellectual or volitional? This issue naturally follows from the moral issue mentioned last in the previous section. Is the present suffering state of man and the cosmos due to intellectual ignorance or willful disobedience, lack of awareness or lack of obedience? Christians have traditionally stressed the volitional dimension of the problem.

Undeniably, most Buddhists stress the intellectual avidja (ignorance, lack of enlightenment) which leads to desire and to attachment which leads to all evil. K. M. Din thinks that the cognitive aspect of sin can be seen also in the prayer of Jesus, "Father, forgive . . . for they *know* not. . . ."[49]

45. John B. Cobb, Jr., "Buddhist Emptiness and the Christian God," *Journal of the American Academy of Religion* 45:1 (March 1977), 11.

46. *Ibid.*, p. 24.

47. *Ibid.*, p. 25.

48. See Lily Quintos, *op. cit.*, p. 171.

49. Khin Maung Din in Douglas J. Elwood, *op. cit.*, p. 101.

Buddhistic liberation is by meditation and analysis for the right understanding or insight into reality that hatred and greed are the cause of suffering.[50] Liberation occurs when one understands "reality as it really is" (karma and samsara). The ascetic ideal fits this view for one has to leave worldly duties to concentrate on attaining "enlightenment" (or full understanding).[51]

Other Buddhists view ignorance not as the root of suffering, but as the personal condition; the root of sin is desire, and the way of liberation is the destruction of desire, i.e., by detachment,[52] which is by struggle of the will.[53] Man has the freedom of will to change the basic course of the self from self-centred desires toward Nirvana which is the transcendent "good self" in one. The focus is on man's consciousness and will to direct the flow of one's phenomenal existence.[54]

Buddhism holds each accountable for the existing disorder due to his previous disobedience. The logic runs like this:

> If we are born in a condition of impermanence, the cause is our previous Karma. . . . Whether we can determine the precise cause or not it remains true that we have forged our own chains: our actual existence depends on our past actions. So it is our own responsibility that we are still in a state of impermanence.[55]

So, Buddhism clearly teaches the possibility of liberation, the deliverance of man from his imprisonment. One can stop and reverse the process of causal sequence by building "good karma," a series of

50. Lily Quintos, *op. cit.*, pp. 9-11 and H. Hudson, "Buddhist Teaching about Illusion," *Religious Studies* 7 (1971), 141-51.

51. Lily Quintos, *op. cit.*, pp. 163-64.

52. Paul K. K. Tong, "A Survey of Thematic Differences between Eastern and Western Religious Thought," *Journal of Ecumenical Studies* 10 (1973), 353-54. Lily Quintos, *op. cit.*, p. 176 classifies this as a minor theme, a part of the process of cleansing from sin.

53. Paul Tong, *op. cit.*, p. 354. Sundar Singh, *op. cit.*, pp. 28-30 discusses the futility of gaining salvation by the extinction of all desire (both good and bad). He gives six arguments: (a) even good desires are based on selfish motives. When desiring to do good, consciously or unconsciously we expect some reward we shall merit; (b) as living beings we cannot exist without emotions or desires; where there are feelings, desires will surely be produced from them; (c) the desire to kill desire is itself a desire, like trying to extinguish fire with fire; (d) the Creator's desire is for us to use rightly his created things, and we sin by not using and by killing our desires; (e) the fact of any desire is proof of the availability of the material to satisfy that need (like water for thirst, sleep for fatigue) and proof that it will be fulfilled (not eliminated); and (f) restlessness increases if desire is not satisfied; but even if desire increases, that infinite Being, which is love, is sufficient and able to fully satisfy all our desires.

54. Richard Drummond, *op. cit.*, pp. 191-92.

55. Quoted in Lily Quintos, *op. cit.*, p. 172.

good mental and physical conduct which will end in the attainment of Nirvana.[56] But again, the issue is: What is the basic cause of evil and suffering? Avidja (ignorance or lack of understanding), karma (the natural law of cause-and-effect) which caused all things (including suffering) to exist, or desire or disobedience?

And correspondingly, what is the answer to the Buddhist samsaric problem: is it the elimination of avidja, desire, or disobedience? The answer seems to be open-ended, from both sides, depending on who are involved in the dialogue.

Means of liberation: attachment or detachment? Christians hold that "love is the greatest," and that Absolute Love participates in the historical existence of man. Do Buddhists have a similar conception of self-sacrificing love, willingness to suffer for the sake of others?[57]

Toynbee and Grether see the outward commonality in both Christianity and Buddhism, but view this as a compromise of Buddhism's essential nature because it is "illogical" and "inconsequent" to the premises on which it is based.[58] Though Buddhism has produced men of compassion who accept suffering with courage and are concerned to alleviate the sufferings of others, they suffered fatalistically ("dtam boon, dtam kam," "according to merit according to karma") and remained untouched above and beyond emotional sorrow; for to have passion is to move away from the ideal. The best way seems to be away from the disturbance of needy people so one meditates to attain peace of mind (and enlightenment) rather than involving oneself to serve others which distracts from attaining Nirvana.[59]

In actuality, no "other" exists, so one cannot "love one's enemy" because there is no enemy to love or hate. The Buddhist practice of mercy (sila paramita) is not concerned with the receiver for he is an "object" of the "world" which neither exists nor does not exist.[60] Contemporary Buddhist thinkers appear to be satisfied with a deep compassion (karuna) since this alone corresponds to the virtue of the "enlightened ones" with their "circuminsessional relation" (a basic term in Kegan philosophy used

56. Richard Drummond, *op. cit.*, p. 191 considers this teaching as "the focus of the entire message of the Buddha"—the third Noble Truth.

57. Fritz Buri in "The Fate of the Concept of God in the Philosophy and Religion of Keiji Nishitani," *op. cit.*, p. 39 calls this a "sphere in which practical consequences of Buddhist teachings become apparent and can be judged."

58. H. G. Grether, *op. cit.*, pp. 446, 455-57, quotes A. Toynbee, *Christianity Among the Religions of the World* (New York: Scribners, 1957), p. 28.

59. H. G. Grether, *op. cit.*, pp. 455-57.

60. Tai Dong Han, "Mediation Process in Cultural Interaction: A Search for Dialogue between Christianity and Buddhism," *op. cit.*, pp. 103-104. See also Fritz Buri, "My Encounter with Buddhist Thought in Contemporary Japan," *op. cit.*, pp. 47-48.

especially by Suzuki and H. Nakamura) of all being and things.[61] But this "enlightenment" is both the foundation and product of Buddhist compassion as a "non-historical absorption in emptiness,"[62] and thus its tendency toward noncommitment to and detachment from historical involvement.[63]

However, some Mahayana Buddhists seem to view others as "sleeping buddhas" (not as nobodies), victims of illusions. Thus the aim of Buddhist teaching and practice of "compassion" is to awaken them out of their sleep through any means appropriate to the person: "there is no limit to the number and nature of the doctrinal devices that may be employed to realize this end."[64] But one should beware of attachment to what appears to be a formulation of it or regarding one device as superior to all others. This would limit "compassion" and our possibility of helping others.[65] Is this not similar to Christian compassion?

Din suggests that this Buddhist perspective of nonattachment can help Christians avoid the error of "over-activism" in the world, which makes one relative aspect of salvation absolute. "Worldly humanists" need to become detached from revolutionary actions, and "other-worldly salvationists" have to be detached from craving for heaven. Salvation is a *mystery* which transcends all human ways of understanding it; no theology of liberation can make absolute claims for itself; and "a truly liberated person is not even conscious of the fact that he has attained salvation . . . the very desire for liberation itself must be transcended before one can acquire final liberation."[66] People should learn to rid themselves of the desire for salvation and the craving for continued existence. The final test is not "knowledge of God," but concrete love for man.[67]

Cobb's earlier view was that "the Buddhist lover is not a self, and consequently, makes no distinction between lover and beloved, whereas Christian love is that of a self for other selves."[68] Winston King finds

61. Fritz Buri, "My Encounter . . . ," *op. cit.*, p. 48.

62. *Ibid.*

63. *Ibid.*, and Kosuke Koyama, *op. cit.*, p. 84. *Karuna* consists of five "do not's": no killing, no stealing, no wrong use of speech, no wrong use of sex, and no wrong use of drugs and intoxicants; cf. Ninian Smart, "Learning from Other Faiths: Buddhism," *Expository Times* 83:7 (April 1972), 212—notice the emphasis on *not doing* this or that.

64. H. Hudson, *op. cit.*, pp. 143-51.

65. *Ibid.*, p. 151. Zen Buddhism seems to differ at this point.

66. Khin Maung Din in Douglas J. Elwood, *op. cit.*, pp. 102-103.

67. *Ibid.*

68. J. Cobb, Jr., *The Structure of Christian Existence* (Philadelphia: Westminster, 1967), quoted in J. Y. Fenton, *op. cit.*, p. 249. Cobb has since changed his view. Compare his following articles, "Buddhism and Christianity as Complementary," "Buddhism and Christianity" coauthored with Seiichi Yagi, both in *The Northeast Asia Journal of Theology* 20 (March 1978), 19-30 and 31-52; and "Buddhist Emptiness and the Christian God," *Journal of the American Academy of Religion* 45:1 (March 1977), 11-25.

in Zen Buddhistic "emptiness" not the obliteration of differences between beings but the freedom of each self and each other to be without coercion or hindrance. He also sees Theravadan meditation on friendliness starting with self-love and moving outward to other-love.[69]

Thus, the issue of the means of liberation is both ontological (is there subject-object personal existence in reality?) and ethical (is the love relationship between persons significantly good or just merely role play?). Is Buddhist compassion (sila paramita or karuna)[70] synonymous with Christian agape? It seems that the treasured virtue of Christians is the troublesome duty of Buddhists (especially Theravadins).

Agent of liberation: self or saviour?   Christians have traditionally emphasized the inability of man to liberate himself from the bad situation of the universe; so outside help (especially from his Creator, called "grace") is necessary. They have also understood that the Buddhists believe in self-determination, that man's destiny is in his own hands, to decide whether or not he will undertake to follow the way to ultimate enlightenment. Can there be dialogue on this issue?

Theravadin Buddhists definitely believe in man's ability to free himself from suffering and the sansaric cycle to obtain Nirvana, without the help of others.[71] Man can advance through four stages: entering the stream as a sotapanna, returning to earth once more before Nirvana as a sakadagamin, not returning to earth as an anagamin, and finally attaining Nirvana as an arahant.

But Drummond suggests that there is a sense in which Buddhistic salvation is not strictly self-help. It is through *participation* in Reality, like plunging into a stream which carries one to the goal. Dharma (teaching or way) as the ideal means has its own dynamism, direction, and quality. It can be viewed as a "gracious Presence," a "dynamic Power" by which people are helped to achieve Nirvana, or a "force that makes for righteousness" in phenomenal existence.[72] Is this not similar to the Christian belief in the presence and work of the Holy Spirit?

As mentioned in the first section, Mahayana Buddhism had developed into deification of Gautama Buddha and some beings, called buddhas (enlightened ones) and bodhisattvas (enlightened-beings who remain on

---

69. Winston King, "Zen and the Death of God," in John Cobb, Jr., ed., *The Theology of Altizer* (Philadelphia: Westminster, 1970), pp. 219-20, quoted in J. Y. Fenton, *op. cit.*, pp. 249-50.

70. A study worth pursuing is the "good deeds" practiced by Buddhists to attain *Nirvana*; the four *viharas* are: lovingkindness (active force), compassion (identification with the condition and sorrow of others), joy (enter the pleasure of others), and equanimity (not indifference but calm detachment from all excitement and an impartial attitude in human relations); cf. U Kyaw Than, *op. cit.*, p. 22.

71. But we cannot say that the Buddhists believe that "man is basically good" (as Alex G. Smith, *op. cit.*, p. 4), because most of them do not believe in the *moral* nature of the universe and the liberation process.

72. Richard Drummond, *op. cit.*, pp. 188-92.

earth to help others),[73] who can give aid and merits to those who pray to them and follow their teachings. Here, one does not need to become an ascetic, but through bhakti (devotionalism) in faith to these celestial or mythological figures (like Amida or Amitabha), one is translated after death to the Pure Land which has good conditions to attain Nirvana or buddahood.[74] One's hope of heaven is through the self-sacrifice of bodhisattvas, who postpone their entrance to Nirvana in order to gain merits which are transferable to their devotees. Grether mentions that many Theravadins in Thailand (and most probably elsewhere) also regard Buddha as a god who lives, knows all, and is able to hear and answer prayer.[75]

Smart seems to be the only person who has tried to formulate a Christology out of a Buddhist framework. He studied the three-body doctrine (trikāya) of the Void School led by Nagaryuna; he found interesting parallels with the Christian logos doctrine.[76] The Void School believes that Absolute Reality is indescribable and insubstantial (sunnata, "suchness" or void) but it takes form in the phenomenal level in three ways: kharmakāya (truth-body, identical with the Absolute), sambhogakāya (bliss-body, showing itself as personal lords, as celestial buddhas), and nirmanakāya (transformation-body, shown on earth as the historical Buddha). He compares this with the Johannine logos doctrine as described by C. H. Dodd:

> The ground of all real existence is that divine meaning or principle which is manifested in Jesus Christ. It was this principle, separable in thought from God, but not in reality separate from Him, that existed before the world was, and is the pattern by which, and the power through which, it was created.[77]

Smart, therefore, surmises: Besides teaching the divine identity-in-differences as seen in sambhogakāya, the trisikas also teach the incarnation as the underlying pattern or principle reflected in the created world

---

73. For some details see David Hesselgrave, *Communicating Christ Cross-Culturally* (Grand Rapids: Zondervan, 1978), pp. 166-67.

74. Ninian Smart, "The Logos Doctrine and Eastern Beliefs," *Expository Times* 78:6 (March 1967), 169-70, and "Learning from other faiths . . . ," *op. cit.*, pp. 213-14.

75. H. G. Grether, "Buddhism in Thailand Today," *Southeast Asia Journal of Theology* 3:1 (July 1961), 34-35.

76. Ninian Smart, "The Logos Doctrine . . . ," *op. cit.*, pp. 168-71 ends up with the observation that the Void School has no belief in the creative dependence on the world of God.

77. C. H. Dodd, *The Interpretation of the Fourth Gospel* (Cambridge: Cambridge University Press, 1957), p. 285, quoted in Ninian Smart, "The Logos Doctrine . . . ," *op. cit.*, p. 161, calling it a "Philonic-Stoic notion of a creative pattern."

as nirmanakāya, a mutatis mutandis.[78] This seems to be a common point for starting dialogue with Buddhists.

Some qustions which can be raised are: Can man be liberated without external help? Who is Buddha—teacher, example, or saviour-god?

Also, who is Jesus Christ in the context of Buddhist model of reality? To Theravadins, can he be presented as the supreme arahant who has broken through samsaric cycle and rules over the karma? Or the true dharma to Nirvana (whatever these terms mean to any Buddhist, qualified of course)? To Mahayana Buddhists, can he be presented as the bodhisattva par excellence? Or the supreme Buddha who enlightens every person? Or the perfect surrata who takes all the threefold phenomenal forms mentioned in the trisikas? Christian dialogue-in-mission may have to take various approaches to Buddhist views into consideration.

The problem of contextualization

To conclude and integrate the discussion in this second main section, two hidden agenda on the mission among the Buddhists have to be raised. Is the status of Christianity vis-à-vis Buddhism unique or relative? And what is the best approach to Buddhism without becoming syncretistic? The two related issues are thus universalism and syncretism.

Means of salvation: one or many? Herein lies the challenge to the absolutist truth-claims of Christianity: Is the Christian faith in the uniqueness and finality of the historical divine revelation in the person and work of Jesus of Nazareth the only single proper commitment and "true truth" by which every person can know and worship God? Are the unique and fuller aspects of reality manifested only in the salvation-history account (focussing on the historical Jesus) recorded in the Christian Scriptures? Depending on their assumptions and convictions, the attitudes of Christians regarding the relationship of Christianity to Buddhism (and all other religions and ideologies) may be classified into four: common faith, no agreement, common ground, and point of contact approaches.[79]

"Common faith" approach: Some theologians believe that Christianity is compatible and complementary with other religions. The religions (of which Christianity is one) are different paths which climb up the same mountain. This may be called the "universalist school."

Two Japanese, theologian Takizawa and New Testament scholar Yagi, found that the ontological basis of man as conceived in the Buddhist experience of autonomy has "profound similarity" with the Christian faith in God. Yagi believes that there is no need to insist on the absoluteness of the "person" of Jesus Christ in a dogmatic way, because

---

78. Ninian Smart, "The Logos Doctrine . . . ," *op. cit.*, p. 170.

79. The author derived this categorization from his interaction with numerous authors and with his students at the Asian Theological Seminary.

the essence of Christianity rests on the "principle" of religious existence which is found universally in other religions also.[80]

"No agreement" approach: In contrast some Christians believe that Christianity is incompatible and completely opposite and different in essence from other religions. They tend to see the incongruence at the level of ontological and metaphysical structures of the religious systems.

Among them Lewis believes that there are basically two opposite worldviews: either the monistic Buddhist-Hindu or the Christian worldview.[81] Carlsen finds the Thai Buddhist beliefs in Nirvana (nonexistence), existence as illusion, desire as cardinal sin, reincarnation and the will to live as the root of evil to be totally opposite to Christian beliefs.[82] Athyal and Hesselgrave find no common ground for fruitful dialogue, especially in the Buddhist beliefs in the nonexistence of God and in the unreality of the world and history.[83] Niles declares,

> The existence of God means the existence of an order of life which is eternal—nicca (permanence). It means that there is postulated for the soul—atta—an identity which is guarded by God's sovereignty, and that sorrow—dukkha—is seen to consist, not so much in the transitoriness of things, as in the perverseness of our wills which seeks these things instead of the things which are eternal.[84]

Also Din sees Jesus Christ as the stumbling block for any faith or ideology which absolutely denies the reality of the Transcendent, which cannot accept the possibility of it becoming immanent, which fails to discern the happening of this possibility in human history, which rejects the biblical witness to Jesus Christ, and which rejects the "kenosis" (self-emptying) of Jesus Christ.[85] Both Han and Koyama find the Christian and Buddhist concepts of history and compassion to be totally different on the structural level.[86]

---

80. Yoshinobu Kumazawa, *op. cit.*, p. 196; see also Kenzo Tagawa, "The Yagi-Tazikawa Debate," *The Northeast Asia Journal of Theology* 2 (March 1969), 41-59. Their conclusions are similar to Don Cupitt's, as described in the last section of this paper.

81. Purushotman M. Krishna, "Presenting One Way to the Universalist," *Christianity Today* 16:21 (July 28, 1972), 4.

82. William D. Carlsen, "Thailand's Religious Roots," *Christianity Today* 22:1 (Oct. 7, 1977), 24-25; also Lucy Powell, "A Lizard for a Roommate," *Eternity* 27:2 (Feb. 1976), 24-25.

83. Saphir P. Athyal, "Toward an Asian Christian Theology," in Douglas J. Elwood, *op. cit.*, p. 77, and David Hesselgrave, *op. cit.*, p. 167. The cosmology of Theravada Buddhism has to be challenged; see also Paul A. Eakin, *op. cit.*, pp. 61-62, and Wan Petchsonkram, *Talk in the Shade of the Bo Tree*, trans. and ed. Frances E. Hudgins (Bangkok: Thai Gospel Press, 1975), pp. 54f., 64f.

84. D. T. Niles, *Buddhism and the Claims of Christ* (Richmond: John Knox Press, 1967), p. 27.

85. Khin Maung Din in Douglas J. Elwood, *op. cit.*, pp. 97-98.

86. Tai Dong Han, *op. cit.*, pp. 102-105 and Kosuke Koyama, *op. cit.*, pp.

"Common ground" approach, also called the "fulfilment" approach. Some Christians view other religions as different preparation for the Christian message, as the Old Testament prepared the Jews for the gospel. To Buddhists, they would say:[87]

> Buddhism needs . . . men who, while proud of being Christians, are yet willing for Christ's sake, to be followers of S'akyamuni in all things lawful and honest; men who can say to the Buddhist, "I will walk with you, and together we will go to Him whom you say S'akyamuni himself bore witness."[87]

Drummond believes that Jesus Christ fulfils what is authentically revealed by God in the teaching and spirit of Buddhism.[88] He finds the common grace of God's general revelation manifested in several aspects of Buddhist beliefs. Examples are the ethical quality of the Buddhist way (dharma) and goal (Nirvana), the possibility of man to attain selfhood by participating in dharma (self-less ethical living), the Mahayana faith in the personal and compassionate nature of the Ultimate, the Pure Land school's devotion to Amida as the one gracious divine figure, and the Zen commitment to ethical conversion and sympathetic appreciation of small and great.[89]

A little differently, De Silva has tried to make the Theravadin Buddhist concepts of Nirvana and anatta fit into the Christian framework. He adjusts Buddhist "not-self" to Christian "personhood" by suggesting that anatta is the negation of egocentricity or exclusive individuality but the affirmation of personality or participative individuality; Nirvana is the community of loving persons who live in complete harmony.[90] He has also tried to show that the Christian Triune God is reflected in the three Buddhist signata.[91]

95-99, 154-56, 137-49, and Kazo Kitamori's view also in Kosuke Koyama, *op. cit.*, pp. 123-24. See also C. G. Williams, *op. cit.*, p. 167, which sees the contrast of Buddhist cyclical faith and *metaphysical* uprooting of self against Christian *linear* and *moral* connotations.

87. Arthur Lloyd, *The Creed of Half Japan* (London: Smith, Elder, 1911), p. 385, quoted in Cyril H. Powles, "Foreign Missionaries and Japanese Culture in the Late Nineteenth Century: Four Patterns of Approach," *The Northeast Asia Journal of Theology* 2 (Oct. 1969), 28. See also Herbert Moore, *The Christian Faith in Japan* (London: S.P.G., 1904), p. 42.

88. Richard Drummond, *op. cit.*, p. 203. He cites the message of Kamegai Ryoun, a converted Japanese Buddhist priest who, though not yet satisfied with the lack of real prayer among *Amida* faithfuls, yet rejoices in the life of thanksgiving and practical morality of this people.

89. *Ibid.*, pp. 169, 205.

90. De Silva in Douglas J. Elwood, *op. cit.*, pp. 116-18.

91. Lynn De Silva, "Theological Tensions behind Points in the Kandy Statement: Relevant Areas of Dialogue with Buddhists," *Study Encounter* 3:2 (1967), 80. His presentation is that man's lost condition is due to the denial of his creaturely

"Point of Contact" approach: This has the same presuppositions as the "no agreement" approach but lays emphasis on finding common points, usually on the existential and ethical level, to evangelize or dialogue with Buddhists.

Many find "contact points" in the Buddhist concern for holy living,[92] the desire for intense devotion (bhakti),[93] the desire for release from bondage,[94] the search for worthy teachers,[95] the authority of personal experience,[96] the search for unselfish state of mind,[97] and its method of presenting and solving problems.[98] Some find the Buddhist meditative techniques and its general profile of mystical life quite compatible with Christian mysticism.[99] Smith finds the existential problems of the fear of death, suffering, and afterlife as "entry points" in talking with Buddhists.[100] Still others consider the "middle way" and many other Buddhist ethical teachings[101] as "points of contact" for Christian-Buddhist dialogue.

The author places himself in the last category but allows fellow Christians the freedom to hold to the second and third views. He believes the first approach tends to universalism and syncretism and thus tends to become unfaithful to biblical Christianity.

---

existence, namely: *anicca* (impermanence), *dukkha* (depravity, not suffering for *du* means comtemptible and *kha* means void), and *anatta* (mortality or soullessness). If these three negatives mean anything, their counterpositive realities cannot be derived from the existential situation itself. The Christian solution is: *amicca* is overcome by God, who is Unchanging Reality; *dukkha* is overcome by Christ, in whom is redemptive grace, and *anatta* is overcome by the Spirit, who gives the ontological reality to the individual.

92. Elwood in Emerito Nacpil and Douglas J. Elwood, eds., *The Human and the Holy* (Quezon City: New Day Publishers, 1978), p. 236; and U Kyaw Than, *op. cit.*, p. 22.

93. Elwood in Nacpil and Elwood, *loc. cit.*, and J. Y. Fenton, *op. cit.*, p. 238.

94. Elwood in Nacpil and Elwood, *loc. cit.*

95. *Ibid.*, and Purushotman Krishna in David Hesselgrave, *op. cit.*, p. 169.

96. Elwood in Nacpil and Elwood, *loc. cit.*

97. T. N. Callaway, "Selflessness in Buddhism and Christianity," *Studies in the Christian Religion* 33:4 (1965), 19-21 and P. M. Tin, "Certain Factors in the Buddhist-Christian Encounter," *Southeast Asia Journal of Theology* 3:2 (Oct. 1961), 30.

98. P. M. Tin, *op. cit.*, p. 30.

99. Rev. Francis Seely in Lynn De Silva, "Theological Tensions . . . .," *op. cit.*, pp. 79-80; J. Y. Fenton, *op. cit.*, pp. 239-47; Ninian Smart, "Learning from Other Faiths: Buddhism," *op. cit.*, p. 212; P. M. Tin, *loc. cit.*

100. Alex G. Smith, *op. cit.*, pp. 23-25 suggests how to find release from *karma*.

101. Sundar Singh, *op. cit.*, p. 54 and Kosuke Koyama, *op. cit.*, p. 163. The latter lists: evil desire as the source of evil, admonition to slow down, control of speech, man's lack of true wisdom, impartiality in judgment, and transitoriness of everything.

Range of expressions: different forms or content?   The other challenge of syncretism confronts those who believe that Christianity is the only true faith
for the liberation of man. Since it presupposes the universality of the
possibility of salvation for all, Christianity has to face the problem of
becoming meaningfully and properly understood by different people with
varying worldviews, each in their respective socio-cultural situations.

Except for a few who try to regard traditional Christian formulations
as absolute, most Christians know that Christian expressions of faith are
relative and penultimate symbols which are no substitute for the absolute
revelation of the transcendent personal God in the person and work of
Jesus of Nazareth.[102] Just as Paul used Greek words (as logos, soter,
mysterion, and metamorphosis)[103] in his theologizing, so Christians can
feel free to express their faith in various cultural (religious or secular)
forms. Thus, in dialogue with Buddhists, Christians should discover contemporary Buddhist thought-forms and proper vocabulary in which the
gospel could be presented more intelligibly and relevantly to Buddhists.[104]

But how much freedom are Christians allowed to adapt and accommodate Christianity to other religions and ideologies before it loses its
essence?[105] Many have considered this concern about syncretism valid,
including the liberal theologians.[106] The danger is of distorting the core
of Christian spirituality (if it indeed be the Truth) which would be tanta-
mount to giving out "candy-coated poison."[107] Many warn that even
in the use of Buddhist terminology, one needs much work to define and
explain such terms (with "endless conditional sentences and explanatory

---

102. Din in Douglas J. Elwood, *op. cit.*, pp. 95, 101-102; also Paul D. Clasper,
"Buddhism and Christianity in the Light of God's Revelation in Christ," *Southeast
Asia Journal of Theology* 3:1 (July 1961), 9-16, and Fritz Buri, "My
Encounter . . . ," *op. cit.*, p. 51.

103. Visser 't Hooft quoted in Kosuke Koyama, *op. cit.*, p. 83-84.

104. P. M. Tin, "Study of Buddhism in Burma," *Southeast Asia Journal of
Theology* 1 (Jan. 1960), 62, especially mentions the Christian concepts of eternal
life, meaning of the cross, Jesus as Lord, and salvation.

105. Elwood in Nacpil and Elwood, *op. cit.*, p. 238, comments that the fear
of syncretism has ended up with the "absolutisation of western Christianity";
he also mentions Rev. Kenneth Fernando's (Sri Lanka) suggestion that
"exclusivism" has been the greater danger for Asian Christians.

106. Even M. M. Thomas accepts Kraemer's definition and warning against
syncretism (adopting elements from other religious trends indiscriminately without
being able to adapt them to the original Christian spirit and structure), yet proceeds to a more liberal call for "radical Christo-centricity in the process of
embodying the universal gospel and the church in societies . . ." (Nacpil and
Elwood, *op. cit.*, pp. 334-35). Elwood also warns about the "relativistic interpretation of religious truth and salvation which fails to understand the uniqueness
of Christ and once-for-all-ness of his saving work" (*ibid.*, p. 237).

107. Kosuke Koyama, *op. cit.*, p. 82.

paragraphs'')[108] to avoid misunderstanding. How can this balance of advocating contextualization and avoiding syncretism be kept?

Two theologians have approached Buddhism on the "theology proper" level and concluded that the Christian concept of God can fit into the Buddhist framework. First, Din sees "God" as transcendent over the personal-nonpersonal and being-becoming dualism.[109] Also Lee believes that the God of dogma is less than the God of Christianity, because God may be better known in a "both-and" Yin-Yang framework than an "either-or" classical Greek framework.[110] He suggests that God is primarily change itself (not the unchanging Being of traditional theology) as the process theologians view "the living God" as "the changing God''; as in Buddhist thought, God is changeless because he is the changing one; he is both changing and changeless at the same time.[111]

Are they syncretizing? Or are they following M. M. Thomas's suggestion of developing a "Christ-centered syncretic process''?[112] The author tends to classify them as overextending the proper bounds for creative theologizing for there seems to be some basic change in the content of the Christian message. The universal Christian worldview revealed in the particular Hebrew and Graeco-Roman cultures must not be relativized. The gospel became a stumbling block to the unbelieving Jews, Pharisees, Sadducees, Romans, and other people in biblical times.

This hermeneutical problem has to be polished further through careful research into cultural perspectives, values, and concepts of the Christian Scriptures and those of Buddhists.[113] This will lead to a more fruitful encounter of God's revealed Truth with Buddhists.

TREND OF "BUDDHISTIZING" CHRISTIAN FORMS?[114]

This last section starts with the suggestion of Don Cupitt in his book *Taking Leave of God* that a form of "Christian Buddhism" with Christian content and Buddhist symbols be adapted for modern man. Implicit is the issue of whether the status of Christianity vis-à-vis secularism is absolute or relative. He suggests what the Christian message is for secular man today.

108. *Ibid.*, pp. 81-82; David Hesselgrave, *op. cit.*, p. 168.

109. Khin Maung Din in Douglas J. Elwood, *op. cit.*, pp. 91-93.

110. Jung Young Lee, "The Yin-Yang Way of Thinking," in Douglas J. Elwood, *op. cit.*

111. *Ibid.*, pp. 188-89.

112. See M. M. Thomas, "Christ-centred Syncretism" in *Varieties of Witness,* ed. D. Preman Niles and T. K. Thomas (Singapore: Christian Council of Asia, n.d.), pp. 9-19.

113. P. M. Tin, *op. cit.*, p. 27, gives high praise for the scholarly approach of Adoniram Judson in translating the Scriptures for Buddhist Burma.

114. This section becomes more subjective as the author evaluates this concern from his evangelical Christian perspective, i.e., historical-doctrinal faith in Jesus Christ *as revealed in the canon of Holy Scripture*.

Summary of Cupitt's view

Don Cupitt claims to advocate "Christian Buddhism" which exalts spirituality over theological doctrine and stresses autonomy. It aims to be "a break from our habitual theological realism, a full internalization of all religious doctrines and themes, and a recognition that it is possible autonomously to adopt religious principles and practices as intrinsically valuable."[115] But he is actually advocating a secularized (for humanistic) religion which is basically Buddhist in both form and content, and has changed the meaning and content of the Christian message. Instead of his stated purpose, in secularizing Christian and Buddhist forms, he has filled Christian form with Buddhist content, interpreted secularly.

Cupitt sees that the highly ideological character of Christianity is an oddity. He foresees that the religious person of the future will have Buddhist-in-form and Christian-in-content faith—a piety which does not need a great deal of "mythological buttressing to prop it up" from the prescientific mythologies in the Christian Scriptures.

Like John Robinson, Cupitt denies the existence of any metaphysical God "out there." The metaphysical expressions of faith in God are thus "not essential but only temporary and culturally conditioned."[116]

Who is the man of tomorrow, according to Cupitt? He will be autonomous man who still needs religion for it is a way of transcendence and a path to deliverance; he will celebrate the "triumph of universal, free, and sovereign consciousness, emancipated from nature and lord over nature."[117] He will speak about God and pray to God as the "mythical embodiment" of all concerned in spiritual life, "the religious demand and ideal," the enshriner of values; "He is needed—but as a myth."[118] Thus, to autonomous man, God is a symbol which represents everything that spirituality requires of man and promises to man; God is "Christian spirituality in coded form"[119] which "represents to us what we are to become and shows us the way to become it."[120] Man's goal is union with God (Nirvana) and the way is the love of God (dharma).

> Like Nirvana, God may be thought of as transcendent yet unspecifiable, an ideal focus of aspiration that does not come as far forward into either objectivity or determinacy as to prejudice the quest for disinterestedness. . . . Ordinarily one ought to live etsi deus non daretur (as if God were not given). . . .[121]

Besides the denial of the relevance of the existence of God in a metaphysical framework, Cupitt denies the importance of historical events

115. Don Cupitt, *op. cit.*, p. xii.
116. *Ibid.*, p. 8; cf. John Robinson, *Honest to God* (London: S.C.M., 1964).
117. Don Cupitt, *op. cit.*, p. 156.
118. *Ibid.*, p. 166.
119. *Ibid.*, p. 14.
120. *Ibid.*, p. 9.
121. *Ibid.*, p. 10.

and doctrinal understanding. He considers the resurrection as a "mythological reality" put in the language of prescientific and prephilosophical cultural setting and not as an objective historical fact.[122] Seeing that doctrine has tended to become ideology and thus make religions seem to become closed, mutually exclusive and irreconcilable ideological blocs, he believes that religious belief should be viewed now as "religious allegiance expressed in symbolic language."[123]

Since Cupitt sees that the main interest of religion or spirituality is the transformation of one's self through total freedom of expression, he finds traditional Christian doctrinal emphasis irrelevant for people of modern technological-utilitarian cultures. What matters is one's full autonomy, especially in religion, where the concept of "God" (in metaphysical theism clothed with mythological language) is discarded, and at the same time replaced with a free and sovereign consciousness of man.

Evaluation of Cupitt's view[124]

Cupitt represents a modern theologian concerned with the secular trend of modern society where traditional religion is fast declining in popularity. The modern mindset seems to view only the material world as real, yet to see everything as transient, contingent, and relative. Modern man thus gropes for new forms of religion to express faith according to his scientific, materialistic, and positivist consciousness; man seems to be controlled by environmental circumstances and seems to become a part of the historical process of evolution on earth. Thus a modern theologian seeks to make the Christian faith viable for the worldview of secular man.[125]

What has become of this concern? A multitude of theologies (or better,

122. *Ibid.*, p. 45. Here Cupitt differs from theologians who view God as immanent, humanistic, evolutionary, and nontranscendent. Instead he tries to preserve the absolute transcendence of God. But he rejects the traditional understanding of the biblical witness to the immanence of God in creation, providence, and salvation-history culminating in the incarnation, life, death, and resurrection of Jesus of Nazareth.

123. *Ibid.*, p. 141, cf. pp. 164-66.

124. The author recognizes that this paper runs the risk of disappointing both conservatives who are satisfied with repetition of past doctrinal systems and theological slogans, and radicals who want to discard traditional and biblical norms to formulate a system according to their own beliefs.

125. Such attempts seem to be uncalled for—for modern peoples do not become irreligious, but instead falter in committing themselves to false religions and ideologies. Social scientists are not predicting the end of religion, but are seeing life, interest, and resurgence of religious life and involvement, especially in the rise of cults and the occult. The secularization process will not lead to full secularism or total secularity. See Peter Berger, *Rumour of Angels* (New York: Doubleday, 1969).

antitheologies)[126] have "demythologized" the premises and concepts of supernatural theism. They view any form of faith as tentative with no claim to finality and uniqueness, because each is supposed to be historically-bound and culturally-conditioned with no transcultural validity.[127] They presuppose that there is no objectively given revelation in history and thus, there can only be subjectively affirmed spirituality in each person's mind; "the relative is the real" and thus no one religion can claim absolute truth.

Besides Cupitt, other theologians have found such belief and its deep relevance for modern man in Buddhist thinking. They see that Buddhist concepts can help Christians devise a better religious system for modern man because they are essentially the same.[128]

Using a different perspective from Cupitt, Cobb, Yagi, and Buri suggest that though both religions are essentially different, they can coexist and help each other become useful for the modern secular world. Cobb in his later writings believes that modern man can seek to understand intellectually the structure of existence advocated (and the important human values attained) by one and partly realized by the other. In fact, Cobb believes that Buddhism has understood the nature of ultimate reality and causality "more correctly and profoundly" than any western philosopher (and theologian?!).[129]

Buri looks at the concept of God as "a symbol of true becoming-human" and the way of true humanity.[130] He believes that "all being, inclusive of man—finally neither in its essence nor in its origin—may be objectified but dissolves into an ungraspable nothing for our unavoidable objectifying thinking."[131] This is not an abandonment of consciousness and thought, but "the realization of being a person who understands oneself as being unconditionally responsible for one's behaviour" (without objectifying), in the "brotherhood of those who have been marked by suffering."[132] This is derived from an ethic of reverence for life. But Buri admits that there are various problems in defining the philosophical basis of this kind of ethics.[133]

126. By antitheology is meant "theologies" which seek to express the absence or denial of faith in supernaturally-revealed truths.

127. Surprisingly these modern theologians seem to believe that their own respective "theologies" are relevant and meaningful transculturally.

128. Among them are the process theologians led by A. Whitehead, the "Death of God" theologians led by T. Altizer, and many critical Bible scholars.

129. John B. Cobb, Jr. and Seiichi Yagi, op. cit., p. 33 and John B. Cobb, Jr., "Buddhism and Christianity" as complementary, op. cit., p. 25.

130. Fritz Buri, "The Fate of the Concept of God . . . ," op. cit., p. 55.

131. Ibid., pp. 55-56.

132. Ibid., p. 56 and Fritz Buri, "My Encounter with Buddhist Thought . . . ," op. cit., p. 53.

133. Fritz Buri, "My Encounter with Buddhist Thought . . . ," op. cit., p. 53.

Is such anthropocentric reinterpretation of both Christianity and Buddhism true to both religious systems? Is this demythologization or secularization of each religious faith valid? Is this the way to present the Christian gospel viably and meaningfully to secular man?

The author disagrees with the view of Cupitt, Cobb, and Buri in their answer to the spiritual dilemma of modern man. They have uncritically accepted the rules laid down by antisupernatural, antitheistic, humanistic, and relativistic thinking of our day. In the process, they have constructed a modern syncretistic secularized religion which has diluted and distorted the Christian message for secularists (including many educated Buddhists today).

Apart from the problem of biblical hermeneutics for proper contextualization,[134] is the main issue to find the absolute transcultural message for all peoples, including secularists? Is there absolute perfect truth? For secular man, the Christian can and should answer, "of course." Though cognizant of the fact that no single conceptual system or set of religious symbols is sufficient to convey the Truth, Christians can and should affirm the validity and relevance of revelation-based Christianity for authoritative, intelligent, and meaningful theologizing, mission, and dialogue with secularists (Buddhist, Christian, or otherwise) today.

If the doctrinal beliefs and historical facts on which Christianity is based are false, what meaning can the Christian message have for today (or the past or the future)? If the personal Creator exists, all lack or denial of true worship of him is subhuman. The secularist closed-word metaphysic does not allow the supernatural intervention of God in history. Is this naturalism not another myth, a modern myth? If the past religious faiths have been relativized, should not the modern secular ideologies be also demythologized? Even modern man is still blind in some ways to some aspects of existential reality.

This paper suggests that the only way to solve the secularist problem of absolute relativity is supernatural norm and intervention; the Absolute has entered history and thus history is not meaningless existence. The Buddhistic-secularist nonhistorical and nondoctrinal structure may have to be remodeled to fit the biblical historical-doctrinal worldview rather than the reverse.

Christians cannot be satisfied with mere repetition of past insights because the understanding of scriptural revelation is not yet exhausted (nor will ever be), and the understood revelation has to be interpreted clearly, coherently, and relevantly to various peoples in different cultures and generations. The common faith in the recorded acts of God in history may be expressed in a rich diversity of languages and perspectives, not in a uniformity of forms and symbols.

Analogies and parallels from the existential human experience can be used to confront modern man with the life and claims of the historical

134. See the section on syncretism, pp. 287f.

Jesus. But clearly, the gospel (which presupposes the existence of a sovereign and wise personal God) cannot be changed to fit some modern form (Buddhistic or secularist or whatever) of consciousness. Let God be God[135]—as revealed in the person and work of the Jesus of Nazareth.

Select Bibliography

Gerald H. Anderson, ed. *Asian Voices in Christian Theology.* Maryknoll: Orbis Books, 1976.

David Bentley-Taylor and Clark Offner. "Buddhism," in Norman Anderson, ed. *The World's Religions.* 4th ed. London: Inter-Varsity Press, 1975.

Don Cupitt. *Taking Leave of God.* New York: Crossroad, 1981.

Lynn De Silva. *The Problem of the Self in Buddhism and Christianity.* Colombo: The Study Centre for Religion and Society, 1975.

——————. *Reincarnation in Buddhist and Christian Thought.* Colombo: The Study Centre for Religion and Society, 1968.

Richard Henry Drummond. *Gautama the Buddha.* Grand Rapids: Eerdmans, 1974.

Paul A. Eakin. *Buddhism and the Christian Approach to Buddhists in Thailand.* Bangkok: R. Hongladaromp, Printer and Publisher, 1956.

Albert J. Edmunds. *Buddhists and Christian Gospels.* Vol. 2. Philadelphia: Invers and Sons, 1909.

Douglas J. Elwood, ed. *What Asian Christians are Thinking.* Quezon City: New Day Publishers, 1976.

David Hesselgrave. *Communicating Christ Cross-Culturally.* Grand Rapids: Zondervan, 1978.

Bhikku Buddhadasa Indapanno. *Christianity and Buddhism.* Bangkok: Sinclaire Thompson Memorial Lectures, 5th ser., 1967.

Kazo Kitamori. *Theology of the Pain of God.* Richmond: John Knox Press, 1965; Tokyo, 1946.

Kosuke Koyama. *Waterbuffalo Theology.* Maryknoll: Orbis Books, 1974.

Kenneth Scott Latourette. *Introducing Buddhism.* New York: Friendship Press, 1956.

Emerito Nacpil and Douglas J. Elwood, eds. *The Human and the Holy.* Quezon City: New Day Publishers, 1978.

D. T. Niles. *Buddhism and the Claims of Christ.* Richmond: John Knox Press, 1967; Colombo as *Eternal Life Now,* 1946.

Wan Petchsonkram, *Talk in the Shade of the Bo Tree*, trans. and ed. Frances E. Hudgins. Bangkok: Thai Gospel Press, 1975.

Lily Quintos. *The Moral System of Buddhism according to the Milainda Panha with a Christian-Theological Reflection.* Quezon City: Ateneo de Manila Press, 1977.

Sundar Singh. *The Search After Reality.* Madras: Christian Literature Society, 1968.

Alex G. Smith. *The Gospel Facing Buddhist Cultures.* Taichung: Asian Theological Association, n.d.

Wilfred Cantwell Smith. *The Faith of Other Men.* New York: Harper and Row, 1963.

Katzume Takizawa. *Buddhism and Christianity.* Tokyo: Hozokan, 1964.

135. Cupitt and Buddhist thinkers could also say this but they would mean a "God" who is totally transcendent and mysterious; whereas by using the following qualifying phrase, this paper refers to a revealing God who is also immanent and knowable.

11. God and Christ in the Context of Buddhism

PRACHA THAIWATCHARAMAS *(Thailand)*

Synopsis

Many Christians in Thailand have failed to address Buddhists in a coherent way because they are ignorant of Buddhist beliefs. The paper surveys the ideas of God and of the Messiah in Buddhist cosmology. It draws on an ancient document promising the coming of a Christlike Messiah, and concludes that an important point of contact already exists in Thai Buddhism for the proclamation of the gospel.

INTRODUCTION

A big gap separates us Christians from the people to whom we preach the gospel. We Christians, who believe in the inspired word of God and are brought up in biblical thoughts, ideas, phrases, and words, must realize that the Buddhist lives in an entirely different world. Therefore, when we share the gospel of our Lord Jesus Christ with them, we must take two important factors into consideration.

First, we must be faithful witnesses to Jesus Christ (2 Cor. 4:5). We must not preach ourselves, our churches, our cultures, our Christian way of living, nor our own theology. For we are appointed to preach Christ Jesus as our Lord and Saviour.

Secondly, our ministry is to reconcile men to God through Jesus Christ (cf. 2 Cor. 5:18ff.). We are ambassadors for Christ to bring peace with God to all men, not to provoke their disbelief in God. I am concerned about this matter because of an incident involving some Roman Catholic priests in Thailand in 1958. They tried to prove that Catholicism was better than Buddhism and also than Protestantism. They published a book comparing doctrinal differences between the two religions in a very unintelligible way. The Buddhists regarded this as hostility to their religion. The Catholic publishing house was closed down. This is not a diplomatic way.

I agree with Lakshman Peiris who spoke on "Communicating the Gospel and Evangelising Buddhists" at the 8th Thailand Church Growth seminar in 1979, that "if we try to show that Christianity is better, they will try to prove that Buddhism is better." While we know that the truth revealed by God is far better than men's wisdom, we should intelligently communicate with them. We must help them realize that the gospel we are sharing with them is the power of God for salvation to every one who believes (cf. Rom. 1:16).

How can we enable the Buddhist to understand the truth as we understand it? We must build bridges of understanding in order to appreciate the common truths which God has revealed in the hearts of men outside Christianity. For it is possible for man to see God's witness in nature, in human reason, or what Christians call general revelation (cf. Rom. 1:19f.). After reaching them with common truths, we shall share with them further truth which they do not know nor understand.

With this understanding we shall look into two kinds of belief confessed by Buddhism, particularly the concept of God and the Messiah. The Buddhism referred to here is the Hinayana Buddhism which is the national religion of Thailand, Sri Lanka, and Burma.

One difference between Buddhism and Christianity is that Buddhists do not regard Buddhism as a revealed religion but as a teaching. Thus, the scripture is regarded as a teaching not as a revelation from God.

Like Jesus, Buddha never wrote any scripture. The Buddhist scripture was transmitted by oral tradition. The task was done by schools of memorizers, who were monks. They learned portions of the discourses by heart from their teachers. In turn they transmitted the memorized text to their students.[1] It took several years after the death of the Buddha to complete the canon.

The two schools of Buddhism differed in their view concerning the canon of the scripture. The Hinayana school held that

> works composed a substantial time after 480 B.C. and not recited at the first council immediately after the Buddha's death could not be authentic, could not be Buddha's own words, and could be no more than mere poetry and fairy tale.[2]

But the Mahayana School regarded the later works as authentic words of the Buddha as well. Nevertheless, there are many additional works in the Pali canon, whose composers are mainly unknown. Few names and dates were indicated. Thus, it is not possible to apply historical criticism to the canon. This does not bother the Buddhists for dhamma itself is the truth which transcended history. They revere their scripture and we should learn to appreciate some truths in it.

IS BUDDHISM ATHEISTIC?

Scholars differ in their views on this matter but what is taught by the Buddha can be catagorized into three opinions.

First, Buddhism is agnostic about the beginning. In this sense some

1. Bhikkhu Khantipalo, *Buddhism Explained* (Bangkok: Mahamakut Raja-vidyalaya Press, 1973), p. 195.
2. *Ibid.*, p. 29.

scholars incline to say that Buddhism is atheistic. But Buddha himself
clearly admitted that

> No beginning can be known to beings, blinded by unknowing and
> driven on by craving who are hurrying through the round of birth-
> and-death.[3]

That is to say that in the present state as a finite being, man can never
know God. Even if there be any God, for the Buddhist it is irrelevant
to the present life. Perhaps what prevents Buddha saying anything about
God is that to assume that there is such a reality, which gives a sense
of security, could be an obstacle for one to realize and understand the
fact of nonegoity or self-emptiness.[4]

Buddha had in mind concern to show people the way beyond all
dukkha. He is more concerned about morality than metaphysics.

But Buddhism is theistic in the sense that first it admitted the idea
of creators in the Hindu's sense and claimed the superiority of the Buddha
over Brahma whom they represent

> as seized by pride when he thought to himself: "I am Brahma, I am
> the great Brahma, the King of the Gods; I am uncreated, I have created
> the world, I am the sovereign of the world, I can create, alter and
> give birth; I am the Father of all things."[5]

These gods were visited by the Buddha and he taught them his dhamma.

These gods, literally the shining ones, are those beings which are more
mighty and live longer than man. They enjoy various states of existence
which accord with the different levels of mental development, which are
also open to cultivation by human beings. Among them are gods in the
formless stage and those subtle form gods. Through meditation man also
may reach the levels of the formless attainments.

The gods of the formless realms abide in their respective stages of infinite space, infinite consciousness, nothingness, and neither-perception.
How long they would live in this stage is impossible for man to conceive.
But when the merit which they gained in their earthly lives is exhausted,
they can no longer abide in this stage. They fall to rebirth in spiritual
realms, i.e., the subtle form gods.[6]

Gods in the realms of form have fine-material bodies and enjoy spiritual
pleasures. They have also a kind of human emotion but no sexual differences. Their lifetime is less than the formless gods but is still better
than the earthly standard. Among them some gods are proud of their
status and claim to be greater than others, the unvanquished, controller,

3. *Ibid.*, p. 61.
4. *Ibid.*, p. 51.
5. Edward Conze, *Buddhism: Its Essence and Development* (Oxford: Bruno
Cassirer, 1951), p. 39.
6. Khantipalo, *op. cit.*, p. 49.

lord, creator, father of all things. But far from being eternal both the
formless and the form gods are merely a myth. This is an element of
Hindu cosmology in Buddhism. These gods are Hindu deities or mere
men who were reborn, vanishing, and reborn in another realm of existence
according to Buddhist cosmology. As Christians we cannot believe it to
be true. Even Buddha himself through his wisdom regarded such dieties
as deluded ones.[7]

Secondly, Buddhism teaches the idea of an impersonal god in the sense
of an ultimate reality unknown to finite man. Any attempt to describe
it leads to nothing and is unprofitable. Buddha maintained silence concerning the matter. He once said

> If there is a causeless cause of all causes, an ultimate reality, it must
> clearly be infinite, unlimited, unconditioned and without attributes.[8]

This idea of God can be seen in the idea of dhamma and Nirvana.

Finally, Buddhism is atheistic in the sense that it rejects the idea of
an omniscient, omnipotent personal creator God. The Buddhist finds it
very difficult to comprehend the concept of a personal God, because if
God is conceived as personal then he must be change, for change is the
essence of "personality." Because of the conventional meaning of the
word "personal" it is difficult to believe in a personal God. The Buddhist cannot understand a God to whom is ascribed some sort of body,
a God who loves, who becomes angry, who wants this or that, and who
can do both good and bad. They assert that the only way to understand
God is to understand him in terms of religious language, as one who does
not have body, does not occupy any place, does not love, does not get
angry, is above all desire, and does neither right nor wrong. Thus, the
Buddhist believes in the impersonal God.[9]

The main arguments against the existence of God are the problems
of human free will and the existence of evil. If God is omnipotent and
omniscient he could not have created such a suffering world for man.
Once Buddha said that

> He who has eyes can see the sickening sight; why does not Brahma
> set his creatures right? If his wide power no limit can restrain, why
> is his hand so rarely spread to bless? Why are his creatures all con-
> demned to pain? Why does he not to all give happiness? Why do fraud,
> lies and ignorance prevail? Why triumphs falsehood truth and justice
> fail? I count you Brahma one the unjust among, who made a world
> in which to shelter wrong. (Bhuridatta Jataka No. 453)[10]

7. *Ibid.*, p. 50.
8. Christmas Humphreys, *Buddhism* (London: Penguin Books, 1978), p. 79.
9. Winston L. King, *Buddhism and Christianity: Some Bridges of Understanding*
(Philadelphia: Westminster Press, 1946), p. 48.
10. Khantipalo, *op. cit.*, p. 64.

Some scholars argue that Buddhism is atheistic because Buddha taught that man is no-self (anatta) which implies that living beings have no eternal souls, that is, no cosmic Self.[11] They assert that the Buddha taught that

> The body, monks, is soulless. If the body, monks, were the soul, this body would not be subject to sickness, and it would be possible in the case of the body to say, "Let my body be thus, let my body not be thus. . . ."[12]

But on another occasion Buddha was asked by the wandering monk Vacchagotta whether there is ego (atta) or not. He did not give any answer. But when the monk left he explained to his close disciple Ananda that

> If I, Ananda, when the wandering monk Vacchagotta asked me: "Is there the ego?" had answered: "the ego is," then that, Ananda, would have confirmed the doctrine of the Samanas and Brahmanas who believe in permanence. If I, Ananda, when the wandering monk Vacchagotta asked me: "Is there not the ego?" had answered: "the ego is not," then that, Ananda, would have confirmed the doctrine of the Samanas and Brahmanas, who believe in annihilation. If I, Ananda, when the wandering monk Vacchagotta asked me: "Is there the ego?" had answered: "the ego is," would that have served my end, Ananda, by producing in him the knowledge? All existences (dhamma) are non-ego? . . . But if I, Ananda, when the wandering monk Vacchagotta asked me "Is there not the ego" had answered: "the ego is not," then that, Ananda, would only have caused the wandering monk Vacchagotta to be thrown from one bewilderment into another: "My ego, did it not exist before? but now it exists no longer!"[13]

Oldenberg asserts that according to Buddha's sayings, he teaches nothing concerning whether the ego is, or whether the perfected saint lives after death or not.[14] In other words he knew nothing about the matter. If so, then Buddhism is agnostic about God rather than atheistic.

We may conclude that Buddhism is not an atheistic religion. It is a theistic religion with the idea of impersonal deity. Buddhists may not see it as we do but the following doctrines show some sign of Godlike or God function in their ideas.

11. Paul Edwards, ed., *The Encyclopaedia of Philosophy* (New York: Macmillan, 1972), vol. 1-2, p. 417.
12. S. Radhakrishnan and C. A. Moore, *A Source Book in Indian Philosophy* (New Jersey: Princeton University Press, 1957), p. 280.
13. Hermann Oldenberg, *Buddha: his Life, his Doctrine, his Order*, trans. William Hoey (London: Williams and Norgate, 1882), pp. 272f.
14. *Ibid.*, p. 274.

THE IDEAS OF GOD IN BUDDHISM

The orderly universe of dharma

Dharma is a word that Buddhism inherited from India. It comes from a root meaning the "foundation" or "basic constitution" of whatever is spoken of. In the course of centuries it has acquired both social and cosmic meanings. It is used narrowly simply as the teaching of the Buddha and also reaches out to include the cosmic order. The contemporary Buddhist usage of dharma may be illustrated in this way:

> All the teachings of the Buddha can be summed up in one word: dhamma (the Pali form of dharma). . . . It means truth, that which really is. It also means law, the law which exists in a man's own heart and mind. It is the principle of righteousness. . . . Dhamma, this law of righteousness, exists not only in a man's heart and mind; it exists in the universe also. All the universe is an embodiment and revelation of dhamma.
>
> When the moon rises and sets, the rains come, the crops grow, the seasons change, it is because of dhamma, for dhamma is the law residing in the universe which makes matter act in the ways revealed by the studies of modern science in physics, chemistry, zoology, botany and astronomy. Dhamma is the true nature of every existing thing, animate and inanimate.[15]

From this definition, we could see a Godlike function in the dhamma, that is God as the law of nature. The Venerable Bhikkhu Buddhadasa Indapanno, in his lecture on Christianity and Buddhism at the Payap College, Chiengmai, Thailand, asserted that this dhamma appeared before all things and thus stands in the position of God. Even Buddha himself regarded the law of nature as the fact without any question. He realized that the only absolute within this changing world is the controlling law of the universe, that of causality. He once confessed that

> where there is no being, but only becoming, it is not a substance, but only a law, which can be recognized as the first and the last.[16]

Bhikkhu Indapanno also sees dhamma as the nature of things which can be compared with the Christian idea of the world with its living creatures. It is something created by God. It is the result of the will of God. He says that we must revere, honour, and pay attention to realize the truth of nature which is to attain God himself. According to him natural phenomena manifest the will of God and in fact constitute the very God.

15. Quoted by W. King, p. 39, from Venerable U Thittila, "The Fundamental Principles of Theravāda Buddhism," in *The Path of the Buddha*, Kenneth W. Morgan, ed. (The Ronald Press Company, 1956), p. 67.

16. Oldenberg, *op. cit.*, p. 252.

He also sees dhamma as duty performed according to the law of nature. This is the will of God that has required man to practice and perform various duties. He says that if God does not have the duty, or is not himself the natural duty, how can he help, love, or punish? Man is to practice and abide in this duty as abiding in the will of God because it is true supplication to God.

Lastly, he presented dhamma as the fruits of practice or of realization. He compares this aspect of dhamma to what Christians call thanksgiving for the grace of God which refers to the highest thing that man can receive as reward from God.

From these elements in dhamma he comes to the conclusion that God in Buddhism is

> neither a person, nor spirit, nor body alone, nor is it both mind and body together! But it is nature which is impersonal, devoid of any self, it has no attributes, has no form or size. It is not under the power of the time and space. It is impossible to say whether it is one or many, for it is beyond the concept of counting or measuring—yet it really exists and it is the fusion or unification of all the countless different things with their different meanings, powers and functions.[17]

In this sense Buddhism presented the idea of an impersonal God which is hidden behind all things.

Avijja: the Creator God

According to Buddhist teaching God is avijja which is the very essence of ignorance itself. Avijja abides in the hearts of every unenlightened person. It does not know the consequences of its own action when developing itself to the point of poisoning and endangering the universe and bringing to itself destruction and dukkha as we see it at present.[18] And since suffering or dukkha is undesirable, this avijja is to be abolished. Buddhism teaches that this God should be conquered and destroyed since it is the cause of suffering and impermanence. Men should try their best to overcome and oppose it until they are free from such ignorance. Therefore, it is impossible for a Buddhist to believe in such a God, worship him, or become his servant.

Karma: the moral order within the universe

Karma is the controller which abides in every being. It witnesses all that humans do. It punishes and rewards them according to their own karma.[19] The law of karma or the law of cause and effect has nothing to

17. The Venerable Bhikkhu Buddhadasa Indapanno, *Christianity and Buddhism*, Sinclaire Thompson Memorial Lecture (Bangkok: Karn Pim Pranakorn Partnership, B. E. 2511, 1968), p. 74.

18. Wan Petchsonkram, *Talk in the Shade of the Bo Tree,* trans. Frances E. Hudgins (Bangkok: Thai Gospel Press, 1975), p. 70.

19. Indapanno, *op. cit.,* p. 71.

do with God. It is solely man himself who is the cause and effect of his own deed as is said in Dhammapada (v. 165):

> By oneself evil is done: by oneself one suffers. By oneself evil is left undone; by oneself one is purified.
>
> Not in the sky, not in the midst of the sea, nor anywhere else on earth is there a spot where a man may be freed from (the consequences of) an evil deed (v. 127).[20]

Thus, man is his own creator and moulder. Karma is a dynamic quality in man which controls and cultivates and which can make him just what he will to be.

> Karma is not only cause and effect in time; rather it is the law which governs the interrelation and solidarity of the universe in all its parts, and hence, in a way, the karma of one such unit is the karma of all. It is the interdependence of Humanity which is the cause of what is called Distributive Karma, and it is this law which affords the solution to the great question of effective suffering and relief. No man can rise superior to his individual failings without lifting, be it ever so little, the whole body of which he is an integral part. In the same way no one can sin, nor suffer the effects of sin, alone.[21]

That is to say all men are under the law of Karma. Even the creatures themselves are not excluded.

Nirvana: supreme goal and heaven

Buddhists would admit that the task of explaining Nirvana is completely hopeless, not only to Christians but also to Buddhists. The reason they give is that the essence of Nirvana is beyond all description or explanation of any sort. However, they are not consistent. For Nirvana is very often described in the Buddhist scriptures and tradition as deathless; the ambrosial; peace; calmness and coolness; release; bliss, the going out of greed, hatred, and delusion; a haven and an unborn, uncompounded (and therefore eternal) essence.[22] It has neither beginning nor ending; nor is Nirvana in any sense spatial; it is not here, there, or yonder. Perhaps we could call it absolutely infinite Infinitude with absolutely no limitations. Again, to Buddhists the word infinite is not an appropriate word to explain. Winston King suggests that

> All that we can say is that Nirvana is utterly different from anything we know about, or perceive in ordinary experience.[23]

20. Humphreys, *op. cit.*, p. 101.
21. Humphreys, *op. cit.*, p. 103.
22. Winston King, *op. cit.*, p. 45.
23. *Ibid.*, p. 46.

Nirvana is impersonal. This implies no change for change is the essence of "personality." Therefore, Nirvana is also conceived as Absolute Permanence as well as Absolute Unchangeability.[24]

Nirvana is utterly desirable, according to Buddhists. For Buddhists see in man suffering (dukkha), anicca or impermanence, and annatta or absence of eternal self. Buddha himself sees that birth-age-sickness-and-death is suffering. Living is also suffering. For it is not simply an existence but a process of becoming something else and that is impermanence, a change. Since man himself consists of no eternal soul, living is also impermanence. Seeing the life-circle is of rebirth, vanishing, and rebirth time and again, Nirvana is most desirable for Nirvana is no change and no rebirth.

Through the spiritual discipline of meditation, both monks and ordinarily devout persons may experience momentarily a Nirvana-like experience of peace and detachment which is the core of the Buddhist conviction of the absolute reality of ultimate Nirvana.

The complex of God-function in Buddhism

The dharma-karma combination of forces governing the world in which we live has many attributes of the Christian God. In Buddhism dharma-karma keeps the order in the universe whereas in Christianity the order is controlled by the personal God, by his changeless decree. Dharma-karma is almost equal to what the Christian calls the sovereign God, in its governing of the universe. Dharma is functioning as if it is God who is behind all natural phenomena by which God is revealed. Dharma in the sense of the law of righteousness and karma as the moral controller seem to remind us of the cosmic judge who will judge men according to their deeds at the end-time.

This God-function, however, is a kind of loose-jointed deity complex rather than any entity that can be called God in the Christian sense.[25] And the two are sometimes in conflict with one another. For example, dharma is the impersonal, found in the natural order. But karma is an absolutely just and impartial moral order. Sometimes the natural order brings calamity, disease, death, pain, and the like upon seemingly undeserving individuals. Yet Buddhist faith makes them one by insisting that even the natural order serves ethical ends.[26]

Can we equate Nirvana with the Kingdom of God with the eternal peace and happiness where we will live with God forever without rebirth and change? In another sense, Nirvana is like God who cannot be described or compared with anything on earth (Is. 40:18). Yet the difference is that Buddhists have to find and make their own way to Nirvana, while God has invited us into his presence with love and care. Let

24. *Ibid.*, p. 48.
25. *Ibid.*, p. 58.
26. *Ibid.*, p. 59.

those who have eyes and ears hear and see the call of God in their heart so that they may decide sincerely with God whether they believe him or not.

Although Buddhism (Hinayana) does not have any idea of the only personal Creator God as we have in Christianity, we cannot ignore some of the spiritual truth which Buddha taught. In reality man knows by his own experience that he cannot have relationship with such impersonal reality but needs to have communion with the personal God.

The proof of this is shown in the later development of the Mahayana school which was formed about A.D. 300 and developed the personal God in the doctrine of the Trikaya, the three bodies of Buddha.[27] This matter lies beyond the scope of the present study.

The Buddhist Messiah

At the scene of his death, Buddha informed his closest disciple that

> I am not the first Buddha who came upon earth, nor shall I be the last. In due time another Buddha will arise in the world, a holy one, a supremely enlightened one, endowed with wisdom in conduct, auspicious, knowing the universe, an incomparable leader of men, a master of angels and mortals. He will proclaim a religious life, wholly perfect and pure; such as I now proclaim. . . . He will be known as Metteyya, which means "he whose name is kindness."[28]

According to a dictionary of Buddhism in Chinese-Sanskrit-English-and-Thai, Metteyya (Maitreya) is described as friendly and benevolent; he is the expected Buddhist Messiah, the Buddha-to-come, the Bodhisattva who will be the next holder of the supreme office of Buddha. In the Mahayana school he ranks as the highest of Bodhisattvas and is most popular in Buddhist art.[29] This Metteyya lives in the Tusita heaven, where he is enjoying unalloyed happiness. One day the conditions in the world of human beings were reported to him and seeing the lawless of mankind, he has to take a human form in order to deliver them. His mission is to reveal the road to the pearly city, the Land of Happiness, Nirvana. He said that

> I shall lift human beings out of the mire of gross ignorance and error, and enable them to cross over from this troubled world to the realm of happiness on the farther shore. Those who are entangled in the meshes of sinful passions, or who still drink the bitter waters of unrighteous desire, or have lost their way in the endless maze of this troubled series of existences; to them shall I preach, revealing to them

27. Conze, *op. cit.*, p. 71.
28. Paul Carus, *The Gospel of Buddha* (New Delhi: National Book Trust, India, 1975), p. 196.
29. *A Dictionary of Buddhism: Chinese-Sanskrit-English-Thai* (Bangkok, 1976), p. 511.

the road to the pearly city, that is the Land of Happiness, Nirvana. Even to those in torment in the four hells, shall I reveal the way to Heaven. I shall sever the cords which now bind men, who are still in this world of trouble and are bound by ignorance and error, having been caught in the snare of evil passions. I shall set them free to go to the Pearly City of Happiness, the Great Nirvana. I shall open with the key of true doctrine. With eye medicine shall I cleanse the eyes, that is the understanding of those whose vision is defective having become blurred by evil desires, or by anger, or hatred, or ignorance. With the medicine, religious instruction, shall I restore them to perfect vision. With the medicine, wisdom, shall I cure the diseases that oppress men, that is old age and death. To those who have lost their way in the wilderness because of the darkness I shall give you light. Those without a refuge I shall deliver from the torments of the four places of future punishment.[30]

Concerning the time of his coming, he said that

I shall take into consideration: (1) The time (2) The nation (3) The tribe (4) The mother (5) The continent.[31]

The document does not explain this matter further, but says that it will be preceded by a period of great wickedness accompanied by a gradual decrease in the length of human life until old age will come at ten years and the natural marriage time will be at five years. During this period, family relationships and natural marriage will be disregarded. Human life will become as cheap as animal's because they will kill each other as they do wild beasts.

How can we recognize who is the Metteyya? To answer this question I refer to a precious document which I received from my father. This unpublished document was a copy of Buddhist scriptures placed at Prasing Temple at Chiengmai, Thailand. In one section of this document which is part of Buddha's prophecy, a certain old brahma asked the Buddha about how to be saved from sin. The Buddha answered that regardless of how many laws you have kept, or even if you pray five times a day, you shall not be saved. Even though you burn yourself as a sacrifice you also cannot be saved. Buddha continues saying that sin is too great to be washed away; even though I become a hermit for more than eight A-song-kai or am reborn for another ten times, I also shall not be saved. The brahma asks what Metteyya's character is. The Buddha answers that his hands and feet are round, his side has a wound which was pierced and his forehead is full with the scars of wounds. He is the golden ship

30. Howard Campbell, trans., "Ariya Metteyya, the Buddhist Messiah," *The Siam Outlook* 6:13 (April 1930), 407.

31. *Ibid.*, p. 405.

to carry you to heaven where you will find Tri-Pra, the Crystal Triune god. Thus, give up following the old way. A spirit from heaven will come and dwell in your heart by which you will overcome your enemies from both four and eight directions.[32]

When I read this document I was so excited for who else can I think of as the Metteyya described by Buddha in this document, if not the crucified Lord Jesus Christ. Can the Crystal Triune God we will meet in heaven, be the trinitarian God and the Spirit from heaven who will dwell in the hearts of men? Can he be the Holy Spirit in the Buddhist concept? These questions have come into my mind and fearing that this document was influenced by Christians in Thailand, I went to the temple in Chiengmai. I got the answer from an assistant professor at Chiengmai University that this Buddha's prophecy was written in the local language of the Old Kingdom located at the present Chiengmai. It was written before the present Thailand was established. Therefore, it is impossible that the writer of this document was influenced by Christianity. This was only his estimation because there is no official data concerning the matter. It, however, gives us some idea of the date of the document.

We shall then present Jesus as Christ or the Messiah, especially his messianic work on the cross. For his death on the cross is not a mere death but it is the fulfilment of his mission. As he claimed in Mark, "The Son of Man also came not to be served but to serve, and to give his life as a ransom for many" (10:45). His death is meant for the forgiveness of sins (Mt. 26:28), which is the highest manifestation of his entire life of service to God and to man. His death is a deliberate act of laying down his life. This is the commandment from his Father (Jn. 10:18). Otherwise no one can take his life from him. We owed the debt of sin which we could not pay. But Christ paid the debt for us with his own life as the atonement offering so that we may live eternally.

Jesus is the Metteyya for the Buddhist as well as for the world. Through him the gate of heaven is reopened. By his death the spiritual struggle with the powers of evil is ended. We have the victory over Satan (Jn. 12:13; 16:11).

Jesus, the Metteyya, is the Holy One (Lk. 1:35). He is called Holy Jesus (Acts 4:27; see also Rev. 3:7), who is the eternal wisdom (Jn. 1:1), who knows the universe as its maker (Heb. 1:2), who is also the master of angels and mortals (Heb. 1:6ff.). Thus, Christ Jesus is also the fulfilment of the one whom Buddha asked his followers to wait for. He is the one for whom the world is waiting. He came almost two thousand years ago but Buddhists have not yet known about his coming. We must share this good tidings with gladness. We must not make the simplicity of the gospel complicated. We must share with them so that the Christ may be known.

32. Unpublished document in the author's possession.

SELECT BIBLIOGRAPHY

Howard Campbell, trans. "Ariya Mettaya, the Buddhist Messiah," *The Siam Outlook* 6:13 (April 1930).

Paul Carus. *The Gospel of Buddha*. New Delhi: National Book Trust, 1975.

Edward Conze. *Buddhism: Its Essence and Development*. Oxford: Bruno Cassirer, 1951.

Paul Edwards, ed. *The Encyclopaedia of Philosophy*. New York: Macmillan, 1972, vol. 1-2.

Christmas Humphreys. *Buddhism*. London: Penguin Books, 1978.

Buddhadasa Indapanno. *Christianity and Buddhism*. Bangkok: Karn Pim Pranakorn Partnership, 1968.

Bhikku Khantipalo. *Buddhism Explained*. Bangkok: Mahamakut Rajavidyalaya Press, 1973.

Winston King. *Buddhism and Christianity: Some Bridges of Understanding*. Philadelphia: Westminster Press, 1946.

Hermann Oldenberg. *Buddha: his Life, his Doctrine, his Order,* trans. William Hoey. London: Williams and Norgate, 1882.

Wan Petchsonkram. *Talk in the Shade of the Bo Tree,* trans. Frances E. Hudgins. Bangkok: Thai Gospel Press, 1975.

S. Radhakrishnan and C. A. Moore. *A Source Book in Indian Philosophy*. New Jersey: Princeton University Press, 1957.

12. Who do you say that I am?
A North American Minority Answer to the Christological Question

GEORGE CUMMINGS *(USA)*

Synopsis

Christological reflection in the early church arose as the early church attempted to discern the meaning of Jesus Christ for their lives. Any contemporary attempt to do Christological reflection must consider the biblical record, the dogmas of the historical churches, and the living presence of Jesus Christ in the lives of Christians as Christology.

Black and Hispanic-American Christians have come to understand that Jesus Christ is the one who delivers them from all oppression—spiritual, social, political, economical, and cultural. They understand the fundamental message of the gospel to be that the God of freedom has acted on their behalf, through the life, death, and resurrection of Jesus Christ. Any overemphasis on any one aspect of Jesus Christ distorts the gospel. Christology is, therefore, challenged to be wholistically true to Jesus Christ.

INTRODUCTION

"Who do you say that I am?" is the Christological question which Jesus of Nazareth posed to those whom he had called together as his followers. Their responses reflected their diverse perspectives. Some identified him as Elijah, others as John the Baptist or Jeremiah, and Peter identified him as the Christ (cf. Mk. 8:27f.; Mt. 16:13f.; Lk. 9:18f.). Even as they responded with many different answers, there is a variety of responses in contemporary times.

No response to the question "Who do you say that I am?" would be complete without an explicit definition of the one who is seeking to respond to the question. Any Christological statement must begin with an acknowledgment of the concrete human experiences within which doctrines are conceived. Theological reflections, and even the framing of theological questions, are inextricably influenced and shaped by the context within which they arise. That context must also be examined on a variety of levels to determine the manner in which it influences one's answer to the question of "Who do you say that I am?" The social, economic, political, religious, historical, and personal context of the

217

theologian substantially shapes his or her approach to the formulation of Christology. The task of this paper is to examine the way in which Christological questions and reflections are pursued by minority theologians in the contemporary North American context.

NORTH AMERICAN MINORITIES

The term "minority" in North America is typically used to designate racial, ethnic, and political status. It is important to recognize the diversity of populations included in this designation: African-Americans, Hispanic-Americans, Asian-Americans, and Indigenous-Americans. Even among each of these populations exists incredible cultural diversity. African-Americans arrived either by force in the context of slavery or by choice, with roots tracing directly from the mother continent of Africa or detouring through the generations and arriving in North America out of the Caribbean experience or elsewhere. Hispanic Americans include those who trace their origins to Mexico, Puerto Rico, Cuba, Spain, and elsewhere in Central and South America and the Caribbean countries. Asian-Americans include Japanese, Chinese, Korean, Vietnamese, and those with still other roots.

Given the enormous cultural diversity represented by peoples defined as "minorities" in the North American context, what possible consensus could exist as each attempts to answer the Christological query "Who do you say that I am?" The differences notwithstanding, a common thread of experience unites all minority people in North America—the experience of disenfranchisement, exploitation, and dehumanization. The kaleidoscope of history has seen this experience imposed upon each of these population groups in a unique way and in varying degrees. But the very fact of identifying peoples of colour as minorities, in terms of influence as well as in terms of numbers, is a key to understanding that experience in the North American context. While all people, presumably, have colour, North Americans use the term to designate nonwhite peoples.

Given my own experience as an African-American in North America, I do not presume to speak for brothers and sisters of colour with other racial and ethnic identification; rather, I am hopeful that in presenting the impact of our status in North America and how that shapes our theological questions and reflections, I will shed some light on the commonality of all minority experiences in contemporary North America and on the Christology that arises in the midst of these experiences.

The black community

Minority peoples in North America live in the heart of western industrial and technological society, and are the victims of the most insidious oppression in the world.[1] The majority of the black community today undergo

1. Cornel West, *Black Theology as a Critique of Western Capitalist Civilization*, unpublished paper. In this paper, Cornel West, a professor of philosophy of religion

a life of daily dehumanization and denigration, cast with a pall of despair which deeply affects the development and the quality of life of all those who experience it. The documentable unemployment rate of black youth is almost sixty percent; drugs and alcohol sedate adults who can find no opportunities to earn a living or to develop and contribute their talents to the society in which they live. In the cities crimes surprise no one, and abandoned buildings are found on every block. Existence for the masses of black and other minority peoples in North America is characterized by a constant struggle to maintain dignity, to preserve respect, and to affirm self-worth in a society which attempts by subtle and obvious means to deny these things.

As a young black man in the early seventies, I remember wondering whether Martin Luther King's death had anything to do with the Jesus Christ he proclaimed and the message of hope he conveyed to black people. In the black church, I listened with interest as black preachers talked about Jesus who was a "heart-fixer" and a "mind-regulator," a Jesus who could "make everything all right." To many of my peers, those words seemed empty, since evidence of such a Jesus at work was sometimes hard to see. We sang a song which told us to

Step to Jesus, and everything will be all right,
Step to Jesus, he'll be your guiding light,
Step to Jesus, all your battles he will help you fight,
Step to Jesus, he'll make everything all right.

And yet my mother still had to work eighteen hours a day to feed her children. Jesus did not seem to enable my parents to resolve their differences, and they were divorced.

The black experience in North America is plagued with these contradictions—belief in a loving, benevolent God coupled with the daily experience of denial, suffering, and poverty; the love of Jesus historically preached at us by white slavemasters who kept us in servitude and even brought us to slavery in vessels with names like "The Good Ship Jesus." Black people were constantly being assailed by the brutal realities of oppression whereas white people were enjoying both the fruits of their own work as well as the labours of black men, women, and children who reaped nothing from their sweat and blood. Black people have begun to reframe answers to the standard theological queries, and to question the questions which have given shape to traditional Christological formulations.

---

at Union Theological Seminary, argues that the kind of dehumanization that occurred to particular minority groups within North America is unique in history. African slaves were uprooted from their land. They were deprived of their culture and forbidden the use of their language and culture. Families were separated. Indigenous Americans were for all practical purposes exterminated, and their cultural forms destroyed. This thorough destruction, West asserts, is unique to those who have been colonized in the heart of western capitalist civilization.

Hispanic-Americans

While Hispanic-Americans do not experience a monolithic reality, they do share a recognition of the oppression and exploitation which characterize their experiences in the North American context.[2] Chicano immigrants struggle against the cheap exploitation of their labour by a capitalist economy which pays for their labour to maximize corporate profit rather than to fairly compensate for its value. Puerto Ricans have sustained for decades their struggle against American colonialism. In October 1978, at the first Hispanic Ecumenical Theology Project meeting, it was declared that in many cases

> the abuse of power by those who run the institutions and the economy is clear. Even clearer are the brutalizing contradictions of a capitalistic system in crisis that requires unemployment, cheap labour, equally cheap raw materials, the transformation of luxuries into necessities, the accumulation of vast wealth by a smaller and smaller minority, consumption as the primary goal in life, and the sacrifice of human beings on the altar of profits.[3]

Consequently, the faith of these marginalized communities emerged as an implicit critique of the dominant religious values and institutions which have been incorporated into the oppressive apparatus of North American Society.

SOURCES OF BLACK CHRISTOLOGY

The black community's experience of Jesus

From the perspective of the marginalized, it has become necessary to reinterpret the faith for ourselves. We have come to recognize that the Christ of the dominant culture is not Christ at all, but rather the powerless shadow of a man domesticated to serve the interests of the status quo. From the beginning, black folk rejected their white masters' interpretation of the gospel which implied that God desired black people to be slaves, and that obedience to God meant willing servitude to whites. In their independent church traditions, the slaves reinterpreted the meaning of the gospel, knowing in their hearts that obedience to God does not imply the denigration of their own self-worth. The encounter with Jesus Christ in the lives of black people who struggle for freedom has been the experience of affirmation, this hope of liberation, and this survival experience has been the primary source of black Christology. Jesus Christ in his expli-

2. For a complete analysis of the Hispanic-American reality, see Virgil Elizondo, *The Mexican-American Promise: A Galilean Journey* (Maryknoll: Orbis Books, 1982).

3. "Message from the Hispanic Project," in *Theology in the Americas Newsletter* 4:2 (April 1979; 475 Riverside Drive, Rm. 1268, New York, NY 10027).

cit identification with the oppressed had identified himself with the black experience in North America.

In our songs, sermons, records, and history, the black community bears witness to the liberating presence of Jesus Christ. This Lord and Saviour enables us to affirm our humanity by struggling against dehumanization, and to affirm God's power in us by overcoming our powerlessness in our struggle for freedom in the North American context. Jesus Christ, in this context, is affirmed as God's liberating Word in the world of those who need a deliverer. God's revelation is understood in an historical sense, for it is in these encounters with God that members of the community meet Jesus in such a way that they often assert that they have "met the Lord for themselves." Jesus was a deliverer and a comforter for them personally in a time of trouble, a "lily of the valley," a "bright and morning star" who appeared in the midst of their darkness.

Nobody understood black existence like Jesus did, since he was a man of sorrows, acquainted with grief. He was whipped, beaten, rejected, mocked, scorned, and crucified as a common criminal for his greatest offence—knowing who he was, and being true to that.

We sing,

Nobody knows the trouble I've seen,
Nobody knows but Jesus.
Nobody knows the trouble I've seen,
Glory Hallelujah.

We, too, were crucified, and can identify with the crucified Lord.

Were you there when they crucified my Lord?
Were you there when they crucified my Lord?
Oh, sometimes, it causes me to tremble, tremble, tremble,
Were you there when they crucified my Lord?

In the spirituals, black people share interpretations of the significance of Jesus Christ when they sing,

He's King of Kings, and Lord of Lords, Jesus Christ,
the first and the last, no man works like him.

For us, Jesus Christ is not an abstractly defined person, nor simply the personification of dogma, but God's act on our behalf and in our history. Jesus is one who vindicates us personally and will ultimately vindicate us historically. The good news of his personal love and touch makes us sing

Go tell it on the mountain,
Over the hills and everywhere,
Go tell it on the mountain,
That Jesus Christ is born.

Jesus did not simply live and die. He was raised by God. This ensured the vindication of God's people in our struggle for freedom, even in the midst of suffering, death, and humiliation.

> Weep no more Martha
> Weep no more Mary
> Jesus rose from de dead
> Happy morning
> Glorious morning
> Glorious morning
> My savior rise from de dead
> Happy morning.

Jesus is accepted as the Christ, because that is who he has been in the black experience. The message of the cross is easily absorbed by a people who have borne the cross of racist oppression and injustice for over two hundred years. The resurrection is seen as the basis of hope for the eschatological vindication of the struggle to be free.

The theoretical difficulties of Chalcedon and Nicaea and the problems of the historicity of the sources were no part of the black experience. They therefore play a relatively small role in black Christological formulations. Jesus Christ is God's liberation in our concrete experience, as well as eschatologically. How else can these great songs of black tradition be interpreted?

> Oh, Freedom! Oh, Freedom!
> Oh, Freedom, over me!
> An' befo' I'd be a slave,
> I'll be buried in my grave,
> An' go home to my Lord an' be free.

or:

> My Lord delivered Daniel,
> Why can't he deliver me?

It was out of this black tradition that Martin Luther King and black theology emerged. Black Christians have always been convinced that many white Christians had misinterpreted the meaning of the gospel when they separated their religion from the rest of life, but utilized the symbols of the Christian faith to rationalize racist domination. The relationship between black Christianity and the long movement of freedom has been well documented by many scholars.[4] Black theologians turn to these black resources as a witness to our primary source for Christology.

---

4. The best and most comprehensive history of black religion in North America may be found in Gayraud S. Wilmore's *Black Religion and Black Radicalism* (New York: Doubleday, 1972). For an excellent historical work on Christianity among the slaves, see Albert Rabateau, *Slave Religion* (New York: Oxford University Press, 1978).

The church

I must now clarify the role of the church in bearing the message of Jesus Christ to black people. I will not develop ecclesiology here. But I understand the church to be a symbol of God's presence with humanity and a demonstration of God's praxis in the world, through human praxis, as it moves toward fulfilment. I do not view the church as the guardian of the gospel for the purpose of bearing it to the world of darkness, but as a location in which the confessing community chooses to enact commitment to God through concrete action. When African slaves encountered the message of the gospel, they were immediately aware of the disparity between what was called the gospel and the lives of most white Christians.

Virgil Elizondo in *The Mexican-American Promise: A Galilean Journey* declares that the Hispanic-American reality—*mestizaje*—encountered the incarnated Lord as the one who signalled the reversal of the power of European domination. He affirms that

> The power of hope . . . came from the fact that the unexpected good news of God's presence was offered to all by someone from whom nothing special was expected: the conquered Indian, the lowest of the low.[5]

Elizondo was primarily writing from the Chicano context, but an interesting section from the novel of the Puerto Rican author, Piri Thomas, illustrates my point within the Puerto Rican experience. Thomas is engaged in discussion with Tia about the role of the Pentecostal church in the community, and asks a question:

> "What does being a Pentecostal mean to you? I mean, like I'm asking without disrespect." Tia smiled like always, sure and secure in her iglesia. "It's what binds much of us poor Puertoriquenos together, it gives us strength to live in these conditions. It's like being part of a familia that is together in Cristo, and we help each other with the little materials we may possess." She talked about us not having silver and gold, but having, instead, peace in our corazon [heart] and salvation as our goal.[6]

Thomas wondered whether it would not be better to have all four simultaneously.

The living presence of the incarnated God unites, strengthens, and enables the Hispanic-American community to continue to struggle in the midst of overwhelming odds. The church has a significant role in this community, much like the black church, and provides the foundations of their protest against those who dominate them. At the first Hispanic Ecumenical Project meeting it was said that

5. Citation drawn from the uncorrected galley proofs of Virgil Elizondo, *The Mexican-American Promise: A Galilean Journey* (Maryknoll: Orbis Books, 1982), p.18.

6. Piri Thomas, *Savior, Savior Hold My Hand* (New York: Doubleday, 1972), p. 21.

From the perspective of Hispanics seeking to follow Jesus, we discover our identity and our evangelizing mission. Rejected and scorned by the powers of this country, we, like the Galileans, are chosen by God to live out and to proclaim the Good News of liberation for all. Like Jesus, we must go up to Jerusalem, to the centres of economic, political and religious power in order to denounce oppression with the strength of the gospel.[7]

The biblical record of Jesus

An encounter with a living presence, however, does not constitute the whole process whereby oppressed people come to know about Jesus Christ. The biblical record is another important source of our knowledge concerning Jesus, for our subjective experiences in the present must have an objective ground external to them.

However, the rise of modern historiography has called into question the biblical basis of our knowledge of Jesus Christ.

No Christological formulation can ignore the impact of post-Enlightenment biblical studies on our understanding of Jesus. Until the nineteenth century, it was generally accepted that the Christology of the New Testament was both recoverable and objectively the Christology of Jesus. The Gospels were accepted as accurate historical records which related the ''bare facts'' about Jesus' life. However, with the onset of biblical critical methods many questions arose concerning their historical validity.

This rigorous study in conjunction with the new wave of dependence on scientific inquiry set off the so-called ''quest for the historical Jesus,'' in the hope that scholars would be able to find some invulnerable grounds for faith in Jesus as the Christ. This first quest concluded when, in a book entitled *The Quest of the Historical Jesus*, Albert Schweitzer argued that there could be no recovering of the historical Jesus, and that there was no necessary logical connection between historical necessity and theological assertions. The essential question, then, became ''Must Christology begin with Jesus himself, or with the message of his community?'' It became necessary to differentiate between the Jesus of history and the Christ of faith, and to explicate the relationship between the two.

Whatever one believes about historical critical methodology, it has made valuable contributions to biblical and theological studies. Some issues for this essay are: Is Christian faith grounded in an objective past event or in a present experience? Even if the ''facts'' about Jesus could be known, by what means and in what sense can twentieth-century persons have access to those events? Is our Christology to be one ''from above'' or ''from below'' as Pannenberg so aptly distinguished?

These questions are posed as if the theologian must choose between the alternatives. I suggest that Christology must be able to explicate meaningfully the relationship between Jesus and his identity as the Christ for

7. ''Message from the Hispanic Project,'' *op. cit.,* p. 8.

people in the world today. Furthermore, Christology must be able to construct a methodology which describes the access of faith by which we come to a knowledge of Jesus as the Christ.

There is no doubt that faith in Jesus Christ must in some way be grounded in a comprehension of the Jew, Jesus. Whether that is possible by way of modern historiography is questionable. The "old quest" was inadequate because it was predicated upon the belief that historical research could recover the "bare facts" about Jesus which would conclusively prove the object of faith. This faith could only lead to a faith which was constantly changing depending on the new archaeological and historical discoveries. Christologies "from above" were inadequate because they overemphasized the divinity/resurrection of Jesus as a faith presupposition prior to a serious analysis of the man, Jesus. The "new quest" is open to the same criticism as the "old quest," though its intention is not so much to establish historical evidence as much as it is to anchor faith in the realm of human life.

I believe an encounter with Jesus Christ in human experience must be in dialogical tension with the historical Jesus, inasmuch as we can recover him. With Jon Sobrino, I would argue the historical Jesus of whom we write is not simply the "bare facts" of the critical historiographers, but Jesus inasmuch as we can recover him in his history. In this sense we are more interested in the history of Jesus, inasmuch as we can discover him in his historical relations. For it is in this history that we can behold his relationship to the people and the society in which he lived. Thus my Christology would not seek an invulnerable area on which to ground faith; rather, I would seek to make the human Jesus an important component of our Christology. This Christology takes seriously not only the risen Lord, but also the man Jesus who died on a cross and was raised by God.

What can we assert about Jesus from the biblical record? In Jesus of Nazareth, we find a man who made some unusual claims to authority with God. Joachim Jeremias has argued with fine documentation that Jesus' unusual use of the words "abba" and "amen" points to the validity of his claims.[8] He was an itinerant preacher who performed exorcisms, healings, and other miracles. The cornerstone of his message was that he had come to inaugurate the dawning of the Kingdom of God. He asserted that this event was good news for the poor, sick, and exploited of the land. After several years of ministry he went to Jerusalem where he was crucified on a tree as a criminal.

The crucifixion is a well-established public fact, based on biblical and other historical records. But it would not mean anything by itself. Other insurrectionists have been crucified. Why did Jesus' cross become so crucial?

Karl Barth said: "The cross of Jesus would have no meaning apart

8. For Joachim Jeremias' complete argument about the use of these terms, see his *New Testament Theology* (New York: Charles Scribner's Sons, 1971).

from the light of resurrection morn!'' Apart from the resurrection claims, the cross would have been meaningless. Nowhere in the Judaism of that period is the idea that the Messiah would be raised from the dead. On the day Jesus died, it would have been folly to project that his sect would continue to exist. As the text itself tells us, they had abandoned him. And yet the reverberations of his death and resurrection are with us even today. Later, they asserted that Jesus Christ had died ''for us'' and Paul declares that ''the word of the cross is power unto salvation.'' I clearly state my belief that there are compelling reasons for accepting the New Testament witness to Jesus' resurrection as true.[9]

The tradition of the church

A third source of our comprehension of Jesus Christ is the tradition of the church, both in its positive and negative form. I will only briefly look at the Christology of the historic ecumenical councils of Nicaea and Chalcedon as they affect our concern. The historic tradition of the church is important if one claims to be a part of that tradition. My own black church tradition is not totally self-sufficient. If I made that assumption, there would be no element of self-criticism and no acceptance of input from outside my tradition with respect to my Christology. While my own encounter with the living Christ begins the process of my Christological formulations, this must be in dialogue with the record of the Jesus of history, and with the traditions of those who claim to be the Christian church down through the ages. This methodology provides a critical element which is external to my own inevitably finite context, range of experience, and conceptualization of how God acts in the course of human events. Thereby solipsism is prevented, and therein lies the beauty of the theological task—the painful, meaningful, and conflict-ridden interaction among differing perspectives on the same God, the same Saviour, the same Lord, the same Christ.

In the struggle at Nicaea and Chalcedon the church patriarchs were

9. I understand the New Testament witness to Jesus Christ to include all that is said about the preexistent logos, the exalted Lord and the Parousia of Jesus. The following diagram will illustrate this:

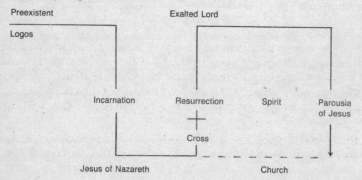

attempting, for their own age, context, and peoples to understand the saving significance of the life, death, and resurrection of Jesus who is called the Christ. Thus the patristic proposals are made not for us, but for those who were present at that time. The agendas established then inevitably differ to some extent from our contemporary concerns. We cannot simply agree with them and reproduce them as our own, nor can we thoughtlessly reject them. In order to gain the wisdom they might have to offer us, we must understand them within their own historical and social context, and *then* decide whether and in what way it is necessary to interpret and apply them to our own situation.

The problem at Nicaea was to understand the status of the divine logos in the man Jesus. Richard Norris argues that everyone at Nicaea assumed that Jesus was a human whose internal identity was the logos.[10] The question was the precise nature of the relationship between the divine logos and his humanity. The Nicaean Council asserted that in the incarnation there was the direct and immediate ingredients of God, which really settled nothing. The Chalcedonian council affirmed its belief in the unity of Jesus Christ "without confusion" and "without division," "one person, in two natures." I will not analyze the complexity of the problem here. But black people have never had any abstract theoretical difficulty in affirming the unity of divinity/humanity in Jesus. At the same time, the Christological tradition has served only as a guideline, not as a rigid dogmatic formula to which the black church must strictly adhere. Our problem with Christology has been much more concrete, because of our desire as black people to see the empirical reference points in our experience which would support the claim that in Jesus Christ, God has performed a decisive act on behalf of our liberation.

It is always in the cooperation of these three sources, the Bible, our experience of Jesus Christ in our lives, and in the traditions, that we are able to come to a clearer knowledge of Jesus Christ. In theological terms there must be a dynamic dialectical tension between them. Black and Hispanic people today would find the first two sources to be of primary importance in their quest for a meaningful Christology, while utilizing Nicaea and Chalcedon only in a secondary fashion. I believe that all three are necessary.

Christian praxis

One last element is important for a complete answer to the question "Who do you say that I am?" Christian praxis—following Jesus in the way of the cross—will contribute greatly to our knowledge of Jesus Christ. Jesus Christ, the Bible asserts, is God's response to the human situation. In him, God has moved into human history and identified God's self with

---

10. For Norris' Christological discussion, refer to *The Christological Controversy,* ed. and trans. Richard A. Norris, Jr. (Philadelphia: Fortress Press, 1980).

humanity. God has become flesh and encamped among us. In doing so, he has taken the cross as his own. Jesus Christ is the sacrifice of becoming flesh in lieu of the privilege of identity as God, for the sake of others. By looking at the history of Jesus, we can see that his scandalous death on the cross was the historical consequence of his life and ministry.

To affirm the incarnation in today's world is to say that Jesus was truly immersed in his historical context, and accepted it with all its implications. He reacted against all types of injustice and oppression because of this understanding of his mission. Jesus struggled in his life to break the power of false religions, the bonds of oppression, and the power of political gods. The cross and resurrection are to be understood as a challenge to all people to call into radical question their being and the present order of things in the world. The crucified God reveals a power, hidden in the suffering, which shall ultimately vindicate itself and raise us from the dead also. Therefore to be a Christian is to follow Jesus in the way of the cross—to call into question our present reality, and to struggle to transform it, as well as to prepare the way for the eschatological Kingdom of God.

"Who do you say that I am?" Inasmuch as we, the Christian community, continue to engage in hopeful struggle to bring radical change to the world, Jesus Christ will be the cornerstone of the struggle. Inasmuch as we are able to gracefully sacrifice ourselves for the oppressed, as Jesus did, he shall be grace. Inasmuch as we follow Jesus into the struggle to liberate the exploited, he shall be hope. For the victims of history, Jesus Christ continues to be the Word of God who is the source of power and hope behind our liberating praxis.

CHRISTOLOGY AND MISSION

In conclusion, I would like to address the connection between this particular witness to Jesus Christ and the mission of the gospel. In early Christianity, the primary data of all theology were reflections upon the significance of Jesus of Nazareth. Christian theology is an activity which arises out of that community whose hope and memory is rooted in Jesus Christ. The significance of Jesus of Nazareth came to expression in the form of gospel. The Greek term for gospel—ευαγγελιον—connotes a verb more than a noun. The full impact of the phrase "to proclaim the gospel" is more accurately translated: "to gospel," "to gospel the gospel," to spread the word, tell the good news. It is word and act. This draws our attention to the fact that the message and the mission of Jesus Christ are inseparable. At its most rudimentary level, Christian theology is reflection upon the gospelling activity of those who follow Jesus Christ. The earliest theological reflection took the form of brief summaries of the testimony of the tradition (I Cor. 15:1-8) which points to the saving significance of Jesus Christ.

As we move into the history of the church, theology is the church's continuing attempt to understand the present-day significance of the gospel *tradition*. In the Gospels the Greek term for tradition (παραδοσις/ παραδιδωμι) is used in two senses. It is used in Luke's Gospel (Lk. 1:2) to signify the handing over of God's Word—Jesus Christ—to the early Christians. This tradition refers to the gospelling activity and the one who called it into being. In Luke 4:18 this gospelling activity is a freedom movement, initiated by God, but enacted by human beings. Freedom is the watchword for the Pauline and Lucan gospelling tradition. However, this tradition also includes a long, complex web of established customs, activities, and reflections which themselves contribute to the present sufferings of oppressed peoples in the world.

The second usage of the term tradition in the Gospels is when Judas traditions (hands over) Jesus into the hands of his captors (Mt. 26:48, etc.). This is a tradition of captivity and enslavement. The Scriptures themselves tell us that many will say "Lord, Lord I have loved you," but they will be rejected (Mt. 7:21-23). The task of theology is to attempt to distinguish between the freedom tradition and the captivity tradition.

In contemporary theology, liberation theology in all its complex manifestations has emerged to focus attention on the feeble attempts of the dispossessed—the disenfranchised, poor, and marginalized—to frame and respond to the Christological question. Liberation theology calls us back to the freedom tradition, initiated by God, in which gospelling activity is a part of God's movement in the world toward freedom for all peoples; to really know the truth, they say, is to do the truth.

May we unite ourselves in common fellowship, as we struggle to follow Jesus the Christ in preaching good news to the poor, proclaiming a release of those who are captives, a recovering of sight to the blind, and a setting at liberty of those who are oppressed, to proclaim this as the acceptable year of the Lord.

SELECT BIBLIOGRAPHY

James Cone. *God of the Oppressed.* New York: The Seabury Press, 1975.
——————. *Spirituals and the Blues.* New York: The Seabury Press, 1972.
Virgil Elizondo. *The Mexican-American Promise: A Galilean Journey.* New York: Orbis Books, 1982.
Benjamin Mays. *The Negroes' God.* New York: Atheneum, 1973.
Benjamin Mays and Joseph Nicholson. *The Negro Church.* New York: Russell and Russell, 1933.
Albert Rabateau. *Slave Religion.* New York: Oxford University Press, 1978.
Piri Thomas. *Savior, Savior Hold My Hand.* New York: Doubleday, 1972.
Gayraud Wilmore. *Black Religion and Black Radicalism.* New York: Anchor/Doubleday, 1972.
Carter Woodson. *The History of the Negro Church.* Washington, D.C.: The Associated Publishers, 1972.

DISCUSSION WITH GEORGE CUMMINGS:

Black American Missions

Q. It is obvious from their songs and their other writings that the American Africans discovered a different kind of Christ very early on after they had settled in a strange land. Why did it take so long for them to have an understanding of missions in the same way that the exploiters and other colonial people did? It would have served us very much in Africa if you had come very quickly to share the new-found Christ with us.

G.C. It is a misconception that the African Americans did not come to an understanding of missions. Afro-Americans sent missionaries to Africa in the 1800s, during slavery. Two big problems were the lack of resources and the state of our existence in the United States. People could not even move out of the farm, country, or location where they worked. Those who did, especially the Africans from the A.M.E. Church, have a very long history of missions to Africa. But since they did not have the resources which white society had, they could not do much about it. Benjamin Mays and Joseph Nicholson describe this period of black missions in *The Negro Church* (New York: Russell and Russell, 1933).

Comment: In the middle of the nineteenth-century a group of Jamaicans who originated from Africa became Christians. When emancipation came, they decided to go back to their home in Southern Nigeria to set up a church. The Presbyterian Church in Nigeria today is strictly speaking a church that came from Jamaica. When they decided to come back to Africa, a Scottish missionary called Hope Waddell who was working in Jamaica decided to accompany them. Once they settled in East Nigeria he made links with the United Presbyterian Church in Scotland and so the United Presbyterian Church took over the mission. This is our history, although it is not written in many of the textbooks.

Identity

Q. It seems to me that Latin American liberation theology proceeds by identification. The black American finds his identity in Christ the suffering servant. Why is there this persistent theme of the suffering servant? For me this suffering servant is a Jew and not a black American. If we proceed by identification, we need some way of linking this with complete reality. What is this suffering? Is it colour or what?

When I read the Gospels, the Christ who challenges me and who challenges us black people, is not the suffering Christ, the suffering servant. It is the risen one who challenges us. It is after the resurrection that Jesus said "All power is given to me, now go and make disciples of all the nations.'' So all nations are now linked with Christ through the resurrection and not through the suffering servant. If you continue with the theme of the suffering servant, I am afraid that you might remain in suffering. The risen one seems to be the real revolutionary whom you are seeking.

G.C. The classic reference point for black people with respect to the identification of our sufferings with the suffering servant in contemporary times is Martin Luther King. He talked in terms of unmerited suffering being redemptive. In that respect I think he was speaking of a particular interpretation of the tradition which finds a point of contact in some parts of black theological tradition but is not by and large the one we would focus on. Our focus is on the risen Christ. The risen Christ allows us to continue the battle after several hundred years of struggle. Because God raised Jesus from the dead, we believe the struggle is hopeful and that it is possible that we shall be free.

Comment: The suffering Christ is very attractive indeed, but among the oppressed of the world today, the Christ that is becoming more attractive and the one they respond to from their own cultures to affirm themselves is the Christ of the miraculous.

Q. Is our identity as Indian or black American going to be simply one of being oppressed and marginalized? Is that the principal identity by which we are defining ourselves? From our Indian context of now thirty-five years of liberation we are no longer so concerned with the oppression issue as an independent nation. We are beginning to see some deeper issues and without setting aside the issue of oppression broaden the context of identity to include the world of religions, belief and unbelief, worldviews, and culture.

G.C. When we speak of Afro-American or Afro-Black, we are speaking not only of our Africanness, which we want to refer to, but to the fact that we are African-Americans also who have been transported to the American context. We are part of the West, but with a decidedly different perspective on things. Black existence, what has happened to us, defines us as a community. It is what we mean when we say ''black'' or ''the black experience.'' We define it togeth er. It is our point of departure for consideration of the Christological question. There are dangers in that. When one takes ideology, abstracts it to a level that it becomes normative for everybody as the Nazis in Germany, then there are a lot of problems. But I am not convinced that we have any other choice. We will not accept and have not accepted, the definition of the gospel which was given to us by white people who were living inconsistently with their claims. I suggest that there are churches in the Two Thirds World who are still buying into their tradition.

Theological method

Q. I am deeply sympathetic toward the suffering, the injustice, inequality, and racism which the black people have experienced. Conservative Christians have practiced segregation more than liberal Christians or Roman Catholics. This is why there are few strong evangelical churches among black Christians in North America. But the whole emphasis of this paper is on one aspect of Christology. It is human liberation theology which does not really represent the full picture of the gospel of Christ. Apart from this horizontal aspect, there is the incarnation, the death, and the resurrection of Christ and his return. Where is the saving grace of Christ in the paper?

G.C. The primary source of our understanding of Christology is the living presence of Jesus. How much more resurrection-oriented can you get than that? What living presence would there be if he was not resurrected? When I refer to Jesus Christ, I refer to all the realities which you mention. (See footnote 9.) That is why Christ is so powerful to us. His redemption is not something horizontal that human beings did. It is powerful because God raised Jesus.

Theology is passionate talk about God. Theology is always subjective as it is human beings who do theology, not God. So I do not claim the myth of objectivity. Our experience in the West is that whites, Catholics, Protestants, conservatives, liberals, and all between are racist. This has very little to do with their theological posture. It has to do with certain attitudes which they have brought into their faith from their culture. In the eighteenth century there was plenty of theological discussion in Germany, but no one was talking about slavery. They acted as if it did not exist. If we assume that people's theological posture decides what they are going to do in relation to certain people in the world, we are believing a fallacy. Racism has to do with buying into the dominant values of the culture, not to do with theology.

Q. In the past we used to discuss Christology from above or Christology from below. But are we not now in danger of building a Christology from inside, from my own existential situation, or building a Christology from outside, from the social context without giving attention seriously to the testimony of the Word of God, God's written revelation? We are now insecure about the historicity of the New Testament because of the historical approach and New Testament criticism. I am not against critical study but I am afraid we may give the impression that we do not trust the New Testament records any more and that instead we build a Christology from inside or from outside.

G.C. What is at stake is an issue of theological method. If you are going to do your Christology by saying that the Bible is the Word of

God which basically states the position and it is obvious what the text
says, then you've got a Christology. If you cannot do that for good
or bad reasons, then you have to find another way to do Christology.
I make the judgement to trust the text. I am doing Christology trusting
the text, but also seeking a Christology that is true to my experience.

Comment: It is not simply a question of white/black issues. It is the
question of the ideology of the racism that appears in the context of the
North American oppressed people. Racism is the instrument that is used
for oppression and that speaks of the white dominant society which is
western society. White society is a transplanted European society.

Whites dominate society in North America, and the same situation
is occurring in Britain, Australia, New Zealand, and South Africa.
Therefore it is western society versus people of colour. That appears very
clearly in the context of North America. Every one of the following groups
have been labelled in nonwhite terms. Go back in history: the Hispanics
are labelled as browns, Asians are labelled yellow, Aboriginal people are
labelled red. Black, brown, yellow, and red. And in each context this
relates to the economic situation. Mexican-Americans are branded brown
in the context in which their land is taken from them by one of the greatest
betrayals, treasons, and double-crossings of history. The great double-
crossing occurred in Texas. When Mexico joined with rednecks who came
from the South, no sooner had they won the war against Mexico than
they took over their lands and they branded them by colour. The same
thing happened with the Chinese, in Los Angeles, and with the Japanese,
in Hawaii. In Hawaii the struggle of World War II did not originate in
the 30s. It goes back to the way plantation owners treated the Japanese
people as a labour movement. To overcome the Japanese labour leaders
in Hawaii they brought twenty-one ships from Puerto Rico in 1900, 1901,
and 1921. And in the process there is the extermination and the overcoming of the aboriginal Hawaiians.

Again the colour lines appear over and over in relation to the problem of class, of power. Whenever white, western dominant society is
threatened, it raises the matter of colour. That is one very crucial issue
for us to bear in mind in terms of racism.

The issue of racism is a fundamental question in theology and specifically in Christology. It profoundly affects the evangelical community in
the United States. The church among the minorities in the United States
is by and large an evangelical church. But the white evangelical establishment which controls the missionary movement has in fact stratified that
minority church so that minority people are the great absentees in the
missionary movement even though we have a very strong missionary
tradition that goes back to the nineteenth century. The North American
Missionary Handbook has hardly any reference to the missionary societies
from the minority people. Black people, Spanish people, and Asian people

have been rejected by the North American Missionary Societies.
Missiological schools have neglected the missionary issues raised by the
minority people inside the United States. The evangelical establishment
in the U.S. only refers to minorities when they want to quote statistics.
Of the 40 million evangelicals in the U.S. at least one third are minorities.
The tendency of the Third World has been to lump all people in the U.S.
together, and not to study and deeply understand the issues taking place
inside North American evangelicalism. An ignorance exists among all
of us including Latin Americans. Until very recently the Latin American
Theological Fraternity refused to accept the issue of the Spanish
Americans as a crucial issue in Latin American theology even though
the largest number of U.S. immigrants come from Mexico, the Dominican
Republic, Nicaragua, and El Salvador.

The minority church in the U.S. is not isolated from world issues.
The black church has a very deep and profound dialogue with Islam.
The Southwest of the U.S. was missionized in the first place by mis-
sionaries who came out of a thousand years' history of encounter with
Islam. The Aboriginal people are people who hold to non-Christian
religions. The missionary encounter with the other religions in U.S. took
place first and foremost in the attempt to evangelize the Aboriginal people.
And the Asians were to come, the Chinese, the Japanese, more recently
people from Southeast Asia and West Asia, with their respective religions.
At the present moment, it is impossible to speak of the minority people
in the U.S. and not speak of interaction and dialogue with the other major religions of the world. But that dialogue takes place from within the
day-to-day life of the people in the ghettoes as they encounter the dominant system.

When we speak of Christology, it is not simply a question of inside
and outside. People of colour, and minority people have had to develop
a Christology from the outside.

The author of Hebrews also developed Christology from outside. He
said: "Let us go forth to Jesus outside the camp bearing the abuse he
endured." We do a lot of reflection on the question of substitutionary
atonement, but very little reflection on the implications of Hebrews
chapter 13 which presents the cross not in terms of something we left
behind, but as something before the church in mission on its way to the
New Jerusalem. That is in fact a Christology from the outside. The issue
is not whether we are going to do a Christology from below or a
Christology from above. Berkhof also suggests that we need also to do
a Christology from behind, bearing in mind the influence of the Old Testament. And we need to do a Christology from the outside because minority
Christians in the U.S. have been outside North American Christianity
and theological method. So, you have to develop a method, sources, and
a discourse that is by sheer history outside of the dominant theological
discourse. Unless we understand this dynamic we cannot really enter into
the very rich and demanding Christological agenda.

When we do Christology we have to bear in mind all these various angles and dimensions; from above because it is a revelatory Christology; from below because it is a Christology that is one in the midst of the struggles of history and that takes seriously into account Jesus of Nazareth; from behind because we have the legacy of the Old Testament; from the outside because we are oppressed people who have been as it were outside of Christendom, and from and for the future because we are on the way to Jerusalem. We are contemplating and anticipating the coming of our Lord because ours has to be a transformative Christology.

We have been brought up in a western evangelical theological school of thought that speaks of true Christology and contemporary Christologies, as if the Christologies that our teachers did were not contemporary Christology. But there is no way of doing Christology that is not contemporary. Reflecting systematically and critically about our belief in Jesus Christ as Lord and Saviour is what Christology is and is for us a contemporary task. My fundamental norm for that Christological task is the Scriptures. For me the canonical Scriptures of the Old and New Testament are the norm of faith and practice. That is something that we agree on. Therefore I am an evangelical through and through. The issue that divides me from mainstream white evangelicals is not whether I believe the Bible to be the Word of God, which I do, but it is that I want to take the Bible seriously because I want to read the Bible from my situation. My situation is one of oppression that gives me a particular vantage point, that is a bit different from some of the other people. My situation is one of Christendom. When I interact from that perspective, inside and outside are two terms which are very important for me. Because inside has been the world of academic theology. "Inside" has been those who have a particular franchise on a form of reading the Scriptures. "Outside" are those of us who do not have a so-called theological culture, who do not necessarily see things through philosophical eyes.

I stand in a dialectical tension with the system which has kept my people in oppression. The result is that I coincide in some fundamental aspects with evangelicals in that system about belief in Jesus Christ. We stand together in church and say we are committed to Jesus Christ who is the Lord and the Saviour. We say we are judged by the same Word. But when we say what does it mean to believe in Jesus Christ, and ask "Who is this Jesus that we confess as our Lord and our Saviour and what does this Jesus command us to do?", at that precise point we start departing from one another.

I am not claiming that my theology is infallible. My Christology is a witness that I bear. I stand under the judgement of the Word, under the judgement of the Lord of history, and under the judgement of the Spirit of Christ and of the church of Christ.

We have to accept a position of humility, vis-à-vis one another, vis-à-vis church history, and vis-à-vis the Kingdom of our Lord which will come. We are dealing with different hermeneutics and with different ways of doing our Christological reflection.

Q. I am not clear whether you want to say that the black community and its tradition is the primary source for Christology with regards to the Scriptures. Is it more important than Scriptures? If there is contradiction do you go with the black tradition? I was intrigued that in *God of the Oppressed* James Cone said that if there is contradiction then one must go with Scripture, otherwise one would have nothing to say to any other tradition. If we are all supposed to take our own particular tradition in history as the primary source and norm, then Latin Americans and blacks have nothing to say to white Europeans when they take their experience as the primary decisive norm and develop an oppressive Christology. If there is a contradiction in some point which do you go with?

G.C. I want to talk about two sources for theology and Christology, my experience and the text of the Christian faith, the Scriptures. You have to talk about what kind of hermeneutical principles you will establish, before you can answer the question about which one will define the other.

The norm of theology is the risen Christ who because God has raised him has promised to vindicate us also. The Scriptures bear witness to that Christ. The testimony of the black Christian tradition bears witness to that Christ.

What if we have a conflict? The norm for my theology will be a norm which comes from both and it is hard for me to say you go with the Scriptures. That is probably what I would do. But it is hard to go with the Scriptures because the Scripture does not stand on its own. Who is interpreting the Scripture? What is the interest of the person who is interpreting the Scripture? Slavemasters taught slaves: "This is what you do, be a good slave, the Bible tells you so." If you mean a conflict between the context and a scriptural interpretation which is contrary to my interpretation of the gospel, I am still going to go with the Scripture because I think the gospel seeks to humanize me. If you suggest a particular kind of problem, say violence, it is hard for me to talk about that abstractly. What is the context? What is going on there? What are the dynamics of the situation? One of the things contemporary theology is struggling with is how to do theology while on one side taking seriously the Christian Scriptures, and on the other hand taking seriously our experience.

13. Miracles, Methodology, and Modern Western Christology

RONALD J. SIDER *(USA)*

Synopsis

One of the most detrimental influences on modern western Christology has been the widespread notion which emerged in the Enlightenment that miracles and scientific thought were incompatible. Convinced that modern scientific thinkers must reject a supernatural worldview, liberal theologians abandoned the deity and resurrection of Jesus Christ. Similarly, modern historical-critical methodology assumed that the critical historian must reject all instances of alleged miracles. There is no philosophical necessity for this widespread assumption. A historical methodology which assumes that alleged miracles must be rejected as legend carries major, unwarranted philosophical baggage. This mistake of western Christology reveals a misplaced contextualization which is also present in evangelical theology that ignores Christ's concern for liberation and in liberation theology that ignores Christ's concern for personal forgiveness grounded in the substitutionary atonement.

INTRODUCTION

Nothing has influenced modern western Christology more profoundly than the eighteenth-century belief that the acceptance of modern science demands the rejection of belief in the miraculous. As an American theologian, Paul van Buren, put it: "The idea of the empirical intervention of a supernatural 'God' in the world of men has been ruled out by the influence of modern science on our thinking."[1] During the Enlightenment, it became part of the accepted wisdom of modern thought that belief in traditional supernaturalism was incompatible with the scientific method. This philosophical judgement, in turn, was decisive for the new historical methodology used by many if not most biblical scholars as the historical-critical approach to the Bible emerged in the nineteenth and twentieth centuries. The result was a fundamental rethinking and redefinition of many central elements of Christian faith, not least the whole area of Christology.

1. Paul van Buren, *The Secular Meaning of the Gospel* (New York: Macmillan, 1963), p. 100.

237

I shall not try to evaluate how far the antisupernatural bias of modern western theology has influenced the church in the Two Thirds World. Rather, I will attempt to outline how the basic notion of the incompatibility of science and miracle has impacted western thought (especially Christology and the understanding of Jesus' resurrection). For modern science and technology tend, as sociologists like Peter Berger have shown,[2] to have a profound secularizing impact wherever they go and therefore western experience may have some value for the entire church worldwide.[3]

THE IMPACT OF MODERN SCIENCE

One can understand why modern science made such a profound impact on modern thought. The scientific method offered a tool that enabled people to explore nature with a precision never before known. The technological developments which flowed from modern science brought immense new power over nature. Many phenomena that previous ages had explained by supernatural causes now received natural explanations. Comets and plagues were no longer supernatural signs of divine displeasure. They were perfectly natural events fully explicable by the new scientific approach.

More and more of the intelligentsia of the West concluded that modern science would soon be able to explain all phenomena in naturalistic terms. Increasingly, people limited reality to what empirical science could explain just as they reduced truth to empirical knowledge. Modern science seemed to banish the miraculous to the prescientific world of medieval superstition.

This new "scientific" outlook became a key element of modern historical methodology as it emerged in the nineteenth century. The belief that miracles do not and never did happen became a central presupposition of historical-critical scholarship. In his influential essay on historical methodology published in 1904, Ernst Troeltsch argued that the historiographical principles of analogy and correlation excluded the

2. Peter Berger, Brigette Berger, and Hansfried Kellner, *The Homeless Mind: Modernization and Consciousness* (New York: Vintage Books, 1973).

3. The issues focussed in this essay are not the only critical ones where modern western Christology has been inadequate. The second phase of the Enlightenment pioneered by Marx raises other critical questions. Elsewhere I have stated my conviction that liberation of the poor and oppressed was one of the central aspects of Jesus' mission. See Ronald J. Sider, *Rich Christians in an Age of Hunger* (Downers Grove: Inter-Varsity Press, 1977); *Cry Justice* (New York: Paulist Press, 1980); and "An Evangelical Theology of Liberation," in *Perspectives on Evangelical Theology*, ed. Kenneth S. Kantzer and Stanley N. Gundry (Grand Rapids: Baker, 1979), pp. 117-34. Any Christology that ignores that important concern as modern western European Christology has largely done is simply unbiblical. Since I cannot discuss everything in a short paper I have chosen to limit my remarks to some problems posed by the first phase of the Enlightenment.

possibility of the historian accepting the historicity of alleged miracles.[4] That view, which has dominated much modern biblical scholarship, received perhaps its most lucid and persuasive expression in Van Harvey's *The Historian and The Believer*.

That such a view would have a profound effect on Christian theology in general and Christology in particular is obvious.

Van Harvey sees modern Protestant theologies in the last two centuries as essentially "salvage operations" designed to reconcile Christian affirmation with the Enlightenment's standard of truth.[5]

Historic Christian theism was supernatural to the core. It is not just that Christians over the ages have believed two monumental miracles in their confession of the incarnation and bodily resurrection—although those two affirmations certainly are the heart of the matter. The miraculous is also integral to the historic Christian understanding of many basic things such as regeneration, the work of the Holy Spirit, prayer, and eschatology. One can, of course, to take the case of prayer, follow Tillich and reinterpret prayer as meditation or self-hypnosis. But only with the presupposition of historic, supernatural theism does intercessory prayer make sense.

From the time of Immanuel Kant in the late eighteenth century to the publication of *The Myth of God Incarnate*[6] in 1977, one can see the direct impact of this rejection of the supernatural.

THE REJECTION OF THE SUPERNATURAL

In his lectures, *What Is Christianity*, published in 1900, liberal historian/theologian Adolf Harnack began with the presupposition that miracles do not happen. He therefore rejected the traditional view of the incarnation and the resurrection, not to mention the miracle stories in the Gospels, as incompatible with modern science.[7] Naturally, he also abandoned historic Christology. Jesus was Son of God only in the *functional* sense that he knew God as father and obeyed him fully. Jesus therefore serves as the unique teacher who shares with us the truth about God. The object of our faith is not Jesus, the God-man, but God. Jesus is simply a great teacher who uniquely reveals God.[8]

4. Ernst Troeltsch, "Uber historische und dogmatische Methode in der Theologie" (1898), *Gesammelte Schriften* (Aalen: Scientia Verlag, 1962), 2:729-53.

5. Van A. Harvey, *The Historian and The Believer* (New York: Macmillan, 1966), p. 246.

6. *The Myth of God Incarnate*, ed. John Hick (London: SCM, 1977).

7. Adolf Harnack, *What Is Christianity?* (New York: Harper Torchbooks, 1957), pp. 24ff. E.g., "We are firmly convinced that what happens in space and time is subject to the general laws of motion, and that in this sense, as an interruption of the order of Nature, there can be no such things as "miracles" (p. 26).

8. *Ibid.*, pp. 124-63.

About the same time, Albert Schweitzer was coming to even more radical conclusions. Schweitzer stressed the eschatological aspects of Jesus' proclamation and thought that Jesus believed himself to be the Messiah. At his trial, Jesus confessed to the high priest his belief in his own messiahship and deity. At this point, however, Schweitzer asks whether Jesus was justified or deluded in his claim. Daniel Fuller puts it as follows:

> To say that he was justified would involve accepting supernaturalism. To say that he was deluded would reject supernaturalism but it would involve something else: a rejection of any worth that Jesus might have for the human race, for of what value are the thoughts of a deluded, apocalyptical fanatic? Schweitzer chose the alternative of saying, in as nice a way as possible, that Jesus was deluded: "Jesus, in the knowledge that he is the coming Son of Man, lays hold of the wheel of the world to set it moving on that last revolution which is to bring all ordinary history to a close. It refuses to turn, and he throws himself upon it. Then it does turn and crushes him. Instead of bringing in the eschatological conditions, he has destroyed them. The wheel rolls onward, and the mangled body of one immeasurably great man, who was strong enough to think of himself as the spiritual ruler of mankind as to bend history to his purpose, is hanging upon it still. That is his victory and his reign."[9]

Schweitzer therefore concluded that the historical Jesus (who of course was only a man and did not rise from the dead) had nothing whatsoever to do with faith. Faith involves some mystical, undefined "spirit of Jesus."

> It is not Jesus as historically known, but Jesus as arisen within men, who is significant for our time and can help it. . . . The abiding and eternal in Jesus is absolutely independent of historical knowledge.[10]

Sometimes modern scholars and theologians have tried to maintain a traditional, historic Christian view of the incarnation and resurrection while accepting the Enlightenment's general view of the miraculous. Such a viewpoint is methodologically and logically inconsistent. If we believe in the incarnation and the bodily resurrection, there is no philosophical or theological reason for not also accepting a supernatural view of the virgin birth, prayer, and miracle stories in the Bible. Conversely, if we agree with Rudolf Bultmann that "it is impossible to use electric lights and the wireless and to avail ourselves of modern medical and surgical discoveries and at the same time to believe in the New Testament world of spirits and miracles,"[11] then we must be consistent and reject not just

9. Daniel P. Fuller, *Easter Faith and History* (Grand Rapids: Eerdmans, 1965), p. 75. The quotation from Schweitzer is from his *The Quest of The Historical Jesus* (2nd ed.; London: A. and C. Black, 1931), pp. 368-69.

10. Quoted in Fuller, *op. cit.,* p. 76.

11. R. Bultmann, "New Testament and Mythology," in *Kerygma and Myth* (New York: Harper Torchbooks, 1961), p. 5.

the miracle stories of the Gospels or a supernatural view of intercessory prayer but also the incarnation and resurrection. If Bultmann and Ernst Troeltsch are right, intellectual integrity demands the logically necessary step of fundamentally reinterpreting all miraculous aspects of traditional Christianity no matter how painful and disruptive it is to ourselves and the church.

The Roman Catholic theologian, Hans Küng, is correct in saying in *On Being a Christian* (first published in 1974):

> We tried to understand the numerous miracle stories of the New Testament *without assuming a "supernatural" intervention—which cannot be proved*—in the laws of nature. It would therefore seem like a dubious retrogression to discredited ideas if we were now suddenly to postulate such a supernatural "intervention" for the miracle of the resurrection: this would contradict all scientific thinking as well as all ordinary convictions and experiences. Understood in this way, the resurrection seems to modern man to be an encumbrance to faith, akin to the virgin birth, the descent into hell or the ascension.[12]
>
> . . . All objections to the disciples' reception of new experiences with Jesus raised to life can in fact be reduced to one. Are we postulating here a supernatural intervention, the very thing that we tried to avoid in regard both to miracles and to the empty tomb? Three points may be considered.
>
> (i) There would in fact be an *a priori* suspicious retrogression to superseded ideas if we were to attempt first to understand the numberous New Testament miracle stories without the unprovable assumption of a "supernatural intervention" in the laws of nature and then at the end to postulate for the miracle of the resurrection just such a supernatural intervention, which is contrary to both scientific thinking and the convictions and experiences of ordinary people. If then we want to speak of the new experiences of the disciples after Jesus' death, they cannot be regarded as miracles canceling the laws of nature, in principle plain for all to see, but merely by accident not seen by the public at large.[13]

It is not surprising that Kung abandons the view that Jesus of Nazareth was born true God and true man. He keeps the traditional language, but fundamentally reinterprets its meaning.[14] Similarly, the authors of *The Myth of God Incarnate* link the abandonment of belief in the supernatural with their rejection of the incarnation. They can no longer accept the historic Christian belief in the incarnation because "idea of supernatural divine intervention was a natural category of thought and faith,

12. Hans Küng, *On Being a Christian* (New York: Pocket Books, 1978), p. 346.
13. *Ibid.*, p. 375.
14. *Ibid.*, pp. 436-63.

in a way that is no longer true of the main body even of convinced believers today.''[15]

Many other examples could be cited to show that the Enlightenment's belief that modern science is incompatible with belief in the miraculous has led to a fundamental reinterpretation of the resurrection and Christology, and of virtually all areas of theology.

It is exceedingly important to challenge this basic presupposition of modern liberal theology and modern historical methodology. To suggest the direction for such a challenge will be my task in the rest of this paper.

THE DOCTRINE OF GOD

What is really at issue is our doctrine of God. If the God of traditional theism exists, then nature is never free from the possibility of his miraculous intervention. If, on the other hand, the Enlightenment is correct and we ought to adopt a deistic view of God, then it would be *theologically* inappropriate to think of supernatural intervention. (A deistic God would be a lousy, incompetent clockmaker if he had to keep intervening to get his technology straight!) Similarly, if the philosophical naturalists are right and nature is all that exists, then of course miracle is impossible. Philosopher Merold Westphal puts it this way:

> When one speaks of the divine activity no conditions outside of God could be obstacles for the realization of what is logically possible. If God exists, miracles are not merely logically possible, but really and genuinely possible at every moment. The only condition hindering the actualization of this possibility lies in the divine will. For the theologian to say that scientific knowledge has rendered belief in miracles intellectually irresponsible is to affirm that scientific knowledge provides us with knowledge of limits within which the divine will always operates. Since the question of morality has been introduced, one may perhaps be permitted to inquire about the intellectual integrity of such an affirmation. Is peace with one's age to be purchased at any cost?[16]

It is sheer intellectual confusion to suppose that more and more scientific information makes belief in miracles more and more intellectually irresponsible. Science simply tells us with greater and greater (indeed breath-taking!) precision what nature regularly does. But no amount of scientific information could, in principle, ever tell us whether there might be a God outside nature who could intervene in nature if he chose.[17]

Modern science does not help us very much in the choice between

15. John Hick, *op. cit.,* p. 4.

16. Merold Westphal in a review of *The Historian and The Believer,* in *Religious Studies* 11 (1967), 280.

17. No book makes this point more clearly and lucidly than C. S. Lewis' *Miracles: A Preliminary Study* (London: Macmillan, 1947).

theism, deism, and naturalism. But if we are not confused by the Enlightenment's deism (or naturalism), many of the reasons for not accepting the historic theistic perspective on the incarnation and resurrection fall away. Furthermore, if we affirm that Jesus was true God and true man and believe that he rose bodily from the tomb, logical consistency demands that we do not use the Enlightenment's antisupernatural, deistic, or naturalistic arguments against traditional views on the virgin birth, the miracle stories of the Bible, the presence of the Holy Spirit, the future return of Christ, and prayer.

It is perhaps at the level of historical methodology that the most subtle forms of antisupernatural bias impact modern Christological thought. Without even citing evidence, predictions of Jesus' passion and resurrection are automatically excluded with the simple assertion that they are *vaticinia ex eventu*—predictions after the event.[18] Miracles do not happen and therefore Jesus' predictions about the future must have been placed in Jesus' mouth after the events occurred. Nor, it is similarly alleged, can the critical historian accept the accounts of Jesus' resurrection.

One of the best ways to explore this antisupernatural approach of modern historical methodology is to examine carefully the arguments of Van Harvey's brilliant book *The Historian and The Believer*.[19]

His position can be summarized under four points. First, Harvey argues that because of the "negative function of scientific laws" it is "impossible" for modern man to believe in the supernatural world of pre-Newtonian man. Second, since miracles are absolutely unique, it is impossible for the historian to know what would count for or against their actually having happened. Third, the comparative study of religion has shown that frequently fictitious miracle stories are told about founders of religion; therefore, the historian can assume that miracle stories about religious leaders are legendary. Fourth, reports of miracles are unacceptable to the modern historian because they come from naive, mythologically minded folk unaware of scientific laws.

THE NEGATIVE FUNCTION OF SCIENTIFIC LAWS

In the case of natural events (e.g., a bodily resurrection), current scientific "laws" have the negative function of telling the historian "what could have happened."[20]

Harvey has not fallen back into Ernst Troeltsch's "never-never land" where one rejects alleged miracles on metaphysical grounds. Harvey fre-

18. E.g., Rudolf Bultmann, *History of the Synoptic Tradition* (New York: Harper, 1963), p. 152.

19. In the following pages, I am using sections of my article "The Historian, The Miraculous and Post-Newtonian Man," *Scottish Journal of Theology* (Aug. 1972), 309-19.

20. Van Harvey, *op. cit.*, pp. 74-75.

quently cautions against saying that miracles are "impossible."[21] When Harvey speaks of the "impossibility" of belief in miracles, he very self-consciously avoids saying that belief in miracles is logically or metaphysically impossible. The impossibility of accepting reports of alleged miracles is a historically conditioned psychological impossibility on the part of the modern historian. Harvey identifies himself with those

> who believe that it is impossible to escape from the categories and presuppostions of the intellectual culture of which one is a part, the common sense of one's own time. . . . We are in history as fish are in water, and our ideas of *possibility and actuality are relative to our own time* [my emphasis]. . . . That is, no doubt, what Bultmann meant when he wrote that "it is impossible to use electric lights . . . and believe in the New Testament world of spirits and miracles." . . . We in fact *do not* believe in a three-story universe or in the possession of the mind by either angelic or demonic beings. It is to say more however. It is to say that we *cannot* see the world as the first century saw it. . . . These beliefs are no longer *practically possible* [my emphasis] for us.[22]

Modern people—or at least *some* modern people—find it practically, i.e., psychologically, impossible to believe in miracles. "This argument is difficult to make clear"[23] because it is specious. Are the psychological difficulties of modern people a criterion of truth?

Peter Berger discusses this point in his book *Rumor of Angels*. The sociology of knowledge shows us how and why we are conditioned to accept current ideas. "It is of course possible to go against the social consensus that surrounds us, but there are powerful pressures (which manifest themselves as *psychological* pressures within our own consciousness) to conform to the views and beliefs of our fellow men."[24] But the sociology of knowledge also relativizes the relativizers:

> When everything has been assumed under the relativizing categories in question (those of history, of the sociology of knowledge, or what-have-you), the question of truth reasserts itself in almost pristine simplicity. . . . The point can be illustrated by recent "radical" or "secular" theology, which takes as both its starting-point and its final criterion the alleged consciousness of modern man. . . . The *past* . . . is relativized in terms of this or that socio-historical analysis. The present, however, remains strangely immune from relativization. . . . The electricity—and radio—users are placed intellectually above the Apostle Paul. . . . It may be conceded that there is in the

21. *Ibid.,* pp. 85, 229.
22. *Ibid.,* pp. 114-15.
23. *Ibid.,* p. 115.
24. Peter Berger, *Rumor of Angels* (Garden City: Anchor Books, 1970), p. 34. My emphasis.

modern world a certain type of consciousness that has difficulties with the supernatural. . . . The diagnosed condition is *not* thereupon elevated to the status of an absolute criterion. . . . We may agree, say, that contemporary consciousness is incapable of conceiving of either angels or demons. We are still left with the question of whether possibly, both angels and demons go on existing despite this incapacity of our contemporaries to conceive of them. . . . What follows is *not*, as some of the early sociologists of knowledge feared, a total paralysis of thought. Rather it is a new freedom and flexibility in asking questions of truth.[25]

The historian, qua historian, cannot assume that traditional theism has been either finally proven or disproven. To do either would be to include a significant metaphysical presupposition in one's historical methodology. The historian must remain methodologically neutral. Personally, the historian may be a theist or a nontheist, but qua historian he ought— according to the morality of historical knowledge—to be an agnostic. As a methodological agnostic, he knows that the God of traditional theism *may* exist and that miracles would therefore be a real possibility. Hence he must decide the historicity of alleged miracles on the basis of the evidence that can be cited for each individual case.

ARE MIRACLES "ABSOLUTELY UNIQUE?"

Harvey describes a miracle as "an event alleged to be absolutely unique, which is to say, an event to which no analogies or warrants grounded in present experience can apply."[26] In the case of something absolutely unique, one would not know what one was talking about nor could one bring arguments for or against it, "for there are no criteria for dealing with an event unlike any other."[27]

> It makes it impossible to isolate data (what kind of evidence testifies to a unique event?), to employ warrants, to offer a rebuttal, or to attach any degree of probability to a claim. The claim that an event is unique, when unique is used in more than a trivial sense, is compatible with an infinite range of contradictory assertions.[28]

Harvey is correct in asserting that one could neither perceive nor conceptualize an absolutely unique event. But are alleged miracles "absolutely unique?" The fact that we can conceive and conceptualize reported miraculous events such as the feeding of the multitude or the resurrection of Jesus shows that they are not "absolutely unique." We can imagine what it would have been like to witness a miraculous feeding because

25. *Ibid.*, pp. 40-42. My emphasis.
26. Van Harvey, *op. cit.*, p. 225.
27. *Ibid.*, p. 228.
28. *Ibid.*, p. 227.

many elements of this alleged event are analogous with our experience. Frequently the only unusual aspects of a reported miracle are its basic structure (e.g., the supposed phenomenon of living again after death) and its apparent inexplicability in terms of present scientific knowledge. Lesser aspects of the total event, on the other hand, are quite common and analogous with present experience. Wolfhart Pannenberg argues that the principle of analogy is a useful tool that must be sharpened so that the historian can expand his knowledge of reality by grasping the dissimilar by means of the similar.[29]

By analogy with one's experience of living people one could in principle at least decide whether or not one were seeing a living person and whether he bore any continuity with some person who had died. The historian would want to examine the accounts of alleged meetings and visits to the place of burial. In principle then, the historian can isolate data and mount arguments on the basis of the nonunique aspects of alleged miracles. Even if in specific instances the historian decides that he lacks sufficient evidence to arrive at a firm conclusion, it will not be because of "the absolute uniqueness" of the alleged event, but because of the inadequacy of the sources. One must conclude that although Harvey correctly asserts that there are no criteria for dealing with absolutely unique events, he has confused the issue by his definition of miracle. Consequently his argument that the historian cannot deal with miracles because of their uniqueness fails completely.

THE HISTORY OF RELIGIONS ARGUMENT

The almost constant connection of frequently fictitious miracle tales with venerated founders of religions is the basis of what might be called the *religionsgeschichtlich* argument against the acceptance of reports of alleged miracles.

> The very existence of miracle stories has itself come to be regarded as a normal and expected occurrence. The contemporary historian expects to find miracle stories in certain kinds of literature.[30]

The human mind tends to produce "myths and legends" especially in connection with religion. "Indeed, if anything has been learned from the comparative study of religion it is that myth and legend are the almost natural forms of expression for the veneration of extraordinary founders, teachers and saints of religion."[31]

This argument is ambiguous. On the one hand the mere constant conjunction of miracle stories with founders of religions tells us nothing about the veracity of the reports. The constant conjunction of fighting in the

29. See his "Heilsgeschehen und Geschichte I: Die Geschichte Gottes und die historisch-kritische Forschung," *Kerygma und Dogma* (1959), 5:264ff.

30. Van Harvey, *op. cit.*, p. 88.

31. *Ibid.*

Middle East with the Arab charge that Israel initiated the hostilities unfortunately fails to identify the original belligerent. On the other hand
Harvey's equation of "miracle stories" with "myths and legends" which
are "almost natural" ways of venerating religious leaders, suggests that
he may have begged the question. If all miracle stories told about founders
of religion are false, then of course they are all false. Let us assume that
he has not begged the question but intends to argue first, that there is
a constant conjunction of miracle stories with religious heroes and, second,
that historical research into the specific reports has shown that very many
are legendary. Do these two findings of *religionsgeschichte* allow the historian
to reject any particular report of a miracle without examining the evidence
for that particular alleged miracle?

What is the status of the historian's generalization that when miracle
stories are told about religious leaders, they are frequently false? We have
already seen that current scientific "laws" do not warrant an automatic
rejection of any particular alleged miracle. The historian's generalization is far weaker than a scientific statement of observed regularity. The
historian cannot experiment and attempt to falsify his generalization in
the way the scientist can. Nor does the historian's generalization have
the mathematical precision of the scientist's "laws."

Further, in the case of some alleged miracles told about religious
leaders, competent people are in disagreement. Scientific "laws" are
suspect when competent observers allege counterinstances. One must conclude that Harvey's generalization (that when miracle stories are told
about religious leaders, they are frequently false) does not justify the
historian in denying the historicity of any alleged miracle apart from
careful examination of the evidence. Of course the conjunction of frequently fictitious reports of miracles with religious founders gives the
historian of religions advance warning to be on the alert for false miracle
stories. However, the historian must evaluate the evidence for each case
quite independently of all the false tales. Hence the frequent connection
of legendary miracle tales with religious leaders does not of itself decide
the historicity of any particular reported miracle.

THE NAIVETE OF PRESCIENTIFIC FOLK

Another argument against accepting reports of alleged miracles arises from
the fact that most miracle stories have been told by "naive and
mythologically-minded folk without any conception of natural law."[32]
"There is a sense in which myth and miracle are natural in some cultures
in a way they are not in our own—so natural, in fact, that the very notion
of an event that 'breaks known laws' (miracles) itself presupposes our
own worldview."[33] Although verbally correct, such a statement exag-
gerates the naivete of people who lived before the rise of modern science.

32. *Ibid.*, p. 10.
33. *Ibid.*, p. 88.

The author of the Fourth Gospel could pen the words: "Never since the world began has it been heard that anyone opened the eyes of a man born blind" (Jn. 9:32; cf. Lk. 1:34). Harvey may be correct in pointing out that since prescientific people observed regularities in nature less precisely than we, they found it easier to accept reports of unusual and miraculous events. This fact activates a warning signal. But one dare not overemphasize this point, or dismiss all pre-Newtonian accounts of alleged miracles solely on the ground that the stories were recorded by "mythologically-minded folk." Again, it is the evidence available for any particular alleged miracle that is decisive.

If the preceding arguments are valid, there seems to be no methodological veto against the historian's positively evaluating some report of an alleged miracle. The historian qua historian could never prove that an unusual event was inexplicable in terms of natural causes, much less that it was due to direct divine activity. At best the historian could say that the evidence for the event was strong enough for him to affirm its historicity even though the event was inexplicable in terms of present scientific knowledge. He could never rule out the possibility that future scientific knowledge would be able to explain the event as one instance of a regularly recurring pattern.[34] But the historian's inability to prove that the unusual event is a "miracle" does not preclude his ruling on its facticity. In the case of the alleged resurrection of Jesus of Nazareth, the historian qua historian could never demonstrate that *God* raised Jesus, but if he found the evidence adequate, he might conclude that Jesus was probably alive on the third day.

I conclude that the scientific method is not incompatible with belief in the miraculous. The Enlightenment's contrary suggestion rested on conceptual confusion and led to theological disaster. If the Christian church in the Two Thirds World learns from the last two centuries of western confusion at this point, its Christology will be the beneficiary.

IMPLICATIONS FOR MISSIOLOGY

The issues discussed in this paper are crucial for contemporary missiological debate. Nothing has done more to weaken the church's zeal to evangelize than the modern Christological view that Jesus is just a great moral teacher whose death has no atoning significance and did not constitute a major supernatural victory over satanic forces, who never rose from the dead, and who certainly will not return at the close of history

34. See Patrick Nowell-Smith, "Miracles," in *New Essays in Philosophical Theology,* ed. A. Flew and A. MacIntyre (New York: Macmillan, 1964), pp. 243-53, and especially p. 245.

to complete his victory over sin, injustice, and death itself. Tendencies toward such a view have largely destroyed evangelism in many western churches. Similar views will do the same elsewhere.

It is important to notice the methodological similarity between the mistakes of modern western Christology discussed here and the problems in some current theologies of liberation. At the beginning of this essay, I suggested that modern western Christology had failed at two important points: its widespread rejection of the supernatural; and its failure to make the historical Jesus' concern for the poor and oppressed and his inauguration of the Kingdom of God central to Christology. In both cases, the failure resulted from a *misplaced contextualization*.

Take the first mistake. Modern "scientific" thought argued that miracles do not happen. Therefore modern theology redefined Christology to eliminate the miraculous. The context—in this case the viewpoint of "modern scientific folk"—led to the abandonment of the very heart of historic Christology.

Methodologically, the same thing has happened as evangelicals have overlooked Christ's central concern for the liberation of the poor and oppressed. In this case the materialistic context of western middle class life seduced us. In our comfort, we overlooked Jesus' concern for the poor. In the process, we ignored a central element of the biblical teaching about Jesus Christ.

We must reject both these one-sided Christologies and return to a wholistic biblical understanding. But the Scriptures, rather than the context, must function as the essential norm. We need contextualized Christologies. Every local church needs to rethink Christ in light of their historical setting without churches from outside imposing a view of Christ from other cultures. But if biblical revelation does not remain the norm, there is no safeguard against subjectivity. One also undercuts any attempt to challenge other Christologies (e.g., North American Christologies unconcerned with the poor).

For instance, if liberation theologians say that since their context is decisive their Christology will deal primarily with Christ's social liberation and will deemphasize forgiveness and the atoning cross regardless of how central this is in the New Testament, they undercut their critique of North American theology. For middle-class North American Christians are justified in retorting from their context of affluence that a Jesus who sides with the poor and oppressed is hardly helpful in converting affluent business people and that therefore they have no obligation to make liberation for the poor central to their Christology.

Only a fully biblical Christ can meet the needs in all our different countries. Only a common commitment to surrender our partial, one-sided Christologies to the authority of God's revealed Word can provide the common ground for mutual discussion, challenge, and correction.

SELECT BIBLIOGRAPHY

Daniel F. Fuller. *Easter Faith and History*. Grand Rapids: Eerdmans, 1965.

Van A. Harvey. *The Historian and The Believer*. New York: Macmillan, 1966.

Ernst and Marie-Luise Keller. *Miracles in Dispute: A Continuing Debate*. Philadelphia: Fortress, 1969.

C. S. Lewis. *Miracles: A Preliminary Study*. London: Macmillan, 1947.

Peter Stuhlmacher. *Historical Criticism and Theological Interpretation of Scripture*. Philadelphia: Fortress, 1977.

Richard Swinburne. *The Concept of Miracle*. London: Macmillan, 1970.

14. Significant Trends in Christology in Western Scholarly Debate

DAVID COOK *(Scotland)*

Synopsis

An examination of how the forces of secularization, pluralism, and relativism condition Christology in the British context with a critical analysis of "The Myth of God Incarnate" and "Spirit-Christology" in the work of Geoffrey Lampe. The paper highlights the dangers of allowing our context to control our Christological understanding in an uncritical way.

INTRODUCTION

I want to express a very genuine gratitude that I have been invited to address you. It is important for the West to be represented, because you have a great deal to give to the West. This is a crucial time for the western theological enterprise. I do not think that western theology alone can solve its problems. We need your help.

But in spite of the past and, some would also say, because of the past, I believe that the West has still something to contribute to the task of mission and to the understanding of theology and of Christology today.

At the same time, I hope that the Two Thirds World will not be guilty of cultural theological imperialism by excluding and ignoring the West theologically. You do not need to look over your shoulder all the time to western theology. Nor do you require permission from anyone. Let the work speak for itself. Let the clarity of its presentation come across, its intellectual rigour be obvious, and its faithfulness to Scripture be clear. Let the sheer quality of work, the truth of its conclusions, and the final proof—the difference it actually makes—let these speak.

I want to say something about context too. This is not to deny particularity, but rather to return to our starting point in the keynote address. Orlando Costas reminded us that in the Latin American scene, in particular, there have been two helpful emphases: the historic Jesus and the cosmic Christ. He stressed the rediscovery of the historicity of Jesus as the starting point of Christology and integral with that, a proper understanding of the cosmic Christ. Both these themes speak to me very clearly of the universal context. The Jesus of the New Testament is the starting point of our Christology, and he is the cosmic Christ, the victor over all and is the Lord, the universal Christ. But that is also to say that Jesus is universal man. He became flesh in the particularity of the incarnation. As a man he was born into a social, economic, racial, and political context like all of us. He was born into a family, a religious, and a cultural context like us. These are universal aspects of context which cannot be ignored. They express the universality of Jesus the Lord: the universality of Jesus the incarnate one.

Kwame Bediako led us to another universal context: that of our human context, because we are all creatures, equally created. We are all equally made in the image of God. We are all sinners, fallen short of the glory of God. We are all women and men for whom Jesus Christ lived and died and rose again. And we are all people created for glory. Our humanity, based on our creation by God, and by Christ's life, death, and Lordship affirms these universal aspects of our contexts.

There is one more universal aspect. Here I act as a prophet, and a prophet is always tested by whether or not what he says comes true. For all our variety, we live in a rapidly shrinking world. It is a dehumanizing world and one of the new tools of dehumanization and of oppression is technology. Of course, technology can be our servant, but it may also be our master, or master us in the hands of others. We are on the verge of the universal, technological context. Even in the slums of Bangkok where people have little or nothing, TV aerials are attached to the slums. Even the beggars in the street often carry transistor radios. This shows the power of the media. This technological context will condition all that we think and do and how we live.

So one important task for the future is to express a Christology for that universal context for the technological world.

A CURRENT DEBATE

A typical evangelistic sermon might well be based on Peter's confession of Christ in Matthew 16:13-20. It would begin with the context and the first question Jesus put to his disciples, "Who do people say the Son of Man is?" This is a vital question in the context of the hill shrines in Caesarea Philippi. A list of prophets follows as possible descriptions of Jesus. Then the direct challenge, so loved of evangelists, is put, "Who do you say I am?" The quantity and variety of Christological writing and debate today shows that the question is still with us. But the responses to the question are as varied now as they were then. The difference, perhaps, is that the variety now exists *within* the church itself.

One key debate in the western theological context which became public in 1977 in Britain sums up many of the pressures on and the content of Christological understanding (or lack of it) in western theology. This "Myth of God" debate is an excellent example of the issues being discussed in Christology, and more importantly, of the different kinds of presuppositions at work from the different sides of the debate.

A number of concerns brought together a group of scholars from Birmingham, Cambridge, and Oxford. They varied from Regius Professors of Divinity to a Principal of an Anglican Theological College. They met, exchanged papers, and agreed to publish a book called *The Myth of God Incarnate*.[1] This was a summary of their thinking to date and an invitation to others to join the debate. All hell broke loose. Sadly, vicious personal responses tended to cloud the real issues. Animosity muddled genuine thought and critique. Replies were produced which culminated in a joint publication of material from a colloquy between the seven essayists and a group of their leading critics. This was entitled *Incarnation and Myth. The Debate Continued*.[2] This has helped to clarify some of the issues at stake.

The heat of the debate shows that Christological issues are not merely intellectual and coldly doctrinal. They are at the very heart of personal beliefs and of the public proclamation of the gospel in a multicultural, secularized, relativistic society. It matters deeply to people who Jesus is and how we are to talk appropriately of him. It is worth following the general lines of the debate, for it will show the Two Thirds World the problems theology faces in the West and its responses to these problems. At the same time it will serve as a warning to theologians and as an invitation to provide some new ways forward in Christological discussion. This is crucial because this is one way in which to begin to redress the imbalance of the past.

"THE MYTH OF GOD INCARNATE"

The essayists in *The Myth of God Incarnate* have differing viewpoints, yet share common concerns. They recognize that Christianity is not a static religion but is dynamic and developing. Part of this development is seen in the shift from a view of the Bible as verbally inspired by God. They have no doubt that the Bible has authority; yet they are equally certain that modern people cannot be intellectually honest and also accept the divine inspiration of Scripture. Humankind is seen as part of the evolutionary processes of nature and in the western culture that means that human beings live, move, and have their being in the context of scientific worldview. Western culture is dominated by scientific models of life, especially in the intellectual realm. Theology is threatened by scientific accounts of reality and scientific standards of procedure, validity, and certainty. The growth of human knowledge and understanding poses an increasing threat to traditional ways of understanding Jesus. The writers of *The Myth* do not believe that for Jesus to have a special role for the Christian he must be divine or God incarnate. Thus they believe that talk of incarnation cannot be meant literally. Rather it is a mythological

1. *The Myth of God Incarnate*, ed. John Hick (London: SCM, 1977).
2. *Incarnation and Myth: The Debate Continued*, ed. Michael Goulder (London: SCM, 1979).

way of expressing who and what Jesus means for us. Hence the provocative title of their collection of essays.

Such views rest on the more general western approach to Scripture and hence to expressions of doctrine in credal or preaching forms, called "demythologizing." Following Bultmann in particular, the notion of "demythologizing" can be expressed quite simply. The New Testament message comes to us in an ancient, mythological framework. The writers of the New Testament believed that they inhabited a three-decker universe, with heaven above, earth below that, and hell below earth. They believed in God and in demonic powers and beings. They believed that both could interrupt processes and control events in history and nature as well as people. They believed in the preexistence, virgin birth, death, resurrection, and glorification of Christ.

This framework of myth is incredible to modern people with their scientific worldview. True Christianity does not and cannot depend on such a primitive mythology. The real purpose of New Testament myth is *not* to give an objective picture of the world, but to express man's self-understanding. Myth is not so much a picture of the cosmos but more a means by which writers understand themselves. We are not to ask whether a myth correctly describes the universe, but whether it is a true understanding of human existence. The New Testament demands demythologizing because some of its mythical positions are contradictory.

We cannot, however, eliminate myth. Theology's task is to interpret myth existentially. Myth is the use of imagery to express the other-worldly in terms of this world and the divine in terms of human life, the other side in terms of this side. Mythological thought looks on divine activity in nature, history, or the life of a person. It objectifies the divine activity and projects it into the plane of worldly happenings. Therefore, myth is misleading for it encourages us to form wrong views of God. By "getting behind" the myths in the Bible, it is possible to reach the irreducible core—the kerygma—the good news of the gospel. This core needs to be reexpressed constantly in order that modern people may be confronted by gospel and grasp it for themselves.

The essayists fasten attention on one particular myth and show that the problems with this myth are so severe that we must seek alternative myths or descriptions. Such demolition is necessary for two main reasons. Firstly, intellectual honesty and a proper concern for truth leave no alternative. Secondly, the living presence and force of other religions both in the world and within the context of each nation must force Christians to accept the pluralism and relativism of our own culture. Note that this plea is a very similar plea to our plea to take the context seriously, but they arrive at a very different kind of conclusion. The appropriate response to the realities of pluralism and relativism is not dogmatism, but tolerance. Thus claims that Jesus is unique must be recast in light of similar assertions in relation to the central figures of other religions. The continued assertion of uniqueness is unwarranted arrogance. Here is a kind of confession of cultural imperialism in theology. The writers of *The Myth of God Incarnate* are more concerned to demolish faulty myths than to construct adequate new ones. They do not claim to be original but to be opening discussion in vital areas. Each writer then pursues a slightly different attack on the "myth" of God incarnate.

The lines of attack

The first attack starts from the variety of ways in which the New Testament and the early church talked of Jesus. The attack is twofold. First it is argued that there is no one correct way of talking about Jesus. There is no orthodox description, but instead a variety of descriptions. The early church interpreted Jesus in supernatural terms, but such terms are inappropriate for modern, scientific people.

Secondly in the history of the church the way of talking about Christ incarnationally has always been problematical. Such incarnational language is today totally unintelligible. This does not mean that there is nothing more to be said. We are left with incarnational *faith*. This faith is real and requires more appropriate "myths" to express its validity for modern culture. At the same time, the object of faith is in Jesus as a model for human life. The writers recognize that this reduction will raise some fundamental problems. How can this Jesus then be Saviour? To worship Jesus would be idolatrous, if Jesus is only man. The advantages would be increased intelligibility and the removal of uniqueness claims. This would pave the way for a more tolerant acceptance of other religions and their central figures.

The second attack seeks to define the essence of and the appropriate language for Christology. It asserts that the language of Christology is the language of confession and testimony, not the language of fact. At best the incarnation is an improbable fact and to assert such a "fact" is arrogant and intolerant. Rather we ought to seek new forms of expression for confessing faith in Jesus as the man for others and thus truly God's man.

The third attack asks why the church has taken so strong a position concerning the incarnation when the New Testament evidence does not support the tradition of the church. It is argued that incarnational myths in Jewish, Greek, and especially Samaritan writings offer a common picture of divinity in terms of incarnation and that, accordingly, Jesus is nothing special. It was natural for the writers of the New Testament to use these sources to portray the special place of Jesus in their own faith. That did not imply that he was actually incarnate. Later church tradition which "objectified" the "myth" of incarnation into terms of "essence" and "being" seriously distorts the intentions of the New Testament writers and their use of sources. Now is the time to get rid of metaphysics with its talk of unity of substance in relation to the person of Christ. In its place, we are to talk of the unity of activity in which a man can do what God wishes him to do and thus act as God in situations.

The fourth attack stems from a forceful presentation of the transcendence of God. There is a concern to let God be God and to recognize the necessity for a differentiation between Jesus and God. Jesus is an historical man, in whom traditional Jewish faith reached its fulfilment and became universal. But it is a mistake to regard Jesus as co-equally divine by nature. If we concentrate on Jesus, we are in danger of shifting the focus of attention from God to man and this leads directly to unbelief in God and to idolatry. We are idolatrous if we worship Jesus when his life and teaching was to lead people to worship God.

The fifth and final attack on the traditional notion of Jesus as the incarnate Son of God draws attention to four myths in Christian thinking. These are the myths of creation, the fall, incarnation and atonement, and resurrection and final judgement. The essayists see a process in theology where each of these myths has been progressively weighed and found wanting. The full flowering of critical and scientific understanding of the Enlightenment has seen the myths of creation, the fall, resurrection, and final judgement run into serious trouble. It has been necessary to reinterpret the traditionally accepted understandings of these doctrines into expressions which are intelligible and acceptable to modern people within their frames of reference. It is now time to reinterpret the "myth" of God incarnate. Thus the essayists see their work not as some new line of attack, but rather merely a part of a long-established process in which Christianity responds to the cultural and intellectual frameworks of real people and seeks new models, "myths," parables, or other forms of communication by which to express the reality of the gospel. They do recognize that such questioning of the incarnation may raise problems concerning the cohesion of Christianity as well as difficulty in discovering new and potent "myths" which will adequately express Jesus for modern man.

RESPONSES TO "THE MYTH"— CONTEXT AND CONTENT

The responses to the essayists and their work have been extremely varied and strongly expressed. In his essay "A Survey of Issues in the Myth Debate," Maurice Wiles writes that, "There are at least four different grounds . . . on which it has been claimed that the position . . . taken by the authors of the book is not merely mistaken but incompatible with genuinely Christian faith."[3] He lists them as the conservative evangelical objection, which protests at the gradual dismemberment of full-blooded Christianity; the Barthian objection, which complains at the resuscita-

3. Maurice Wiles, "A survey of issues in the myth debate," in *Incarnation and Myth,* p. 1.

tion of tired and discredited nineteenth-century ideas; the conservative Roman Catholic objection which complains at the conflict with and rejection of the church's self-definition at the Council of Chalcedon; and the "historical faith" objection, which protests that the form of Christianity in *The Myth of God Incarnate* is so different from what people normally understand as Christianity that it is misleading to call it Christianity.

Neither western theology nor our conference theme would benefit from the simple recital of these critiques and the claims and counterclaims. Nevertheless the debate following the publication of the original essays raises fundamental issues for Christology itself and the expression of Christology in a modern, scientific world. Western theology may be in danger of continuing down a cul-de-sac here and requires constructive, theological input from the Two Thirds World. I shall try to pinpoint the issues where such help is needed.

The important questions which require some treatment before an adequate Christology can be propounded in the West today fall under the two headings of *context* and *content*. The contextual questions centre on the nature of the western scientific, instrumentalist culture. The content questions centre on philosophical and theological issues. In terms of context, we need to consider relativism, pluralism, and reductionism. In terms of content, we need to examine the nature of being, knowing, and language as well as the nature of God, Scripture, Jesus Christ, and orthodoxy in terms of philosophical and theological categories.

CONTEXT

Secularization

Our context in the West is that of a secularized society. Theology suffers from the same disease as all else. The church and the Christian are affected by a transition from a culture where the beliefs, activities, and institutions presupposed beliefs of a Christian kind to a society and culture where the beliefs, activities, and institutions are based on atheistic views. Western society has been and is being effectively de-Christianized, de-divinized, and de-demonized. The categories of the sacred, mystery, holiness, transcendence, and otherness are increasingly foreign and mystifying to the modern person who has an empirical, pragmatic grasp of reality. This is accompanied by pluralism. We are confronted by a variety of competing worldviews and presuppositional frameworks. With the presence of others within our culture—other religions, other races, other cultures—everything is open to question, especially the areas of life which traditionally have been accepted in an uncritical way. For theology, the presence of other religions with their counterclaims of revelation, uniqueness, moral standards, and religious experience sows seeds of doubt in the minds of the Christian theologians. To this must be added the challenge of relativism. Meaning, truth, and falsity are simply relative to a particular culture at a particular time. There are no absolute universals. Morality and religious truth are culturally dependent and can only have relative truth and authority. Understanding can only be found within a limited context and no final judgement can be made between different cultures, attitudes, or ways of life.

One response to the challenges of pluralism and of relativism is reductionism. If everything is open to challenge, then a tactical withdrawal reducing the number of hostages to fortune, and only defending what is essential, seems a highly sensible manoeuvre. This reductionism is supported by the scientific temper of our culture. The critical, analytical style and practice of science tends to move from the wholistic and complex to the simple and irreducible by a process of reduction. It is also interesting to note how the second wave of the Enlightenment—Marx, Freud, and those like them—are interpreted in this kind of ''scientific'' and reductionist way. Marxists in the British context are more concerned with such philosophical analyses than with identifying with oppressed groups and people. Even Marxism is often reduced to a grasping of economic laws. This looks like a move toward greater certainty and immunity from criticism. Such a position has great attractions for the theologian. But that immunity is bought at too high a price. We have been critical of each other here and critical of each other's grasp of Christology. This is vital if we are to redefine our ideas and grow in understanding. We must not be immune from criticism.

Given that these aspects of culture are both real and condition the content and practice of theology, it is vital for theology to respond. It would be foolish to underestimate the normative role these cultural forms exercise on Christology. The frames of reference which theologians bring to their study are part of their cultural baggage. But need this be the case? There seems to be a too ready acceptance of the force of modern culture as necessary and appropriate without any real question. Are we inevitably subject to cultural presuppositions? Are we able to test such presuppositions and to make decisions to change or adapt our presuppositions? The liberal critic tends to function in the following way. The biblical writers had presuppositions. It is difficult for us to understand what they were really saying and meaning. Even if it is possible to discern that meaning and essence, it is so framed in a foreign context that we are unable to share those old-fashioned presuppositions. We are modern people and must use modern criteria.

There are, however, a number of problems. Is it fair to assume that we are unable to accept other presuppositions than our own because we are totally certain of our own set? Are we so sure that modern presuppositions are the correct ones? Are we so certain that we know what these ''modern'' presuppositions are? There is a tension here within our modern world. While it is true that modern science continues to have a vast impact on our knowledge and understanding, there is equally a reaction to scientism. Existentialism and existentialist theology, which seek to demythologize in order to discover the true essence of theological and biblical statements, proclaim that a personal nonsystematic, existential grasp of truth is proper to the nature of truth and to the nature of people. Theologians are guilty of drawing both from the scientific and existential emphases without realizing the tension between the two. This tension must call in question the "uniformity" of modern cultural presuppositions. There is much greater variety within our western culture than is clear from an analysis of theological reflection on that culture.

It is also doubtful whether the implications drawn from these presuppositions are necessary. In contrasting scientific accounts with other "mythical" accounts (like biblical stories), it is assumed that the scientific account is not mythical. The more careful admit that this is not the case, yet argue that the scientific "myths" are more appropriate than biblical ones. This allows scientific models a greater power than most scientists would claim for them. In picturing the nature of phenomena, scientists freely use atomic or subatomic "myths" and models. The scientists themselves make no claims that this is how things are, but rather that this is a way of describing how things behave under certain specified conditions. This pragmatic, flexible approach seems much less of a threat and more muted in its claims than the scientific models described by theologians. The danger is that the theologian may misunderstand the scientist and his claims and in the misapprehension allow the scientific worldview a normative role it does not claim and cannot sustain. Some would go further and argue that to seek to fit theology to the scientific worldview is to fail to do justice to theology. Its practices and forms are more those of the humanities than of the sciences.

Alternatively, a robust few are happy to affirm the scientific worldviews (properly understood in their muted form) and argue that there is a proper science of theology which is based on the same fundamental principle as all scientific knowledge: that to be rational is to be conditioned by the nature of the object. This is what the true theologian does in his approach to the object of theology, God himself. Our argument here is to question whether we have a proper grasp of the nature of modern culture and in particular whether scientific forms of investigation can or do pose the kinds of threat which seem to force theologians along the path of reductionism.

Much of the hesitation concerning the doctrine of the incarnation is an unease concerning the possibility of divine interaction with and involvement in the historical and natural processes. Modern science rules out an interventionist God, it is claimed. But traditional Christianity, based on the Bible, finds no embarrassment in talk of God's activity in history, in nature, and in the lives of people. Indeed, to understand any and all of these, reference to God is essential. We would need to be very clear what scientific presuppositions were being applied here such as to exclude God from activity in his universe. It is too easy to talk about science in general and thus fail to discover that no particular scientific model could so operate without destroying its own status as a model and its claims to be scientific.

Even if it were possible to specify some detailed scientific presuppositions which are the very essence of modern culture and to contrast those with the presuppositions of biblical writers, this of itself does not imply that there is no one more correct way of looking at the world than another. Nor indeed does it necessarily imply that the modern view is obviously more correct. Such a judgement rests not so much on the difference in frameworks, as in the belief that humanity's judgement and understanding are developing and thus are "more correct" now than in any previous time. This need not be the case and requires proof for its assertion.

There seems too a hesitation to recognize that we can reflect on, criticize, and change our presuppositions. The essayists in *The Myth of God Incarnate* seem to believe that the poor old biblical writers had to accept their worldview and we, fortunate, enlightened souls, have to accept our worldview. This is far too static a view of presuppositions. We are able to specify our presuppositions and to reflect critically upon them. While we cannot criticize them all at once, it is possible to criticize each and every one in turn and to revise them. The very fact of the fundamental changes in presuppositions in any kind of political, scientific, or religious conversion shows that this is clearly no case of special pleading. It is a necessary fact of life for new knowledge to be discovered and present mistakes corrected. It is in this questioning of the presuppositions of western culture that the Two Thirds World has a vital role to play. Such a contribution would provide tools for the critique as well as preventing cheating by western theologians begging the questions in their own favour.

Pluralism

The next feature of the context to be examined is pluralism. The presence of other religions and the special roles of their religious founders is held to constitute a fundamental challenge to the claims of uniqueness for Christ. Mutual toleration is the proper safeguard against such misguided arrogance. There is a genuine possibility of undercutting this challenge. If Two Thirds World theologians are able to expound a full-blooded Christology both in spite of and yet in relation to Islam, Hinduism, Buddhism, traditional religions, and the sociological analyses of liberation movements, then the supposed threat from other cultures to Christology and its traditional exposition is dissolved. The cure of tolerance would thus be the antidote for a nonexistent disease. One is puzzled how the sheer fact of a plurality of positions is held to act as a brake in the affirmation of any one correct view. The fact of many opinions does not, in itself, mean that there is no one true view. This is applied directly to the analysis of the Christology of the New Testament by reference to Jewish, Greek, and Samaritan redeemer myths. It may be true (but it is by no means universally accepted by Inter-Testamental and New Testament scholars) that there are close parallels between these myths and that the New Testament writers used these myths to express their understanding of Christ. But this is not the same as to assert that Christ is therefore of the same standing as the other "redeemers." The genetic fallacy is at work here, where the explanation of origin does not explain the full essence and content of a view.

Relativism

Relativism seems, however, to constitute a major challenge to Christian claims concerning the truth of the incarnation. There is, though, the danger of too uncritical acceptance of relativism. A total relativistic claim, that everything is relative to a particular culture and time, is subject to its own test and scrutiny. The judgement that "everything is relative" is itself relative to a particular culture and time. Thus to establish its primacy is to go beyond the proper claims of relativism. Such an attempt leads to contradictions. If "everything is relative" and this absolutely so, we find that everything is not relative, for we have one absolute which affects everything. If, in contrast, everything is not relative, then the strong threat from relativism is mere shadow and a proper caution to interpret things in their appropriate contexts.

The relativist must also establish that no facets of man or of the world continue through the various cultures and times. Such an exercise and proof would need to be very exhaustive and thorough, and many, Christian and non-Christian alike, look to the nature of people, morality, religion, and the nature of the world as the ground of genuine continuity between and among cultures. If, however, it could be established that relativism were correct, then it is important for the relativist (and those who seek to reduce or adapt Christianity to meet that challenge) to realize that the relativist knife cuts more than one way. The objectivity of theology and its claims may be questioned, but so may those of science and modern culture. One cannot stop being relativistic at whatever point one chooses. Theology and so Christology are in no worse (and no better) a position than any other discipline, if relativism is correct. We certainly do not find every period of history and every cultural setting equally difficult to understand and we can identify common features with our own culture and time. We must examine why particular cultures and times may be especially difficult for modern people to grasp. It is hard to see what is so extremely difficult in the cultural setting of first-century Palestine, that we are so hesitant in understanding that, while readily accepting much earlier and equally "foreign" cultures of Greece, China, and many others.

Reductionism

The final feature for comment in terms of content is reductionism. We know from the paradoxes of Zeno that, while in theory we may continue to cut slices from a cake leaving some cake still to be cut ad infinitum, in practice there comes a point where there is, in fact, no more cake. Reductionism likewise leads in the end to nothing. The reductionist replies that a minimum something is left. Here the debate for Christology is how far it is possible to reduce the account of the nature of Christ and yet retain some account which is in recognizable continuity with orthodox views of Jesus. The irreducible minimum would have to be an absolutely certain base, or the move would have been pointless. If the line between scientific and other myths cannot be clearly drawn, greater certainty will not come if one moves to a purely scientifically acceptable account. No one who reads the New Testament and who studies church history and doctrine can fail to realize the variety of expressions concerning Jesus. This variety has been held together to point to the complex fact of Jesus, God incarnate. There is a real family resemblance and continuity between these various expressions and motifs. There is a real Christian shape to the doctrine of Christ. To seek to reduce that complexity to one facet alone seems to do violence to the reality of Jesus.

We shall see how Geoffrey Lampe's attempt to reduce Jesus to the overarching concept of Spirit inevitably does violence to the preexistent and postexistent Christ, with all the work which is his and his alone in the biblical accounts. Such a reduced Christ, like the reduced Christ of the mythographers, is a very far cry from orthodox Christianity. This is the ground for seriously questioning their standing as Christians within the tradition of Christendom. Are all views open and freely to be propounded by those called Christian theologians? Is there no standard of orthodoxy and heresy left? The writings of the mythographers certainly imply rejection of such sharp distinctions. It is as if such a dividing line is itself almost sub-Christian.

Yet in the end they do and must recognize some limits. They appear to favour the test of appropriateness. However, this still leaves open the questions, "Appropriate to whom? Appropriate to what? Appropriate for what purpose?" The traditionalist points back to Scripture and the doctrinal tradition as the ground of appropriateness, resting ultimately in the reality of Christ himself. The mythographers point instead to modern culture and scientific terms as the actual standards of intelligibility and appropriateness.

If we are being asked to reject scriptural and traditional formulations there must be an overwhelming ground for such a change. Also the "reduced" account must be shown to be much more intelligible and appropriate to the reality of Christ for modern people. It is not obvious that the kind of Christ pictured by the mythographers or Lampe, as an exponent of Spirit-Christology, is any more believable to modern people, far less that this is a more adequate view of Jesus.

CONTENT

In our reflection on the pressures at work in the task of expounding Christology to western people we move now from the issues of context—

secularization, pluralism, relativism, and reductionism—to those of content. The link between context and content may be seen in terms of presuppositions. If one accepts, even critically, the reality of secularization, pluralism, and relativism, how does this affect one's presuppositions concerning the general issues of ontology, epistemology, the relation of language to reality, and the specific issues of the nature of God, Scripture, Jesus Christ, and orthodox doctrine? If one accepts the necessity and force of these contextual presuppositions, this will mean a fundamental shift in the kind of content presuppositions one holds. It will seem necessary to adapt the content of traditional biblical and doctrinal accounts to fit the context of modern culture. In contrast, if one is highly skeptical as to the normative nature and content of the modern context itself, one is even more wary of adapting traditional biblical and historical accounts which lay claim to some objective ground, to fit the passing subjective fancy and spirit of a passing age.

One clear lesson from church history is to avoid an overdependence on the philosophy and cultural norms of the day. One leading western theologian, T. F. Torrance, propounds the doctrine of Christ in light of and in relation to the modern scientific theories of relativity and of quantum mechanics with special reference to the nature of light, space, and time. But any cultural shift from these models of scientific understanding means the collapse of any description and doctrine of Christ which is totally integrated with those models. While Christian doctrine and Christology must be as intelligible as possible within any culture, no particular doctrine must be reduced to the models and terms of that culture without some remainder.

While we may share the presuppositions of modern culture as modern people, we are not totally the prisoners of such presuppositions. We can reflect critically upon our own deeply held presuppositions and change these in light of new understanding of truth or of new insight into old truth. When we approach the specific categories of being, knowing, and the relation of language to reality, we find the normative role played by cultural spectacles. Reality is what is there. But what is that and how are we to describe it?

For Christology the problem comes most sharply in the debate over what constitutes a fact. When this is applied to the historical realm we run into divergence. The traditionalist is quite happy to talk of the facts of the life of Jesus and the fact of the various expressions of his divinity recorded in the Gospels. From these facts it is perfectly proper to infer that Jesus is fully God and fully man from his words, works, his life, death, and resurrection. For the mythographers, these cannot be facts for they run contrary to the presuppositions of modern culture. They are unintelligible if taken literally and can only be understood as myths pointing more to the response of faith by the writers of the New Testament than to objective facts. Such a narrow view of fact is neither appropriate to the theory and practice of science today, nor to the integrity of the

New Testament writers. The standards theologians would like to apply to Scripture are far more stringent than scientists and historians use in their work.

EPISTEMOLOGY

Behind this tension between the mythographers and the traditionalists is a different stress in epistemology. For the mythographers, knowing is to be conformed to scientific criteria. But in practice they reject the biblical account as subjective, while accepting the "subjective" scientific account as if it were objective. The interaction of the subjective and objective aspects of knowing are universal and this shows the folly of too narrow a view of epistemology based purely on so-called "empirical facts" or "feelings." In relation to knowing God, the criteria are often applied in such a way as to deny any concept of the supernatural. Naturalistic reductionism seems to be the operative force here. If we rule out any activity of a transcendent, supernatural God in relation to his creation purely on the grounds of modern scientific understanding, we set too great store by one set of "myths" and force these "myths" to do a job they were never intended to do.

If one starts with a God totally removed from or simply identical with his creation, then it is difficult to see how God can "act" in the world and the affairs of people. If, however, our understanding of God rests ultimately on the point of intersection of transcendence and immanence, the God-man Jesus, then there is no necessary gap between divine and human action. This is equally true in our understanding of the person of Christ. It is claimed that we can make no sense today of talk of divine and human natures existing united in one person. Yet we find no difficulty at all in talking of people in general in two radically different ways. We ascribe to them physical, material properties and talk to them as objects in the physical world. We also describe people by reference to mental events and to the activity of the mind and the nature of their personality. It is difficult to say exactly how these two aspects of people's nature relate and are integrated, but we are certain that a person has these different aspects and that to talk properly about a person one must use both frames of reference.

If one starts with a divided Christ, it is difficult to see how the aspects of divinity and humanity can be matched. If, however, the historical reality of Christ is from the very moment of his conception a living expression of a united nature, which is referred to by different terms, there seems to be no real problem. The New Testament writers had no such problems and move freely between the two frames of reference. Problems arise when these frames of reference are reduced to or analyzed into categories stemming from particular ontologies and philosophies which do not begin with the fact of divine-human unity in Christ.

DAVID COOK

Our knowing then must be true to the object to be known. God's revelation of himself is to be found in creation, history, and most of all in Christ. We must say most of all in Christ, if we are to take seriously the fall and its implications for human knowing. There is now an ambiguity in creation and in history, which means that our grasp of God and his activity in these spheres is not crystal clear. It will be protested that there is still ambiguity in apprehending Christ. It is in the resolution of the ambiguities that the difference emerges. If I recognize God in creation and history, I assent to a fact and may have feelings in light of that. In assenting to Christ, one is transformed by the power and presence of the living Christ; hence the sharp distinctions in the New Testament between darkness and light and the children of darkness and the children of light. The knowledge of Christ transforms if it is a fully personal and community knowing.

We have argued that we must avoid too narrow an account of epistemology. Polanyi makes the point that we know much more than we say.[4] This is as true in knowing Christ as in our other experiences. This gap between reality and how we talk of that reality leads us to the relationship of language to reality. The mythographers recognize that language is subtle. They are concerned that talk of "historical fact" misleads. Mythical language is what is actually at work. There is a proper concern here. In all our talk of God and of Christ, there must be an element of inadequacy in our language and expressions. We cannot produce a final linguistic account which will totally encapsulate the reality of God in Christ. But this is, in a very important sense, no less true of all our language whether it be scientific or literary. Thus theology needs no more desperate measures than other disciplines.

But the fact that we cannot say everything absolutely, does not mean that we can say nothing, nor that what we say is unreliable. The skeptical doubt which threatens all knowledge is lurking ominously and it is a crucial mistake to take the skeptic too seriously. We have perfectly proper ways of checking doubts and dealing with ambiguities in language. Our linguistic usage is extremely refined. In theology, there are ways of talking in terms of sense and reference, which we acquire as we study theology and engage in theological debate and discussion. We need not be afraid to speak of God, realizing that there are proper questions of meaning to be put by philosophers. These questions are not in themselves destructive. They are invitations to greater clarity. We need not fear such questions nor such clarity.

The content of ontology, epistemology, and language's relation with reality are very closely interwoven. There is a dominant western model at work. It is not at all clear that this model is correct nor that there are

4. Michael Polanyi, *Personal Knowledge: towards a post-critical philosophy* (London: Routledge and Kegan Paul, 1973).

no viable alternatives. Two Thirds World theologians must help us to establish such alternatives. In terms of the other aspects of content—God, Scripture, Jesus, and orthodox doctrine—the starting point is crucial. The answers one arrives at are a result of the questions one asks. The mythographers seem to write with the kind of answer which will be acceptable in mind. This either sees God as totally transcendent or totally immanent. Jesus is truly human and may be affirmed as the proper person for us to emulate and follow in the quality and character of his life. Scripture is an expression of how the early church understood its own faith and feelings and offers us stories which encapsulate the intentions of the writers. Orthodoxy is too important to be left to the church because of the danger of begging the questions in favour of the church. Our modern culture and its criteria of sense, nonsense, meaning, and truth must be the appropriate setting for deciding what can be believed.

These presuppositions are open to dispute. We have already seen major problems within the notion of the modern context and in its applications to theology and Christology. The attitude to Scripture typifies the divergence between traditionalists and the mythographers and has a fundamental effect on Christology as well as the doctrine of God. There is no disagreement about the necessity for close New Testament analysis and a proper grasp of the contemporary literature. How we interpret the Bible is the issue at stake. Are we to set the standards for the interpretation of Scripture, or are we to sit under the authority of the Bible? Do we believe that the Bible is the Word of God and carries with it authority for doctrinal understanding and expression? If not, there is no use in looking at John 1, Philippians 2, Colossians 1, and Hebrews 1, or any other central Christological passage in the New Testament. If my own authority is to weigh equally with that of Scripture, I may paint a portrait of Christ in my own image. At least then it will be a relatively modern portrait. This is ultimately a dispute about revelation and what constitutes the given for Christology. My own experience cannot be the sole criterion, for it requires something objective, outside myself to constitute experience and to give reality instead of self-delusion. Logically and theologically, we must turn to Scripture and the accounts of the realities of God and Christ. If we do not believe that there is historical fact in the New Testament, Christological study seems a pointless exercise. Yet theologians who share the presuppositions of the mythographers continue to do Christology. What that Christology is like we shall see from an analysis of Geoffrey Lampe's book *God as Spirit*, and his essay "The Holy Spirit and the Person of Christ."[5]

5. Geoffrey Lampe, *God as Spirit* (Oxford: Clarendon Press, 1977); "The Holy Spirit and the Person of Christ," in *Christ, Faith and History,* ed. S. W. Sykes and J. P. Clayton (Cambridge: Cambridge University Press, 1972).

DAVID COOK

SPIRIT-CHRISTOLOGY: A CASE STUDY

For Geoffrey Lampe, Christology has been overdependent on the concept of Word and failed to do justice to the concept of Spirit. The advantages of the concept of spirit over all others for "articulating the Christian experience of God" are that it is less open to hypostatization, less confined to rational categorization, less liable to be misunderstood as implying a go-between God, and more flexible for the task of representing personal relationships. Lampe is aware of his departure from traditional norms, "I shall certainly not claim that the views I have expressed are compatible with the way in which the ancient creeds articulate our faith."[6] Lampe's claimed intention is not to "reject the model of incarnation as the key to Christology and replace it with the model of inspiration."[7] For, he argues, " 'Incarnation' and 'inspiration' are not in fact two quite different alternative models for Christology."[8] Nevertheless, when he tries to describe the relationship of God and Jesus, he suggests that, "the concept of God as Spirit seems to provide a more satisfactory theological model than that of God the Son."[9]

Lampe denies that God performed an act of salvation once and for all at a particular moment in history. He cannot accept the idea of a divine interruption into a fallen world to rescue it from the power of evil, to save man from sin and from the consequential wrath of God, and restore him to the divine likeness in which he was created. He writes,

> If these traditional pictures, or any others which depict salvation as a decisive act of God performed at a definite point in history, represent that which God has done for us in Jesus, then no doubt the best model for Christology is the divine person of the pre-existent Son who comes down into the world of human sin and demonic tyranny, defeats the devil in the battle of Good Friday and Easter, and bears the penalty of sin or offers the perfect sin-offering in the human nature which he assumed, free from the inheritance of original sin. If, however, we reject these myths of redemption, we may give a different answer to the question, "What has God in Jesus done for man that man himself could not do?"
>
> We do reject these pictures. . . .[10]

Lampe's answer follows immediately. God has, in Jesus, "brought the process of creation to the point where perfect man appears for the first time."[11] Thus we must look at the person of Christ in Lampe's

6. *God as Spirit*, p. 228.
7. *Ibid.*, p. 12.
8. *Ibid.*
9. *Ibid.*, p. 13.
10. *Ibid.*, pp. 15-16.
11. *Ibid.*, p. 17.

analysis in *God as Spirit* and "The Holy Spirit and the Person of Christ," an essay in *Christ, Faith and History* edited by Sykes and Clayton.

Lampe elsewhere challenges the notion of the preexistent Christ and the incarnation. He writes of the way to interpret Jesus "coming down" to the human sphere in his person. He argues,

It might be expected that the most appropriate concept for the expression of this image would be Spirit-possession. God's Spirit is his own active presence: God himself reaching out to his creation. It also stands for the immanence of the presence of God within men's souls. The Spirit may possess a man and in some measure unite his personality to God. Yet this is without any diminution of his humanity; rather, it means the raising of his humanity to its full potentiality, the completion of the human creation by the re-creating influence of the creator-Spirit. Through Spirit-possession a man may be divinely motivated and act divinely—he may be at one with God—and become at the same time, and because of this, fully and completely human.[12]

This means,

Spirit christology cannot affirm that Jesus *is* "substantially" God. . . . It does not follow that Jesus is only "adjectivally" God, that is to say, God-*like* or "divine" in the sense of being a man who possessed to an excellent degree the qualities that we attribute to God. An interpretation of the union of Jesus with God in terms of his total possession by God's Spirit makes it possible, rather, to acknowledge him to be God "adverbially."[13]

Such a Spirit-Christology

has the advantage of enabling us to dispense with certain mythical concepts, such as a pre-existent Son (for it is the possessing and inspiring Spirit that is the eternally pre-existing deity which operates humanly in Christ), a descent from heaven of a personal being who chooses to be born and become an infant, a divine being who may either exercise and voluntarily suspend his omniscience.[14]

In *God as Spirit* Lampe adds,

Nor do we need the concept of a "post-existent" continuing personal presence of Jesus, himself alive today, in order to interpret our own continuing experience of God's saving and creative work. The Kingdom of God which Jesus called men to enter is here today. . . . Those people who in some measure respond in a Christlike

12. *Christ, Faith and History*, p. 117.
13. *Ibid.*, p. 124.
14. *Ibid.*

way to God the Spirit within them are a body in which God the Spirit is concretely manifested and through which he is at work in our world.[15]

For Lampe this Spirit-filled Jesus is authentically human, but is no mediator between man and God.

> For when we speak of God as Spirit we are not referring to a divine mediator. The early church's theology demanded a mediator between God and his creation. . . . Yet in fact we need no mediator. It is God himself, disclosed to us and experienced by us as inspiring and indwelling Spirit (or Wisdom or Word), who meets us through Jesus and can make us Christlike.[16]

When dealing with Paul's concept of Christ's resurrection by God for our justification, Lampe is clear.

> We do not share his (Paul's) Pharisaic presuppositions, and we should be very cautious about following him in his belief that Jesus was dramatically vindicated in a resurrection-event. . . . it is also a dangerous temptation to think that Good Friday was reversed by Easter. . . . If Easter were needed in order to assure us that God set the seal of his approval on Jesus, this would mean that our faith was altogether less advanced than that of the heathen centurion.[17]

On the same theme he writes a few pages later,

> In taking this view we need not fear . . . that if the bones of Jesus lie somewhere in Palestine we can have no confidence that death has been overcome, and, in consequence, no hope and faith for the future of ourselves as individuals or for the ultimate salvation of the human race. We may leave aside the literal question concerning the whereabouts of Jesus' bones. . . . they cannot be supposed to be elsewhere than in Palestine. That question is of little importance.[18]

This leads to Lampe's account of the final consummation in eschatological terms.

> We can, perhaps, retain the idea of a visible *parousia*: not in the impossible sense of a personal return of Jesus from a heavenly throne, but in the form of the consummation of God's creation of mankind, when human society will have been so fully transformed into the likeness of the archetypal "Adam" that Christ will have reappeared in the form of a Christlike community, where God's incarnate Spirit is manifestly present—a "coming" of the Lord Jesus in, rather with,

15. *God as Spirit,* p. 33.
16. *Ibid.*, p. 144.
17. *Ibid.*, p. 155.
18. *Ibid.,* pp. 158-59.

his "holy ones." This is a *parousia* of God as Spirit in his perfected creation—God, the Spirit who was in Jesus.[19]

Thus Lampe brings us to his view of eternal life.

> Once Christians have discarded the mythical picture of the goal of human history as a personal *parousia* of a post-existent Jesus, and of divine judgement as a great assize at the end of the world, over which he will preside, there is no need for them to maintain the Pauline distinction between life "in Christ" now and life "with Christ" hereafter.[20]

Lampe's position in Spirit-Christology has a positive and a negative aspect. Positively, he believes that God is one person not three, and that the Spirit therefore is not a distinct divine person but is simply the unipersonal God in his activity toward and in the world. Negatively, Lampe rejects the adequacy of traditional expressions of the person of Jesus. Jesus is not the eternal Son and Word, the second person of the Trinity, nor incarnate in human nature. Rather, Jesus is a man in whom God as Spirit is uniquely and incomparably active.

In relation to the person of Jesus, Lampe explicitly rejects preexistence, incarnation, atonement (in terms of penal substitution), bodily resurrection, ascension, the high priestly role, glorification, second coming, last judgement, and the ultimate Lordship as traditionally understood. The concept of Spirit is, he claims, a better model by which to interpret and express the realities behind these doctrines. Our task is to grasp the intentions of the New Testament writers and to formulate those intentions of light of our modern understanding.

SPIRIT-CHRISTOLOGY: A CRITIQUE

Lampe is right to complain that there has been too little understanding of Christology in light of the concept of the Spirit. There has been too little pneumatology and experience of the power of the Spirit in the life and witness of the church. He claims to recognize a variety of models in relation to Christology, but rejects all models but his own preferred model based on the Spirit. We may question the new tyranny of Lampe's account by some of the grounds he uses to reject the old tyranny of Word—and Wisdom—Christology. If there are a variety of models, then any one of these pressed too far to the exclusion of others and their corrective influence, is bound to lead to disaster and less than a fully biblical and true account. In short, both Word and Spirit are necessary as complementary models.

However, more serious than the selective use of one model to exclude others is Lampe's acceptance of a normative role for modern culture.

19. *Ibid.*, p. 171.
20. *Ibid.*, p. 172.

It is because of the dominant forms of thought in our scientific age, and the inability of traditional and biblical accounts to come up to the standards of meaning and truth of this age, that Lampe embarks on his reconstruction. Unfortunately, the demolition smacks more of reduction than reconstruction. Mascall comments,

> Many, I think, will feel that the main achievement of Dr. Lampe in these lectures has been to show how little remains of the biblical and patristic faith when one forces it into a conceptual scheme that is logically inconsistent with it.[21]

The questions which we have raised about how the presuppositions of the modern conceptual scheme operate are equally pertinent to Lampe's exercise in reduction and reconstruction. Brian Hebblethwaite draws attention to this reductionism in Lampe,

> Here are two examples from Lampe: "In order to interpret God's saving work in Jesus we do not need the model of a descent of a pre-existent divine person into the world." "If . . . it is God's Spirit, his own real presence, which is active in and through the reciprocal love and trust of human beings, then there is no need to project human personality on to Trinitarian "persons."[22] . . . (these) illustrate the common use of the criterion of "economy." We are to cut out all unnecessary theologically accretions. This is a very dangerous criterion especially when used alone. It is not surprising that, on this ground, Unitarianism is preferred.[23]

Hebblethwaite is concerned, like Mascall and many others, that Lampe's end result will be Unitarianism. But this concern is not only about the application of the reductionist theme of economy. It is also that such an account in terms of Spirit alone will fail to do justice to the sheer comprehensiveness of Christology and the biblical (as well as traditional) evidence. We must take account of all the evidence and supply a Christology adequate to it. It is doubtful whether we have an adequate replacement for Incarnational Christology, not least because Lampe's concept of Spirit is somewhat vague and unanalyzed. Does this concept on its own have real and sufficient content for us to know God adequately in personal terms?

In approaching the content of Spirit-Christology, we must ask two questions. Is there sufficient ground to distinguish Jesus from the Spirit? What is the specific content of Christology that questions Lampe's reductionist understanding of Jesus? Johannine teaching clearly distinguishes

21. Eric Mascall, Review of God as Spirit in Journal of Theological Studies 29 (Oct. 1978), 620.

22. God as Spirit, pp. 33, 139.

23. Brian Hebblethwaite, "Recent British Theology," in One God in Trinity, ed. P. Toon and J. Spiceland (London: Bagster, 1980), pp. 161-62.

Jesus and the Spirit. The Spirit is promised by Jesus. The Spirit is *another* paraclete. The Spirit will witness to Jesus, glorify him, bring him to mind, and interpret the true meaning of the words of Jesus (Jn. 14–16; Jn. 20:21–22; Acts 1:8). Lampe recognizes that Paul and John do not identify Jesus and the Spirit consistently (1 Cor. 12:3).[24] Christians do not believe that it is possible to understand Jesus solely in terms of inspiration. Christians believe in the decisive nature of God's expression of himself in Jesus Christ. This is because God *became* man in a way which is distinct from even the highest form of inspiration.

There can be no adequate account of Jesus in terms of Spirit-control, for Christian prophets are not simply controlled by the Spirit to a different degree from Christ. There is more radical disjunction. For the Spirit who fills the prophet is the Spirit mediated through Jesus (1 Cor. 2:16; 1 Cor. 14:29-34). This is not to deny that Jesus is inspired. However, Jesus is more than endowed with Spirit. Jesus is the giver and instigator of the coming of the Spirit (Jn. 1:33; Acts 2:33; Eph. 4:7ff.; Jn. 14:16; 14:26). Thus there is sufficient biblical ground to distinguish Jesus from the Spirit.

We have seen how Lampe rejects various traditional aspects of Christology. Is this adequate to deal with the evidence? A full account of Christology is necessary to respond to Lampe. We must be content here with a summary. The ultimate reason for holding to an incarnational understanding of Christology lies in the earliest evidence of Christian understanding of Jesus. The New Testament writers believed in a preexistent Christ (Jn. 1:1-4; Heb. 1:2; Phil. 2:6; Col. 1:15-17). Preexistence and incarnation go hand in hand in these accounts. The Christologies of Galatians, Romans, and Corinthians are highly developed and lay great stress on the divinity, transcendence, and unity of Jesus with God. This is not some later philosophical incursion but part and parcel of the language and concepts required to account for the reality and experience of Jesus. He is not simply a god disguised as a man, nor a man inspired by a god. He is God incarnate (see also Jn. 1:4; Heb. 1:3; 2:14; Col. 1:15-19; 2:9; Phil. 2:7; 1 Tim. 2:5 and the helpful account of C. F. D. Moule in *The Holy Spirit*).[25] Likewise the doctrine of the virgin birth in Matthew and Luke points to a unique incarnation.

These accounts, whether taken literally or symbolically, propound a view of Jesus as far more than an inspired man (Lk. 2:23; Mt. 1:18-25; Lk. 1:34; Gal. 4:4; Rom. 1:3; Phil. 2:7). The New Testament writers have no doubt that Jesus' death is an atoning death (Heb. 1:3; 1 Pet. 2:24; 1 Jn. 2:2; 1 Cor. 5:7); that Jesus rose bodily from the dead (1 Cor. 15; Lk. 24; Mt. 28); that the ascended Christ is at the right hand of God in power (Heb. 8:1; 9:15); that Jesus fulfils a high priestly role (Hebrews; Rom. 8:31-39); that Jesus is coming again (Acts 1:11; Mt. 24:27, 30;

24. *God as Spirit*, pp. 116-17.
25. C. F. D. Moule, *The Holy Spirit* (Oxford: Mowbray, 1979).

2 Thess. 2:8; 1 Cor. 15:23; Phil. 2:9); that Jesus will judge the world (Mt. 25:31-34; Jas. 5:9); and that Jesus is Lord (Phil. 2:9). There are many more biblical passages to build on and that is where the heart of the debate with Spirit-Christology must take place. Does the view propounded do justice to the witness to Christ in the pages of the New Testament? Lampe's account patently does not.

CONCLUSION

The importance of *The Myth of God Incarnate* in the western Christological debate is twofold. It highlights the tension between modern western culture and traditional Christianity. We have tried to analyze both the context and content of the presuppositions at work. Some will feel that there has been too little dealing with the essential matter of Christology and too great a concentration on the form of Christology. This is the case, for the issues of methodology are primary in the western Christological debate and it is vital that evangelicals respond properly to the issues of method. The second importance of the essayists' work is that they all reject the language of incarnation which belongs to a framework of thought which is no longer valid. They are still ready to affirm Jesus as supremely inspired. In this way their work and methods lead very naturally to the theme of Spirit-Christology. Attention has been given to the work of Geoffrey Lampe and the conclusion drawn that any fully biblical account of Christology must retain a full-blooded notion of incarnation, as well as inspiration. We have tried to show ways in which the truth of God incarnate may be appropriately understood and expressed in modern culture.

DISCUSSION WITH DAVID COOK

Q. Is our problem not common between the West and the Two Thirds World, namely, how we are to criticize our culture?

D.C. There are three particular ways in which we criticize our own culture. First, we can reflect critically within the culture, because we understand it best. Simply because I understand it I am not debarred from having a critical interaction and understanding not simply that this is so, but why is it so and asking whether it ought to be so. That is the way in which we must reflect individually on our own culture.

The second way we reflect critically in our culture is in relation to each other. I opted for dealing with these themes in the hope that it would stimulate the other cultures to reflect critically on my culture. I think that in the world in which we live and within the Christian faith in which we function we have much to learn from each other. God has given us each other within different cultures, to speak to each other and help, clarify, and judge.

The third way to criticize culture is in light of the categories of Scripture. This is in interaction with Scripture. I come to the Scripture, I look at my culture and I ask what the Scripture has to say to this. And I then take some of the problems of my context to Scripture and I interact with it. There is no reading off of a solution, but there is a growing understanding of the Word and a growing interpenetration of the Word into my context. That is an on-going dynamic kind of activity.

Q. Why do the writers use "myth" and not "metaphor"?

D.C. I think that the word "myth" was used because those theologians wanted us to realize very forcefully the serious problem they propound. They want us to be provoked to very serious thinking and "metaphor" in one sense may be an answer to the problem of "myth." They want to bring us back to that problem of how we are to interpret the Bible today.

Q. You have grounded much of your discussion on the problem posed by the Enlightenment, but it has all been limited to what has been known as the first phase of the Enlightenment. You have hardly mentioned the second phase which is critical historical thinking and the impact of Marx into an industrial society which manifested itself in your own context of the British Isles as the Workers' Movement. How do you reconcile your partial discussion of the Enlightenment background with the totality of the Enlightenment?

D.C. British theology has not taken seriously any kind of Marxist kind of analysis and finds it difficult to both respond to the question and even to understand the question. I think that Marx is very much a creature of the Enlightenment. While it would be possible and instructive for me to follow through the Marxist second phase of the Enlightenment I still tend to see him in relation to that first stage and given an average choice I come to the first phase first.

Comment: If it is true that the issue of Christology or theology in the western world is the scientific worldview of the West, then the response will be one thing. What many have argued is that there is a second moment to the Enlightenment, that is the Marxian question which has to do with the question which those people who have not been recognized in history have been asking: women, black people, indigenous people. What is the relationship between their question and this scientific question, which is relative within the philosophical context of the western world. That is what we mean when we refer to the two phases of the Enlightenment.

Q. How is your implicit analysis of Christology as it appears in the West but concentrated on the British Isles related with other Christological discussions and models in the British Isles itself such as Leslie Newbiggin's trinitarian approach and, on the continent, the approach of Moltmann, Berkhof, and Pannenberg?

D.C. It is not possible in the time given to describe adequately all the strains of Christology in the western world. Part of the difficulty in my context is the very narrow definition of what constitutes a theologian. In British terms, there is much greater concern with the writings of Moltmann and Pannenberg, than with folk like Newbiggin. This finds expression in the doubt whether mission is a proper subject for theology.

In choosing a way of coming at the problems of the western theological context, Moltmann and Pannenberg would have been an excellent choice. I believe that they are attempting to write responses to that kind of context. But to some extent they are providing (or trying to provide) the answer to the kinds of questions which have been the focus of my paper. Now whether or not they are sufficiently answers, in the sense of taking seriously enough the problem, is the area of debate. I think their kind of work is an attempt to give an answer to these kind of contextual problems. But to some extent I wanted to concentrate on the actual setting of the problems, and thus have focussed on context and content.

Q. In our attempts to formulate a contextualized Christology, did you suspect some tendencies to follow these mythologizers in one way or the other? Are you giving us your analysis of western Christology as a warning?

D.C. There was no intent to make that point explicitly. But in working through the material, it did strike me that in many ways their missiological concerns are very near to our concerns. We have much to learn from the way they have done their task and the conclusions they have come to. There may be crucial negative lessons as well as positive lessons.

Q. Is not the absence of missiology one of the major weaknesses in the whole spectrum of contemporary theology in the West? How does Christological discussion then relate to missiology?

D.C. I agree with your analysis of western theology. It seems to me that mission means sending and the one who sends is the Christ who sends and the message that we proclaim in being sent is Christ. So in terms of the proclaimer and the proclaimed, the mission and the missioner is Jesus himself.

Q. One purpose of this consultation is to search for an evangelical Christology. The West has a tradition of theology for 2000 years. I would ask you from the West to give some suggestion to us of what could be the evangelical Christology we are searching after.

D.C. I think there are three questions there in relation to methodology and the attitude of Scripture. I homed in on the attitude to Scripture because that is the basic context that the mythographers use. If you are going to respond to their context you have to express the nature of Scripture and use it properly. Western people and British people in particular perhaps, think about Scripture in a highly intellectualized way. This is a basic problem in the churches, where there is a tremendous gap between knowing and doing. George Cummings was saying that to know is to do. That is just not true in the western context. We know millions of things but never do them. There is a gap between theory and practice. The problem is seeing that religion is genuinely a part of our humanity because it has been squeezed to the periphery. The religious life is certainly not a ''natural'' thing for British and western people. We may have much to learn there.

Some may feel that I have not given a western evangelical route by which to develop a Christology for the Two Thirds World. I was very conscious of the difficulty of my position here. I did not want to come with any particular answers that I think you must all take account of, that I know and none of you know. I came to do exactly the same thing as all of you; to try to struggle with Christology in my context.

I do believe in struggling with that Christology in my context, which has been influential. There may be many bad things but that is the way it is. And to some extent we come to a point where we must accept our past and respond to it.

CONFERENCE FINDINGS
15. Towards a Missiological Christology in the Two Thirds World

We (twenty-five) evangelical mission theologians from the Two Thirds World met at Bangkok, Thailand from March 20-25, 1982 to consider various Christologies arising from the poor, the powerless, and the oppressed and non-Christian worldviews in order to faithfully proclaim Jesus Christ. We were deeply conscious of our continuity not only with historic evangelicalism, but also with the different Christian traditions, both of western and of nonwestern origin, which exist in the Two Thirds World.

As established and emerging theologians with our different cultures and languages, we struggled together to discover the meaning and content of Christology for the agenda of mission. We worked with a common commitment to Scripture as the norm, not only in matters of faith and conduct but also for theology. We were, however, also deeply aware that the agenda for our theological activity must be given to us by our respective contexts. In these contexts, it is always necessary to reflect on the biblical passion for justice, the biblical concern for the "wholeness" of salvation, and the biblical concept of the universality of Christ. It is necessary for us to engage profoundly and theologically not only with the reality of oppression, powerlessness, and poverty, but also with other religions, in their various dimensions, which command massive support in some of our contexts.

The proceedings of the conference, both the papers and the discussions, reflect our concern that our hermeneutic should both be loyal to historic Christianity and arise out of our engagement with our respective situations. The tasks that face us require that we seek fresh ways to articulate our faith in Christ Jesus as Lord.

The western missionary enterprise has been largely instrumental in the emergence of many new Christian communities. But it did not, in general, engage in a serious encounter with the religious quests of, and the social realities in our respective contexts. So, churches of the Two Thirds World are in danger of bondage to alien categories. These do not permit them to meet adequately the problems and challenges of proclaiming Christ in our contexts. This does not mean that we reject our past. Rather we assume it, and make its legacy part of our apostolate in our time.

We seek to apprehend the Good News in more of its fulness, because we believe that we have been apprehended by Christ Jesus our Lord (Phil. 3:12). He became one of us (Jn. 1:14) in order that we might become, through the operation of the Spirit, conformed to his image (Rom. 8:29). Thus Christ calls us to obey him faithfully in our whole existence and participate in his redemptive mission in the world. As he has entered into the fulness of our human predicament (Heb. 4:15), so he calls us to identify with the sufferings of the world, which he came to redeem, and so to be ministers of his Good News in a broken and alienated creation.

As mission theologians from the Two Thirds World, we can play a part in seeking to articulate the unspoken questions of the marginalized, to understand their longings, and to demonstrate the meaning of the Good News of Jesus Christ in their situation. We are also conscious that vast numbers of people in our world continue to pay allegiance to alternative "ways of salvation." It is our responsibility to find ways of articulating the biblical witness that grace and salvation, which are ours in Christ Jesus, can become theirs also by faith in him.

We have therefore paid serious attention to the religious pluralism of our respective contexts, and have explored ways in which our Saviour and Lord, Christ Jesus, can answer the questions and needs of all people everywhere. We recognize, therefore, that our Christological task is carried out in dialogue with people from other religious traditions. We undertake to assume our responsibility to take up this task in all our contexts.

Many of us have been called from within other religious traditions, and we are confident that through the enabling power of the Spirit, and in the light of God's Word, this task can be done.

It will be necessary to read, hear, and see the presentation of papers and the discussions which followed to understand how we seek to express and live the reality of Christ amid Buddhism, Islam, Hinduism, the primal religions, and in the context of social, political, economic, and racial oppression.

Nevertheless, we can identify a number of vital areas for further discussion and reflection in the task of mission in the Two Thirds World. We express these as our humble contribution toward a missiological Christology.

1. The Christological task is twofold. It stresses the historical reality of Jesus, the man of Nazareth in Galilee, in his concrete socio-economic, political, racial, and religious context. This Jesus is also the incarnate Word of God. At the same time, we affirm the universal Lordship of Jesus Christ. A full Christology must include both these understandings and one aspect cannot be stressed without reference to the other.

2. We reflected on many different approaches to Christology. We recognized that there were questions to be asked of all of us who appear

to emphasise only one such approach. For example, how does the actual life of Jesus Christ relate to Christology from "above"? How does the saving death of Christ relate to Christology from "below"?

3. We affirmed the crucial importance of the Scriptures as normative for Christology, and the necessity for a careful and obedient hermeneutic, true to the whole of Scripture, and sensitive to our contexts.

4. We discussed in what ways our various contexts ought to be judged and tested by Scripture. We sought to grapple with the ways in which the life and mission of the church are continuous with our various cultures and to explore how these are discontinuous. We affirmed both explorations as necessary for the faithful and relevant proclamation of the gospel. We also examined ways in which the nature of Christ himself transcends cultural boundaries and enables us to do so in the power of the Spirit.

5. We were aware of the need for clear methodology in Christology and its correlation with missiological terms and contexts. Our methods must be faithful to Christ and to Scripture and be sensitive to our respective ecclesial traditions, and to our socio-cultural realities.

6. We recognized the necessity not only for dialogue between mission theologians from various regions, but also for a proper interaction with the philosophical presuppositions, cultural values, social structures, mission histories, and religious traditions of our contexts.

7. We expressed our human solidarity with the poor, the powerless, and the oppressed of the world, with those who are followers of other religions and with all people everywhere. We recognized that we are all made in God's image, yet fall short of his glory. Christ came, lived, died, and rose again for us all. We are all under the sovereignty of the Lord Jesus Christ, whom we are committed to proclaim to all, especially our brothers and sisters in the Two Thirds World.

We acknowledge that our work will be judged by whether it helps the church in the Two Thirds World to proclaim Jesus Christ more faithfully, effectively, and authentically.

16. Emerging Issues for the Ongoing Debate

VINAY SAMUEL and CHRIS SUGDEN *(India)*

MISSIOLOGICAL HISTORY

In addressing the basic question of the conference, what does it mean to proclaim Jesus Christ, to be forgiven by him, and to confess him in our various contexts, participants recognized that the contexts from which we were addressing the question included our missiological history. The issue emerged of how to evaluate this history by biblical criteria. The process of reviewing missiological history was important for discovering our own identity as Christians *in* the Two Thirds World and *of* the Two Thirds World. Kwame Bediako's paper gives an exhaustive treatment of this issue in the particular context of Ghana. Such a process also means that we are beginning to grapple with areas of theological thought and even speculation that have remained taboo for decades.

STARTING POINTS FOR CHRISTOLOGY

Varying images of Jesus emerged in the presentations from different contexts. It was evident that one prime reason for this divergence was the different starting points for the Christological task. For some the starting point was the incarnation and the historical Jesus. For others it was an ontological Christology derived from the Bible and handed down from the past. Both seek universal meaning and particular application. One position seeks concrete historical paradigms in the life of Jesus for Christian action today. The other stresses that we know Christ as ascended Lord and this informs our entire understanding of his person and work. What is the relationship between these two starting points?

PLURALITY OF CHRISTOLOGICAL CONFESSIONS

In the interests of affirming the universality of Christ we could define the context in universal terms which describe all men as sinners needing to be saved by grace. But this is not an adequate description of the context. A more realistic and concrete description would see not only all men

280

as sinners, but some as sinned against in a particular sense. The sinful condition of man would be further explicated by terms such as "oppressed-oppressor" and "poor." The confession of Christ in such particularity would obviously stress Christ's special relationship to the poor and his distinct relationship to the rich. Thus a focus on the particularity of the context will result in a different Christological emphasis relevant to that context and distinct from the Christology emerging from a description of the context in universalistic terms. What is the relationship between the two?

INTRA-CONTEXTUAL ISSUES

Issues were also raised which primarily concerned Christian witness within particular contexts. African Christians addressed the issues of ancestor worship and sacral kingship which have long been considered taboo subjects for creative theological reflection. Black American Christians addressed the issue of whether oppression defines our Christian identity: whether we are to be defined by the forces of oppression or by what God has done. Asian Christians addressed the issue of what priority should be accorded to naming the name of Christ in Christian mission. Latin American Christians as they research the reality of the oppressed Indian groups are rediscovering the importance of the religious dimension in the social existence of communities.

It is important to note that while these issues were of prime importance to a particular context, contributions and even challenges from other contexts played a significant role in developing new perspectives on the issues. Thus while our contexts are distinct from one another, it is important that they remain open to each other.

17.Participants

KWAME BEDIAKO (Ghana)
Minister of the Presbyterian Church of Ghana.

BONG RIN RO (Korea)
Executive Secretary of the Asia Theological Association, Taiwan.

MALCOLM BRADSHAW (USA)
Associate Director, World Vision International, Asia Region, Philippines.

WILSON W. CHOW (Hong Kong)
Dean of the China Graduate School of Theology, Hong Kong.

DAVID COOK (Scotland)
Senior Lecturer in Theology, Westminster College, Oxford and Lecturer in Theology, Regent's Park College, Oxford.

ORLANDO E. COSTAS (Costa Rica)
Thornley Wood Professor of Missiology, and Director of Hispanic Studies, Eastern Baptist Theological Seminary, Philadelphia, USA.

GEORGE CUMMINGS (USA)
Assistant Professor, Chicago Theological Seminary.

PHINEHAS DUBE (Zimbabwe)
Director of Scripture Union, Zimbabwe.

DAVID M. GITARI (Kenya)
Bishop of Mount Kenya East.

ROLANDO C. GUTTIEREZ (Mexico)
Pastor of Horeb Baptist Church, Mexico D.F.

HAN CHUL-HA (Korea)
President of the Asian Centre for Theological Studies and Mission, Seoul, Korea.

DAVID LIM (Philippines)
Assistant Professor and Dean of Extension Studies, Asian Theological Seminary, Manila.

MICHAEL MAELIAU (Solomon Islands)
General Secretary of the South Seas Evangelical Church, Solomon Islands.

WAYAN MASTRA (Indonesia)
Chairman of the Protestant Christian Church of Bali.

MICHAEL NAZIR ALI (Pakistan)
Provost-Vicar of Lahore Cathedral.

EMILIO A. NUNEZ (Nicaragua)
Director of Postgraduate Studies, Central American Theological
Seminary, Guatemala.

RENÉ PADILLA (Argentina)
Editor, Latin American Mission, Buenos Aires.

PALUKU RUBINGA (Republic of Central Africa)
Dean of Bangui Evangelical School of Theology.

VINAY SAMUEL (India)
Presbyter-in-Charge, St. John's Church, Bangalore and Executive
Secretary of Partnership in Mission Asia.

NORBERTO SARACCO (Argentina)
General Secretary of the Fraternity of Latin American Pentecostals and
President of the Extension Centre for Theological Education of the
Association of Churches of God.

RONALD SIDER (USA)
President of Evangelicals for Social Action and Associate Professor of
Theology, Eastern Baptist Theological Seminary, Philadelphia.

CHRIS SUGDEN (England)
Assistant Director of The Association for Theological Extension Education, India.

PRACHA THAIWATCHARAMAS (Thailand)
Lecturer, Bangkok Bible College and Thailand Baptist Seminary.

PEGGY YEO BEE TIN (Singapore)
Executive Director, Asian Christian Communication Fellowship,
Singapore.

KEY YUASA (Brazil)
Vice-President and Director of Education, Evangelical Holiness Church,
Brazil.

18. THE COVER PAINTING
Christ the Archer

NYOMAN DARSANE *(Bali, Indonesia)*

My painting compares Hindu and Christian lifestyles in Bali and their differing methods of entering heaven. Christians have only one way which is simple and direct. The Hindu way is more complicated.

The dragon symbolizes the devil. He has one body but two heads. The blue head represents the female dimension of humanity, and is soft and gentle. The red head symbolizes the male dimension and is strong and aggressive.

The fire coming out of the dragon's mouth tries to destroy faith in God. So the action of the devil during our lives it to confuse us and force us to make false comparisons between right and wrong. In this way he pushes people into sinful ways. At death, the dragon waits for the spirits of people who pass away and tries to stop them entering heaven. The tail of the dragon is held by the Hindu temple priest who in Balinese belief is the only person with power to weaken the force of the dragon.

In the middle of the picture, men are carrying funeral biers which are crowned with towers. The levels of the towers represent the caste of the deceased person being carried in the bier: the more levels on the tower, the higher the caste of the deceased. Because the tower is used to carry the dead, it also symbolizes darkness. The large number of people carrying the tower indicates that many Balinese adhere to the Bali Hindu faith. The cloud of darkness covers many of them. But no women carry the towers since on such occasions they prepare the sacrificial offerings for the cremation ceremony.

The calf symbolizes the carriage for the journey to heaven. It is usually red or black for people of low caste, and white for people of high caste. The people on the boat are spreading the ashes of a dead person on the ocean to enable the spirit to join God through the waves. The birds symbolize the spirits of people who have died and gone to heaven.

The archer is God who shoots the dragon. This indicates that God has power over the devil. His white loin cloth indicates that Jesus Christ is pure and holy, and is available to us in this present life. The single arrow represents the Christian way of living, the one true way of life which is through Jesus Christ.